Calvin's Theology
of the Psalms

Texts and Studies in Reformation and Post-Reformation Thought

General Editor

Prof. Richard A. Muller, Calvin Theological Seminary

Editorial Board

Prof. Irena Backus, University of Geneva

Prof. Susan M. Felch, Calvin College

Prof. A. N. S. Lane, London School of Theology

Prof. Susan E. Schreiner, University of Chicago

Prof. David C. Steinmetz, Duke University

Prof. John L. Thompson, Fuller Theological Seminary

Prof. Willem J. van Asselt, University of Utrecht

Prof. Timothy J. Wengert, The Lutheran Theological Seminary
    at Philadelphia

Prof. Henry Zwaanstra, Calvin Theological Seminary

Books in the Series

Caspar Olevianus, *A Firm Foundation: An Aid to Interpreting the Heidelberg Catechism*, translated and edited by Lyle D. Bierma

John Calvin, *The Bondage and Liberation of the Will: A Defence of the Orthodox Doctrine of Human Choice against Pighius*, edited by A. N. S. Lane, translated by G. I. Davies

Law and Gospel: Philip Melanchthon's Debate with John Agricola of Eisleben over Poenitentia, by Timothy J. Wengert

Martin Luther as Prophet, Teacher, and Hero: Images of the Reformer, 1520–1620, by Robert Kolb

Melanchthon in Europe: His Work and Influence beyond Wittenberg, edited by Karin Maag

Reformation and Scholasticism: An Ecumenical Enterprise, edited by Willem J. van Asselt and Eef Dekker

The Binding of God: Calvin's Role in the Development of Covenant Theology, by Peter A. Lillback

Divine Discourse: The Theological Methodology of John Owen, by Sebastian Rehnman

Heinrich Bullinger and the Doctrine of Predestination: Author of "the Other Reformed Tradition"? by Cornelis P. Venema

Architect of Reformation: An Introduction to Heinrich Bullinger, 1504–1575, edited by Bruce Gordon and Emidio Campi

An Introduction to the Heidelberg Catechism: Sources, History, and Theology, by Lyle D. Bierma with Charles D. Gunnoe Jr., Karin Y. Maag, and Paul W. Fields

Calvin's Theology of the Psalms, by Herman J. Selderhuis

Sweet Communion: Trajectories of Spirituality from the Middle Ages through the Further Reformation, by Arie de Reuver, translated by James A. De Jong

Calvin's Theology of the Psalms

Herman J. Selderhuis

Baker Academic
Grand Rapids, Michigan

Published by Baker Academic
a division of Baker Publishing Group
P.O. Box 6287, Grand Rapids, MI 49516-6287
www.bakeracademic.com

Printed in the United States of America

Library of Congress Cataloging-in-Publication Data is on file at the Library of Congress, Washington, DC.

ISBN 10: 0-8010-3166-4
ISBN 978-0-8010-3166-3

Funding for translation costs associated with producing this book was provided by the Netherlands Organisation for Scientific Research (NWO)

Contents

Series Preface

The heritage of the Reformation is of profound importance to our society, our culture, and the church in the present day. Yet there remain many significant gaps in our knowledge of the intellectual development of Protestantism both during and after the Reformation, and there are not a few myths about the theology of the orthodox or scholastic Protestant writers of the late sixteenth and seventeenth centuries. These gaps and myths—frequently caused by ignorance of the scope of a particular thinker's work, by negative theological judgments passed by later generations on the theology of the Reformers and their successors, or by an intellectual imperialism of the present that singles out some thinkers and ignores others regardless of their relative significance to their own times—stand in the way of a substantive encounter with this important period in our history. Understanding, assessment, and appropriation of that heritage can only occur through the publication of significant works (monographs, essays, and sound, scholarly translations) that present the breadth and detail of the thought of the Reformers and their successors.

Texts and Studies in Reformation and Post-Reformation Thought makes available (1) translations of important documents like Caspar Olevian's *A Firm Foundation* and John Calvin's *Bondage and Liberation of the Will*, (2) significant monographs on individual thinkers or on aspects of sixteenth- and seventeenth-century Protestant thought, and (3) multiauthored symposia that bring together groups of scholars in an effort to present the state of scholarship on a particular issue, all under the guidance of an editorial board of recognized scholars in the field.

The series, moreover, is intended to address two groups: an academic and a confessional or churchly audience. The series recognizes the need for careful, scholarly treatment of the Reformation and of the era of Protestant orthodoxy, given the continuing presence of misunderstandings, particularly of the latter era, in both the scholarly and the popular literature and also given the rise of a more recent scholarship devoted to reappraising both the Reformation and the era of orthodoxy. The series highlights revised understandings regarding the relationship of the Reformation and orthodoxy to their medieval background and of the thought of both eras to their historical, social, political, and cultural contexts. Such scholarship will not only advance the academic discussion, it will also provide a churchly audience with a clearer and broader access to its own traditions. In sum, the series intends to present the varied and current approaches to the rich heritage of Protestantism and to stimulate interest in the roots of the Protestant tradition.

Richard A. Muller

Acknowledgments

Now that the publication of the English edition of *God in het midden: Calvijns theologie van de Psalmen* is a fact, I would like to express my gratitude to those who have made it possible. First, I want to thank Victor d'Assonville and David Holmlund for having worked so diligently on the translation. A generous grant from the Netherlands Organisation for Scientific Research (NWO) was the sine qua non for making a translation possible. I want to thank Richard A. Muller for his willingness to take this book into his series and Brian Bolger of Baker Academic for the pleasant communication we had on this project. I hope every reader enjoys reading this book as much as I enjoyed writing it.

Herman J. Selderhuis

Introduction

Here I must relate a memorable story. While we were supping in a certain inn and speaking of the hope of the heavenly life, a profane despiser of God happening to be present treated our discourse with derision and now and then mockingly exclaimed, "The heaven of heavens is the Lord's." Instantly afterwards he was seized with dreadful pain and began to vociferate, "O God! O God!" and, having a powerful voice, he filled the whole apartment with his cries. Then I, who had felt indignant at his conduct, proceeded in my own way to tell him irritated[1] that now at least he perceived that they who mock God are not permitted to escape with impunity. One of the guests, an honest and pious man and withal facetious (as a matter of fact he is still alive), exploited the opportunity thus, "Do you invoke God? Have you forgotten your philosophy? Why do you not permit God to remain in peace in heaven?" And as often as the one bawled out, "O God!" the other, mocking him, retorted, "Where is now thy *Coelum coeli Domino*?" Eventually his pain was indeed mitigated; nevertheless, the remainder of his life was spent in sinful contempt of God.[2]

Calvin calls it a memorable occasion (*memorabilem historiam*) and that "memorable" does not concern him only but also them who keep busy in researching Calvin. This incident tells something about Calvin's self knowledge when he acknowledges himself to be quite irritable and short-tempered. Precisely because of this, the story also tells us something about his adoration for this "honest and pious man" who knew how to tackle this problem more effectively than Calvin himself. Yet, in even greater significance, this story tells us something about Calvin's view of God as the one who does not spend his time resting in heaven, secluded from the turbulent events of the world, but rather as a God who is undeniably present in the reality of daily existence and who acts in this world in a dynamic way.

---

[1] "perrexi meo more, stomachose denuntians," Ps. 115:16 (*CO* 32, 191). In this study, "*CO*" indicates the various passages by Calvin from the *Ioannis Calvini Opera quae supersunt omnia*, ed. Wilhelm Baum, Edward Cunitz et Edward Reuss (Brunsvigae-Berolini: C. A. Schwetschke et filium, 1863-1900), and these 59 volumes are also found in volumes 29–87 in the *Corpus Reformatorum* (*CR*), ed. Bretschneider (1834 ff.); the correspondence between the editions follows the pattern of *CO* 1 = *CR* 29; *CO* 2 = *CR* 30, etc.

[2] Ps. 115:16 (*CO* 32, 191).

1. Theology of the Psalms

The search which has now been carried out for many years to find the central dogma in Calvin's theology still has not produced anything. The reason for that simply could be that Calvin's theology is nothing else than *theo*-logy; by this I mean to say that the whole of his theology as well as all of its parts constantly deal with God. All themes in Calvin's thought are discussed with God as both the point of departure and the unifying interest. On the one hand this impedes finding an organizing theme in Calvin's theology, but on the other hand this makes his theology so captivating. The complexity and liveliness of Calvin's theology is especially manifested in his commentary on the Psalms.

Three facts are brought forward by Erwin Mülhaupt in his argument to explain Calvin's affection for this Bible book.[3] First of all the Psalms were of special significance to Calvin personally. He recognized much of himself in David and in difficult times he found comfort and strength in this book of the Bible. Secondly the Psalms are the only book from the Old Testament from which Calvin preached on Sundays. Thus the Psalms were the only exception to his customary practice to preach from the New Testament on Sundays while the Old Testament was reserved for weekdays. Thirdly Mülhaupt mentions that Calvin has furthered the singing of Psalms during the church service like no other.[4]

No justice would be done to Calvin's theology of the Psalms if it were only described in view of various themes. For instance, Calvin never speaks about the church without taking into account the Lord of the church or the members of the church. Calvin does not speak about creation without taking into consideration the Creator himself or those he created. Furthermore, Calvin does not speak about election apart from discussing God or apart from discussing the believer. In each case the mutual relationship between God and man comes to the surface repeatedly.

Calvin constantly rejects the idea of a fixed or static God. Instead, God is the living God, the God who makes history and who experiences history with man. This moved and moving God reveals himself to man from the perspective of different relationships. In a similar way as one and the same man can be an employee, a parent, a friend, a colleague or a neighbor

---

[3] *Der Psalter auf der Kanzel Calvins; bisher unbekannte Psalmenpredigten herausgegeben und eingeleitet von Erwin Mülhaupt* (Neukirchen-Vluyn: Neukirchener Verlag, 1959), 9–10.

[4] In his introduction to the publication of Calvin's unpublished sermons on the Psalms, Mülhaupt gives the same three reasons, but he then mentions the one of the singing of the Psalms first. Johannes Calvin, *Psalmpredigten, Passions, Oster- und Pfingstpredigten*. Herausgegeben von Erwin Mülhaupt, see *Supplementa Calviniana*, vol. VII (Neukirchen-Vluyn: Neukirchener Verlag, 1981), xxiv–xxviii.

according to his various relationships to each person, this also applies to God with regard to his various relationships with man. In this way Calvin's theology of the Psalms is described from the different relationships of God with man. By thus taking in each chapter the point of departure in God, man with his history is inevitably concerned as well. Calvin of course states even at the beginning of his *Institutes* that it is impossible to speak about God without speaking about man, just as is it impossible to speak about man without referring to God.[5] In this respect Calvin distinguishes, for the sake of clarity, between two kinds of our knowledge of God: that is, the knowledge of God as Creator and of God as Redeemer. The commentary on the Psalms functions as an outline upon which various themes could be elaborated (see below). Yet, the nature and content of the Psalter limit which subjects are in fact treated in a more comprehensive way. The main theme of the *cognitio Dei et hominis* is dealt with in such a way that it sheds light on the whole of Calvin's theology. In the framework of this book the titles and arrangement of chapters cannot be appreciated in any other way than as an *ordo docendi*.

2. Argument

An analysis of Calvin's theology on the basis of only *one* of his commentaries could seem to contradict to his own principle of differentiating sharply between commentary and *loci*.[6] Commentaries serve to offer a verse-by-verse exegesis, which should not be interrupted by excursuses on specific topics. The intention of this book, however, is in no way to be contradictory to Calvin's own methodological principles. Instead, I have opted to start from merely one locus of Calvin's thought, namely, the *locus de Deo*. In this way I will attempt to gain some insight into Calvin's theology without simply summarizing the *Institutes* in a nutshell or presenting a *loci communes* on the basis of the Psalms commentary. The fact that our investigation begins with a commentary and not with the *Institutes* reflects the emerging consensus of Calvin research that the *Institutes* ought to be read in the light of the commentaries and not the other way around.[7]

The judgment that one commentary on an Old Testament book gives insight into the theology of Calvin proceeds from his view on the unity of the

---

[5] Jean Calvin, *Institutio christianae religionis* (Genève, 1559), I.1.2.

[6] Richard A. Muller has shown from a number of the prefaces of Calvin how the Reformer kept this principle. See his *The Unaccommodated Calvin: Studies in the Foundation of a Theological Tradition* (New York: Oxford University Press, 2000), 21–38.

[7] "The *Institutes* must be read in the light of the commentaries and on the assumption that Calvin's basic, positive theological formulations are at least as likely to appear in the commentaries as in the Institutes," Muller, *Unaccommodated*, 116. Muller agrees here with the insights of Calvin scholars like Brian Armstrong, Elsie McKee and David Steinmetz.

old and new covenants. For example, Calvin summarizes Book II of the *Institutes* (in which Christology in particular is treated) with the following heading: "The knowledge of God the Redeemer in Christ, first disclosed to the fathers under the law, and then to us in the Gospel." According to Calvin the Old and the New Testament differ in clarity and not in essence. Hence his commentaries on the Old Testament are just as informative about his theology as his exegesis of the New Testament. Furthermore, for Calvin the book of the Psalms assumed greater and greater significance in his theological development. In the first edition of the *Institutes* (1536) the Psalter is the least-quoted biblical book, in the last edition it is quoted more than any other with the one exception of the epistle to the Romans.[8]

In order that Calvin not be limited in any sense, a comparison with other commentaries on the Psalms, such as those by Bucer and Musculus, is presently omitted.[9] The similarities between Calvin's theology and that of Luther shall be pointed out though.[10] Although research on the influence of Luther on Calvin may have a long tradition, it is still quite limited in its interests and conclusions.[11] This study therefore seeks to make a modest contribution to the ongoing research on the relationship between the theological work of each Reformer.

After a general introduction the book starts with a first chapter dealing with the relation between Calvin's biography and his theology according to his commentary on the Psalms. This chapter makes clear that this particular commentary gives us insight into his theology as well as into his spirituality, and it also cannot be understood without his biography. In the following ten chapters the theology of Calvin's commentary on the Psalms is discussed thematically according to the thesis that neither Christology nor Pneumatology is central to Calvin's thought but rather it is the *doctrina de Deo* which fundamentally informs his biblical interpretation. For the most part it is my

---

[8]   F. L. Battles, *Interpreting John Calvin* (Grand Rapids: Baker Books, 1996), 145.

[9]   In his preface Calvin writes with appreciation about these two commentaries: "Et priusquam enarrationem aggrederer fratrum meorum rogatu dixeram quod verum erat, me ideo supersedere quod fidelissimus ecclesiae doctor Martinus Bucerus summa, quam in hoc opere praestitit, eruditione diligentia et fide, id saltem consequutus erat ne tantus esset operae meae usus. Nec vero de Wolphgangi Musculi commentariis" Praefatio (*CO* 31, 13).

[10] Mülhaupt has already pointed out the similarities in the central themes on which Luther and Calvin focus in their respective interpretations of the Psalms: "Es ist eigenartig und zeigt wieder einmal die tiefe geistliche Verwandtschaft Calvins und Luthers, daß die Schwerpunkte der Psalmenverkündigung Calvins dieselben sind, die auch Luther am Psalter hervorhebt," Mülhaupt, *Psalter*, 24.

[11] W. van 't Spijker has done some research on Luther's influence on Calvin; in his study he gives a survey of literature on this theme: see W. van 't Spijker, *Luther en Calvijn: De invloed van Luther op Calvijn blijkens de Institutie*, Apeldoornse Studies No. 20 (Kampen: Kok, 1985).

purpose to let Calvin speak for himself as far as it is possible; therefore references to and interaction with other studies of Calvin's theology are by and large omitted. Similarly it is appropriate that, as this study is primarily concerned with the content of Calvin's theology, the emphasis is on *what* he said and not on the question of from whom he derived his ideas. In order to focus on the Psalms commentary in particular, very little reference is made to other works of Calvin. After the theological analysis, the book ends with a postscript giving some evaluative conclusions.

Furthermore, in this analysis of the commentary on the Psalms there is no separate reference to Calvin's sermons on the Psalms. Various reasons can be given for this choice. Not only would the footnotes be more extensive, but also a reading of the sermons shows that the theological content of the sermons does not deviate from that of the commentary. What is more, some examination has been done on the substance of these sermons already.[12] The most important reason though is that very few of Calvin's sermons from the Psalms have been preserved down to the present day, and those which we still possess were delivered over the course of many years during Calvin's pulpit ministry.[13] The commentary however forms a whole in itself and was published at a time when Calvin's theology had reached its complete and mature form—just two years before the appearance of the last Latin edition of the *Institutes*.

As our point of departure, the Latin edition of the commentary on the Psalms has been chosen because it was the source for the French translations of 1558[14] and 1561.[15] Unfortunately, it is still not quite clear how involved Calvin was in the French translation of his commentary.

The Bible verse references in the footnotes do not always precisely correspond with the correct biblical text since Calvin generally elaborates on

---

[12] P. Opitz, "Ein Thorapsalm als ABC des christlichen Glaubens; Beobachtungen zu Calvins Predigten über Psalm 119," in *Calvin's Books: Festschrift dedicated to Peter de Klerk on the occasion of his seventieth birthday*, ed. Wilhelm H. Neuser, Herman J. Selderhuis, and Willem van 't Spijker (Heerenveen: J. J. Groen, 1997), 117–31; Mülhaupt, *Psalter*, 19–24, gives a review of the "Schwerpunkte der Verkündigung in Calvins Psalmpredigt."

[13] For example, in sermons which have been published during Calvin's lifetime, namely two sermons on Psalm 115 and 124 (1546), four sermons on Psalm 16, 27, and 87 (1552) and 22 sermons on Psalm 119 (1554). The 72 sermons that existed in handwriting were lost during the eighteenth century.

[14] Jean Calvin, *Le livre des Pseaumes exposé* (Genève, 1558). For bibliographical references, cf. Rudolphe Peter/Jean-François Gilmont, *Bibliotheca Calviniana. Les oeuvres de Jean Calvin publicées au XVI siècle: Écrits théologiques, littéraires et juridiques*, 2 vols. (Genève: Droz, 1991-1994), vol 2, 672–74.

[15] Jean Calvin, *Commentaires sur le livre des Pseaumes* (Genève, 1561). In the subtitle it is mentioned that this is a corrected translation: "Ceste traduction est tellement reveuë, & si fidellement conferee sur le Latin, qu'on la peut iuger estre nouvelle." Cf. Peter/Gilmont, vol. 2, 801–3.

a few verses at a time while only citing the first of the verses. Also, the quotations of biblical texts are mostly based on Calvin's own translations. Calvin himself did not favor a particular existing translation; from the commentary it is evident that he mainly translated directly from the original Hebrew or Greek text.[16] The quotations which are taken from Calvin's Latin commentary are translated or verified by myself and then adjusted according to the original. The most recent Dutch translation of the commentary on the Psalms dates back to 1898 and has several flaws.[17] As for the other more recent translations, one must say that there are certain problems concerning their use. The English translation of the Calvin Translation Society[18] not only uses a more archaic type of English, but it also reflects too much of the image of Calvin at that time instead of presenting the words of Calvin itself.[19] In 1965 Parker published a revised edition of the oldest English translation which was produced in 1571 by Arthur Golding. Parker's main argument for the republishing of this edition was that it originated from a time "before scholastic Calvinism had taken Calvin's words and given them definite and irrevocable meaning."[20] The most recent German translation appeared in 1930[21] and translates less than what Calvin has said. Not only are some sentences occasionally omitted, but most of the passages in which Calvin engages in controversy against Rome have been systematically removed without any explication from the translator. Furthermore the function of some essential Latin theological terms is generally overlooked by all existing translations.

3. God at the Center

Calvin expresses the heart of his theology when he offers the programmatic statement that God is at the center. This remark comes in the context of his discussion about the essential difference between heavenly philosophy and pagan philosophy. In regard to the latter, Calvin has some appreciation since, for example, it also acknowledges that wealth and pleasure do not last and

---

[16] Regarding Calvin's handling of Bible translations, cf. W. de Greef, *Calvijn over de Bijbel. Enkele brieven, inleidingen en hoofdstukken uit de* Institutie (Houten, 1998).

[17] *Het boek der Psalmen verklaard door Johannes Calvijn*, vertaald en uitgegeven onder toezicht van den weleerw. heer J. Boer Knottnerus V. D. M. (n.p., 1898). Een ongewijzigde tweede druk verscheen in 1970 bij W. A. de Groot-Goudriaan.

[18] *Commentary on the Book of Psalms, by John Calvin, translated from the original Latin and collated with the author's French version by the Rev. James Anderson*, 5 vols. (Edinburgh, 1845–1849).

[19] See below, chapter 8, "God the Hidden."

[20] *A commentary on the Psalms by John Calvin in four volumes*, vol. I, trans. Arthur Golding in 1571, revised and edited by T. H. L. Parker (London: James Clarke, 1965), 10. Only volume I was published.

[21] *Johannes Calvins Auslegung der Heiligen Schrift: Die Psalmen, in deutscher Übersetzung*, 2 vol. (Neukirchen: Buchhandlung des Erziehungsvereins, 1930).

that they offer no lasting support. When it concerns a "happy life" (*beata vita*), though, they are looking for support simply in virtue and by this alone they are going to fall into despair. The problem with pagan philosophy is that it does not place God, who rules the world, in the center,[22] it is thus left with uncertainty. In every matter Calvin places God in the center.[23] The intention of this book is to demonstrate this pattern of Calvin's thought from his commentary on the Psalms.

All statements about God in these texts assume and sometimes state explicitly that our knowledge of God is only partial. Among the very few times in the commentary that Calvin engages in controversy, it is more often than not polemic against the presumptuousness of those theologians who assume they know more about God than he has revealed about himself. The way in which Calvin judges our knowledge of God can be seen in his exegesis of Psalm 104:2. In that verse the psalmist speaks about God as one who veils himself in the light as in a cloak. Calvin then warns that we should not focus on that of God which is hidden but rather on that which God has revealed about himself. Thus, in Calvin's words, this verse explains,

> although God is invisible, yet his glory is conspicuous enough. In respect of his essence, God undoubtedly dwells in light that is inaccessible; but as he irradiates the whole world by his splendor, this is the garment in which he who is hidden in himself appears in a manner visible to us. The knowledge of this truth is of the greatest importance. If men attempt to reach the infinite height to which God is exalted, as though they could fly through the clouds, they cannot but fail in the midst of their course. Those who seek to see him in his naked majesty are certainly very foolish. That we may enjoy the light of him, he must come forth into view with his clothing; that is to say, we must cast our eyes upon the very beautiful fabric of the world in which he wishes to be seen by us and not be too curious and rash in searching into his secret essence.[24]

Calvin has a great aversion to theological speculation because he is convinced that things will go wrong when theology exceeds the limits of our knowledge of God. In this book the question should indeed be asked of Calvin whether he himself has been faithful to this principle.

---

[22] "non constituunt Deum in medio," Ps. 49:2 (*CO* 31, 482).

[23] In this context the parallel is remarkable with Bonhoeffer's speaking of "God in the center" with the associated conclusion that the life of man is only saved from derailing when man leaves God in the center. See Dietrich Bonhoeffer, *Schöpfung und Fall: theologische Auslegung von Genesis 1-3*, hrg. von M. Rüter und I. Tödt (München: Chr. Kaiser, 1955), 77–78.

[24] Ps. 104:1 (*CO* 32, 85).

The analysis of the commentary on the Psalms not only makes a contribution to a fuller comprehension of Calvin's theology, but it explains some of the distinctives of Calvinism. These characteristics, for centuries the same, are found among Calvinists throughout the church universal, and they originate in particular from Calvin's theology of the Psalms. In this respect this study is not concerned with only a search for the roots of Calvin's thought; it is rather concerned with the description of his thought in order to explain how Calvin's theology put its stamp on the spirituality of that which we now know as Calvinism. Calvin's commentary on the Psalms not only tells us much about the man Calvin and his theology, but it also explains many characteristics of his theological descendants, those generations which lived after him and sought to follow in his theological tracks.

1

Calvin and the Psalms[1]

1. The Heart of Calvin

A general short summary of Luther's view on the Psalms runs as follows: "In the Psalms we have a view of the inner heart of the faithful."[2] Though Luther never went on to say that "In their commentaries on the Psalms we have a view of the inner heart of theologians," the intensity with which Calvin devoted his attention to the exposition of the Psalms leads us to think that it would not be unfair to say this of the other great Reformer in Geneva. In short, the question is: Do we look into Calvin's heart when we read his commentary on the Psalms? This question is necessarily preceded by another, namely, whether Calvin did have a heart at all—for no Reformer was pictured as more heartless than this Frenchman.[3] Indeed *"hard"* and *"without heart"* were the image that was created even during his own lifetime; later this image of Calvin was seen as a feature of Calvinism as well.

This caricature has flourished, firstly, because of a widespread ignorance of the work and person of Calvin and, secondly, because of a remarkable one-sidedness of research on Calvin. As regards the ignorance, evidence of Calvin's heartless character is located in the part he played in the case against Michael Servet, a part which is still not yet sufficiently demythologized.[4] As for the one-sided research, for many years special attention was only given to one book—the *Institutes*—as if the whole Calvin and every facet of him could be found in it. The distortion is on par with a tourist who estimates the

---

[1] This part is an elaborated version of my *Calvijn als asielzoeker*; Apeldoornse Studies 35 (Apeldoorn: Theologische Universiteit, 1997).

[2] "In this way it not only passes their words regarding their works on to us, but also opens their heart and the deepest grounds of the richness of their souls, to enable us to get a view on the background and the source of their words and works, *i.e.* in their heart." Cf. WA B, 10, I, 98-105.

[3] Regarding the origin and the refutation of this picture of Calvin, see Richard Stauffer, *L'humanité de Calvin* (Neuchâtel: Delachaux et Niestle, 1964). Cf. Olivier Millet, "L'humanité de Calvin," *La Revue réformée* 191 (1996/5): 9-24 and the literature mentioned by him.

[4] For a more balanced version of Calvin's role in the Servet case, see Ernst Pfisterer, *Calvin's Wirken in Genf* (Neukirchen: Verlag der Buchhandlung des Erziehungsvereins, 1957).

value of a city through merely a study of its ground plan. Fortunately, scholars of Calvin's theology are now turning their attention more and more to his sermons, letters and commentaries.[5] His commentary on the Psalms, however, has not received its share of scholarly attention[6]—in spite of the fact that it is one of the most frequently translated and widely published biblical works of Calvin. An exception to this rule is the book by J. van der Haar[7] which provides a systematical synopsis of the Commentary on the Psalms. Because of this work's meditative character, however, it is limited to but a description of Calvin's view on personal religious life.

---

[5] For a review on current Calvin research, see R. C. Gamble, "Current trends in Calvin Research, 1982-1990," in *Calvinus Sacrae Scripturae Professor*, ed. W. H. Neuser (Grand Rapids: Eerdmans Publishing Company, 1994), 91-112.

[6] The monograph of John Walchenbach does not treat the Commentary on the Psalms but only the influence of David and the Psalms on Calvin: John R. Walchenbach, "The Influence of David and the Psalms on the life and thought of John Calvin" (Th.M. thesis, Pittsburgh Theological Seminary, 1969). Almost without exception the rest of the literature is limited to smaller studies on narrower subjects from the Commentary on the Psalms. In those cases where the relation between David and Calvin is treated, the research is primarily confined to the *Praefatio* of Calvin's commentary. See K. Bakker, *Opmerkingen over Kalvijn's voorrede bij den commentaar op de psalmen* (Amsterdam, n.d.); W. Balke, "Calvijn over de geschapen werkelijkheid in zijn Psalmencommentaar," in *Wegen en gestalten in het gereformeerd protestantisme: Een bundel studies over de geschiedenis van het gereformeerd protestantisme aangeboden aan Prof. Dr. S. van der Linde* ed. W. Balke (Amsterdam: T. Bolland, 1976), 89-104; E. Blaser, "Vom Gesetz in Calvins Predigten über den 119. Psalm," in *Das Wort sie sollen lassen stahn: ein Festschrift für A. Schädelin* (Bern, 1950); E. A. Gosselin, *The King's Progress to Jerusalem: Some Interpretations of David during the Reformation Period and their Patristic and Medieval Background* (Malibu: Undena Publications, 1976); James A. de Jong, "'An Anatomy of all Parts of the Soul': Insights into Calvin's Spirituality from His Psalms Commentary," in *Calvinus Professor*, 1-14; H. J. Kraus, "Vom Leben und Tod in den Psalmen: Eine Studie zu Calvins Psalmenkommentar," in *Biblisch-Theologische Aufsätze* (Neukirchen: Neukirchener Verlag, 1972), 258-77; Robert Martin-Achard, "Calvin et les Psaumes," in *Approche des Psaumes* (Paris, 1969), 9-17; J. L. Mays, "Calvin as an Exegete of the Psalms," in *Calvin Studies IV: Presented at the Colloquium on Calvin Studies at Davidson College and Davidson College Presbyterian Church, Davidson, North Carolina*, ed. J. H. Leith and W. S. Johnson (1988), 95-104; Peter Opitz, "'Asperges me Domino hyssopo, et mundabor': Beobachtungen zu Sadolets und Calvins Exegesen von Psalm 51 als Frage nach dem '*proprium*' reformierter Schriftauslegung," in *Reformiertes Erbe: Festschrift für Gottfried W. Locher zu seinem 80 Geburtstag*, 2 vol., ed. Heiko A. Oberman, *et. als* (Zürich: Theologischer Verlag, 1993), 297-313; *idem*, "Imitation of David: David as Paradigm for Faith in Calvin's Exegesis of the Psalms," *Sixteenth Century Journal* 24 (1993): 843-63; S. H. Russell, "Calvin and the Messianic Interpretation of the Psalms," *Scottish Journal of Theology* 21 (1968): 37-47; H. Schützeichel, "Ein Grundkurs des Glaubens: Calvins Auslegung des 51. Psalms," *Catholica* 44 (1990): 203-217; and H. J. Selderhuis, *David, Calvijn en ik* (Barneveld: De Vuurbaak, 1995).

[7] J. van der Haar, *Het geestelijke leven bij Calvijn* (Utrecht: De Banier, 1960).

2. The Commentary on the Psalms in Historical Context

My research is directed to the theology of Calvin's commentary on the Psalms. In order to arrive at a proper understanding of Calvin's theology, however, it is necessary to relate it to his biography. Theology is never timeless, and it cannot be studied in a historical vacuum. Therefore, an astute theologian must not only have a thorough knowledge of the cultural, social, political and religious situation of his era, but he will also be conscious of the fact that these aspects of his time influence his own theological work. This truth applies of course to Calvin. The first part of the above-mentioned dictum is in any case applicable to him. His involvement in the European Reformation naturally roused in him a high degree of political interest and activity. His correspondence also reveals that Calvin was well informed about scientific and cultural developments. It is thus the influence of his historical context on Calvin's theology which merits a closer investigation, and this study seeks to contribute to such an investigation.

Calvin's high esteem for the Psalms is already visible in his preface to Louis Budé's French translation of this biblical book in 1551.[8] There Calvin writes that the kindness of God as well as the encouragement to thank him for his benevolence are never better expressed than in this Old Testament book. Indeed, David is a God-given mirror in whom we can see what must incite us to prayer and what must move us to praise him when he answers our prayer. In this preface Calvin pens the memorable statement which he will repeat in the preface to his commentary: the Psalms are "an anatomy of all feelings of the soul."[9] All emotions of the human heart—joy, anger, temptation and sorrow—can be found there. In stating this, Calvin repeats what Luther had said: that in the Psalms one can look into the inner heart of the faithful. Subsequently Calvin proceeds to give a lengthy exposition of things we can learn by reading the Psalms. Calvin's emphasis on the teaching aspect of the Psalms is rather conspicuous. The Psalms uncover sins that would otherwise have remained hidden to us. They teach us how necessary it is to call on God's help when we encounter trials. The Psalms teach us that Satan is our greatest enemy. In this book we learn how it is justified that God punishes our sins. By reading from the Psalter we are taught of both our own need and our duty to pray for our neighbor as well as for the whole church. Through the Psalms the Spirit instructs us to embrace God's mercy in the

---

[8] The text of this preface is in Rodolphe Peter's "Calvin et la traduction des Pseaumes de Louis Budé," *Revue d'histoire et de philosophie religieuses* 42 (1962): 175-92.

[9] "...les Pseaumes contiennent comme une anatomie de toutes les affections de l'ame...," *Calvin et la traduction*, 186. In his preface to the commentary on the Psalms, Calvin writes: "Librum hunc non abs re vocare soleo *anatomen* (Greek) omnium animae partium...," (*CO* 31, 15).

midst of all difficulties. Calvin concludes that he who wants to make progress in the school of God needs the Psalms.[10]

The commentary on the Psalms appeared in 1557 during the last few years of Calvin's life.[11] Thus he was able to draw from a lifetime of theological reflection in producing this book. This certainly would seem to be the case with the Psalter since this commentary emanated from his teaching at the Academy in Geneva. He started to lecture on the Psalms in 1552, and he began writing his commentary in 1553. It was, however, a few years earlier that he developed a great interest in the Psalms, for since 1549 he preached on the Psalms every Sunday afternoon almost continuously, finishing the series with the last Psalm in 1554.[12] Even afterwards he often preached from this book on Sunday afternoons. During these years, moreover, Calvin treated the Psalms every week in the *Congrégations* (the public Bible studies with his colleagues on Fridays).[13] Additionally, his high esteem for the Psalter is evident from the fact that this was the only Old Testament book from which he preached on Sundays.

In his preface to the commentary Calvin takes pains to explain that it was always other people who incited him to an exposition of the Psalms. Apparently Calvin here intends to deny the idea that the commentary was ever meant to increase his own fame.[14] On the contrary, it was not even Calvin's choice to write,[15] but since it now exists, he says it must solely serve the edification of the church.[16] Indeed, initially Calvin did not intend to lecture on the Psalms either. He regarded Bucer's commentary to be so

[10] "Telles et si grandes utilités nous monstrent assez en quelle recommandation nous devons avoir le Psautier, si nous desirons de profiter en en l'eschole de Dieu," Peter, "Calvin et la traduction," 188.

[11] For bibliographical notes, see Rodolphe Peter et Jean-François Gilmont, *Bibliotheca Calviniana: Les Oevres de Jean Calvin publiées au XVIe siècle*, 2 vol. (Genève: Droz, 1994), vol. 2, 627-32. A French translation of the commentary was published the next year. A summarized version of the French edition was published in 1558: *Le Psaultier déclaré pas annotations extraites des commentaires de M. Jean Calvin.* See Peter/Gilmont, 682-83.

[12] For a chronological review of Calvin's sermons, cf. T. H. L. Parker, *Calvin's Preaching* (Louisville, KY: Westminster/John Knox Press, 1992), 150-2.

[13] Calvin discussed the Psalms during these meetings from 1555 up to August 1559. See T. H. L. Parker, *Calvin's Old Testament Commentaries* (Louisville, KY: Westminster/John Knox Press, 1993), 15 and 29-31.

[14] At the end of the preface Calvin mentions that there are people who rather would have preferred a thicker book with polemics and erudition, for that would bring more fame for Calvin himself: "...ex multiplici congerie suggerere materiam ambitiosi splendoris," *Praefation* (*CO* 31, 15).

[15] "Is certe metus ad opus texendum magis me pertraxit quam tulerit libera voluntas," *Praefation* (*CO* 31, 15).

[16] "...sed nihil pluris fuit, quam ecclesiae aedificatione consulere," *Praefatio* (*CO* 31, 35).

excellent as to render his own exposition entirely superfluous.[17] When he, having been prompted by friends, decided to lecture on the exposition of the Psalms, though, there was an idea to publish his lectures. In order to have something available for his own people, Calvin planned to write on the Psalms in French.[18] Just before starting with this, however, he began to comment on one Psalm in Latin, and, seeing that it went so well, he simply continued in the same vein. Once more it was others who prompted him to comment, but now Calvin himself became convinced that while working on the exposition, he saw the possibility of helping people not so well versed in reading to understand this Bible book better. Therefore he avoided controversy as far as possible and treated dissenting views only when keeping silent about them would create unnecessary confusion among his readers.

Meanwhile, this was also a very eventful period in the history of the city of Geneva. Around the year 1550, the city had about 13,000 inhabitants. However, because of the immigration of Protestant refugees who came primarily from France and Italy, the population increased to more than 21,000 by 1560.[19] These numbers show that the group of people to whom Calvin preached and administered pastoral care consisted more and more of refugees. In addition in all his publications he kept in mind the needs of the persecuted refugees in his fatherland, France.

From a political and an ecclesiastical point of view the period during which Calvin wrote his commentary was a time of transition from intense struggle to peaceful labor in constructing an orderly ecclesiastical life. After an intense internal conflict during 1553 and 1554 the Council decided in January of 1555 to uphold the church order of 1541. To Calvin this came as a complete surprise. The results of the local elections during the following month were also favorable to Calvin's policy—a fact to be taken into account when rating his exegesis since he writes out of a position of a winner.

Calvin's commentary on the Psalms provides an excellent case study in the relation between theology and biography. The character of the Psalms

---

[17] *Praefatio (CO* 31, 13). Bucer's commentary was published in Strasbourg in 1529 with the title *S. Psalmorum libri quinque ad ebraicam veritatem versi, et familiari explanatione elucidati.* On the order of Bucer it was published under the pseudonym Aretius Felinus. In retrospect, says Calvin, he could also have mentioned the commentary by Wolfgang Musculus. It was published in 1551, and Calvin had not known it yet when he started his lectures on the Psalms. For information about the editions of the commentary by Musculus, see Marc van Wijnkoop Lüthi, "Druckwerkeverzeichnis des Wolfgang Musculus," in *Wolfgang Musculus (1497-1563) und die oberdeutsche Reformation,* ed. Rudolf Dellsperger, *et al.* (Berlin: Akademie Verlag, 1997), 379-85.

[18] "...aliquid gallice...," *Praefatio (CO* 31, 13).

[19] William G. Naphy, *Calvin and the consolidation of the Genevan Reformation* (Manchester, NY: Manchester University Press, 1994), 140.

leads to a clear expression of the theology and spirituality of the commentator not only in sermons but even more so in a commentary upon them. The choice for taking this commentary is confirmed by the value Calvin himself attributes to the Psalms. He writes:

> Nowhere else can the favor of God towards his church and all his other works be found revealed more clearly. Nowhere else are so many deliverances by God recorded. Nowhere else do we find so many splendid evidences of the fatherly providence and solicitude of God towards us. In short, nowhere else are we more perfectly taught the right manner of praising God nor the reason by which we are most powerfully roused to the performance of this religious service.[20]

3. Biographical Aspects

Calvin expressed his motto of life in his personal emblem. The emblem shows an outstretched hand holding a large heart in such a way that the hand is evidently presenting the heart: *"Cor meum tibi offero, prompte et sincere"* ("My heart I give you, promptly and sincerely"). A question that has kept scholars busy for ages thus follows: What is embodied in that heart of Calvin? What are the thoughts and emotions within this man who preferred not to talk about himself?[21] It is the question about Calvin's spirituality.

Much is known about his life and works, but the person behind the reformer is largely unknown.[22] Yet he reveals more about himself than is apparent at first sight. Precisely his statement that he dislikes to speak about himself shows the way to study Calvin's spiritual biography. Sometimes research on Calvin assumed that Calvin stated that he had not said anything about himself. In reality, though, he merely said that he was not eager to do so.[23] So he does indeed speak about himself although it is infrequent and minimal because he disliked it. Therefore Calvin's words need to be read very carefully, for only then can we discover that between the lines he tells us quite a lot about himself.[24]

---

[20] *Praefatio* (*CO* 31, 19).

[21] "De me non libenter loquor," as Calvin answers Sadoleto, *CO* 5, 389.

[22] In an elaborate study Büsser has captured the way Calvin saw himself very clearly: Fritz Büsser, *Calvins Urteil über sich selbst* (Zürich: Zwingli Verlag, 1950).

[23] The importance of the quoted statement is formulated by Oberman as follows: "...to reflect on especially these five words, "De me non libenter loquor" is worth the trouble. The reason is that it is possible to draw a line from these words to Calvin's personality, to his vocation and above all to the centre of his theology, which has been sought for so long." Heiko A. Oberman, *De erfenis van Calvijn* (Kampen: J. H. Kok, 1988), 15-6.

[24] Cf. Bouwsma: "Nevertheless, I think that Calvin reveals a great deal about himself to those who have learned his oblique modes of communication," William J. Bouwsma, *John Calvin: A Sixteenth Century Portrait* (New York: Oxford University Press,

Apart from the occasional remark in his letters or the information we receive from his contemporaries, we have a rich source of knowledge about the person of Calvin in his commentary on the Psalms, for it is particularly through David that Calvin makes himself known to us. In the preface of his commentary he says that the Psalms reveal to us all the stirrings of the heart.[25] From this typically short passage it is clear that Calvin speaks first and foremost about his own heart. William Bouwsma has presented these stirrings of Calvin's heart in a refreshing new way. It took a non-theologian to help us see Calvin as a man, as a human being. But as soon as the non-theological viewpoint of Bouwsma is forgotten, there is the risk that Calvin, like formerly Luther, might fall prey to a primarily psychological interpretation.[26] Therefore Bouwsma's results need to be assimilated and possibly corrected by a theological approach to Calvin.[27] Indeed, in his exposition of the Psalter Calvin opens his heart to us. However, when research on Calvin goes further than this, it can obscure Calvin's purpose in writing this biblical commentary, which was to present people with a view of the very heart of God.

In any case, the unveiling of Calvin's heart in this commentary offers an intimate picture of the Reformer. Calvin himself writes in the preface: "I must confess that by nature I have not much courage and that I am timid,

---

1988). Oberman has analyzed some autobiographical notes of Calvin painstakingly. By that he shed more light on the meaning of Calvin's "conversion" and on the contextuality of Calvin's theology. Cf. his *"Subita conversio*: The conversion of John Calvin," in *Das reformierte Erbe*, 279-95, and *"Initia Calvini*: The Matrix of Calvin's Reformation," in *Calvinus Professor*, 113-54.

[25] Cf. Alexander Ganoczy, *Le jeune Calvin: Genèse et évolution de sa vocation réformatrice* (Wiesbaden: F. Steiner, 1966), 295-304. Ganoczy presents in the context of his study on the young Calvin an analysis of the *Praefatio* and draws the conclusion that it is not an autobiographical document. According to Ganoczy, Calvin for example does not tell how and when he was converted; instead he wants to demonstrate by virtue of his own experience the way in which way the grace of God is stronger than the resistance of man. Millet agrees with Ganoczy's conclusion by stating in a similar way that the character of the preface is not biographical but typological. He admits that the text contains biographical aspects, though: "A cette perspective, non pas biographique mais typologique ...," Olivier Millet, *Calvin et la dynamique de la parole: Étude de rhétorique réformée* (Paris: H. Champion, 1992), 522. In my opinion, the typological character includes the autobiographical aspects rather than excluding them. Specifically from the typology there are some clear lines to Calvin's person.

[26] Regarding Luther, see Erik H. Erikson, *Young man Luther: A study in psychoanalysis and history* (New York: Norton, 1958).

[27] "One hopes, however, that this paradoxical, troubled, sublime thinker will yet find an interpretation in which Bouwsma's contribution is incorporated into a more unified understanding of Calvin's theology and conscious intentions," Edward A. Dowey, Jr., *The Knowledge of God in Calvin's theology* (Grand Rapids: Eerdmans Publishing Company, 1994), 274.

faint-hearted and weak."[28] In reading the text of this commentary on the Psalms the truth of this self-evaluation is confirmed. Taking note of Calvin's life experiences, it is no wonder that he found the Psalms intriguing. His child died shortly after birth. His wife, Idelette van Buren, passed away only eight short years after they were married. Moreover, Calvin's exceptionally weak health throughout his adult life caused him to suffer from various ailments, bringing with them constant pain and fatigue.[29] Add to this the attempts on his life, the incessant slander from his critics, the endless hard work, the political intrigues, and—not to be forgotten—the enduring pains of homesickness.[30] It is telling of the Frenchman's experience when, having said that the Psalms describe the whole spectrum of human feelings, he only enumerates the negative ones: "pain, depression, fear, doubt, hope, worries, anxieties, confusion—in short, all the feelings that swing man's inner being to and fro."[31] Although the Psalter also describes many feelings of joy, certitude, and thankfulness, Calvin's remark is somewhat characteristic of his personality. While many in the Reformed tradition consider Calvin to be, as the title of one book on him puts it, "the giant of Noyon,"[32] we instead find in the commentary on the Psalms someone who seems more like Tom Thumb.

To better understand this commentary, it is important to notice the time at which it was written. In a letter to Bullinger dated March 27, 1557, Beza remarks that Calvin is often forced to endure injustice and that he finds consolation in his work commenting on the Psalms.[33] Having endured many things, Calvin finds events in the Psalms comparable to his own experience. Because he views these events from the perspective of the Psalms, Calvin's interpretation sometimes reflects more his own experience than the historical facts.[34] The notion of identification is strengthened by the fact that Calvin also experienced the world in which he lived as completely chaotic. It is a

---

[28] This biographical coloring of the *Praefatio* fits into a long tradition of exegetes of the Psalms who similarly wrote of themselves. Millet, *Calvin et la dynamique de la parole*, 523, mentions in this regard the names of Athanasius, Cassiodorus, Luther and Bugenhagen.

[29] Concerning Calvin's health (or lack of it), see T. H. L. Parker, *John Calvin: A biography* (Philadelphia: Westminster Press, 1975), 150-5.

[30] Oberman, *Calvinus Professor*, 154, note 152, in this regard also refers to the following texts: "...et scimus hoc est durius, ubi quis longe abstrahitur a patria," Jer. 22:28 (*CO* 38, 399); "Scimus enim durum esse exsilium," Lamentations 1:3 (*CO* 39, 511).

[31] *Praefatio* (*CO* 31, 15). Regarding Calvin's troubles see also the way he bore it in: Büsser, *Urteil*, 83-9.

[32] P. A. de Rover, *Calvijn, de reus uit Noyon: Levensroman*, 2nd edition (Den Haag: Voerhoeve, 1980).

[33] "Calvin que est très injustement accablé comme tu le sais, se console en écrivant des commentaires sur les Pseaumes." See *Correspondence de Thèodore de Bèze*, vol. 2 (Genève, 1996), 58.

[34] For examples, cf. Naphy, *Consolidation*, 84-120.

world in which everything turns around and nothing is sure,[35] in short, a world where confusion rules.[36] This chaos particularly strikes Christians who live like sheep among wolves[37] and wander about on this earth.[38] Not a day passes that we do not experience pain and trouble, says Calvin.[39] It is small wonder, therefore, that his own experience has so molded his exposition as he himself admits:

> Moreover, if my readers derive any fruit and advantage from the labor which I have bestowed in writing this commentary, I would have them to understand that the small measure of experience which I have had in the conflicts with which the Lord has exercised me has in no ordinary degree assisted me, not only in applying to present use whatever instruction could be gathered from these divine compositions, but also in comprehending more easily the design of the writer in each of the Psalms.[40]

Humanistic exposition of texts implies a subjective involvement of the expositor. The expositor is more than someone who simply passes on the meaning of the text. Therefore, he is not the *trait d'union* between the text and the reader of its exposition, but by involving himself in the context of the text, he attempts to pass on the meaning as efficiently as possible.[41] It is a matter of communication, not only between expositor and text but also between the expositor and the reader of the exposition. This humanistic textual exposition has the consequence that the exposition also reveals much about the expositor. The result of this view is indeed that, when the reader has some profit from Calvin's commentary, it is mainly due to Calvin's own experience. Because he knows that his audience in Geneva (most of whom were refugees) and the readers in France face the same sorts of troubles, he continually speaks in terms of "we" and "us." Through this rhetorical style he establishes a relation with his readers.[42] When the text describes various kinds of troubles, Calvin uses his own experience as a starting point. Therefore,

---

[35] "...in rota volvatur mundus ...," Ps. 18:8 (*CO* 31, 216); "...hac caduca vita ...," Ps 23:6 (*CO* 31, 242).

[36] "...confusa perturbatio...," Ps. 25:13 (*CO* 31, 258).

[37] "...in medio luporum...," Ps. 34:8 (*CO* 31, 338).

[38] Calvin speaks about "vagari," Ps. 37:9 (*CO* 31, 371).

[39] "Conditio nostra, fateor, tot miseriis in hoc mundo implicita est, tantaque varietate agitatur, ut nullus fere dies sine molestia et dolore praetereat, deinde inter tot dubios eventus fieri non potest quin assidue anxii simus ac trepidi," Ps. 30:6 (*CO* 31, 294-5).

[40] *CO* 31, 19.

[41] Millet, *Calvin*, 523.

[42] Regarding Calvin's use of the rhetoric, cf. Serene Jones, *Calvin and the Rhetoric of Piety* (Louisville, KY: Westminster/John Knox Press, 1995).

when he speaks about "us" and "we,"[43] it should be understood as "me" and "I," references to the first person by the man who claimed, "I do not like to speak about myself."[44] He who reads "I" in many of the places where "we" is written expands his knowledge about Calvin the man.[45] Calvin's comment that the Bible serves as the spectacles that a man needs in order to notice God's hand in creation is well-known.[46] Similarly it should be kept in mind that Calvin, while commenting on the Psalms, is himself wearing spectacles, namely those of his own experience. In Calvin's case though they are sunglasses: even bright things acquire a dark shade.

While this commentary then presents us with an insight into Calvin's heart, it ought to be considered if and to what extent this commentary illumines the heart of Calvin's theology. Therefore I want to discuss further the theological importance of Calvin's commentary on the Psalms, beginning with a look at Calvin's relation to David.

4. David and Calvin

Reading the commentary on the Psalms soon shows us that Calvin recognizes himself in David.[47] This recognition is given both by Calvin's emphasis on the analogous situation between the church of Israel and the church of Geneva[48] and even by the common situations face by David and Calvin himself. When Calvin reads the Psalms, it is as if he is so re-reading his own life-history, "...as if in a mirror I can see both the beginning of my calling as

[43] Concerning the way Calvin uses the word "us," see Millet, *Calvin*, 532-7; W. H. T. Moehn, *God roept ons tot Zijn dienst: Een homiletisch onderzoek naar de verhouding tussen God en hoorder in Calvijns preken over Handelingen 4:1-6:7* (Kampen: Kok, 1996).

[44] This approach does not mean a correction, though it offers a significant addition to the data of Büsser. He restricted himself to the "I"-statements.

[45] Millet refers to passages in other works of Calvin where the latter speaks about "us" but primarily thinks of "me." (Millet, *Calvin*, 532-537, has named this section fittingly: "Du 'nous' ou 'je.'") Calvin speaks about "us" to mention himself not explicitly but to include himself unambiguously. Mülhaupt believes that the same applies to the sermons on the Psalms: "Wenn irgendwo in seiner Predigt die Herztöne seines Christentums vernehmbar sind, dann ist dies in seinen Psalmpredigten zu erwarten," Mülhaupt, *Psalmpredigten*, xxviii.

[46] *Inst.* I.6.1.

[47] Dowey formulates it by saying that, for Calvin, David is "his own nearest counterpart in the Bible." Dowey, *Knowledge*, 194.

[48] See *inter alia* Calvin's introduction on Psalm 10: "...descriptio vivam publici status corrupti et perversi imaginem quasi in speculo repraesentat...," (*CO* 31, 108); similarly "...si eadem sit sua conditio, quae olim fuit Davidis..," Ps. 12:1 (*CO* 31, 126); see also Ps. 118:19 (*CO* 31, 207-8). According to Gosselin, *Progress*, 70, we find this idea of an analogy with the situation of David also in the case of other Reformers like Bucer and Melanchthon: "...as they were caught up in what they believed were parallel crises, duties and feelings."

well as the further course of my work."[49] The church of Geneva and the church of Israel likewise present identical situations. The existence of many hypocrites in the church and many enemies outside the church as well as the sins of idolatry and wickedness are found both in the Psalms and in Calvin's letters. Similar also is the relation between throne and altar, between city hall and temple; for in Geneva Calvin wanted to institute his ideal of the Christian society à la Israel.[50]

Calvin attributes a large number of Psalms to David even though not all of these Psalms have the inscription "of David." He favors this interpretation of authorship and setting because the situation described in the Psalms often fit David best. He even applies this to a Psalm where, for instance, Asaph is cited as the author.[51] Yet, Calvin can also question Davidic authorship by means of this same argument.[52]

Calvin admires the constancy of David's faith,[53] and the example of David's courage, fidelity and determination supported the Reformer during some difficult years.[54] Calvin felt that he also was opposed by militant Philistines and troubled by local traitors, but, just like David who persevered in such circumstances, Calvin intended to endure such hardship if he might obtain an equally successful result as well. The attacks on his person, the casting of suspicion on him, and the scorn of those who formerly conducted themselves as his friends and brothers hurt him badly. Calvin thus describes the precarious position of David in such a lively manner that it appears as if he himself experienced it.[55] When he says that insult and false accusations are more painful than a hundred deaths, he is surely speaking from experience.[56] In short, Calvin encountered in Geneva the same kind of trouble caused by the same sort of people as those against whom David had fought.[57] Therefore, he recognizes himself in the pains that David experienced, and thus it is no wonder—indeed it is an illuminating admission on the part of the Reformer—when he writes:

---

[49] *Praefatio* (*CO* 31, 21).
[50] Calvin calls the relation between the role of the king and that of the priest in Israel: "sacrum vinculum," Ps. 20:3 (*CO* 31, 208).
[51] Ps. 73: introduction (*CO* 31, 673).
[52] Ps. 44:1 (*CO* 31, 436).
[53] "...pietatis constantiae...," Ps. 116:14 (*CO* 31, 199).
[54] Ps 88:1 (*CO* 31, 806). Even on his dying bed the example of David was comforting Calvin, see Beza's *Vita Calvini* (*CO* 21, 165).
[55] "...ut petulantius vexarent miserum et profugum hominem, quem videbant omni auxilio destitui," Ps. 64:4 (*CO* 31, 600).
[56] Ps. 69:5 (*CO* 31, 639).
[57] See *inter alia*: Ps. 26:1 (*CO* 31, 264); Ps. 31:12 (*CO* 31, 307).

My readers, too, if I mistake not will observe that in unfolding the
internal affections of both David and others I discourse upon them as
matters with which I have familiar experience. [58]

With more detail than is permitted by the biblical text, Calvin considers the
scorn that David had to suffer from those who simply wanted to vilify his
good name. David vehemently resisted these people, Calvin writes, not
because of his name but for sake of the well-being of the church.[59] The reader
of the commentary will thus understand why Calvin took up a position in
Geneva the way David did and why Calvin has to condone this position.

Hence, when Calvin speaks of David, he is often speaking of himself.
This circumstance opens the door to a rich source of information about
Calvin. From the remark of Calvin quoted above it is no wonder that this
biographical information is most of all to be found in the Psalms written by
David. If, for instance, Psalm 2 mentions the enmity David has to endure, it
provides Calvin with the occasion for an extensive discussion on fear, temptation and human emotions.[60] The subjective involvement with the Davidic
Psalms is all the more conspicuous against the backdrop of a certain reserve
in his exposition of the other Psalms.

Calvin's recognition of himself in David almost approximates an identification with "the anointed of the Lord." This identification is apparent
especially when the special position of David comes up for discussion.
Calvin discusses extensively how David was called by the Lord and therefore
has a legal claim to be king; what is more, because of his unique position he
has the right to defend himself against attacks as well as to permit himself a
certain course of action.[61] Calvin understands his own position in a similar
manner because, like David, he has been called from anonymity to the
highest office of being a servant of God. Both this identical career and the
consciousness of being called were clearly very important to Calvin. It
sounds like a defense of his own attitude when Calvin states that David
himself did not pursue his high office since that truly would be a sign of
"haughty thoughtlessness."[62] Divine calling was to David as well as to Calvin
the legitimization of his continuing work in defending the church and her
true doctrine. By extension Calvin points out that this *vocatio Dei* implies
that to resist David is to resist the anointed of the Lord and thus the Lord

---

[58] *Praefatio* (*CO* 31, 33).

[59] "Haec ratio est cur tam sollicite et vehementer contendat David in asserenda causae
suae iustitia," Ps. 18:21 (*CO* 31, 181).

[60] "Nec vero dubium est quin anxie cum gravissimis tentationibus ei luctandum fuerit,"
Ps. 2:1 (*CO* 31, 41-2).

[61] See especially the exposition on Psalm 2 (*CO* 31, 41-52). Similarly Ps. 18:1 (*CO* 31,
169-70); Ps. 106:16 (*CO* 31, 122-32); Ps. 106:31 (*CO* 32, 128).

[62] Ps 101:1 (*CO* 32, 56).

himself.[63] From this perspective of such an identity between David and Calvin, the latter's actions in Geneva are more comprehensible. Calvin is fascinated by David's unexpected election to the throne.[64] This parallel might even shed light on Calvin's *subita conversio*. Calvin's conversion was not sudden like that of Paul but unexpected like God's election of David as king.[65] In this way Calvin feels a personal connection to David which is evident in Calvin's remark that David, having been unexpectedly elected by God, was equipped with special gifts to fulfill his task. As Calvin points out, God did the same with the apostles, and he is still equipping his chosen servants today.[66]

This identification also leads to an interpretation of David's circumstances from Calvin's situation. The enmity that David experienced according to Psalm 2 is also evident, says Calvin, in the novelties (*res novae*) his opponents bring, although this text does not speak of such a thing. The same applies to the remark that David was accused of being the cause of conflict with Saul, and this because of David's appetite for power (*regnandi cupiditas*). While absent from the text, this charge was issued against Calvin.[67] Moreover, does not Calvin speak from self-knowledge and therefore about himself when he says that we often provoke opposition because of our lack of self-control?[68]

It is this identification with the psalmist that furnishes us with reasons to deduce autobiography, specifically a spiritual autobiography, from Calvin's expositions. However it is noteworthy that this identification neither leads to an idealization of David nor even to an ideological use of David. This would not only be contrary to Calvin's aversion to idolatry but also to his view of man. David is often presented to his readers as an example, and from Calvin's choice of his words it is indeed clear that David is an admirable model. All of the faithful can learn a great deal from this king.[69] Calvin would have liked to have the patience and zeal of this king of Israel. Yet Calvin sometimes does not hesitate to criticize David when he deviates in words and deeds from God's commandments.[70] In Calvin's exposition of Psalm 42 one hears a note of critique where David complains about his

---

[63] "Sed notanda est fiduciae ratio quod scilicet non temere vel privato motu se ingesserit ad regnandum, sed tantum Dei vocationem sequutus sit. Unde colligit in sua persona Deum impetu...," Ps. 2:1 (*CO* 31, 42). See also Ps. 4:3 (*CO* 31, 60).

[64] For example, Ps. 89:20-1 (*CO* 31, 818-9). Cf. Ps. 118:22 (*CO* 32, 208-9).

[65] Cf. Oberman, *Subita Conversio*, 279-295, who also translates "subita" as "unexpected."

[66] "Et eandem hodie spiritus gratiam in suis ministris exserit," Ps. 89:20 (*CO* 31, 818).

[67] Ps. 7:4 (*CO* 31, 80).

[68] Ps. 7:4 (*CO* 31, 81).

[69] Ps. 25:17 (*CO* 31, 261); Ps 26:1 (*CO* 31, 264); Ps. 34:7 (*CO* 31, 338).

[70] Ps. 30:6 (*CO* 31, 295); Ps. 34:1 (*CO* 31, 335); "...vitioso excessu...," Ps. 39:5 (*CO* 31, 339).

inability to go to the temple. Calvin remarks that people who are accustomed to difficulties since childhood are generally more steeled against adversities and would probably not complain so easily.[71] That this perseverance is not seen in David is a conclusion that the reader himself can draw.

Calvin's descriptions of the moral aberrations of David often give us information about the way Calvin has struggled with his own shortcomings.[72] To this must be added the circumstance that this identification has had a negative effect on the exposition of the Psalms. To what extent his own experience influenced the exposition of the Psalms can be seen in his exposition on Psalm 18, when he says that though God has called David to the office of king, David himself would rather have stayed with the sheep and in the secure vicinity of his father.[73] There are, however, no indications of such wishes in the text. We do know about Calvin that he would have preferred to remain in the tranquil sheepfold of his study. In this way Calvin transfers his own feelings to the text. In commenting on Psalm 101:2, Calvin rejects the view held by many exegetes that David was expressing a wish in saying, "When will you come to me?" According to him, it is not a wish (in the form of a lamentation) but a statement: "till you come to me." Calvin, though, immediately adds that David surely did have reasons for such a wish because, having been an unknown shepherd, he was better off than now. Now he is banished from his fatherland and has to endure shame and hatred.[74] David made the statement; the wish however belongs only to Calvin.

What Calvin passes on to the readers of his commentary is so colored by his own experience that a certain one-sidedness is apparent. As has been said, Calvin summarizes mainly negative feelings like pain, doubt and loneliness. His personal experience, including his poor health, evidently contributed to this exposition. As for this commentary's exposition of the religious life and its expression in the Calvinistic tradition, it means that part of its character conforms more to Calvin's experience than to God's revelation.

5. The "Asylum" Motif

There is one parallel in particular between David and Calvin that leads to a better understanding of the correspondence between Calvin's biography and his theology. It concerns what I would like to call the "exile" motif. David's Psalms were mostly composed at times during which he was banished from Jerusalem, at first because of death threats by Saul and later because of Absalom's revolution. According to Calvin a life in exile is the worst that

---

[71] "Scimus, qui a prima pueritia malis sunt assueti, callum contrahere et ipsa malorum assiduitas generat in nobis quandam duritiem...," Ps. 42:5 (*CO* 31, 428).

[72] Ps. 7:4 (*CO* 31, 80-81); Ps. 26:1 (*CO* 31, 264); Ps. 39:2 (*CO* 31, 397).

[73] Ps 18:19 (*CO* 31, 179).

[74] Ps. 101:2 (*CO* 32, 57).

one can encounter.[75] Calvin therefore found himself moved by this theme, and these very words also described his "stirrings of the heart." For Calvin the parallel is startling. This can be seen in his summary of David's afflictions: David was exiled from his fatherland, deprived of his wife, separated from his family and left without financial means.[76] David's position was clearly a reconstruction of that of Calvin. It is widely known that Calvin was always aware of his status as a foreigner in Geneva.[77] He had to flee from France, and he settled in Geneva against his intentions. He was later expelled from this city also, but when trouble started there he realized that he must return, even if it were against his will.[78] During the three years between his departure from and his return back to Geneva he found asylum in Strasbourg where he became a minister of the French speaking congregation. This congregation consisted of French Protestants who had to flee their country because of their faith, and they sought refuge in Strasbourg which at that time was the largest center for refugees in Europe.[79] Thus Calvin, himself an asylum seeker, became a minister to asylum seekers. The same situation arose again in Geneva where French refugees formed a large part of his congregation. Having lost almost everything after they had to flee because of their Reformed convictions, they found asylum in Geneva. These biographical elements connect Calvin with David. Thus it is no wonder that the concept of "asylum" is often found in the commentary on the Psalms. In Calvin's exposition of the Psalms this concept appears 24 times,[80] while, in contrast, the word "asylum" is not even found in the corresponding passages of the Vulgate. In the context of two of these 24 cases, the Vulgate renders *"refugium"*[81] while Calvin speaks about "asylum." "Asylum" is a legal term that Calvin not only encountered in the Bible,[82] but he would undoubtedly also have encountered it in his legal studies. Both canon law and the laws of the early Christian emperors stipulated the right of asylum.[83] Canon law asserted that the protection provided by asylum is only valid as long as the refugee remains at the place of asylum, usually the church. The extension of

---

[75] "Nam sicuti nihil tunc miserias fuit quam in exsilio degere," Ps. 126:2 (*CO* 32, 318).

[76] "Quum patria extorris, uxore spoliatus, cognatis orbatus, cunctis denique opibus privatus foret...," Ps. 27:4 (*CO* 31, 273).

[77] Büsser, *Urteil*, 80-1.

[78] "...quanto tamen cum moerore quantis lacrymis et quanta anxietate, Dominus mihi optimus testis est ...," (*CO* 31, 27).

[79] See *inter alia* Christian Wolff, "Strasbourg, cité du Refuge," in *Strasbourg au coeur religieux du XVIe siècle: Hommage à Lucien Febre* (Strasbourg: Librairie Istra, 1977), 321-30.

[80] Ps. 7:9; 10:6; 11:4; 25:11; 27:5; 31:5; 32:6; 42:7.

[81] Ps. 31:5 (Vulgate 30:4) and 32:6 (Vulgate 31:7).

[82] *Inter alia* Ex. 21:13-14; Num. 35:9-34.

[83] Regarding these laws, what they contain and their history, see: *TRE* vol. 4, 315-27, s.v. "Asylrecht."

this principle into looking to God for asylum is obvious. Calvin incorporates a juridical principle into his theology: One only finds protection against penal prosecution and punishment when you have resort to God.

6. The Parallel between David and the People of God

Calvin is not only interested in the connection he has with David regarding their respective individual fates, but he also envisions a common experience between the fate of David and that of all the other Reformed refugees who were exiled unjustly. To them also David is an example.[84] Calvin numbers himself among them, and this is another reason for Calvin's inclusive use of "we" and "us." In his exile he is united with his exiled brothers and sisters— the asylum seeker in the pulpit and in his cathedra is united with the asylum seekers in both the church and the classroom. This is clear from his exposition of Psalm 94:21, where the twisting of justice into injustice is applied to the authorities who oppress the faithful. Here Calvin would have had the French government specifically in mind, for he states that the system of justice degenerates into a criminal conspiracy to condemn the guiltless.[85] But this indictment is not merely limited to the abuses in France, for to Calvin the church of the Old Testament, the church of the New Testament and the church of post-biblical history is one single church. What happens to David, to Calvin, and to the members of Calvin's congregation is the common destiny of the whole church always and everywhere.[86] David is the model ("specimen") who shows all of the faithful how God's favor leads them.[87] Particularly in the Psalm where David, because of his enemies and pains, cries to God from the deepest distress, Calvin remarks that David is the representative of the whole church and is describing the lot of all of the faithful.[88] Calvin means here that David intentionally uses general terms when it actually concerns just him in order to point out to all of the faithful that God deals with them in the same way as he dealt with David.[89] David is the mouth of Christ and of all those who belong to Christ.[90] Calvin therefore calls him the teacher of the entire church.[91]

---

[84] Ps. 39:2 (*CO* 31, 397). In the exposition on Ps. 34:4-7 (*CO* 31, 337-8) David is called "exemplum" four times.

[85] Ps. 94:21 (*CO* 32, 28).

[86] Ps. 2:2 (*CO* 31, 43-4); Introduction to Ps. 18 (*CO* 31, 169); "Porro sub hoc typo sciamus invictam regni Christi statum fuisse adumbratum...," Ps. 18:38 (*CO* 31, 188).

[87] Ps. 116:16 (*CO* 32, 200).

[88] "...in quo nobis propnitur communis piorum omnium conditio," Ps. 69:1 (*CO* 31, 637).

[89] "Ac generalem sententiam (ut dix) proferre maluit...," Ps. 30:6 (*CO* 31, 294).

[90] "Iam quum loquutus fuerit David quasi ex ore Christi et ex ore piorum omnium, quatenus sunt Christi membra...," Ps. 69:4 (*CO* 31, 638).

[91] "...toti ecclesiae ... magister et doctor...," Ps. 37:1 (*CO* 31, 386). Cf. Ps. 42:1 (*CO* 31, 425): "Communis erat totius ecclesiae doctor et insigne spiritus organon...."

This identification of David with the whole church serves as a consolation and an encouragement. If this man was sometimes struck by anxiety, present believers should not be ashamed of their own fear.[92] If such a virtuous man was slandered, we who are inferior to him in sanctification should not be surprised when we endure the same disgrace.[93] David's faults were in any case a reassurance for Calvin because if, according to Psalm 39:2, even a man like David had difficulty in controlling his tongue, it is small wonder that we often experience the same difficulty.[94] David is also an example of someone who suffers juridical injustice, yet he can bear it in faith.[95] In fact, this reference to bearing injustice in faith implies that Calvin had a message for certain groups in the Reformation: David did not react by taking up arms, and neither should we.[96] Apart from its consolation the parallel also contains an admonition as can be seen from Calvin's remark that David, even away from his fatherland, continued to keep God's law, and even in exile he continued to experience joy in the law.[97] Yet the theological element, directly connected to the historical situation, is more important than the biographical and somewhat psychological aspects mentioned above.

7. The Theological Aspects

As has already been remarked, Calvin wrote and published the commentary on the Psalms towards the end of his career. Consequently, a whole lifetime of theological study and discussion was integrated in this commentary. Because the Psalms do not give equal weight to all of the theological *loci*, one would not expect to find sufficient material in the commentary to represent the whole extent of Calvin's theology. However it contains more than enough to represent the essential aspects of his theology.

Research on Calvin has repeatedly sought a central theme in the theology of this Reformer.[98] The problem in this body of research is that such a theme would need to be sufficiently broad so as not to overlook other themes from his theology. The result of the study of the commentary on the Psalms is, as has been mentioned already, that Calvin's theology does not appear to be anything except *theo*-logy in the sense of treating and defending God's

---

[92] Ps. 25:17 (*CO* 31, 261).

[93] Ps. 64:4 (*CO* 31, 600). Cf. Ps. 119:22 (*CO* 32, 224).

[94] Ps. 39:2 (*CO* 31, 397).

[95] "...discamus non solum iniustam violentiam aequo animo ferre, sed indignas etiam calumnias quibus praeter meritum gravamur," Ps. 94:21 (*CO* 32, 28).

[96] See also Ps. 140:5 (*CO* 32, 388): "Itaque eius exemplo, quoties insolenter hostes nostri se efferent, discamus ad Deum confugere...."

[97] Ps. 119:54 (*CO* 32, 238).

[98] H. Bauke, *Die Probleme der Theologie Calvins* (Leipzig: Hinrichs, 1922); E. Saxer, "Hauptprobleme der Calvinforschung—Forschungsbericht 1974-1982," in *Calvinus Ecclesiae Genevensis Custos*, 93-111.

essential character, his being-God. The generally accepted idea in the past of a central theme (like the sovereignty of God, for example) is not entirely satisfying because the totally otherness of God is not sufficiently expressed. Sovereignty indeed expresses a *gradual* but not an *essential* difference between God and man.

In the beginning of the *Institutes* Calvin points out that theology concerns both the knowledge of God and of knowledge of ourselves. It is impossible for Calvin to describe man detached from his relation to God. Nor can he picture God apart from his dealings with man. Seeing that the Psalms first and foremost treat the relationship between God and man, Calvin finds in the Psalms these central and essential elements for his theology. Indeed, his *Institutes* commences with the declaration:

> Nearly all the wisdom we possess, that is to say, true and sound wisdom, consists of two parts: the knowledge of God and of ourselves.[99]

The same vital connection between the knowledge of God and the knowledge of man is described in the commentary on the Psalms. In this sense Calvin's commentary on the Psalms is a practical elaboration of his *Institutes*. Everything systematically set out in the *Institutes* as biblical doctrine acquires a practical character in the commentary. The practical side of the commentary is evident when Calvin points to the question of what this God *being God* actually means for man. On the one hand it means the salvation of man. Because of his very essence God is able and willing to work salvation by means of righteousness,[100] to guide history according to his plan and purpose,[101] and to render faultless and secure protection to his church in the midst of global chaos. Time and again Calvin stresses that God is not idle.[102] On the other hand God being God also causes a struggle of faith. This struggle may stem from affliction over one's own sins which provoke God's wrath,[103] from the incomprehensibility and the inscrutability of God's ways with people,[104] or from the difficulty of the righteous punishment of God.[105]

However, the God-being of God is mainly a source of reassurance, especially insofar as this is lacking in the notion of God as pictured to the people by Rome. According to Calvin, Rome makes the people afraid of

---

[99] *Inst.* I.1.1, as translated by Ford Lewis Battles in *Institutes of the Christian Religion*, ed. J. T. McNeill, trans. F. L. Battles (Philadelphia: Westminster Press, 1960), 35.

[100] Ps. 32:1 (*CO* 31, 314-5).

[101] Ps. 37:34 (*CO* 31, 384).

[102] *Inter alia* Ps. 9:9 (*CO* 31, 100); Ps. 10:12 (*CO* 31, 115). See also discussion in chapter 4 below.

[103] Ps. 6:6 (*CO* 31, 76).

[104] Ps. 11:6 (*CO* 31, 125); Ps. 37:19 (*CO* 31, 375).

[105] Ps. 6:6 (*CO* 31, 76).

God. On the one hand this is done by presenting salvation as being dependent on human effort, creating constantly a nagging doubt as to whether one has ever done enough. On the other hand God is mainly presented as a just Judge. The Psalms, however, reveal to us the true God—a God who is so great as to be able to "forgive sins free of charge."[106] "In this book," writes Calvin, "the most important thing we can wish to have is presented to us, namely, not only that we might be on intimate terms with God but also that we might openly confess to him the weaknesses which, casting shame on us, we kept hidden from others."[107] The otherness of God comes to light not only in his "un-, human" holiness but also in his "un-human" goodness and mercy.

Calvin's accent on God being God leads him, like his teacher and colleague Luther, to a wholly personal theology of the cross.[108] God's acts are often untraceable and his way of working often seems to us to be unreal and contradictory. We believe, for instance, that God creates order amidst chaos every day while almost none of this is visible.[109] In practical terms Calvin's "*theologia crucis*" considers the Christian life as a life of cross-bearing.[110] Communion with Christ, which is so often accentuated by Calvin,[111] implies communion with the crucified Christ. Consequently the cross plays a part not only in justification but also in sanctification. The Christian life is a life of mortification, a life in which God sometimes poses a cross as a burden to train us in faith and patience;[112] a life in which God leads us into darkness in order to bring us into the light;[113] where God's hand strikes us down in order to teach us that his hand alone can lift us up and raise us again.[114]

In this connection Calvin often speaks about the hiddenness of God,[115] even though he is not always consistent. Sometimes God's hiddenness means that God keeps himself hidden to us while at other times he merely *seems* hidden to us. For instance, Calvin compares God to a worm that works

---

[106] Ps. 32:1 (*CO* 31, 316).

[107] *Praefatio* (*CO* 31, 19).

[108] Walter von Loewenich, *Luther's Theology of the Cross*, trans. H. Bouman (Minneapolis: Augsburg, 1976), 6. For a review of Luther's "theologia crucis," see also Bernhard Lohse, *Luthers Theologie* (Göttingen, 1995), 49-52.

[109] Ps. 7:12 (*CO* 31, 85).

[110] Ps. 30:6 (*CO* 31, 294).

[111] Regarding this, see W. van 't Spijker, "'*Extra nos*' en '*In nobis*' bij Calvijn in pneumatologisch licht," in *Geest, Woord en Kerk*, ed. C. Augustijn, W. H. Neuser en H. J. Selderhuis (Kampen: J. H. Kok, 1991), 114-32.

[112] "...nos Deus cruce exercit...," Ps. 23:4 (*CO* 31, 240); Ps. 9:9 (*CO* 31, 100).

[113] Ps. 30:8 (*CO* 31, 297).

[114] Ps. 44:10 (*CO* 31, 441). See also chapter 8 below.

[115] This subject needs further examination. Cf. Gerrish's formulation: "Surprisingly, however, there is no such body of literature on what Calvin thought about God's hiddenness," B. A. Gerrish, "'To the unknown God', Luther and Calvin on the Hiddenness of God," in *The Old Protestantism and the New: Essays on the Reformation Heritage* (Chicago: University of Chicago Press, 1982), 141.

underground and therefore is invisible,[116] yet he also writes that God sometimes conceals his power to us.[117] We also encounter Calvin's *"theologia crucis"* when he says that God sometimes shrouds himself in darkness in order that our eyes may be enlightened.[118]

His constant accent on God's providence is connected to his historical situation. In times of chaos, injustice and suffering, one only finds stability and peace in the knowledge that God rules. All events must thus be related to God, preventing pride during prosperity and despair in adversity.[119]

Calvin stresses the difference in *rank* between God and man rather than emphasizing the *distance* between them. Of course there is a difference, but this is bridged by God through his accommodation to man in both speech and action. This concept of *"accommodatio,"*[120] however, is utilized by Calvin to denote the total otherness of God. God's accommodation to our capacity of understanding implies that in reality he is different. Therefore, it is impossible to draw conclusions about God's essence from his accommodation.[121] We cannot fully know God; we are unable to entirely grasp him. Calvin's intention is most clearly expressed in his frequent and unconcerned speech about God as our Father. God reveals himself as Father in order that we may understand how and who he wants to be for us. This *accommodatio,* however, does not entail that we should picture the Lord to be like an earthly father.

In spite of his criticism of Roman Catholic theology, Calvin is in a certain sense afraid of God. It is important however to distinguish between two kinds of anxiety. The first is anxiety as "mortal fear," by which I mean a kind of terror that can seize one in certain situations. Calvin sometimes experienced this type of anxiety when he was persecuted.[122] Distinct from this and yet closely related to it is the "dying struggle," the anguish to appear before a just God. Calvin means that this second variety of anguish grows in proportion to

---

[116] Ps. 39:11 (*CO* 31, 403).

[117] Ps. 18:47 (*CO* 31, 192).

[118] Ps. 30:8 (*CO* 31, 297).

[119] Ps. 9:4 (*CO* 31, 97-8).

[120] Ps. 10:1 (*CO* 31, 108); Ps. 18:26 (*CO* 31, 183).

[121] This interpretation of the concept of *"accommodatio"* is reminiscent of the influence of Duns Scotus. Together with the question about the relation between Calvin's theology and calvinistic theology the question about the influence of Scotus on Calvin needs to be investigated. See *inter alia* Oberman, *Grenzen Grootheid*, 27. F. Wendel has already done some research into this: *Calvin: Sources et évolution de sa pensée religieuse*, 2nd edition (Geneve: Labor et Fides, 1975), 92-4. Cf. also S. van der Linde, "Gereformeerde Scholastiek IV, Calvijn," *Theologia Reformata* XXIX (1986, no. 3): 244-66.

[122] Oberman, *Calvinus Professor*, 137, refers to a sermon on 2 Samuel 5:12-17 (1562) in which Calvin tells in retrospect about his mortal fear: "...j'ay esté en ces distresses là, que i'eusse désiré voulu estre quasi mort pour oster ces angouisses."

one's dedication to and knowledge of God.[123] That both types of anxiety played a part in Calvin's life is detectable, and one can also observe how he tries to free himself from the fear of death. Calvin found the fact that David knew such anxiety to be reassuring.[124] Yet the mortal fear of God is a terrible reality that Calvin knows from experience.[125] In his well-known letter to Sadoleto, for instance, he tells that, because of his early exposure to Roman Catholic doctrine, an extreme anxiety was instilled in him towards God, the final judgment, and death.[126] On the other hand Calvin emphatically states that we do not need to fear death.[127] We thus see in Calvin a struggle to move from anxiety toward God to a proper fear of the LORD.

Nevertheless the enduring element of anxiety before God explains why Calvin was no less than two times (first by Farel and later by Bucer) moved to do as others wished. According to Calvin's description of these events he yielded in both cases to obedience when reference was made to God's judgment.[128]

Calvin's theology is concerned with the divinity of God. It is especially evident in passages where God's providence is discussed. The power and glory of God is revealed, Calvin says, not only in the creation of this world, but also in its government.[129] Divine guidance is concealed to us throughout; indeed it remains so hidden that God's acts may seem contradictory to us. God's providence can not be predicted, and yet it is not unpredictable.

The concept of an *"ordo,"* basic for Calvin's ecclesiology and the ensuing principles of canon law, is also related to God being God. In and through creation God has established an order in which man must function as head. By means of a wrong theology, especially a wrong image of God prompted by Satan, man in paradise lapsed into *"superbia."* This pride resulted in a break with God, and consequently in the disruption of order so that creation fell into chaos. Only God's merciful intervention led to the restoration of order. This order is restored in Christ and takes the form of an ordered Christian and ecclesiastical life. Therefore the last judgment is presented by Calvin as the moment when God will restore order totally and definitely. But as long as the Judge is in heaven, "this world remains in confusion."[130] These theological statements must be seen against a biographical backdrop. Calvin

---

[123] Ps. 6:6 (*CO* 31, 77).

[124] Ps. 4:2 (*CO* 31, 59).

[125] Ps. 6:6 (*CO* 31, 77).

[126] "Quoties enim vel in me descendebam, vel animum ad te attollebam, extremus horror me incessebat, cui nulla piacula, nullae satisfactiones mederi possunt" (*CO* 5, 412). Regarding Calvin's anxiety or fear, see also Oberman, *Das Reformierte Erbe*, 291-3.

[127] Ps. 31:5 (*CO* 31, 303).

[128] *Praefatio* (*CO* 31, 24-5).

[129] Ps. 8:1 (*CO* 31, 88).

[130] "...res in mundo miscentur...," Ps. 1:5 (*CO* 31, 40).

lived in chaotic times which he could not tolerate, and he was longing above all else for a peaceful order.[131]

Through all these themes the motif of the "exile" is still present. The situation of Calvin and his congregation is an image of the situation of the church and of the believers on earth: we are seeking for asylum, which means we are outside our fatherland. We may live and work here, but this is not our home: we are staying here temporarily while awaiting the journey home.[132] This theme is taken still further until, in this way, biography brings us to theology: we are not only physically but also spiritually driven away and dislodged. Because of our sins we truly have landed outside of paradise and in the desert. Being in this situation we must and we may seek asylum from God, meaning that we find asylum in his mercy.[133] But as soon as we find this asylum, it will bring us again to exile, oppression, and disgrace; yet, while bearing the cross because of our faith, we may seek and find asylum in the mercy and in the care of God.[134] Thus we live on earth as asylum-seekers, as people who have found asylum by God, and therefore we are strangers, guests, and foreigners on earth. He to whom God has granted asylum in the meantime becomes an asylum seeker in this world again.

This concept can help us to better understand Calvin's doctrine of predestination. Too often—and to the detriment of preaching and pastoral care in the Calvinist tradition—Calvin's doctrine of predestination was artificially removed from its experiential and historical context. Firstly it must be said that the doctrine of predestination has a modest place in the commentary.[135] Secondly, when Calvin speaks about predestination, he is looking at an audience of asylum-seekers. They are the elect because the mark of election is oppression, disgrace, and forced exile; in short, the mark of election is the cross. The cross of Christ is a means of election, but as in cross-bearing it is also a fruit of election. Calvin speaks inclusively about *"our* election in Christ"[136] because in front of him he sees refugees like himself, people who had to leave their possessions behind; these people have lost husband, wife or child—all this because of the theology of the cross. Therefore the distinction between the elect and the reprobate is very clear: those who are persecuting are the rejected; those who are persecuted are the

---

[131] Calvin strived for *"interior tranquilitas"* in the midst of *"motus turbulentos,"* Ps. 37:29 (*CO* 31, 381).

[132] "...peregrinantur in mundo...," introduction on Ps. 37 (*CO* 31, 365).

[133] "...ad gratiae asylum confugere," Ps. 32:1 (*CO* 31, 316).

[134] "...ad misericordiae Dei asylum confugere...," Ps. 25:11 (*CO* 31, 256).

[135] This commentary supports the opinion of Bauke, *Probleme*, 81, that "die Lehre doch im Verlauf der Geschichte der Calvinischen Kirche und Theologie infolge des konfessionellen Gegensatzes ein grösseres Gewicht bekommen, als sie im Rahmen der eigentlichen Theologie Calvins hat."

[136] "...quia gratis in Christo nos elegit...," Ps. 28:8 (*CO* 31, 285).

elect.[137] Hence Calvin's doctrine of predestination is not to be seen apart from the historical situation in which it has its roots. As has been said, this doctrine has but a modest place in the commentary and it did not originate in the silence of the study but in the struggle of daily life.[138]

8. Conclusion

A knowledge of Calvin's biography leads to a better understanding of his theology. Meanwhile a careful reading of his theological works in their historical context compliments his biography. Thus we find in this commentary on the Psalms both the heart of Calvin the man and the heart of his theology. Just as Calvin called the Psalms a treasure chest filled with all sorts of beautiful treasures,[139] we might also conclude that his commentary on the Psalms is a treasure chest filled with his insights both into his theology and his spiritual biography. The following chapters will give a description of these treasures.

---

[137] Ps. 36:5 (*CO* 31, 361).

[138] "Für Calvin ist die Prädestination nicht eine abstrakte Idee, die über der Wirklichkeit schwebt, sondern sie ist die beherrschende innere Ursache in der Entwicklung des Lebens und seiner Zustände," Reinhold Seeberg, *Lehrbuch der Dogmengeschichte*, 4 vol. (Erlangen: A. Deichert, 1920), vol. 4.2, 579.

[139] "Quam varias ac splendidas opes contineat hic thesaurus ...," *Praefatio* (*CO* 31, 15).

2

God the Triune

1. *Vera Theologia*

Calvin's theology is a God-centered theology—a theology which, as its root word (*theo-*) suggests, reflects Calvin's concern "to recognize God as God."[1] The concept one has of God and the doctrine of God that one consequently holds is of essential importance according to Calvin. The way in which Calvin speaks in his commentary on Psalm 100:1 about the attitude of man towards God explains that, in his view, only two possibilities exist: either man fashions God into his own image or God fashions man into his image. Sin inevitably leads man to fashion God into his own image. The result is that man virtually worships himself[2] by ascribing to his own power what belongs to God's power alone. It is God's grace when man is formed in the image of God. Man must recognize God as God and render to him alone all glory. This is the only true theology and, in Calvin's view, also the only true piety. "The definition of piety is that the true God is perfectly served when he alone is so exalted that no creature obscures his divine majesty."[3] On this point the papacy also errs because various superstitions obscure God's glory.

What troubles Calvin concerning idols is not that the creation of images as such is wrong. (Calvin does not censure the arts!) The problem is that when men form themselves an image of God, they haul God down from heaven, and they think they can attach him to such an image.[4] The eternal God however cannot be represented by a corruptible image for it is repugnant to his essence to dwell in something like stone or wood. We are allowed one single concept of God alone, namely, that of his heavenly majesty.[5] God simply cannot be "captured" in our representation of him. An accurate summary of Calvin's theology is that men must recognize God as God. That means they must live with the reality that God's revelation to them is limited.[6]

---

[1] "…cognoscere iubet quid Deus sit Deus," Ps. 100:1 (*CO* 32, 54).
[2] " …quisque tamen sibi Deus est, et se ipsum adorat," Ps. 100:1 (*CO* 32, 54).
[3] Ps. 97:7 (*CO* 32, 45).
[4] "…quasi ipsum elicere e coelo: in eius locum substitutiae mare falsitas…," Ps. 115:8 (*CO* 32, 187).
[5] Ps. 115:4 (*CO* 32, 186).
[6] Dowey, *Knowledge,* 11.

Just how fundamental Calvin regards the doctrine of God is clearly shown by his commentary on Psalm 83:19, where it confesses that God's name is the LORD, the Most High over all the earth. In his discussion of the relation between a general knowledge of God and a true knowledge of God, he describes how only a correct view of God leads to correct doctrine and life. In the commentary's discussion of this verse, concepts like "*vera religio*," "*verus Deus*," "*vera doctrina*," "*verum cultus Dei*," and "*vera definitio pietatis*" are almost used as synonymous phrases. Moreover, Calvin's linkage of these concepts shows that a deviation from the "*verum*" in the case of one concept has a negative effect on all the others. Calvin refers to "Turks, Jews, and Papists" as examples of those who, because of an erroneous doctrine, do not in fact acknowledge the true God.[7] In this respect, there is no difference between these groups. Calvin's criticism of the papacy therefore includes the indictment that it does not give God the honor which he is due and that he is consequently not acknowledged as God.[8] A wrong theology or a distorted image of God leads to a restless life, for only he who knows God truly can also have confidence.[9] He who is convinced of God's omnipotence has an invincible support against temptations.[10]

Though no one can comprehend the immensity of God, his glory, so far as it is profitable to us, has been sufficiently manifested to leave the entire world without the excuse of ignorance.[11] We can also clearly discern God's character by merely looking at his works with the naked eye.[12]

True knowledge of God is not obtained by "cold speculations" but only by faith.[13] "It is not God's will that we should scrutinize his secret essence," Calvin cautions, but rather that we should note what he has revealed about himself to us. If we do so, we learn that he is wise, good, righteous, and merciful.[14] The problem with speculation, however, is that it keeps the minds of men busy with things which can profit no one.[15] Indeed, it is foolish to seek God "in his naked majesty."[16] Calvin's criticism of scholastic theology is that it denies the being-God of God because, by

---

[7]   "Quae eadem ratio nunc quoque valet, nam apud Turcas, Iudaeos, et Papistas scimus extinctam esse verae doctrinae lucem, quare aliter fieri non potest quam ut obstupefacti iaceant in suis erroribus: quia impossibile est, nisi *agnito vero Deo*, redire ad sanam mentem, ut eos errorum poeniteat," Ps. 97:7 (*CO* 32, 45).

[8]   "...certum est pro Deo non agnosci," Ps. 100:1 (*CO* 32, 54).

[9]   Ps. 91:14 (*CO* 32, 8).

[10]   Ps. 93:1 (*CO* 32, 16).

[11]   "...ut totus mundus careat ignorantiae praetextu...," Ps. 135:5 (*CO* 32, 358).

[12]   "...quae oculis nostris occurrunt virtutes, in quibus relucet viva eius imago," Ps. 103:8 (*CO* 32, 78).

[13]   "...veram Dei notitiam semper ad fidei sensum referri debere...," Ps. 103:8 (*CO* 32, 78).

[14]   Ps. 103:8 (*CO* 32,78).

[15]   Ps. 103:8 (*CO* 32, 78).

[16]   Ps. 104:2 (*CO* 32, 85).

scrutinizing him apart from his virtues and consequently despoiling him of his attributes, it leaves him as nothing but the bare name "God."[17] According to Calvin theology must in any case be relevant to the church and to the individual believer. He warns against idle and subtle philosophizing which "in fleshly pride wants to wing its way to heaven."[18] Our weakness compels us to look at what God has revealed about himself because "we cannot rise with our thoughts to God's eminence."[19] Those who do not stop at this boundary will wander about in a labyrinth and finally arrive in the abyss.[20]

While Calvin warns against "*curiositas*," he also rejects that we give in too early to the idea that we cannot know anything about God (*crassam inscitiam*). In spite of God being exalted far above us, we must nevertheless exert ourselves "more and more to draw near to him" by enquiring about his works.[21] God reaches out his hand to us, and therefore we must know what he has revealed about himself. It is "foolish and unprofitable"[22] to just keep silent about God's decrees under the pretext that they are inaccessible to us.[23]

2. God's Revelation as Accommodation

The Bible accommodates itself, Calvin asserts, to our "*ruditas*."[24] For instance, it is God's style to adapt himself to human capacities by using images from the visible world to express something about the invisible.[25] God's acts are thus described in an anthropomorphic way in order that even those who are "uncivilized and malicious" can perceive that God is their Savior.[26] To speak about God's hand, for instance, is "a simile borrowed from men."[27] When it is said in the ninth Psalm "Lord, arise," it is also metaphorical speech. "To arise is a word that does not befit God,"[28] but we understand it visually as if God arises when we see him intervening in

---

[17] "Unde sequitur, papistas veram deitatem quantum in se est abnegare, quum Deum fraudantes suis virtutibus, nudum fere nomen ei relinquunt," Ps. 86:9 (*CO* 31, 795).

[18] Ps. 86:9 (*CO* 31, 794).

[19] Ps. 86:9 (*CO* 31, 794).

[20] "...in suis ambagibus vagari, quarum finis semper erit inextricabilis abyssus," Ps. 86:9 (*CO* 31, 794).

[21] Ps. 40:6 (*CO* 31, 409).

[22] Ps.40:6 (*CO* 31, 410).

[23] Contra Bouwsma, *John Calvin*, 107: "But the God of the nominalist was transcendent, unknowable and chiefly concerned that his human creatures acknowledge and pay tribute to his glory. This God too was a philosophical construction." Bouwsma blames Calvin for using the Aristotelian concept of God—see 105.

[24] Ps. 106:45 (*CO* 32, 134).

[25] "...stylum accommodat...," Ps. 86:6 (*CO* 31, 807).

[26] Ps. 18:14 (*CO* 31, 177).

[27] Ps. 110:1 (*CO* 32, 161).

[28] Ps. 9:20 (*CO* 31, 106).

salvation. When David writes that God is looking down from heaven, God lets himself be represented as an investigative judge in order to adapt himself to what we can imagine. In this way we learn bit by bit to understand God's hidden providence for we cannot grasp it at once.[29] The petition in Psalm 35:2 that God should take the shield is likewise figurative language.[30] It is the Holy Spirit who uses such images in order that we should have a better understanding of God's help. We are unable to conceive of God's secret and invisible power. While God condescends to us in these images, they help our faith to ascend to his heavenly power. In this way God accommodates himself to our weakness.[31]

In Psalm 31 the psalmist asks God to open his eyes to take care of our distress. This is also figurative speech for it implies mutability in God, a characteristic which does not belong to him.[32] The same applies to Psalm 14:4 where God is represented as being astonished at what he sees. "God does not actually experience such affections but invests himself with their form and similitude that the effect of dread is enhanced in us."[33] God's *accommodatio*, therefore, has an exclusively pedagogical aim since it is neither possible for Calvin nor for his audience to live with a God who has closed eyes.

Humbling and (as it were) transforming himself, God allows himself to be compared to a hen protecting her chickens[34] in order to strengthen our faith. The wealth and prosperity of Christ's kingdom are presented in terms of an earthly kingdom. In this way the prophets adapt their words to the understanding of the people.[35] Based on his own experience man speaks about God in the same terms.[36] Yet Calvin speaks about God's sympathy without qualifying it as an *accommodatio* when he says that God is moved by our distress. The more we experience misery, the more kindness he shows to us.[37] The issue that arises from this—how "the accommodated God" is related to the real God and how the one is distinguished from the other is—not treated as such by Calvin.

---

[29] Ps. 14:2 (*CO* 31, 137).

[30] "Improprie hoc ad Deum transferri certum est…," Ps. 35:2 (*CO* 31, 346).

[31] "…certum est nostrae infirmitati hoc concedi…," Ps. 35:2 (*CO* 31, 346).

[32] "…tribuitum Deo mutatio, quae proprie in Deum non competit," Ps. 31:16 (*CO* 31, 308).

[33] "Tales quidem affectus in se Deus non suscipit, sed eorum induit formam et similitudinem…," Ps. 14:4 (*CO* 31, 139).

[34] "…quodammodo transformat…," Ps. 17:7 (*CO* 31, 163).

[35] "…sed prophetae, quum suam doctrinam accommodare vellent ad captum populi…," Ps. 45:7 (*CO* 31, 453).

[36] "…ad externam rei speciem et sensus nostras refertur…," Ps. 9:20 (*CO* 31, 106).

[37] "…sed miserarium nostrarum sympathia tangi dicitur, ut sit nobis eo humanior, quo magis sumus miseri…," Ps. 145:8 (*CO* 32, 415).

3. The Being of God

God's being is hidden and incomprehensible to us. Therefore, Calvin observes that the Bible does not speak directly about God's essence but rather about his name as an indication of his majesty as it is revealed to us.[38] God's name represents all that we can know about him. What has been revealed about his attributes is intended for the sake of believers and not for philosophical speculation. God's eternity, for instance, must be related to his commitment to always care for us.[39]

God's attributes must always remain interrelated. It is not possible to separate God from his being. This means, for example, that he may not be separated from his powerful works.[40] God cannot be idle. Neither can his majesty be separated from his goodness, for his majesty alone would render people awestruck while his goodness alone would leave people without respect for him.[41] Moreover, God's glory assumes his power. The one who conceives of God without his power has rather a dead than a living God.[42] You rightly acknowledge God as the ruler of the world not when you coldly speculate about his power but when you apply it to your own personal benefit.[43] Calvin holds that God's power sets us at rest but his mercy brings joy. "Our reason for praising God is found more clearly in his mercy than in his sheer power and justice."[44]

Calvin's fundamental criticism of Rome is that they think of God in limited terms. For example, to think that God does justice only to those who are worthy is "a cold and narrow view" of his character.[45] If it were true that man first has to prepare himself for grace, nobody would come to God. Calvin indeed acknowledges a "*gratia praeveniens*," but only as it denotes the grace that precedes all human acts of faith.

In contradistinction to man, God's existence is independent. "A particularity of God is that he exists in himself and that he exists by his own power."[46] Calvin cannot tolerate the idea of a God who is dependent or mutable or even has emotions.[47] That means, indeed, that he has to look for a solution to the problem that God had initially decided to extinguish Israel,

---

[38] "…occulta et incomprehensibilis est eius essentia…," Ps. 9:10 (*CO* 31, 101).

[39] Ps.102:14 (*CO* 32, 67).

[40] Ps. 68:18 (*CO* 31, 627).

[41] Ps. 138:6 (*CO* 32, 375); see also Ps. 65:12 (*CO* 31, 592): "…hanc Dei potentiam et bonitatem quas a Deo separare non fas est…."

[42] Ps. 96:6 (*CO* 32, 39):"…quia mortuam potius essentiam imaginantur, quum vivum deitatem, qui eius potentiam ab eo separant."

[43] "…non eos qui frigide speculantur Dei potentiam, sed qui in usum praesentem ususm aptant…," Ps. 33:12 (*CO* 31, 330).

[44] Ps. 118:1 (*CO* 32, 202).

[45] Ps. 25:8 (*CO* 31, 255).

[46] Ps. 96:4 (*CO* 32, 39).

[47] "…non quod in Deum cadant passiones humanae…non quod Deus in se ipso sit flexibilis…," Ps. 106:23 (*CO* 32, 125).

but subsequently, because of Moses' prayer, he purposed to forgive them. The problem is solved by explaining that God all the while had decided to forgive, the announcement to destroy Israel only being meant to humble them.[48] Calvin's concept of God, which to his mind is also required in view of his audience, constrains him to this logic. God is immutable, yet he "puts on a human mask" (*persona*) in order that we might feel the seriousness of his wrath.[49] Calvin even says that God is constrained to put on a mask when he wants to present himself as wrathful.[50] Here Calvin utilizes a notion which is also used by Luther to explain that God represents himself to be different from what he truly is.[51] The God of wrath is therefore not the true God. God is by nature merciful and propitious, and his severity is only accidental.[52] When God is wrathful and vengeful, he speaks in an unusual way, actually assuming another character.[53] He is naturally inclined to forgiveness by which he draws us to himself.[54] Even when he is wrathful, he does not set aside his fatherly love.[55] "*Persona*" is thus quite different than "*natura*."[56] When speaking about God's nature, the concept of "*accommodatio*" is not under discussion. By nature God is a Father, and he cannot divest himself from this nature.[57] God can be nothing but merciful.[58] God does not change his nature, and so thus it is certain that, even after a

---

[48] Ps. 106:23 (*CO* 32, 125).

[49] "...inducere cogitur hominis personam...," Ps. 106:23 (*CO* 32, 125).

[50] The French translations of 1558 and 1561 clearly express the coercive character. In Ps. 18:26, he writes, "...contraint Dieu de forger nouvelles manières de parler, et comme disguizer...." In Ps. 106:23, "...il est contraint de prendre la personne d'un homme...."

[51] "He is a God of life, glory, salvation, joy, and peace; that is his true face though he sometimes puts on a mask through which he appears as a God of wrath, death, and hell." In this connection, Luther utilizes both "larva" (e.g. WA 44, 601) and "persona" (e.g. WA 40 I, 174). See further W. J. Kooiman, "Gods maskerspel in de theologie van Luther," in *Maskerspel: Feestbundel voor W. Leendertz* ed. M.A. Beek *et al.* (Bossum, 1955), 49-83.

[52] "...scriptura naturaliter clementem et propitium praedicans, quasi accidentale esse significat si quando severus ac rigidus est," Ps. 86:14 (*CO* 31, 797).

[53] "...et quasi alienam personam induere," Ps. 18:26 (*CO* 31, 183).

[54] "...sicuti natura ad beneficentium propensus est...," Ps.107:43 (*CO* 32, 145).

[55] Ps. 89:3 (*CO* 31, 812).

[56] J. Raitt concludes that Calvin utilizes the concept "*persona*" in more than one sense. She mentions Altenstaig's sixteenth century dictionary where the primary meaning of "persona" is to play a role in a drama. In spite of this, however, she pays relatively little attention to this meaning in her article. J. Raitt, "Calvin's use of '*persona*,'" in *Calvinus Ecclesiae Genevensis Custos: Die Referate des Internationalen Kongresses für Calvinforschung vom 6. bis 9. September 1982 in Genf* ed. Wilhelm H. Neuser (New York: Lang, 1984), 273-87.

[57] Ps. 77:8 (*CO* 31, 714).

[58] Ps. 77:10 (*CO* 31, 715).

long time, he shows compassion towards his own.[59] Having such a nature, it is impossible for God *not* to be merciful towards those to whom he has once shown himself to be a Father.[60] God is not a source of fear, but rather he inspires confidence.[61] Compassion belongs to his nature.[62] According to Calvin's understanding of God's being, it follows "that God is by nature so merciful and ready to forgive that he delays and even hides his punishments to the point that he would never punish us but for our obstinacy which compels him to do so."[63]

This other quality, the divine *persona* or mask, is for the wicked in order that they might "perceive in him nothing but cruelty, wrath, and ferocity."[64] God accommodates himself to people in general, but the form of this *accommodatio* unto the faithful differs from that unto the wicked. God can only show favor to us believers by putting aside the mask of a judge[65] and forgiving our sins.

In summing up, Calvin says about God: "He is just, fair judge of this world, a compassionate Father, and a faithful protector of those who belong to him."[66]

4. The Freedom of God

Calvin accentuates the very orderliness of God's creation. Furthermore, he emphasizes God's faithfulness to his own word. However, this rejection of any arbitrariness in God does not somehow limit God's freedom. Calvin provides examples of exceptional circumstances where God can lead his elect to act in a way which is not part of their calling. This applies to Phinehas (Num. 25) and to Moses, who "was moved by the invisible impulse of God"[67] to slay the Egyptian though he was not yet invested with the *"potestas gladii."* We are here concerned with actions which, in Calvin's opinion, "ought not to be estimated by the ordinary standards."[68] God has a certain ordinary way to call people to his service. This however does not prevent him, when necessary, from inciting his elect to extraordinary acts by the hidden operation of his Spirit.

Calvin's constant denial of a *"deus otiosus"* also has implications for God's freedom. God did not establish perpetual fertility once and for all in

---

[59] "Quia Deus animum et ingenium non mutat, fieri non posse quin suis tandem appareat propitius," Ps. 77:12 (*CO* 31, 717).

[60] Ps. 77:8 (*CO* 31, 714).

[61] "...fiduciam iterum colligens ex Dei natura," Ps. 69:14 (*CO* 31, 644).

[62] "...eius misericordiae, quae naturaliter in ipso residet...," Ps. 78:38 (*CO* 31, 734).

[63] Ps. 86:14 (*CO* 31, 797).

[64] Ps. 18:26 (*CO* 31, 183).

[65] "...nisi deposita iudicis persona...," Ps. 143:2 (*CO* 32, 400).

[66] Ps. 89:15 (*CO* 31, 816).

[67] Ps. 106:31 (*CO* 32, 128).

[68] Ps. 106:31 (*CO* 32, 128).

creation so that he might merely sit idly afterwards (*otiosum sedere*). On the contrary, he renders the earth fruitful from year to year, "affording us thereby a manifestation of his goodness."[69] God exercises his freedom also in the occasional withholding of fertility. This freedom also concerns God's grace. Seeing that he has the whole scope of the universe at his disposal, he was under no obligation to choose man from among all he made to uniquely display his grace. Therefore this choice of God was totally free and unrestricted, not being connected to anything in man.[70]

Calvin is quite conscious of the difficult questions surrounding God's intentions. He can indeed do anything if he is so inclined, but we do not always perceive what he wants.[71] The only way to live with this question, Calvin explains, is to be convinced that God cares for each person in particular. Those who hold that God governs the world only in a general manner, without attending to individuals, leave people in great anxiety and uncertainty. No one but he who is persuaded of God's guardianship will persist in prayer.[72] In Calvin's view then both God and man "need" God's omnipotence, for without it God would not receive his due honor.

Calvin's rejection of a God who acts arbitrarily implies that adversity has to be related to sin. The only other explanation left is that God leads people into trouble without cause, and if this were true, we would fashion him whom we know to be the just judge as being in fact a tyrant.[73] If he were the God of "*potentia absoluta*," he would be deprived of his righteousness. When we want to honor God and refrain from presenting or harboring a false concept of him, we "have to connect our sins with his wrath."[74] Resisting the idea of a tyrannical and arbitrary God, Calvin rather has to postulate a direct relationship between God's wrath and the sins of men.

Calvin's readers struggling with questions are consoled with the paradox of the *theologia crucis*. God laughs while we are weeping, meaning that while we are suffering from our enemies and imagining that God's arm is too short to help, he is already laughing at the fruitless efforts of those very enemies. He even delays his wrath in order to expose such enemies to an even greater derision. "Let us, therefore, hold that if God does not immediately stretch forth his hand against the enemies, it is his time of laughter."[75] As often as it pleases him, God can playfully remove his

---

[69] Ps. 85:13 (*CO* 31, 790).

[70] Ps. 8:4 (*CO* 31, 91).

[71] Ps. 121:3 (*CO* 32, 300).

[72] Ps. 121:3 (*CO* 32, 300).

[73] "...non esse tyrannum qui iniuste saeviat, sed aequum iudicem qui nunquam irascitur nisi offensus," Ps. 38:4 (*CO* 31, 387).

[74] Ps. 38:4 (*CO* 31, 387).

[75] Ps. 2:4 (*CO* 31, 44).

enemies.[76] This knowledge not only assuages our grief, but it also "wipes away our tears."[77]

If God has cared for us while we were children, he cannot but extend his loving care until the close of our lives.[78] God is infinitely good and will not suddenly change his attitude towards us, for, as Calvin writes, "he is not mutable like men."[79]

5. The Otherness of God

The otherness of God implies that he cannot be measured by our standards.[80] Whenever meditating about him, we must actually soar above heaven and earth,[81] and that is precisely what humans cannot do.[82] For instance, he who prescribes how God should act constricts "God's immeasurable power within certain limits."[83] What is expected of God should not be measured according to human standards. Therefore we should not elevate our norms to serve as God's norms.[84] Calvin warns against the danger of extolling human experience as a transcendent norm. In his opinion it is very risky to draw conclusions from human experience about God and his plans.

The otherness of God is also seen in his sublimity. Because of his majesty there is an immense distance (*longam distantiam*) between God in heaven and us on earth. Yet this does not prevent him from descending to us, showing himself to be near at hand, associating with us, and providing for our salvation.[85] God's sublimity is described in almost spatial terms, namely, "that he needs not change place when he would condescend to take care of us."[86] From his sublime position he can stoop to any location. In this way Calvin combines God's immutability with his actions of deliverance.

Note the paradox: precisely from his exalted position God casts his eyes on the humble and lowly.[87] The inconceivable glory of God does not cause him to be so distant from humanity that he does not any longer see human need.[88] Men are inclined to imagine such a great distance between God and themselves that their faith is thereby hampered. Calvin utilizes in this

---

[76] "…sed hoc ludendo facturum quoties libuerit," Ps.2:4 (*CO* 31, 44).
[77] Ps. 2:4 (*CO* 31, 44).
[78] "…fieri non posse quin sibi ad extremum consilet," Ps. 71:17 (*CO* 31, 660).
[79] Ps. 71:17 (*CO* 31, 661).
[80] Ps. 90:2 (*CO* 31, 834).
[81] Ps. 90:2 (*CO* 31, 834).
[82] "…quia supra mundum non respicimus…," Ps. 90:3 (*CO* 31, 834).
[83] "…immensam Dei potentiam in arctum cogere," Ps. 61:3 (*CO* 31, 581).
[84] Ps. 61:3 (*CO* 31, 581).
[85] Ps. 113:5 (32, 178).
[86] Ps. 138:6 (*CO* 32, 375).
[87] Ps. 138:6 (*CO* 32, 374).
[88] "Incomprehensibilem Dei gloriam non esse causam distantiae…," Ps. 68:5 (*CO* 31, 621).

context the term *"imaginari"*[89] to distinguish the human portrayal from reality. As far as the faithful are concerned, the distance has been bridged by the covenant whereby "a chain of holy unity" with God has been established.[90] Hence Calvin celebrates both the remoteness and the nearness of God. He lives among men and invites them kindly to him.[91] Therefore God's nearness must be proclaimed especially to those who think that they must travel far to find him.[92]

6. The Disposition of God

Calvin speaks often and freely about God's disposition to act as Savior—a characteristic that flows from his being (*pardonner est son métier*). A variation on Voltaire's dictum, "to forgive is his profession," could then faithfully represent Calvin's theology: *"sauver est son métier."* It follows that "nothing is more suitable to the nature of God than to help the destitute."[93] God simply cannot bear to see people's affliction. Therefore, the more one is oppressed and the more one is destitute of human aid, the more God is inclined to help him.[94] According to Calvin this lies in "God's character to redeem."[95] His office is to save,[96] especially in light of the threat from the gates of death.[97] It belongs to God, Calvin says, "not only to lift up his servants from the mud but also to liberate them from the grave."[98] The Reformer calls it God's proper work is to bring the dead to life.[99] Furthermore, it is typical of God to avenge injustice.[100] His ordinary, daily office is to help his servants who are wronged.[101] In the Bible God ascribes to himself the task of raising the dead to life again.[102] Calvin mentions God's beneficent disposition so frequently so as to reassure his readers.[103] Meanwhile God will surely fulfill his office for he cannot change his nature.

---

[89] "Iam ne longa distantia, quam imaginari solemus inter nos et Deum, cursum fidei nostrae abrumpat," Ps. 68:18 (*CO* 31, 627).
[90] Ps. 68:18 (*CO* 31, 627).
[91] "...unde familialiter eos ad se invitat...," Ps. 68:5 (*CO* 31, 621).
[92] Ps. 68:5 (*CO*, 31, 621).
[93] Ps. 86:1 (*CO* 31, 791).
[94] Ps. 86:1 (*CO* 31, 791).
[95] Ps. 130:8 (*CO* 32, 338).
[96] Ps. 7:2 (*CO* 31, 80).
[97] Ps. 9:14 (*CO* 31, 104).
[98] Ps. 37:34 (*CO* 31, 384).
[99] Ps. 6:3 (*CO* 31, 75).
[100] "...quia proprium Dei munus est...," Ps. 94:22 (*CO* 32, 29).
[101] "...ordinarium Dei munus...," Ps. 103:6 (*CO* 32, 77). Cf. Ps. 119:85 (*CO* 32, 252): "...quia proprium Dei munus estpauperibus iniuste oppressis succurrere...."
[102] "...munus excitandi a morte in vitam," Ps. 68:23 (*CO* 31, 630).
[103] Ps. 75:3 (*CO* 31, 702).

These merciful actions serve to the ends of both the glory of God and the salvation of man, yet, between the two, God's glory has the priority. He gives us everything by grace in order that his goodness may be made known. Hence the gift of faith and salvation to sinners is not merely intended for their own sakes but for the praise of God's name.[104] God therefore has an interest in helping us; for if he were to leave us to ourselves at the close of life, his honor would at the same time become obscure. Likewise, if God would be merciful to us for only a moment, his glory would also last no more than that moment.[105] Likewise God has an interest in the well-being of his church, for when he takes care of her, she has a continual reason to exalt him. Therefore God will not cease to be benevolent towards his church.[106]

When we do not trust him wholeheartedly, we defraud God of his honor.[107] While Luther sees self-righteousness as a cause of doubt, Calvin sees it as a defrauding of God. When men trust their own zeal, wisdom, and toil, they usurp God's exclusive right to glory for the well being of his people.[108]

7. The Person of Christ

Calvin certainly reads and expounds the psalms in their Old Testament context. However, this entails that the advent of Christ should also be taken into account. In the introduction to his commentary on Psalm 21, Calvin says that it was the Holy Spirit's intention in this Psalm to lead the minds of the faithful to Christ because he was the ultimate and true expression of the reign depicted by this Psalm.[109] The exposition must account for Christ, but its initial historical context is the Old Testament situation. The result of this method is that Calvin's commentary on the psalms also provides significant data for a reconstruction of his Christology.

In his exposition of Psalm 45 Calvin introduces a number of observations which belong in Christology. This psalm is a song of praise to Solomon, but, having expounded its literal meaning,[110] Calvin draws attention to the parallel between Solomon and Christ. Though the parallel and its meaning are evident to many of the faithful, they demand more attention because Jews and other unbelievers deny that the psalm concerns Christ. Therefore, Calvin is also either addressing Jewish readers directly or

---

[104] "...ut Dei nomen celebretur: sicuti minime in alium finem nobis optanda est salus," Ps. 79:12 (*CO* 31, 753).

[105] Ps. 71:17 (*CO* 31, 661).

[106] "...quia non desinit suam ecclesiam assiduo favore prosequi," Ps. 55:2 (*CO* 31, 603).

[107] Ps. 73:25 (*CO* 31, 688).

[108] "...usurpant quod Dei proprium est...," Ps. 73:25 (*CO* 31, 688).

[109] Ps. 21: introduction (*CO* 31, 212). Cf. Ps. 47: introduction (*CO* 31, 466): "Vaticinium tamen de futuro Christi regno continent"; Ps. 65:2 (*CO* 31, 604); Ps. 66:1 (*CO* 31, 610); and Ps. 68:19 (*CO* 31, 628).

[110] "Huc usque literalem sensum exposui...," Ps. 45:7 (*CO* 31, 452).

partaking in the ongoing controversy with the Jews. Some of the things mentioned here simply cannot be applied to Solomon and therefore have to be transferred to Christ, as, for instance, when an everlasting duration of the kingdom is promised.

Calvin's interpretation Psalm 45:7 also clearly teaches the divinity of Christ. Although this psalm concerns Solomon, he is here called *"Elohim,"* and this name, Calvin reminds the reader, is not suitable to a human being.[111] Christ's deity is essentially important in his role as mediator. These two should never be separated, for his deity alone does not help us and his mediatorship without his deity cannot assure us that he will always be our savior and protector. As this passage again indicates, Calvin always applies doctrine to the practice of faith.

Psalm 22 offers to Calvin the opportunity to describe Christ's human nature and feelings. Christ was a man in the true sense of the word, and therefore he was not immune to the weakness of the flesh. Even though it did not cause him to sin and his nature remained perfectly pure, he was nevertheless subjected to human feeling. However, these human feelings were limited that they might not lead to sinful excesses.[112] It enabled Christ, even in the midst of excruciating pain, to keep a *"compositi animo"*[113] and to subject himself to God. Calvin expresses the connection between Christ's deity and humanity by stating that Christ is "God revealed in the flesh."[114]

Calvin's defense of the humanity of Christ has a pastoral intent. For instance, he blames some expositors (without mentioning them by name) for explaining the words "My God" in Psalm 22 in such a way that they do not express the desolate feelings of Christ but rather the emotions of those who saw him hanging on the cross. This explanation is motivated by a fear of charging Christ with a wrong attitude. However, such commentators do not realize, says Calvin, the extent to which the consolation of the faithful is diminished by intimating that Christ was exempt from the terror of God's judgment, something which we sinners know very well. Precisely *as* our representative, he suffered all this pain and terror, but he of course did not yield to any sinful temptation which may have been contained therein.[115] Because he is "the servant of God and our brother," Calvin affirms that his anguish and pain should be a consolation to believers.[116]

Commenting on Psalm 8, Calvin is confronted by the fact that verse 6 ("You have made him only a little lower than the angels") is applied in

---

[111] Ps. 45:7 (*CO* 31, 454).
[112] It is remarkable that Calvin localizes sin in terms of human feelings: "...sed moderatur tantum ne excessu sint vitiosi," Ps. 22:15 (*CO* 31, 228).
[113] Ps. 22:15 (*CO* 31, 228).
[114] Ps. 21:14 (*CO* 31, 219).
[115] Ps. 22:2 (*CO* 31, 222).
[116] "...servus Dei est, et frater noster," Ps. 45:7 (*CO* 31, 454).

Hebrews 2:7 to Christ. According to Calvin, the author of Hebrews is entitled to do so because Christ had a complete human nature. Also the gifts given to Christ in this passage are gifts of grace because, firstly, he also was a mortal man, and, secondly, the gifts conferred on him are actually intended for us humans.[117]

Calvin rejects the opinion of the Greek and Latin church fathers who claim that the soul of Christ would have been in hell. This view makes Christians appear ridiculous in the eyes of the Jews. Moreover, it is a confusing idea that can easily lead us into a labyrinth of other subtleties.[118] What is meant here, he explains, is simply Christ's body in the tomb.

Calvin accentuates the nearness of Christ. Like the ark resting in the temple, Christ is continually present among us.[119] Christ resides amongst us for that was his promise, and those who are not led by it to abundant joy are ungrateful and stupid.[120] Indeed, although Christ has ascended bodily into heaven so that as far as his flesh is concerned there is a great distance between him and us, there is yet a hidden communion between him as our head and us as his members,[121] and our souls are still spiritually fed by his body and blood. As regards his deity, he is not localized.

Because he mainly concentrates on the presence of God the Father, Calvin hardly treats the presence of Christ in his commentary on the Psalms.

8. The Offices of Christ

According to Calvin the priestly office of Christ is the most important, for without his mediatorship "we would all be prevented from seeing God."[122] It is Christ himself who restores the human race.[123] Reconciliation with God is only possible through Christ, "whose gaze scatters all the clouds of our sins."[124] Because even the praise of our lips is impure, it is only acceptable to God through Christ. He helps us in our service to God.[125] Furthermore, we can only honor God if we honor him in Christ.[126] This priesthood of the Son is indissolubly connected with his office as king.[127] Just as temple and

---

[117] "...quod mortalis homo et filius Adae...," Ps. 8:6 (*CO* 31, 93).

[118] Ps. 16:10 (*CO* 31, 157).

[119] Ps. 122:2 (*CO* 32, 303).

[120] "Quare ingrati sumus et stupidi, nisi in summum gaudium nos rapiat illa promissio," Ps. 122:2 (*CO* 32, 303).

[121] "...arcanae inter caput et corpus societatis...," Ps. 68:19 (*CO* 31, 628).

[122] Ps. 110:4 (*CO* 32,164).

[123] "...humani generis instaurator...," Ps. 8:6 (*CO* 31, 93).

[124] Ps. 84:9 (*CO* 31, 783-784).

[125] Ps. 66:15 (*CO* 31, 615).

[126] "Summa est, Deum honore suo fraudari nisi in Christo colitur," Ps. 2:12 (*CO* 31, 50).

[127] "...atque regnum Christi a sacerdotio inseparabile est," Ps. 132:13 (*CO* 32, 349).

palace were connected in the case of David, so Christ's kingship and priesthood are connected.[128] Concerning the relationship between Christ and predestination, Calvin in this commentary only makes the remark that predestination is "in Christ,"[129] but he gives no further explanation to this remark.

The bond between Christ and the church is inseparable, for there is a "hidden communion between the head and the body."[130] Christ being the head and we the body leads Calvin to say that, committing his spirit to the Father while dying on Golgotha, Christ simultaneously committed the souls of those who belong to him to the care of God.[131] This assures believers that, in spite of all temptations, they will not lose their faith. Christ is the custodian of our salvation.[132] Calvin sees Christ's suffering not only as a vicarious atonement but also as a demonstration of the afflictions his followers have to suffer from unbelievers.[133]

9. David and Christ

David is a type of Christ and therefore a type of the church as a whole. What was typologically started with David is subsequently fulfilled in Christ and in the church, implying that the whole church and every believer individually will similarly suffer from external enemies as well as internal foes.[134]

The reason for Calvin's view of David as a type of Christ[135] is that the Psalms mention things about David and his kingdom that were never applicable to David himself. Psalm 18:43 is one such example. Here David says that God has appointed him as the head of the nations. Imbued with the Spirit of prophecy, David knew that Christ first had to be debased before his exaltation, and therefore he puts his own person forth as a type of Christ.[136]

Therefore, Calvin holds that David's reign is a prefiguration and image of the kingdom of Christ, which means that Christ's triumph against all resistance is assured.[137] From this analogy there is also a returning movement in the sense that David's acts are justified because he was a type of Christ. Like Christ, who will judge those who refuse to acknowledge his

---

[128] Ps. 2:6 (*CO* 31, 45).

[129] "...quia gratis in Christo nos eligit," Ps. 28:8 (*CO* 31, 285).

[130] Ps. 68:19 (*CO* 31, 628).

[131] "...quod Christus animam suam moriens patri commendans, omnes suorum animas custodiendas suscepit," Ps. 31:5 (*CO* 31, 302).

[132] Ps. 89:19 (*CO* 31, 817).

[133] Ps. 69:21 (*CO* 31, 646).

[134] Ps. 41:10 (*CO* 31, 422).

[135] "...in hoc typo spiritus sanctus regnum Christi depingat...," Ps.118:44 (*CO* 32, 190).

[136] Ps. 22: introduction (*CO* 31, 219).

[137] Ps. 18: introduction (*CO* 31, 169).

authority, David was allowed to kill his enemies. Yet, what David preferred above all else (at least according to Calvin) was to show clemency to the penitent just like Christ would later do.[138]

Because David knew that he and his kingdom were prefigurations of Christ and his kingdom, he could already himself call on the mediator Christ for forgiveness of sins. In order to do so, he appealed to his anointing that made him a type of Christ.[139]

10. The Spirit and the Believer

Calvin's warning against reading Christ prematurely back into the Old Testament also holds for the way Scripture speaks about the Holy Spirit. For instance, he turns down the exposition of "ancient exegetes" who used Psalm 33:6 as proof text for the deity of the Holy Spirit against Sabellianism since it proved to be an interpretation that these words do not allow.[140]

The Spirit of God flows through Christ unto the whole Church,[141] and therefore God gives his Spirit only to the elect.[142] By the "internal illumination of the Spirit" we are prevented from despising our calling in carnal blindness.[143] In his commentary on the Psalms, Calvin focuses more on the sanctifying than the justifying operation of the Spirit. As he says in one place, he who has received the "Spirit of adoption" is meek, can endure injustice, is not revengeful, and can even give a hand to the very enemies who have caused his affliction.[144]

The Spirit exhorts us to fulfill our duties towards God[145] and to draw near unto him in prayer.[146] We need the Spirit for he leads us to a correct lifestyle.[147] The Spirit is "the commander and the leader" who helps us lest we react in difficult situations with vengeance and slander.[148] All our thoughts and directions are wrong and confused until the Spirit imposes the right rule upon them (Calvin contrasts confusion with this "*regulam*").[149]

Calvin utilizes strict cognitive concepts when depicting the operation of the Spirit. Man's heart must be refashioned to consent with God's will.[150]

---

[138] Ps. 18:38 (*CO* 31, 187-8).
[139] Ps. 84:9 (*CO* 31, 783-784)
[140] Ps. 33:6 (*CO* 31, 327).
[141] Ps. 89:19 (*CO* 31, 817).
[142] "Quia ergo spiritus sui participatione non dignatur, nisi quos diligit, et in suis reputat." Ps. 51:12 (*CO* 31, 519).
[143] Ps. 16:7 (*CO* 31, 154).
[144] Ps. 7:5 (*CO* 31, 81).
[145] Ps. 31:24 (*CO* 31, 313).
[146] Ps. 20:2 (*CO* 31, 208).
[147] Ps. 19:14 (*CO* 31, 207).
[148] Ps. 26:4 (*CO* 31, 266).
[149] Ps. 143:10 (*CO* 32, 405).
[150] Ps. 143:10 (*CO* 32, 405).

There are three ways in which God is our teacher: "he instructs us by his word, secondly, he illuminates our minds by his Spirit and, thirdly, he engraves his teaching (*doctrina*) upon our hearts.[151] It is the Spirit who leads the faithful to a true knowledge of the law, and therefore Calvin calls him "the Spirit of knowledge."[152] Yet it always concerns a knowledge of the mind and of the heart. The mere hearing and understanding of the word is not enough unless it is combined with "a willing obedience of the heart."[153]

11. Conclusion

In his commentary on the Psalms, Calvin is vitally interested in the first person of the Trinity. Consequently Christology and Pneumatology lie on the periphery. He stresses the fact that we can only talk about God in terms of his attributes. The *nudus Deus* is of no help. Calvin therefore proposes an image of God which would give maximum consolation and assurance to man. His use of the terms "*accommodatio*" and "*persona*" must be seen against this background. Thus, Calvin mainly accentuates the "positive" attributes of God. His rejection of any other concept of God (since any other concept would defraud him of being God) is born of the conviction that such would be incapable of doing justice to either God or man.

---

[151] Ps. 143:10 (*CO* 32, 404).
[152] "...spiritus intelligentiae...," Ps. 119:33 (*CO* 32, 228).
[153] Ps. 143:10 (*CO* 32, 404).

3

God the Creator

1. The Purpose of the Creation

From Calvin's utterances about the creation it is evident that he continuously points to God's active and ongoing concern with the whole universe he has made. Although his commentary on the Psalms is especially concerned with man's part in creation, the whole created order itself is also discussed. For example, Calvin disputes quite vehemently the idea of the Greek philosopher Epicurus (341-270 BC) that the earth emerged by chance from the random collision of various atoms.

> The world is not eternal and has also not emanated coincidentally from particles, but the splendid order which we see has originated at once from God's command.[1]

It is ridiculous to believe that such an artistic and splendid construction like the earth could have originated from a mere combination of atoms.[2] Neither has the world emerged from itself,[3] but it has been created through the Word, the only-begotten Son.[4]

Already in his act of creation God is seen to be gracious because in his approach towards man he pushes the water back to form the land where man can live. For Calvin it is one of the biggest wonders in God's works that water is not everywhere but that God instead made space for land (dry ground).[5] According to Calvin the water is a threat; therefore he sees grace in that separation which God orders between water and land. God continues to take care that the water is kept under control, and floods show what could happen if God's hand were not to stop the water.[6]

---

[1] Ps. 148:7 (*CO* 32, 435).

[2] Ps. 104:24 (*CO* 32, 94).

[3] Ps. 104:5 (*CO* 32, 86).

[4] "...mundum per aeternum Dei sermonem, qui Filius est unigenitus, fabricatum esse," Ps. 33:6 (*CO* 32, 327). Calvin takes over the Erasmian practice of using the concept "*sermo*" when the written word of God is not specifically mentioned. Cf. Olivier Millet, *Calvin et la dynamique de la Parole: Étude de rhétorique réformée* (Paris: H. Champion, 1992), 210-11.

[5] Ps. 136:4 (*CO* 32, 364).

[6] Ps 104:9 (*CO* 32, 88). Calvin mentions the example of a flood in the Baltic Sea which caused *inter alia* damage for the population of Flanders.

The fact that God gives life does not imply a deification of living beings in any way. Calvin thus criticizes the proponents of Manicheism who, according to him, maintain erroneously that the human soul is part of the spirit of God. Still worse though is the philosophy of that "filthy dog Servet" who dares to claim that even oxen and donkeys are part of the divine being (essence). That God gives "breath," Calvin maintains, means that the origin of life is within the breath of God and not that the divine breath is divided into little pieces and subsequently distributed.[7] In his defense of God's true involvement in creation, Calvin safeguards the distance between God and man.

As one of the basic principles of Calvin's theology, the creation implies the honor of God and salvation of man. Calvin says that God has created everything in order that man would glorify his name;[8] therefore Calvin considers it as sacrilege when any human being does not praise God.[9] We are born into the world with the purpose of glorifying of God.[10] All people are created and are kept alive to devote themselves to the praise of God.[11] "We know that we are put down on this earth to praise God unanimously and that this is the purpose of our lives," he writes.[12] Men and women were so situated on the earth that they might, as it were, celebrate the praises of God with one voice; meanwhile, all other things were made principally for the use of men that they might thereby recognize God as their Father.[13] For angels and for men there is not a more excellent service than to praise God,[14] and there is "no corner in heaven or on the earth where God is not praised."[15]

It is almost as though Calvin presents a new monastic rule when he says that "for man there is no other rule to live in a good way than to strive to please God and to be approved of by him."[16] This is also the reason why God keeps us alive.[17] The purpose in man's creation is "eternal blessedness."[18] Calvin assumes that from the beginning it was not intended that man would live forever on the earth. This inference is clear in Calvin's remark that God

---

[7] Ps. 104:29 (*CO* 32, 96).

[8] Ps. 113:1 (*CO* 32, 177).

[9] "...et sacrilegium esse silentium...," Ps. 113:2 (*CO* 32, 178).

[10] Ps. 11:10 (*CO* 32, 170).

[11] Ps. 145:4 (*CO* 32, 413).

[12] Ps. 6:6 (*CO* 32, 76). Cf. Ps. 115:17 (*CO* 32, 191).

[13] Ps 115:17 (*CO* 32, 191).

[14] Ps. 103:19 (*CO* 32, 83).

[15] Ps. 103:22 (*CO* 32, 84).

[16] Ps. 19:14 (*CO* 32, 207).

[17] "...a Dei laudibus, ad quas celebrandas nati sumus et conditi...," Ps. 30:10 (*CO* 32, 298); "...quia statuat non aliam sibi esse vivendi causam nisi ut se exerceat in Dei cultu...," Ps. 119:17 (*CO* 32, 221).

[18] "...beatam aeternitatem, ad quam creati sunt...," Ps. 90:12 (*CO* 32, 840).

has given man as much space as he needs for his temporary stay here on earth.[19]

In the same way that man is created for God's sake, the rest of the world is created for the sake of man.[20] Therefore Calvin can define the end of creation in relation to man:

> God has created men and put them in this world in order to be a Father for them.[21]

All the riches with which the world abounds proclaim aloud what a beneficent Father God is to mankind.[22] For our sake God has so magnificently filled the earth in order that we may not only be spectators of this beautiful theater but also enjoy the great abundance and variety of good things which it presents to us.[23] In this further way God receives the honor he is due since the enjoyment of his gifts leads to his praise.

Hence the only reason for God to take care of this world is that he wants man to take notice of his fatherly care.[24] According to Calvin, this of course implies that we people of flesh and blood are created to enjoy God's kindness in this world. It also implies that one's life has been meaningless when he has not known God as his Father. Life is short, and when we do not taste something of God's generosity in this short life, we will in the end find out that we have lived to no purpose.[25] Calvin adds that life is so short that, unless God hastens to give us some taste of his benefits, the opportunity to taste his kindness is lost.[26] Hence Calvin does not emphasize the tragedy of *being lost* without God so much as that of *having lived* without God. Calvin furthermore says that a person has not only missed very much but also that it would be even better for him not to have been born since, in living now without God, he languishes away "in continual sorrow."[27] These words underline that Calvin sees God principally as a caring Father under whom one finds comfort for his troubles. He who does not know this God will perish gradually from his own sorrow. Calvin expresses the ideal of a life with God using the Greek concept of *"euthumia,"*[28] which denotes cheerfulness as well

---

[19] "...quod scilicet Deus terrae spatium hominibus destinaverit quantum ad hospitium sufficeret," Ps. 74:16 (*CO* 32, 698).

[20] "...hominis causa mundum esse creatum...," Ps. 147:7 (*CO* 32, 428).

[21] Ps. 89:47 (*CO* 32, 828-829).

[22] "...paternumque erga humanum genus amorem...," Ps. 115:16

[23] Ps. 104:31 (*CO* 32, 96). Cf. Ps. 89:47 (*CO* 32, 829): "...in hunc finem conditos esse mortales ut fruantur Dei beneficentia in mundo."

[24] Ps. 115:16 (*CO* 32, 190).

[25] Ps. 89:47 (*CO* 32, 828).

[26] Ps. 89:47 (*CO* 32, 829).

[27] Ps. 89:47 (*CO* 32, 829).

[28] "Scimus praecipuum batae vitae caput esse euthumian...," Ps. 16:9 (*CO* 31, 155).

as contentment. Only he who knows God's grace and God's providence knows this *euthumia*.

Calvin's overarching interest with God does not imply that his fellow man disappears from the scope of his concerns. Whereas Satan wants to extinguish the name of Christ, it is the duty of Christians to do all they can in order to keep his name high and well-known in order to promote the eternal salvation of men.[29] Calvin's conception of God, his *theo*-logy, brings fellow-man into the picture for its own sake. Since man is created to praise God, the believer would tell about God in order that other people would also praise God. Calvin makes clear that whereas God never does nothing (*non-otiosus*[30]); God also does not tolerate that his people do nothing. Just as God is active, they have to commit themselves to other people, and they should take care of one another.[31]

2. "*Ordo*"—Calvin's Cosmology

Calvin's view of the created natural order is best presented in his exposition of Psalm 75:4. The earth occupies the lowest place in this universe. It does not rest on a foundation, but it is supported only by water and hangs in the air.[32] It is so saturated with water that, if God were not to preserve it with his hidden power, it would dissolve at once. How can the earth hang suspended in the air if it is not upheld by God's hand?[33] Nothing in this world is stable except in as far as it is sustained by the hand of God.[34] It happens frequently that cities perish by earthquakes, but the earth itself remains, and this is only possible because God sustains it.[35] The terminology which Calvin uses in his description indicates how deeply he is troubled by the vulnerability of the earth and its inhabitants.

When Calvin points to the great variety and beauty of fruit,[36] it is apparent that he had an eye for the splendor of the creation. He calls this world "the theater of God's kindness, wisdom, justice and power."[37] God has made the stars as decorations because the sky would have been empty without stars.[38]

---

[29] Ps. 45:18 (*CO* 31, 459).

[30] Cf. the chapter below on "God the Caring."

[31] "Neque enim suos Deus otiosus esse patitur, sed in commune suas operas conferre, ut alii aliorum commodis, mutuo consulant ac studeant," Ps. 34:15 (*CO* 31, 342).

[32] "...solis aquis fulciatur," Ps. 104:5 (*CO* 32, 86); "...suspensa est in medio aëre...," (*CO* 31, 702).

[33] Ps. 93:1 (*CO* 32, 17).

[34] "...nihil in mundo esse firmum, nisi quatenus Dei manu fulcitur," Ps. 104:5 (*CO* 32, 86).

[35] Ps. 104:5 (*CO* 32, 87).

[36] Ps. 24:1 (*CO* 31, 244).

[37] Ps. 125:13 (*CO* 32, 361).

[38] "...nam si hoc ornatu carerent coeli, quodammodo vacui essent," Ps. 33:6 (*CO* 31,327).

The whole earth is a mirror of providence[39] and the power of God.[40] Calvin values the heavens as the most splendid part of the creation—more striking in his estimation than even the earth.[41] The heavens and their exquisite, artistic orderliness by which God has created them are a mirror of God's glory.[42] He who has learned to know the glory of God by looking to the heavens also acknowledges God's power and wisdom on the earth as it is evident in even the smallest plants.[43]

The sin of man has brought the whole creation under God's damnation.[44] Because of sin the whole order of nature is so disturbed that it results in the severest failures of crop.[45] Hunger in the world is not to be blamed on God, but rather it occurs because of man's sin. As a result, says Calvin, not only human beings but also all living creatures have to endure hunger. Calvin's attention to even the animals is apparent when he writes about little sparrows which are so lonely that their distress exceeds all sorrow.[46]

The major contours of Calvin's view concerning the structure of reality are well-known to Calvin scholars.[47] Before the fall of man there was an established and regular (*legitimus*) natural order by virtue of God's creating act. Because of sin, though, this order is disturbed, and mankind is fallen apart "in a mournful state of dissipation."[48] Since then, order and disorder exist next to each other and even against each other, for sin means not to follow God, and it results in disorder and hence in chaos.[49]

At creation the order of nature was determined by God. In this order the same sun, moon and stars are always present in the sky, and believers and unbelievers are kept alive with the same food and air. This order is the result of God's love: "The whole natural order is a testimony of God's fatherly love

---

[39] Ps. 24:2 (*CO* 31, 244).

[40] Ps. 134:3 (*CO* 32, 356).

[41] Ps. 19:1 (*CO* 31, 194).

[42] "...eius speculum in coelorum machina et exquisiti ordinis artificia proponit...," Ps. 19: introduction (*CO* 31, 194).

[43] "Nam ubi quis ex coelit intuitu Deum agnoverit, non modo in terrae superficie, sed in minimis quibusque plantulis eius sapientiam et virtutem reputare et mirari discet," Ps. 19:1 (*CO* 31, 194).

[44] Ps. 145:9 (*CO* 32, 415).

[45] "Nam post Adae lapsum, vitiis nostris saepe labascit pulcerrimus ille naturae ordo quem ab initio Deus instituerat," Ps. 145:16 (*CO* 32, 417).

[46] Ps. 102:7 (*CO* 32, 63).

[47] For an overview of Calvin's thought on the natural order, see Susan E. Schreiner, *The Theater of His Glory: Nature and the Natural Order in the Thought of John Calvin* (Grand Rapids: Baker Books, 1995).

[48] "...in hac lugubri dissipatione...," Ps 8:8 (*CO* 31, 95).

[49] "Unde sequitur, suos profanis hominibus conatus et studia retrorsum cadere, quia Deum non sequendo confuse et inordinate omnia pervertunt." Ps. 90:16 (*CO* 31, 842).

towards us."[50] However, as long as godlessness keeps the heart of man occupied, everything on earth is confused, and a "horrible disorder" dominates this earth which in the meantime has become dark.[51] An illustration of this view is seen in the way Calvin writes about wild animals. It is a wonderful example of God's care that lions stay in their dens during the daytime in order that man may move about freely. But when the animals diverge from this order, this is a result of Adam's fall during which man lost domination over the animals,[52] for since the fall it seems as if wild animals are only born to cause harm to mankind.[53]

"*Ordo*" and "*pietas*" are closely connected to each other in the Reformer's thought. As proof that every sense of piety has vanished Calvin mentions that the whole order is disturbed and that there is no longer a distinction between justice and injustice.[54] As there is no stability without God, one should not be astounded about disorder. In the place where the creator is not acknowledged, disorder is inevitable.[55]

With Christ as their head, God now brings people together with the aim of restoring the order to let those who are reunited in Christ once again enjoy something of that which was lost in Adam.[56] Calvin's declaration that "no order can be said to prevail in this world until God would erect his throne and reign amongst men"[57] not only contains an eschatological reference, but it also implies that prior to Christ's second coming order prevails only where the reign of God is acknowledged. The reign of Christ is spiritual, and this reign sees to it that everything perfectly returns again to its original order.[58] Since the reign of Christ is acknowledged only by believers, religion is of cardinal importance for society. Calvin explains,

> Religion is the best teacher for instructing us mutually to maintain equity and uprightness towards each other; and where a concern for religion is extinguished all regard for justice then perishes along with it.[59]

---

[50] Ps. 65:11 (*CO* 31, 609). Calvin here means the rain which soaks the earth such that something grows.

[51] Ps. 96:10 (*CO* 32, 41).

[52] Ps. 104:21,22 (*CO* 32, 92-92).

[53] Ps. 104:22 (*CO* 32, 93).

[54] "...exuisse omnem pietatis sensum: nempe quia ordinem omnem perverterint...," Ps. 14:1 (*CO* 31, 136).

[55] "Quae enim vastitas magis deformis est, quam ubi creator ipse non agnoscitur?" Ps. 96:10 (*CO* 32, 41).

[56] Ps. 8:8 (*CO* 31, 95).

[57] Ps. 96:10 (*CO* 32, 41).

[58] "...quo omnia instaurantur in perfectum ordinem...," Ps. 72:2 (*CO* 31, 665).

[59] Ps. 14:4 (*CO* 31, 139).

In fact, Calvin draws a direct correlation between Christ's second coming and the restoration of order. At this stage everything on earth is still in confusion—the order as it was originally given by God has disappeared. It is not going to stay this way though since the moment will come when God will restore the order.[60]

It is clear that a direct link connects this vision with Calvin's effort for order in the church. The church is the body of Christ, and therefore the restored "legitimate" order of the creation is being realized somewhat in the church. Furthermore, there is no stability in the whole of universe with the exception of the church since the church is built on the foundation of God's word. For Calvin the church is the only fixed point in this world because of the bond with God through the word.[61] The church is a fragment of paradise on earth. Consequently Calvin remarks that, when the wicked overthrow the lawful order in the midst of the church, the church is converted into a Babylon or an Egypt.[62] But where God is present any confusion caused by the impious immediately ceases.[63]

Calvin always distinguishes the tranquility and stability of the heavens with the mobility and instability in the world.[64] Everyday the heavens circle at a high speed, and yet their continuous steady motion is not disrupted because of this velocity.[65] Calvin speaks about the antithesis between heaven and earth.[66] According to him there is "a shrill contrast between the turbulent and confused situation in the world and God's heavenly reign."[67] On earth we see total disorder. Calvin's experience is that the earth in its entirety is suffering from shock.[68] He even speaks about a "disgusting" disorder which causes the order in God's providence to darken.[69] In this world nothing at all is stable or fixed.[70] The intensity with which one can experience the disorder is clear when Calvin says that things can be so confused "that the heavens seem as if they were to fall with great violence, the earth to be displaced and the mountains to be torn up from their very foundations."[71] However, in the

---

[60] "...sed res non semper ita fore confusas: ubi autem in legitimum ordinem reductae fuerint...," Ps. 1:5 (*CO* 31, 40).

[61] "...nulla sit coeli et terrae stabilitas, ecclesiae tamen salutem, quia suffulta est aeterna Dei veritate...," Ps. 102:26 (*CO* 32, 72).

[62] Ps. 14:7 (*CO* 31, 142).

[63] Ps. 76:9 (*CO* 31, 708).

[64] "...stabilitatem solii Dei conferre cum versatili mundi agitatione...," Ps. 92:8 (*CO* 32, 13).

[65] Ps. 93:1 (*CO* 32, 17).

[66] "Subest enim inter coelum et terram antithesis," Ps. 11:4 (*CO* 31, 123).

[67] Ps. 123:1 (*CO* 32, 308).

[68] "...totius mundi concussio...," Ps. 46:2 (*CO* 31, 561).

[69] Ps. 92:6 (*CO* 32, 11).

[70] "...mundo, in quo nihil fixum est vel stabile...," Ps. 92:8 (*CO* 31, 139).

[71] Ps. 46:2 (*CO* 31, 461).

antithesis, when we take a look at the heavens we can see that God is quietly sitting there as a supervisor while he governs[72] and that we can expect from him "the restoration of the collapsed order."[73] Under heaven everything moves continuously, and we see that human life is only "a whirling river." God however remains in a state of undisturbed tranquility. Although he subjects the world to many alterations, "He remains unmoved."[74] With this explanation Calvin seeks to comfort people who find themselves "in the whirling river." It is significant to see that Calvin does not condemn the antithesis between heavenly order and earthly chaos, but instead he wants to fill it positively in a pastoral way. Believers, for example, know to whom they should address themselves "when no hope of aid is left for them on earth, yea, when their condition is desperate—just as if they were laid in the grave or lost in a labyrinth."[75]

However, the initial order has not entirely disappeared. Calvin speaks about the "beautiful order according to which God has given every star its own position and in terms of which he directs the course of each star."[76] The order shows that the heavens have not originated coincidentally but rather that there is obviously an architect who planned everything. The order in the world and in human life is visible to everyone, and it has the character of revelation. Even if God had not said anything about it in the Bible, the heavens themselves all call out loudly that they have been created by his hands.[77] God has regulated the whole order of nature in such a way that he even sees to it that even such despicable birds as ravens are fed.[78]

The alternation of day and night is also no matter of coincidence but depends on the order which God imposed on it.[79] The daily and annual course of the sun and moon is for Calvin an evident proof of God's glory. The sun chooses everyday another course and yet, after a year, it is back again at the same place in the sky. The planets wander without losing their fixed position.[80] God made the law of this course in such a way that it agrees every day and every year again. The sun ascends by degrees while at the same time it approaches nearer to us, and afterwards it bends its course so as to depart from us little by little. By this means the variation of the lengths of days and nights is regulated by a law so uniform as to recur invariably at the same

---

[72] "...et rebus in mundo turbatis ac confusis, Deum sedere nihilominus in coelo moderatorem," Ps. 28:5 (*CO* 31, 283-4).
[73] "...collapsi ordinis restitutio...," Ps. 11:4 (*CO* 31, 123).
[74] "...aeterna haec ac immutabilis Dei constantia...."
[75] Ps. 123:1 (*CO* 32, 308).
[76] Ps. 8:5 (*CO* 31, 91).
[77] Ps 19:1 (*CO* 31, 195).
[78] Ps. 147:7 (*CO* 32, 429).
[79] "...non fortuito inter se succedere noctes et dies certis vicibus, sed Dei arbitrio praefixum fuisse hunc ordinem...," Ps. 74:16 (*CO* 31, 698).
[80] Ps. 93:1 (*CO* 32, 17).

points of time in every successive year.[81] Hence there is order even in the variation among days and nights.

Calvin is quite impressed that, although the universe is such an enormous construction with all sorts of movements and rotations within it,[82] the symmetry and harmony of the universe is conserved. For ages there has been a beautiful order which remains uninterrupted. For Calvin therefore all of these things demonstrate an order which is maintained continuously by God. The whole of the order in nature provides many reasons to praise God[83] because the wonderful order in nature proves the kindness of God.[84] Although only a part of the initial created order has remained, this is the part which still enables human life on earth, and Calvin predominantly observes disorder. This disruption in nature is the result of sin in paradise; in the relations among men it is also the result of the specific sin of not acknowledging Christ's reign.

By discussing the purpose of creation, the purpose of research in the natural sciences is also given. It is the task of such science to examine the mysteries of the works of God in such a way that man comes closer to God.[85] Natural scientific research is only valuable then when the examination or the analysis itself leads to the maker of nature.[86]

The way that Calvin describes the universe as a revelation of God's glory gives insight into why an impulse towards the study of the natural sciences can ultimately be attributed to Calvin. At the same time, the sciences with their results also set Calvin's mind at ease. He mentions the *"philosophi"* (a designation for natural scientists)[87] who have more understanding of the created reality and know the extraordinary order in the system of stars although there is no confusion (*confusus*) in the great multitude of stars.[88] To man, who is threatened with uneasiness of mind and even anxiety over the confusing affairs of earth, every discovery of order, regularity or pattern in the scientific laws of the universe brings peace of mind.

---

[81] Ps. 19:2 (*CO* 31, 196).

[82] Calvin speaks about *"rapidus motus"* and *"diversae revolutiones,"* Ps. 68:31 (*CO* 31, 636).

[83] Ps. 8:1 (*CO* 31, 88).

[84] Ps. 145:16 (*CO* 32, 417).

[85] Ps. 65:11 (*CO* 31, 609).

[86] "Esset quidem utilis et iucundae arum rerum investigatio, si nos, ut decebat, manu duceret ad ipsum naturae autorem." Ps. 29:5 (*CO* 31, 289).

[87] Paracelsus considers the *"philosophi"* as the investigators and the ones with knowledge about the nature who, because of their "secret" knowledge, have a longer and better life. See Will-Erich Peuckert, *Die Grosse Wende: Das apokalyptische Saeculum und Luther* (Darmstadt: Wissenschaftliche Buchgesellschaft, 1966), vol. I, 95-102.

[88] Ps. 19:2 (*CO* 31, 195).

The stimulus to study science, though, is found directly parallel to Calvin's criticism of science which does not reckon with God. Calvin points here to scientists who speak so myopically about secondary and lower causes that they, in effect, separate God from his works.[89] From all the secondary causes in nature they weave a curtain so that God, who is the first cause, is no longer visible. Calvin at this point refers by name to Aristotle, who mentions various causes in his book about meteors but forgets the most important cause—God himself.[90]

There are scientific explanations for rain and wind, but behind them is God's hand. It is also not sufficient to admit only generally that God is the author of rain, stormy weather or wind. God determines every single raindrop, Calvin asserts. These things do not take a blind, "natural" course, but it is God who determines when it is cloudy and when the sun shines.[91]

Calvin's discussion about the order in creation is not meant as a theoretical or theological analysis. He points to this order with the aim that man, who especially experiences chaos, might find peace of mind in recognizing order and might then praise God because of it.

3. Creation and Revelation

Calvin speaks about the creation as a source of God's revelation.[92] The silent creation teaches all people that there is *one* God.[93] God lives in inaccessible light, and therefore we cannot come to him, but he—who is hidden in conformity with his essential nature—reveals himself in creation. Creation is the clothing (*vestis*) in which God appears to man.[94] According to Calvin this has two consequences. In the first place it is foolish to seek God "in his naked majesty."[95] God wants us to see him the way he approaches us in creation. The beauty of creation shows us who he is. The theater of this world displays so many clear truths about him (such as *who* he is) that these indications are sufficient to lead someone to belief.[96] In the second place the excuse that God cannot be known since he keeps himself hidden in darkness is unconvincing.[97] Although a knowledge of creation is not sufficient to lead

---

[89] Ps. 29:5 (*CO* 31, 289).

[90] "De his ebus acutissime Aristoteles in Meteoris disputat, quantum ad propinquas causas, nisi quod praecipuum caput omittit." Ps. 29:5 (*CO* 31, 289).

[91] Ps. 135:7 (*CO* 32, 360).

[92] Stauffer illustrates from Calvin's sermons that the Reformer sees the creation as the revelation of God. See Richard Stauffer, *Dieu, la création et la Providence dans la prédication de Calvin* (Bern and Las Vegas: P. Lang, 1978), 19-51.

[93] Ps. 19:7 (*CO* 31, 199).

[94] "...haec vestis est in qua visibilis quodammodo nobis apparet qui in se ipso erat absconditus," Ps. 104:1 (*CO* 32, 85).

[95] Ps. 104:1 (*CO* 32, 85).

[96] Ps. 19:7 (*CO* 31, 199).

[97] Ps. 104:1 (*CO* 32, 85).

people to real piety, it does deprive all mankind of the excuse for the lack of knowledge.[98] He who already knows God can learn more about him by looking to the creation. Consequently, he who wants to enjoy God's face, according to Calvin, should not look to heaven but to the earth.

Through this approach Calvin resists any investigation into the hidden nature of God which is based upon sheer curiosity.[99] He does not advocate a "*theologia gloriae*" which penetrates into the heavens by searching out who God is. God dresses himself in the garment of creation, and in this living image of creation God shows himself in this world.[100] He writes, "There is nothing in the ordinary course of nature throughout the whole frame of heaven and earth which does not invite us to the contemplation of God."[101] As proof for this, Calvin appeals to a passage from the *Odes* of Horace, who "was not only a heathen poet but also an Epicurean and a vile derider of God."[102] Yet, even Horace, being under the impression of the violence of nature, had to admit that there exists something like a God.

Calvin emphasizes these convictions with strong expressions. He says, for example, that the succession of seasons loudly cries out that there is a divine being in the heavens who rules over everything.[103] The wisdom and power of God can be found in the smallest and most despicable corners of the earth.[104] But God also reveals himself in the more striking matters of the world. Is not the whale conclusive proof of the impressive strength of God, stirring up not only the sea but also the heart of man with its movements?[105] The kindness of God is revealed in the fact that, even in the most barren areas, trees are growing, birds are singing and there is even water for the wild animals.[106] High trees also declare God's strength, for how can moisture rise from the earth to the very tops of such trees without God's strength?[107] Just a view of the sun should also lead us to respect God.[108]

Calvin repeatedly speaks about God's revelation in the thunderstorms. The power of God is revealed through the vehemence of such natural phenomena like violent and stormy weather.[109] When we cannot see God's

---

[98] Ps. 19:7 (*CO* 31, 199). "...la révélation cosmique n'a d'autre rôle que d'enlever à l'homme tout alibi...," Stauffer, *Dieu*, 32.

[99] "...ne perperam in arcanae essentiae investigatione simus curiosi," Ps. 104:1 (*CO* 32, 85).

[100] Ps. 104:3 (*CO* 32, 85).

[101] "...quod nos ad Dei notitiam non invitet...," Ps. 29:3 (*CO* 31, 287).

[102] Ps. 29:3 (*CO* 31, 287-288).

[103] "...aperte clamitat aliquod regnare in coelis numen," Ps. 147:15 (*CO* 32, 431).

[104] Ps. 19:1 (*CO* 31, 194).

[105] Ps. 104:25 (*CO* 32, 94).

[106] Ps. 104:10 (*CO* 32, 89).

[107] Ps. 104:16 (*CO* 32, 92).

[108] Ps. 19:4 (*CO* 31, 198).

[109] Ps. 29:3 (*CO* 31, 288).

face, his presence becomes very clear in the thunder of stormy weather.[110] To shake believers awake and to let hardened unbelievers hear his voice, God from time to time will let the weather rage in order to impress all people.[111]

This revelation in nature however does not suffice as true knowledge about God. In nature God's voice is heard indeed, but he who wants to understand the voice must go to church, where God speaks clearly and understandably. What is more, in nature God draws attention to his existence by frightening people, but in the church he invites people to him in a friendly way.[112] Nature is a school where one receives some knowledge about God, but one does not progress in such a manner that one actually submits himself to God.[113] On the other hand, the mirror of nature displays God's spiritual glory to us only when we look with the eyes of faith.[114]

To know God and to praise him, one needs another voice in addition to the voice of stormy weather, bushes and mountains.[115] We stay deaf to the voice in nature if he does not teach us more clearly and let us taste something of his fatherly love.[116] Without the help of the word, man stays blind in respect to the glory of God as he reveals himself in creation.[117] In nature there are sufficient visible signs to deprive everyone of the excuse of ignorance.[118] Namely, there is so much visible of God's glory that no one can say that he does not know anything of God.[119] However, the knowledge about God which stems from creation and providence leads to a fallacy if it is not completed by the knowledge from the Bible. This latter form is the knowledge of true doctrine because God thereby approaches us clearly as Father. From God's creation and rule of the world one should progress to doctrine, and for Calvin that is made known in the word of God.[120]

4. Man as God's Creature

In the opening pages of the *Institutes of the Christian Religion*, Calvin states that it is not possible to speak about man in isolation from his relation to

---

[110] Ps. 81:7 (*CO* 31, 762).

[111] Ps. 29:3 (*CO* 31, 288).

[112] Ps. 29:9 (*CO* 31, 290).

[113] "Quia ergo non eo usque proficiunt homines in illa universali schola, ut se Deo subiiciant...," Ps. 29:9 (*CO* 31, 290).

[114] Ps. 104:3 (*CO* 32, 86).

[115] "...ad Deum vere cognoscendum...alia voce opus esse...," Ps. 29:9 (*CO* 31, 290).

[116] Ps. 29:9 (*CO* 31, 290).

[117] Ps. 19:7 (*CO* 31, 199).

[118] Ps. 135:5 (*CO* 32, 358).

[119] "...satis est nobis exposita, ut totus mundus careat ignorantiae praetextu," Ps. 135:5 (*CO* 32, 358).

[120] "...a creatione mundi et gubernatione necessarios esse progressus ad eam doctrinam qua Deus familiariter ad homines accessit, ne perperam vagentur," Ps. 68:35 (*CO* 31, 636).

God.[121] Man is always in a relation with God since even unbelief means a certain (in this case, negative) relation with God. This is the reason for discussing Calvin's anthropology not in a separate chapter but together under the theme of God as the creator.

According to Calvin's commentary on Psalm 32.2, there are in fact only three types of people: believers, hypocrites and those who openly despise God.[122] The last-mentioned group has a realization of guilt alright, but they so enjoy committing their sins and so harden themselves in their unbelief that this cognition of guilt does not lead them to God. In contrast, when hypocrites are troubled by their guilt, they know various excuses to avoid any need to seek pardon from God. Common to hypocrites and those who despise God openly is that neither group is looking for true joy in God's fatherly love. This division in three groups explains how Calvin can speak so inclusively about "we believers" and "we chosen" since there is no uncertainty about the question of who belongs to which group.

In this regard it is also important to see that for Calvin the attitude of faith is the normal attitude of life. Faith is not understood as something added; rather unbelief is presented as a serious defect. This point of view transpires in Calvin's commentary on Psalm 49:15 where he mentions that unbelievers are going to perish in the realm of the dead. Calvin blames them because "they have by their offense deprived themselves of the better life to which all of us were destined."[123] It is apparently normal in Calvin's opinion that a life with confidence in God leads to a better life with God, but disbelief deprives one of that life. The biggest misery of man therefore consists in the fact that he does not know God.[124]

Unlike the believer who finds his security in God's providence, Calvin discerns in the case of unbelieving people an all absorbing sense of unrest. The heart of the unbeliever is "full of tumult, drawn asunder, and scattered about as it were in fragments," and only God can unite it again.[125] It is this antithesis between tranquility and unrest, unity and disunity, order and chaos—all of these analogous to and inherent in the antithesis between faith

---

[121] *Inst.* I.1.1. There is a huge body of literature about Calvin's anthropology. For an analysis of it together with the results of new research, see J. van Eck, *God, mens, medemens: Humanitas in de theologie van Calvijn* (Franeker: Van Wijnen, 1992); Eva-Maria Faber, *Symphonie von Gott und Mensch: Die responsorische Struktur von Vermittlung in der Theologie Johannes Calvins* (Neukirchen-Vluyn: Neukirchener, 1999); and Schreiner, *Theater*, 55-72.

[122] "Hac particula fideles discernit tam ab hypocritis quam a stupidis contemptoribus...," Ps 32:2 (*CO* 31, 317). See also Ps. 33:1 (*CO* 31, 324).

[123] Ps. 49:15 (*CO* 31, 489).

[124] "...quia sicuti nihil homine miserius est absque Dei notitia...," Ps. 103:7 (*CO* 32, 78).

[125] Ps. 86:11 (*CO* 31, 795).

and unbelief[126]—which Calvin separately mentions. Hence, although everyone has a clear natural longing to enjoy happiness, most people do not follow the correct way to this happiness.[127] The unrest of the unbeliever is proof for Calvin that a certain idea of God lives within every person:

> We know that the heart of everyone is occupied by religion in such a way that nobody could actually openly and totally turn away from obedience to God although most people turn away to endless bypaths.

Everyone is religious, and according to Calvin this religiosity can be traced back to an original orientation towards God. Calvin relates this "religion" to a view of life that still shows signs of obedience to him, although it is not aimed at God. Likewise they who deny God show behavior which sometimes conforms to God's commands and flows apparently from God's will. When this religious behavior of all humankind is investigated, one has to conclude as Calvin does:

> There has never existed a nation so barbarous as not to have worshipped some deity; but every country forged particular gods for itself.[128]

All people have a certain ingrained religious notion, no matter how this apprehension by which we conceive of God is immediately distorted.[129] As Calvin says in Psalm 107:22: "Nature itself teaches that some kind of homage and reverence is due to God; this is acknowledged by even the heathen themselves who have no other instructor than nature."[130] Proof of this orientation towards God is also apparent when people who normally do not occupy themselves with God suddenly face troubles. They are then "moved by a secret instinct of nature to have recourse to him."[131] How otherwise does it happen, asks Calvin, that through the ages those people who view religion as a fairy tale are sometimes forced by distress to seek help from God? According to Calvin they do not do it as a joke, but it emanates from "a secret instinct of nature." This instinct is defined more accurately as "the seed of religion that is planted in their hearts."[132] Every human has the ineradicable

---

[126] "Est autem tacita antithesis inter vagos et erroneos discursus...et rectum fidei ductum...," Ps. 5:4 (*CO* 31, 67).

[127] Ps. 119:1 (*CO* 32, 215).

[128] Ps. 83:19 (*CO* 31, 779).

[129] "Ingenita est hominibus religio aliqua...," Ps. 97:7 (*CO* 32, 44).

[130] Ps. 107:22 (*CO* 32, 140).

[131] "...arcano naturae instinctu...," Ps. 81:7 (*CO* 31, 762). Calvin also uses the phrase "*arcano quodam instinctu*" for the urge in animals for food, Ps. 145:15 (*CO* 32, 146).

[132] "...insitum sit eorum cordibus religionis semen," Ps. 106:6 (*CO* 32, 137).

perception that God has to be honored,[133] but since it is also true that man is not able to worship him in a spiritual way, he creates a visible substitute for God and makes this the object of his worship while he denies any service to the true God.

For Calvin, however, the natural sense of God does not imply some bridge to the true knowledge about God. Thus he states that trust in God is not inborn, but we receive it partly from God's word and partly from his works. Nevertheless, "the view of the works of God can ignite the light within us in no way, as I have said before, unless God first illuminates us by his word and shows us his benevolence."[134]

In his commentary on Psalm 83:19 Calvin also raises this same matter. There it is confessed that the name of God is "LORD, the Most High over all the earth." In this passage Calvin states that everyone actually has a sense that something like God exists, but when correct knowledge is lacking this sense leads to the creation of idols. Because this true knowledge about God is lacking, according to Calvin it can be rightly said that "religion is the beginning of all superstition."[135] The Reformer carefully distinguishes here between "*Dei cognitio*" and "*deitatis sensum,*" a difference he compares to that between light and darkness. Hence it is not dealing with a *gradual* but an *essential* difference, just as he underscores when he says that "not only the weakness of our minds but our blindness and stupidity cause our apprehension of God to be immediately corrupted."[136] Weakness would be a gradual difference, but blindness indicates an essential difference for Calvin. As living proof for this he considers certain inhabitants of Geneva, who, though they are freed from superstition, yet fail to serve God and consequently live even more shamefully.[137] When the light of God's Spirit does not break through, all "*sensus deitatis*" remains just sinful idolatry. Every person is almost forced to acknowledge that there is a God who made everything, but this glory is dispersed at once and allocated to various idols. For Calvin this is practically "nihilism," since man in this very way reduces the God-being of God to nothing.[138] When unbelievers nevertheless pray to God in their distress, it is because of God's plan to take them deliberately into such situations in order to "squeeze"[139] the concession from them, teaching them that help is only to be expected from God as well as forcing

---

[133] "Principium illud naturaliter omnium cordibus infixum est, nec potest excuti, Deum esse colendum," Ps. 50:14 (*CO* 31, 501).

[134] Ps. 40:5 (*CO* 31, 407).

[135] "...hinc fit ut religio initium sit omnium superstitionum," Ps. 83:19 (*CO* 31, 778-9).

[136] Ps. 97:6 (*CO* 32, 44).

[137] Ps. 97:6 (*CO* 31, 45).

[138] "Atque hoc modo ipsa divinitas, quantum in ipsis est, redigitur in nihilum," Ps. 100:1 (*CO* 32, 54).

[139] "Atque hoc modo confessionem illis Deus extorquet...," Ps. 107:6 (*CO* 32, 136).

them to call upon his name. Invoking God's help in crisis is no sign of a true knowledge about him since there is a fundamental difference between religiosity and faith. Religiosity falsely builds upon the *"semen religionis,"* whereas faith is the God-given reformation of that seed.

However, with most believers, they do not deny the existence of God on purpose, nor do they put up learned disputes to prove it. Rather they most often pretend as if God is locked up in heaven such that they can peacefully go their way on earth without him. The outcome of this way of life is that every sense about God is suppressed, and "religion at the end lies dead on the ground."[140]

5. Man as Image of God

Since everyone has a type of awareness of God and because all people long for a paradisaic condition, we come now to the matter of Calvin's understanding of man's original situation as a creature of God.

The Reformer claims that humanity is the mirror that lets us see the glory of God most clearly.[141] Calvin explains the contents of this glory in his exposition of Ps. 8:5, where the psalmist writes that man is created almost divine. Man has this high position since he

> was formed after the image of God and created to the hope of a blessed and immortal life. Moreover, man is provided with reason by which he can distinguish between good and evil and the seed of religion which is planted in him. People can communicate with each other in that they are bound to each other by certain sacred bonds. Respect and shame are found in people, and they are restrained by laws. All these are certainly no obscure signs of the highest and heavenly wisdom.[142]

Summarizing the concepts which are used by Calvin, we can say that being created in the image of God consists in having the following gifts: *"ratio,"* *"religio,"* *"communicatio"* and *"moderatio."*

Man is "the most illustrious ornament on earth."[143] If it were not for man, Calvin says, it would be a terrible and desolate desert here on earth. God also intended the creation to be for the sake of man, and this is an opinion which reflects a significant point of agreement with Martin Luther.[144] According to Calvin the reason why there is such a variety and quantity of beautiful fruit is

---

[140] "...donec emortua iaceat religio," Ps. 14:1 (*CO* 31, 136).

[141] Ps. 8:1 (*CO* 31, 88).

[142] Ps. 8:6 (*CO* 31, 92).

[143] "...homines...qui maxime illustre sunt terrae ornamentum et decus...," Ps. 24:1 (*CO* 31, 244).

[144] For Luther, see Albrecht Peters, *Kommentar zu Luthers Katechismen, 2nd vol.: Der Glaube* (Göttingen: Vandenhoeck & Ruprecht, 1991), 90-1.

that God has created them with no other purpose than the use by and comfort of man. The same can be applied to the animals; they also enjoy creation, but in the end they are created for man in order that man would acknowledge God as Father through these gifts.[145] Calvin is amazed by the gifts with which God has decorated the soul, but likewise he admires the "artistic formation of the human body." He heartily comments an old saying which calls man a "*micro-cosmos*."[146] The human body is created with such care and purpose, he writes, that, even if one were to remove a single nail from the hand, the fingers could no longer be used without difficulty.[147]

However, here as well the impressive structure of the human body ought to lead one to glorify God. Calvin asks rhetorically, "Which embroiderer, with all his eagerness and precision, would be able to execute but a hundredth part of this complicated and diverse texture?"[148] Thus the creation of man in particular is very clear proof of God's hidden wisdom.[149] At the same time, though, Calvin stresses the immense distance between God and man. He contrasts, for example, "the incomparable heavenly majesty" of God with "us small worms" who are so vulnerable, living on earth in misery.[150] Yet Calvin emphasizes this distance not to see the position of man only in relative terms but to clarify the grace of God still more.

Man distinguishes himself from the animals by "the light of understanding and reason."[151] For Calvin the concepts "*intelligentia*" and "*ratio*" are synonymous. For instance, while commenting upon Psalm 145:15 he says it is by our "*ratio*" that we differ from the animals,[152] but when he remarks on Psalm 119:169 it is the possession of "*intelligentia*" which he says raises man above the animal.[153] Here Calvin additionally states that this is the organ by which man approaches God in the closest way and where man, in being God's image, finds the best expression.[154]

To capture the complete uniqueness of man Calvin also uses the concept of "*anima*." The soul is the seat of reason and the feelings.[155] The soul has the body as its home, and at the end of life God calls the soul back to himself.[156]

---

[145] Ps. 115:17 (*CO* 32, 192).

[146] Ps. 139:6 (*CO* 32, 378).

[147] Ps. 139:15 (*CO* 32, 381).

[148] Ps. 139:15 (*CO* 32, 381).

[149] Ps. 139:17 (*CO* 32, 383).

[150] Ps. 8:5 (*CO* 31, 91).

[151] Ps. 119:73 (*CO* 32, 246).

[152] Ps. 145:15 (*CO* 32, 416).

[153] Ps. 119:169 (*CO* 32, 291). See also Ps. 62:10 (*CO* 31, 589).

[154] "...intelligentiae lucem, qua praecellimus bruta animalia, et proxime ad Deum accedimus," Ps. 119:169 (*CO* 32, 291).

[155] Ps. 103:1 (*CO* 32, 75).

[156] "Quia animae domicilium est corpus...morte enim illam ad se Deus revocat," Ps. 146:2 (*CO* 32, 422).

Calvin admits that the soul is the most important part of man, but he also says that the soul does not have any power in itself although it keeps on living after the body dies. Without the grace of God, the Reformer suggests, the soul cannot exist anymore, being only a breath of air just like the body.[157] In addition to being the image of God, man is also appointed as a ruling guardian of the creation. Calvin judges it as a sign of God's love that he has entrusted man with ruling over everything.

> It is a rare and incomparable honor that mortal man may rule the world as the representative of God (*mortalis homo vice Dei*) as if it is his right and that he, wherever he should look, sees that nothing which is necessary for a joyful life is lacking.[158]

However, here also this original position has been lost through the fall of man. Although something of the rule of man is still visible in the fact that horses and sheep are obedient to him,[159] in general it must be said that man has become a prisoner instead of a ruler.

> He is not only deprived of so distinguished and honorable an estate and dispossessed of the former dominion, but he is also now captive under a degrading and ignominious slavery.[160]

Nevertheless, at this point Calvin directly mentions Christ who gives back to believers what they had lost in Adam although they are going to receive the paradisiacal dominion only after his second coming.

6. Man as Fallen Image

The contrast between man as he was created and man as he has become through sin is pointed out clearly by Calvin in his commentary on Psalm 62:10. According to Calvin, sin has left no particle of the original unimpaired condition in which man was created.[161] The sinful human is less than insignificant, he asserts.[162] Man is "a miserable being without any value" who crawls together with other miserable creatures over this earth.[163] The human race is, in its entirety, committed to lies and deceit. Without any exception everyone seeks an excuse to go the wrong way. In Calvin's opinion, this is not only the case with a few people, but it characterizes the nature of every

[157] Ps. 103:14 (*CO* 32, 81).
[158] Ps. 8:7 (*CO* 31, 94).
[159] Ps. 8:7 (*CO* 31, 95).
[160] Ps. 8:7 (*CO* 31, 94).
[161] "...quae nullam integritatis guttam in hominibus reliquit...," Ps. 62:10 (*CO* 31, 598)
[162] "...vanitate sint vaniores...," Ps. 62:10 (*CO* 31, 598).
[163] Ps. 8:4 (*CO* 31, 91).

human. Therefore it does not make much sense to ask what has been left of "reason, wisdom and free will." Against the objection that there could still be some remainders left over, Calvin answers that "although men have been endowed with splendid gifts, these have been corrupted by the fall and have vanished into nothing."[164]

The image of God is almost entirely wiped out, and the remainders of it are said to be only a ruin.[165] The original glory is still recognizable in the remainders, but these are nevertheless mere remnants. That which is left over has value only when it is bound with a true knowledge of God, Calvin explains. From his frequent usage of the concept of *"vanitas"* in this passage, it is apparent that the Reformer is not concerned with the remaining presence[166] of natural gifts so much as the remaining value of them, and this value is clear: "Everything which man knows by himself is insignificant and in vain."[167] There are still some remnants of prelapsarian humanity left within us from that time before the fall, but the situation is so bad that Calvin thinks the soul is almost dead.[168] Possessing *"intelligentia"* distinguishes man as a creature from the animals, but sin has so blinded the understanding that man is more like a brute beast. From Calvin's remark we see that God must enlighten our reason if we are not to live like cattle anymore.[169] Reason has been so blinded by sin that we no longer have the ability to distinguish between good and evil, and we do not realize the end to which we are actually living anymore. The biggest part of humankind has obscured the light which God had given to everyone with the consequence that man now does exactly the contrary from that which God intended. Any thought about the future life is buried under our daily worries; hence man lives for the world alone and is alienated from God.[170] According to Calvin it *should* be just the opposite.

Nevertheless, unbelievers remain superior to cattle since they still show certain traces of God's image through the possession of reason and knowledge.[171] To Calvin it is therefore a step too far to put humans who are living without God on an equal level with the animals—a point he says explicitly in his exposition of Psalm 49:13 ("But man, despite his riches, does not endure; he is like the beasts that perish"). Calvin rejects the interpretation of those who subsequently think that people who deny the origin of their souls

---

[164] "...et evanescere in nihilum...," Ps. 8:4 (*CO* 31, 91).
[165] Ps. 8:6 (*CO* 31, 93).
[166] Ps. 103:14 (*CO* 32, 81).
[167] Ps. 73:15 (*CO* 31, 682).
[168] Ps. 19:7 (*CO* 31, 200).
[169] Ps. 119:169 (*CO* 32, 292).
[170] Ps. 119:144 (*CO* 32, 280).
[171] "...praecellunt brutis pecudibus, quia ratione et intelligentia praediti notas adhuc aliquas imaginis Dei retinent," Ps. 49:21 (*CO* 31, 494).

are disgraced to the level of animals. In Calvin's opinion the psalmist only wants to raise the matter of unbelievers who are so swollen with pride since they do not realize that they have to pass away just like the animals.[172] They have in common with animals that their end will also be without honor since they have misused the gifts of God.[173]

In spite of the distance between God and man, the value of being human does not entirely disappear according to Calvin. He makes this clear for instance, in his exposition of Psalm 147:10. When it says that we should not rely on the power of horses, this does not mean that one may not use the strength of a man or an animal. Instead, that type of strength is discarded which fails to honor God.[174] For Calvin being human keeps its meaning, and he acknowledges a general sense of fairness and moderation. Calvin's estimation of fallen man thus depends on the specific relation of the individual. When it concerns the relation with God, then the image is only negative; but when the relationship between man and creation is in view, the retained characteristics of humanity are emphasized.

7. The Natural Condition of Man

Through sin man has reached a condition of "terrible nasty helplessness."[175] God's attitude towards man has changed. His benevolence has not disappeared fully yet, but after the fall very little of it can still be noticed.[176] In addition, the Bible is clear about the natural situation of man. Human nature is prone to vanity and lies.[177] By nature we are deaf, and we remain deaf until God pricks our ears for us.[178] Our hearts are rebellious and full of sinful thoughts, and our nature seeks everything that is wrong.[179] The fall concerned not only one part of man, "but [it] took possession of the whole soul and the whole body."[180] Calvin confirms this in his explanation of Psalm 119:37, where the poet asks God if he would turn his (the psalmist's) eyes away from evil. Calvin here refers to the eyes as two doors. As soon as we open the doors, Satan can enter into our hearts. Hence every sight with the eyes, every commotion of the feelings, and every thought is afflicted with sin.[181] David prays in Psalm 51:12 that God would create a new heart in him. For Calvin

---

[172] Ps. 49:13 (*CO* 31, 487).
[173] Ps. 49:21 (*CO* 31, 494).
[174] "Unde colligimus non aliam fortitudinem damnari nisi quae Deum honore suo fraudat," Ps. 147:10 (*CO* 32, 429).
[175] Ps. 8:6 (*CO* 31, 93).
[176] Ps. 8:6 (*CO* 31, 93).
[177] Ps. 119:29 (*CO* 32, 226).
[178] "...donec eas perforet Deus," Ps. 40:7 (*CO* 31, 411).
[179] "...corda nostra nihil nisi vitiosum concipere...," Ps. 119:36 (*CO* 32, 230).
[180] Ps. 119:37 (*CO* 32, 230).
[181] Ps. 119:37 (*CO* 32, 231).

this word "create" is proof that the heart of man is entirely corrupted by nature since "create" indicates that something totally new has to appear.

Calvin however is here not consistent in his logic and his use of biblical texts. If the usage of "create" is proof of the total corruption of man's heart, the fact that David prays this prayer after his sin with Bathsheba would mean that either he was no believer at all beforehand or that he had fallen by this sin from the state of grace. Calvin, however, does not want to choose either of the two conclusions; he even states outright that grace cannot be lost. The peculiar consequence of this interpretation by Calvin is that the one who prays verse 12 of Psalm 51 is not born-again, but the one who prays the words of verse 13 must be a believer!

The organ in which the bond between God and man finds expression is the conscience. For Calvin the conscience plays a very important function in controlling and correcting human actions. It can be used by God to force even the most wicked person through distress to acknowledge God's strength and majesty.[182] Within everyone there is this notion that he or she has done something wrong in his life and needs forgiveness for it. According to Calvin there is no one on this earth who has no burden from his conscience and who does not know that his conscience accuses him before God's throne of judgment. Even among bad people, "nature wrings out" the confession that we are only fine when God has forgiven us our sins.[183]

Because of sin the free will does not amount to anything anymore, as Calvin indicates from the confession of David in Psalm 86:11. The poet indicates here that he does not have any understanding and uprightness and that the Spirit has to endow him with it. Calvin comments that both capacities—to know appropriately and to act correctly—are attributes of the will.[184] The same is stated by Calvin in commenting on Psalm 119. When the poet prays that the Spirit will give him an obedient heart, it is clear how senseless it is to speak about a free will.[185] The prayer for the Spirit is proof that the will itself does not have the power to make correct decisions. This alone is sufficient to disprove any merit to the notion of a free will.[186]

A clear argument against free will is also raised by Calvin in his exposition of Psalm 95:8 ("Do not harden your hearts"). He remarks how absurd it is that Rome handles this text to defend free will. By nature, he maintains, the heart of man is already hard. The text means that when somebody hears the word of God and still does not bow before it, he hardens his heart further.

---

[182] Ps. 14:1 (*CO* 32, 231).
[183] "...extorquet ipsa natura...," Ps. 32:1 (*CO* 31, 314).
[184] Ps. 86:11 (*CO* 31, 795-796).
[185] Ps. 119:80 (*CO* 32, 249).
[186] Ps. 143:10 (*CO* 32, 405).

Moreover, man himself has chosen this natural hardness. Calvin calls this hardness "inborn but voluntarily indeed."[187] He who does not obey God cannot therefore be justified in blaming somebody else.

In the matter of free will also, Calvin is ultimately concerned about God's glory. Against the *"sophistae,"*[188] Calvin states that God's honor has been obscured; consequently God is done injustice if some room is given to the will of man in justification such that the will of man merely has to concur with grace.[189] Only without any free will of man does God receive the whole credit. In his exposition of Psalm 51:7 ("Surely I was sinful at birth, sinful from the time my mother conceived me"), Calvin must elaborate, of course, on the question of how Adam's sin became the sin of all mankind.[190] First of all, Calvin starts by repudiating the Pelagian idea that man does not sin because he is sinful but because he has sinful examples. That this view is unbiblical according to Calvin is apparent from the words of David. He does not blame his parents but puts himself before the throne of God's judgment and confesses himself to have been a trespasser of God's law already before his birth. Calvin believes that this view exposes the error of papal theologians according to whom inborn sinfulness is merely reduced to an inclination to sin. Furthermore they wrongly say that sin has its seat in a lower part of the soul and in the more physical desires. Finally, while experience teaches that sin affects the whole life, the papists state that the sinful nature disappears upon receiving baptism.

Calvin however holds the opinion that we have a good doctrine of sin only when we understand that sin rules in all parts of the soul and that the heart and thoughts of man are totally corrupted. The question of how sin is transferred from the parents to the children remains, though. Some believe this problem is related to the question about the origin of the soul since sin can be transferred from parents onto children only when the soul of a child originates from the soul of its parents. Calvin though does not find it necessary to "enter these labyrinths,"[191] and he offers another solution: it is sufficient to say that Adam lost his original righteousness and that his mind

---

[187] "Caeterum quamvis ingenita sit nobis talis pravitas, quia tamen voluntaria est...," Ps. 95:8 (*CO* 32, 33).

[188] By the *"sophistae,"* Calvin means specifically the scholastical theologians of Paris. See in this regard Richard Muller's "Scholasticism in Calvin: A Question of Relation and Disjunction," in *Calvinus Sincerioris Religionis Vindex*, ed. Wilhelm H. Neuser & Brian G. Armstrong (Kirksville, MO: Sixteenth Century Journal Publishers, 1997), 247-5.

[189] Ps. 51:12 (*CO* 31, 518).

[190] Ps. 51:7 (*CO* 31, 513-4).

[191] Ps. 51:7 (*CO* 31, 514).

and will were obscured because of his sin. When he then conceived children, they of their own accord also displayed these characteristics.

An objection to this solution might hold that, while one body indeed originates from another, the defects of the soul cannot be transferred. Against this argument Calvin states that Adam has to be seen in paradise as the representative of the whole human race, therefore as sweeping all his descendants along with him in his fall. In Adam all mankind was provided with the gifts of the Spirit, and therefore with Adam all mankind has also lost all these gifts. Yet, not all are affected to the same degree with such inborn sinfulness. It is true, Calvin writes, that

> we all were born bad, and we who know as Adam's posterity an inborn corruption cannot do anything good as long as our own spirit is guiding us. Yet we know that in most cases God restrains evil with hidden reins in order that they do not express it in various scandalous deeds.[192]

Calvin draws this conclusion on the basis of that which he sees around him.[193] In spite of the fact that the whole human race is infected with sin, it is clear that there are many people who do live decently. Next to them there is a group who admittedly does wrong things, but still it remains within the bounds. Trouble arises most often though in the case of the third group—those who are by nature so bad that their behavior is not allowable.[194] In his commentary on the Psalms Calvin does not answer the question of why some are more openly affected by an inborn sinfulness than others.

8. The Role of Satan

Where Calvin's view on creation and the fall is discussed, one should also give attention to his view of Satan's activities. It is strange that in Calvin research there has been very little reflection on Calvin's understanding of Satan's nature and work. This is remarkable since Calvin mentions Satan quite often as we observe in his commentary on the Psalms. Yet Calvin's method of exposition does not treat every different theme individually (as in an excursus, for example), and so one finds no separate discussion about Satan in his work. Moreover, it is typical of Calvin to describe the work of Satan in continuous connection with the relations between God and man. Thus, we will notice only a few characteristics at this point, but in the chapter about God the Father more will be said about Satan.

---

[192] Ps. 58:4 (*CO* 31, 560).
[193] "...experientia tamen ostendit...," Ps. 58:4 (*CO* 31, 560).
[194] "...alios vero naturae adeo perversae, ut sint prorsus intolerabiles," Ps. 58:4 (*CO* 31, 560).

Calvin gives no attention to the question about Satan's origin, but instead he simply presupposes his destructive presence. Some thoughts about the background of Satan and his kingdom are manifested though when Calvin speaks about the "rejected angels."[195] These angels are also bound to God's permission, but, since they obey God's commands only from sheer necessity and not from their hearts, they are not servants of God like "normal" angels.

Behind the enemies of God's church, Satan is hiding. In fact, Calvin calls him a "craftsman in fraud"[196] who suggests to the opponents of Christ's congregation how they could cause the most harm. As the "father of lies," Satan seeks to inflict so much indignity on Christians that it would appear as though they were the "excrement of the world"[197]—a designation which we would expect from Luther rather than Calvin. Since Satan wants to destroy the church of God, he is constantly provoking hatred and aggression against the church among his followers.[198] For the atrocious behavior of some who deliberately act maliciously against God's people, Calvin has no other explanation than that they "are blinded by the devil."[199] Calvin therefore believes that he is warranted in identifying Satan's strength in the papacy.[200]

Satan is also the one who holds the power to exorcize evil spirits from people and animals. Calvin believes this power exists and is being practiced. If this weren't possible God would not have forbidden it, Calvin argues.[201] Unmistakable here, though, is the implication that the power of Satan is limited. Although God permits Satan to manipulate unbelievers with this power, he does not allow him to do so among those "who are enlightened with his word and Spirit." The emphasis here is on the intervention of God and thus on God's honor. As long as a human is not saved from his sins by God, he remains under the tyranny of Satan and is not capable of overturning injustices.[202] For man there are thus only two possibilities—that he stands either under the guidance of God or under the guidance of Satan. Therefore when people emancipate themselves from God to go their own way, they are therefore going to be guided by Satan.[203] Moreover, when God takes his Spirit away from people, this means that he gives them into the hands of Satan.[204]

---

[195] Ps. 35:4 (*CO* 31, 348).

[196] "...Satan, fraudum omnium artifex...," Ps. 5:11 (*CO* 31, 71).

[197] "...ac essent faeces et excrementa mundi...," Ps. 109:3 (*CO* 32, 147).

[198] Ps. 83:5 (*CO* 31, 774).

[199] Ps. 14:4 (*CO* 31, 139).

[200] "...Satanae et papae imposturas..." Ps. 119:136 (*CO* 32, 277).

[201] "Certe si nullae essent incantationes, frustra lege Dei prohibitae ac damnatae essent, Deut. 18,11," Ps. 58:5 (*CO* 31, 561).

[202] Ps. 119:133 (*CO* 32, 275).

[203] Ps. 81:12 (*CO* 31, 765).

[204] Ps. 109:13 (*CO* 32, 152).

9. Fall and Renewal

For the rest it is significant that Calvin raises the matter of rebirth after he has spoken about man in his lost condition. In his exposition of Psalm 103:4, he presents the natural situation of man as being "dead and handed over to the grave," but he points directly afterwards to the fact that the renewal of one's spirit is equal to a resurrection from the grave.[205] From our mother's womb we are mastered by depravity and wickedness. This situation remains in a person until a rebirth through the Spirit has taken place and we have been reformed into new humans.[206] Our eyes form the entrance gates for Satan until the Holy Spirit acts as the sentry.[207] Man is dead by nature until he is brought to life again through the knowledge of heavenly doctrine.[208]

This rather radical description of sinful man must be seen within the context of Calvin's message urging the reader to put all his or her hope in God. The aim of Calvin is not to give a negative view of man but instead to assure that man will expect everything from God alone when he sees that he cannot expect anything from himself anymore.[209] Man has to examine himself before the face of God; then it will become clear that he needs forgiveness. Satan however teaches another anthropology, and he tries to deprive us from an awareness that by nature we are lost humans.[210] Therefore a person has to come to the understanding that he or she cannot be helped by mere upbringing and education but that such blindness can disappear only when God through the illumination of his Holy Spirit carries out a reformation of the heart.[211] The description of the condition of man must result in seeking after God. The scope of the *"cognitio hominis"* is therefore the *"cognitio Dei."* In this regard God sometimes uses drastic means. Calvin writes that man is so blind to God being a savior that he first has to meet eye to eye with death before he will see him.[212] We are born, Calvin continues, without any comprehension of God, and in the first years of our lives it is not sufficiently clear to us that he is our maker. Yet if we suffer need and God renders help, the help is like a resurrection in which we see the grace of God reflected.[213]

Along with the change in our relation to God, the renewing work of the Spirit also has consequences for our humanity. Through rebirth the Spirit

---

[205] Ps. 103:4 (*CO* 32, 75).

[206] Ps. 14:2 (*CO* 31, 138).

[207] Ps. 119:37 (*CO* 32, 231).

[208] Ps. 119:144 (*CO* 32, 280).

[209] "...quum homines ipsa vanitate sint vaniores, nihil aliud restare, quam ut spes omnes suas ad unum Deum referant," Ps. 119:144 (*CO* 32, 280).

[210] Ps. 32:2 (*CO* 31, 317).

[211] Ps. 119:73 (*CO* 32, 246).

[212] "Nam ad mortem usque descendere necesse est ut Deus appareat redemptor," Ps. 71:20 (*CO* 31, 662).

[213] "...resurrectio ipsa nobis illustre est gratiae eius speculum," Ps. 71:20 (*CO* 31, 662).

liberates man from "deceit and vanity."[214] Calvin here uses the word "*corrigere*," which points to an act that brings something back into a previous state. It is a matter of *re*-formation into the image of Christ. "Christ is the living image of God, and in conforming to this image we have to be reformed."[215] The previous state is characterized as a perfect insight. In Calvin's opinion it is thus the most important promise of the Spirit that he will give man understanding and enlighten him with true and sound wisdom.[216] This light gives the opportunity to follow in God's ways. "We should ask nothing more from God than for guidance through his light so that we are not equal to the ignorant cattle anymore." The concepts used here— "*prudential*," "*ratio*," "*intelligentia*," "*caecitas*" and "*lux*"—indicate that the cognitive impact of Calvin's theology is meant to be practical since correct knowledge must lead to correct action. When God enlightens the mind, man is enabled to follow in the right way again.

The will which God has given us, although by the fall still prone to commit sin, has nevertheless been changed positively by God such that we "voluntarily" strive after righteousness.[217] In spite of this, the old characteristics of the sin do not fully disappear after rebirth. Even one who wants to aspire to peaceful and right behavior sees that, when around you injustice is not punished, the temptation is to react in blind fury.[218]

The renewal given by God means a restored "correctness of the heart." This internal renewal of the heart rests on a rebirth through the Spirit who renews us to the image of God.[219] Elsewhere Calvin writes that God restores the corrupted nature through the Spirit of rebirth.[220] Grace is not an addition to nature, but rather through grace there arises *another* nature.

10. Conclusion

Calvin's cosmology in the Psalms commentary is significantly informed by the antitheses between God and Satan, order and chaos, and fall and renewal. He makes a strenuous effort to recognize the beauty of creation and its creatures while also admitting the reality and consequences of sin. Calvin's biggest fear is the idea that God and creation in one way or another could stand separate from each other. Thus Calvin raises the rebirth in his anthropological comments as soon as he has mentioned man being lost. Also

---

[214] Ps. 62:10 (*CO* 31, 589).
[215] Ps. 8:6 (*CO* 31, 93).
[216] Ps. 119:169 (*CO* 32, 291).
[217] "...ut libere appetamus iustitiam...," Ps. 40:8 (*CO* 31, 412).
[218] Ps. 17:4 (*CO* 31, 161). It is significant that Calvin changes the subject in the sentence from "they who" to "we." Can he perhaps identify with this temptation?
[219] Ps. 96:10 (*CO* 32, 42).
[220] Ps. 25:8 (*CO* 31, 255).

the emphasis on the concept of "order," by which Calvin makes use of platonic terminology, can be elucidated from his effort to keep God and creation bound to each other.

4

God the Caring

The Providence Carer

1. An Existential Theme

One of the aspects of Calvin's theology that has been researched most thoroughly relates to his doctrine of God's providence.[1] Since the Psalms address the way God deals with his people, this matter surfaces in Calvin's commentary on the Psalms more frequently than any other theme. Calvin designates God's providence as "one of the most important principles of heaven's philosophy."[2] Creation and providence are inextricably tied together, and therefore this chapter follows the chapter on "God the Creator." According to Calvin, one will only believe that God cares for this world if one acknowledges him as the creator. Furthermore it is evident that the providence of God is a consequence of his role in creation.[3] In this chapter Calvin will speak for himself rather comprehensively in order to elucidate this important doctrine, and we shall see how his reflections on God's providence in particular had a later influence on Calvinistic spirituality.

Here, perhaps even more than in the case of other themes, one can appreciate that Calvin interpreted the Bible within the context of his own time and with an eye towards his and his readers' circumstances. Calvin knows from personal experience how many dangers threaten one's life. The account of these in his *Institutes* is quite memorable in a paragraph that forms a subdivision of the chapter dealing with providence. These very same convictions resonate in his commentary on the Psalms.[4] Calvin knows how vulnerable life is: "One's life is exposed to a thousand deaths. It hangs by a thin thread of silk and presents nothing more than a breath that passes away suddenly."[5] He was certainly acquainted with the dangers of traveling,[6] he was familiar with the plight of a refugee, he knew the fear of

---

[1] Still essential is J. Bohatec's "Calvins Vorsehungslehre," in *Calvinstudien: Festschrift zum 400. Geburtstage Johann Calvins* (Leipzig: R. Haupt, 1909), 339-441. For a more recent analysis, see Schreiner, *Theater*, 7-37; Stauffer, *Dieu*, 261-302; and Faber, *Symphonie*, 139-67.

[2] Ps. 49:1,2 (*CO* 31, 481).

[3] Ps. 33:6 (*CO* 31, 327).

[4] *Inst.* I, 17, 10.

[5] Ps. 31:5 (*CO* 31, 302).

[6] For the dangers of traveling in Calvin's times, see: Emmanuel Le Roy Ladurie, *Le siècle des Platter (1499-1628)* (Paris: Fayard, 1995).

being endangered by compatriots and fellow citizens, and from daily experience he was acquainted with mourning, disease and pain. Calvin repeatedly refers in autobiographical terms to "our fears."[7] At the same time he realizes that he is preaching, teaching and writing to those who have experienced by and large the same things.

For Calvin there are only two possibilities. World affairs are either determined by chance or by God's hidden providence[8] even though God's providence can sometimes be so hidden that it seems as if chance rules.[9]

The term "providence" is otherwise inadequately suited to articulate what Calvin intends to say. The notion may sound static, but the issue in question is rather dynamic. The word "providence" is often associated with a detailed and designed plan engineered even before the creation of the world that inevitably and immutably will come to consummation. Calvin however speaks of providence as the continuing intervention of God in world affairs. The sky does not coincidentally become overcast, a raindrop does not merely fall from the clouds and a gale does not start blowing at random. All these things are set in motion by a secret resolution of God.[10] He gathers together the winds so that the ocean swells and rages. Mariners can tell from present weather conditions that a storm is approaching, but sudden changes proceed only from God's appointment.[11] Moreover, God's care and guidance cover every single aspect of life.[12] Bearing in mind these explanatory notes, I will keep using the word "providence" due to colloquial speech.

2. Calvin contra Epicurus and Aristotle

Fundamental for Calvin's view of the providence of God is his intense rejection of the opinion that God could be idle (*otiosus*). God does not merely sit in heaven looking down upon the earth to observe what we are conducting among ourselves.[13] Calvin calls the belief that God is *otiosus* a disease under which most people labor.[14] He therefore strongly reacts against those who would imprison God in heaven and pretend as if he

---

[7]   *Inter alia* Ps. 3:2 (*CO* 31, 53).
[8]   "Neque enim imaginanda est nobis fortunae rota, quae temere omnia volvendo misceat …nempe occulta Dei providentia impelli," Ps. 73:18 (*CO* 31, 683); "…arcana providentia…," Ps. 5:5 (*CO* 31, 68).
[9]   "…sed arcano suo consilio moderetur quae videntur maxime fortuita…," Ps. 135:6 (*CO* 32, 359).
[10]   Ps. 149:7 (*CO* 32, 434).
[11]   Ps. 107:23 (*CO* 32, 141).
[12]   "…nempe quae singulus vitae nostrae partes praesenti virtute moderatur," Ps. 75:9 (*CO* 31, 704).
[13]   Ps. 10:14 (*CO* 31, 117).
[14]   "…morbo communiter laborant cuncti mortals…," Ps. 10:12 (*CO* 31, 115).

merely sits there inactive.[15] Calvin, like *inter alia* Luther, Zwingli and Bucer had done before him, designates this group of people as "Epicureans."[16] These ideas of the Greek philosopher Epicurus (341-270 BC) were introduced anew by a number of humanists that the gods do not interfere with matters on earth because their ultimate contentment is that they do not have to meddle with such mortal affairs.[17] A god who lives in a state of idleness and makes light of everything in this world is inconceivable though in Calvin's view. You can offer no greater affront to God than to imprison him in heaven because that, in essence, implies that you would bury him. What kind of life would God's be, Calvin asks, if he neither saw nor took care of everything?[18] God cannot simply do nothing although Calvin admits that the temptation to believe that God remains seated at ease in heaven indeed intensifies when one becomes aware of the apparently mundane ways of the world.[19] Related to this image of the ever-active God is Calvin's depiction of heaven. Heaven is not the place where God indulges in leisure, but rather it is the seat of government from which he exercises his reign over earthly affairs. Heaven is not a palace but a parliament.[20]

Simultaneously, Calvin fears the image of a God who functions merely as "first unmoved mover," as can be seen from his exposition of Psalm 127:3, where the birth of children is mentioned. He rejects the idea that God in the beginning equipped man with a certain ability of reproduction and that consequently children are begotten by a "secret instinct of nature." He likewise opposes the opinion held by some believers that God does not descend from heaven for each individual conception of new life. Solomon's description of children as a heritage from the Lord bears witness to the fact that God is directly involved in the origin of each new human being. Having children is not the fruit of chance, nor is it entirely due to natural ability, but instead it is an honor which God bestows upon people.[21] Hence, God's care discloses itself in child-birth. Even before the birth of a baby, it could have died already a hundred times, and directly after it is brought into the world,

---

[15] Ps. 139:1 (*CO* 32, 377).

[16] Cf. Marc Lienhard, "Les Épicuriens à Strasbourg entre 1530 et 1550 et le problème de l'épicurisme au XVIe siècle," in *Croyants et sceptiques au XVIe siècle* (Strasbourg: Librairie ISTRA, 1981), 17-56; Peuckert, *Wende,* 89-94.

[17] For an analysis of Epicurus' ideas, see R.W. Sharples, *Stoics, Epicureans and Sceptics: An Introduction to Hellenistic Philosophy* (London and New York: Routledge, 1996).

[18] "Qualis enim Dei vita, si nihil cernat, vel curet?," Ps. 33:13 (*CO* 31, 331).

[19] Ps. 92:6 (*CO* 32, 12).

[20] "Significat enim, coelam non ad delicias, ut somniant Epicurei otiosum esse palatium, sed regiam e qua imperium suum per omnes mundi partes exerceat," Ps. 33:13 (*CO* 31, 331).

[21] "Contra pronuntiat Solomo, patres fieri quos Deus hoc honere dignatur," Ps. 127:3 (*CO* 32, 324).

all kinds of threats and anxieties descend upon it when it cannot even lift a finger to help itself.[22] Calvin, therefore, warns of two risks: the Epicurean thought that God does not concern himself with this earth and the Aristotelian belief that God is merely the primary cause.

3. *Praesentia Realis*

Calvin entitles the providence of God "the true theology." That alone is the genuine doctrine of God when we do not envisage him as Epicurus did, namely, as an unoccupied and self-contained god without any concern for mankind.[23] This "absurd idea" nevertheless obtained wide currency amongst many.[24] This is also a theology that bears consequences. The existence of God is indeed not denied, but this view pretends that God is shut up in heaven in order that on earth one can act as he likes without being punished.[25] This thought that God has no concern whatsoever for the world smothers all piety.[26] The doctrine of God subsequently determines ethical decisions, and this is yet another reason why Calvin fears this Epicurean thought. Even though man does not deny the existence of God, it is nonetheless true that whoever renounces God's care for this world has in fact abolished him.[27] God's being though is characterized in particular by the fact that he is not directed to himself but that in love he is directed to others. Therefore by his very nature he must be engaged with his creation.

For these reasons every version of God's providence in which he beforehand only *knows* the course of events is foreign to Calvin. This also counts for the idea that there is only some pre-framed plan that God now has put into effect. The events in nature do not merely proceed according to particular laws that God impressed upon them in the beginning only to stand by idly as these events unfold. After he had created all things, God did not entirely entrust the world to a course of its own in terms of fixed physical laws, but instead he guards over his creatures and absolutely nothing takes place without his continuous intervention.[28] Here Calvin speaks of a *"praesens arbitrium,"*[29] an active presence and continuous

---

[22] Ps. 22:10 (*CO* 31, 226).

[23] "Atque haec vera theologia est Deum non imaginary, cum Epicuro, vacantem otio vel deliciis, et que se uno contentus humanum genus negligat...," Ps. 9:9 (*CO* 31, 100). See also Ps. 10:5 (*CO* 31, 112): "...sicut Epicurei Deum palam negare non audentes, fingunt in otio deliciari."

[24] Ps. 135:6 (*CO* 32, 359).

[25] "...imo Deum coelo inclusum fingentes, quasi nihil sibi esset cum eo negotii, sese ad spem impunitatis confirment," Ps. 10:5 (*CO* 31, 112).

[26] Ps. 121:3 (*CO* 32, 300).

[27] "Deum itaque...abolent quicunque mundum non subiicunt eius providentiae...," Ps. 10:4 (*CO* 31, 111).

[28] Ps. 148:7 (*CO* 32, 435).

[29] "...nec quidquam nisi preasenti eius arbitrio moveri...," Ps. 149:7 (*CO* 32, 435).

involvement of God. It is not the distance of a plan coming to an end but it is the nearness of God who not only observes reality but also determines it. Nor is it some vague "universal providence" as some maintain, but rather Calvin's view encompasses a "particular providence."[30] He who holds that God does not provide in everything, Calvin charges, despoils him of his power and casts a shadow upon his strength.[31] Hence God's care extends over the whole of creation, including each living creature.[32] Even concerning weather it is true that God not only created an order but he intervenes in the particulars of events. It does not rain because nature forces it to do so but because God decides to let it rain.[33] Storms do not burst by chance, but they are scourges from God just as it is a signal of his goodness when he moderates the excessive heat by a gentle cooling breeze.[34]

God's uninterrupted intercession does not signify a persisting threat or even an interruption of the physical order. Calvin calls it "the glory of our faith"[35] for the very reason that God does not abandon the order which he himself established. Calvin illustrates this by referring to a nursing infant. A tongue that is not even able to pronounce a single word has, on account of a mysterious instinct provided by God, the skill to suckle. In fact, there is only food for such a newborn to eat because God wonderfully changed blood into milk within the mother.[36] So we see that God's intervening hand is hidden behind an established order. Those who reject this intervention of God and explain an event simply in terms of nature are in fact waging a war against God. Calvin however admits that it is not always easily discerned because "the dreadful disorder that devastates man's life vehemently obscures the order of God's providence."[37]

At times, though, God intervenes abruptly in the order of the creation, and, according to Calvin, this is always with a specific intention. Particular events are not signs of coincidence but rather tokens of God's providence "because, if the course of events were always uniform, men would merely sound forth, 'It is nature, it is nature!'"[38]

The repeated denial of a "*deus otiosus*" or a God that is far away amounts to the acknowledgement of the active "*praesentia realis*" of God in this world. The correspondence with Calvin's doctrine of the Lord's Supper is clear: God is present in the created reality and his presence is

---

[30] Ps. 135:6 (*CO* 32, 359).
[31] Ps. 135:6 (*CO* 32, 359).
[32] Ps. 147:10 (*CO* 32, 429).
[33] Ps. 137:7 (*CO* 32, 360).
[34] Ps. 104:3 (*CO* 32, 85).
[35] Ps. 11:4 (*CO* 31, 123).
[36] Ps. 8:3 (*CO* 31, 89).
[37] Ps. 92:6 (*CO* 32, 11).
[38] "...iactarent omnes, naturam, naturam," Ps. 113:7 (*CO* 32, 179).

always an operative presence though God is by no means a component of the created reality. Concerning God's presence in world events, then, the *extra-Calvinisticum* holds good as well.[39] Providence is so essential to Calvin that its denunciation in fact equals the denial of God's existence. Likewise God is only worshipped appropriately when his providence is known from one's own personal experience. Meanwhile a cold knowledge of God—that is, to know him merely as a judge or supervisor—does not evoke true devotion.[40]

The confession that God is "*non-otiosus*" touches upon the office of God. Instead of idly sitting around, God is diligently at work caring for those who belong to him. The care that he provides for his faithful is so essential to his being that Calvin repeatedly maintains that it is God's vocation to nurture. When the faithful are troubled by the enemies of the church, they can confidently trust because it is God's office to guard them against the attacks of the impious.[41] For these reasons, God's providence is a source of comfort:

> Let us therefore observe when we are distressed and anxious (*anxii*) to seek comfort in God's providence, for amidst the awesome solicitudes we ought to be fully persuaded that it is God's peculiar office to come to the aid of the wretched and afflicted.[42]

When Calvin writes that it is God's duty to care for the believing, he goes beyond his discourse on the office of God whereby he relates the obligation to care with God's nature once again.[43] It is a chore that God laid on himself, and it is true to his essence to comply with such obligations.

While God has his duties, he also has rights. When Calvin says that God can claim our praise and gratitude when he delivers us, one hears the judicial element in Calvin's thinking. He who does not appreciate God's providence in any deliverance robs him of that right.[44] Simultaneously there exists a clear relation between God's office to care for us and the duty of man to execute his task on earth. This relation between the confession of

---

[39] Cf. Heiko A. Oberman, "Die '*Extra*' Dimension in der Theologie Calvins," in *Die Reformation: Von Wittenberg nach Genf* (Göttingen: Vanderhoeck & Ruprecht, 1986), 253-82, where Oberman has already indicated how the *extra-Calvinisticum* is also applicable to other themes in Calvin's theology.

[40] "Neque vero sufficit frigidam de iudicio Dei notitiam concipere...," Ps. 10:4 (*CO* 31, 111).

[41] "Uno itaque complexu Deo tribuit suos tuendi et servandi munus contra omnes impios qui ad oppugnandam eorum salutem insurgunt," Ps. 7:7 (*CO* 31, 163).

[42] "...proprium eius esse munus...," Ps. 10:1 (*CO* 31, 108).

[43] "Ita prius argumentum sumptum est ab ipsius Dei natura, et quasi a proprio officio...," Ps. 25:4 (*CO* 31, 252).

[44] "...fraudari Deum iure suo, nisi hac in parte agnoscitur eius providentiae...," Ps. 107:22 (*CO* 32, 140).

God's providence and a so-called "typically Calvinistic" work ethic is emphasized by Calvin: they who know that God nurtures us until death or even until after death "are not so distracted by fear as to cease from performing their duty."[45] He who knows that God cares can calmly and faithfully do his work.

4. The Significance of the "Secondary Causes"

Calvin rejects all the philosophers who dismiss divine providence by their appeals to "middle causes."[46] Such thinkers, Calvin says, try their best to bury God's providence. The Reformer mentions by name Aristotle, who, although a man of genius and learning,[47] was nevertheless a pagan and therefore concentrated on covering up God's providence in various speculations. However every layman who has but a little faith outshines this philosopher because Aristotle in his contemplation of meteors includes all the natural causes (and Calvin readily believes that to this degree he is right!), but he does not point to the most important cause of all, God.[48] According to Calvin Aristotle's case is so grievous in that he used all the knowledge that God gave him to extinguish every light. On this matter these philosophers are in reality even more unacceptable than his Epicurean contemporaries. Calvin has these Aristotelian philosophers in mind when he writes that there have been theologians in the church who have sought an acceptable explanation for this question by aligning themselves with pagan philosophers. The consequence, however, was that they arrived at the doctrine of free will and of good works simply because they could not venture to utter what God proclaims in his word. Even Augustine would have pursued this course had God not prevented it by knocking him from this fallacy as if with a hammer.[49] Rather Calvin follows a Scotist line of reasoning for the sovereignty of God when he rejects the notion that causes are so connected to each other that God himself is also bound to them.[50] Faith looks beyond the causes and sees there God's hidden decree, by which he directs all things according to his intentions in complete sovereignty.

Calvin admits that this confession can arouse resentment because it presupposes some restriction on human agents. Such a complaint however

[45] Ps. 31:5 (*CO* 31, 302).
[46] "…in excundendis mediis causis…," Ps. 107:43 (*CO* 32, 145).
[47] "Aristoteles tam ingenio quam doctrina maxime excelliut…," Ps. 107:43 (*CO* 32, 145).
[48] Ps. 147:15 (*CO* 32, 430).
[49] "Deus autem quasi melleo eum expoliem…," Ps. 105:25 (*CO* 32, 109).
[50] Ps. 105:19 (*CO* 32, 107). Wendel notes that the resemblance between Scotus and Calvin is expressed in the view that God is bound by his decisions without being compelled to them in a causative way. Wendel, *Calvin*, 92-4. See also Stauffer, *Dieu*, 112-6.

can only arise from arrogance. According to Calvin it all comes down to a choice between the authority of God's word and the normative mandate of human reason. For Calvin there is thus no option:

> What insanity is it to embrace nothing but what is pleasant to human reason? What authority will God's word have if it is not admitted any further than we are inclined to receive it?[51]

Calvin admits that there are also unbelievers who maintain the doctrine of God's providence. But when matters turn out contrary to their expectations or hopes, they openly deny what they previously professed. The reason for this is that the non-believer is not regenerated by the Spirit of God who would enable him to persist in the confession of God's providence in spite of impediments.[52]

Calvin does not deny the existence and significance of the "*causae secundae*," provided that these do not preclude the disclosure of God's providence behind them.[53] His critique is that the great majority of people adhere to the "*media*" and effectively overlook the "*prima causa*."[54] What proceeds from God is then ascribed "*ad medias causas*."[55]

Calvin is convinced that the providence of God is not detrimental to *human responsibility*. Calvin states clearly that God takes under his protection those who entrust themselves to him whole-heartedly.[56] He voices his outlook in the introductory comments to Psalm 34, which was written by David after he pretended to be mad—conduct which, incidentally, rescued him. Calvin regards the behavior of David a disgrace because it belies a lack of trust in God's deliverance and above all David provoked disdain. Yet, the praise for this deliverance is ascribed to God. The question as to how both relate is simply explained according to Calvin. When God wishes to rescue, he can do it even though people err in choosing the means that God provides for salvation. "Consequently, the deliverance was the work of God, but the intermediate sin which is on no account to be excused ought to be ascribed to David."[57]

5. Distinctions in General Providence

In order to perceive the pastoral dimension to Calvin's theology, it is critically important to bear in mind Calvin's distinctions which have

---

[51] Ps. 105:25 (*CO* 32, 109).
[52] Ps. 73: introduction (*CO* 31, 674).
[53] "…sed mediae causae Dei providentiam obscurare non debent…," Ps. 147:7 (*CO* 32, 428).
[54] "…sed praepostere in externa quae circumstant media…," Ps. 33:13 (*CO* 31, 331).
[55] Ps. 46:9 (*CO* 31, 464).
[56] Ps. 16:1 (*CO* 31, 149).
[57] Ps. 34:1 (*CO* 31, 335).

reference to God's providence. First, there is a universal providence by which God regulates the entire scope of world affairs. Moreover, God's providence is especially certain in his guidance of and care for his church. To this particular providence God offers special attention within his universal providence because it concerns the extent and character of his care. While it is true that his providence benefits the whole of mankind, his distinctively paternal care as a true father in heaven is destined only for his own children.[58] God thus differentiates between the ways he cares for his creatures, and he reveals this as well in order that the faithful can find peace of mind in the knowledge that they live under the special care of God.[59] God takes it upon himself to care for the church, and he therefore pledges his providential governance to her more than even to the rest of the world. Because of this exceptional attention, Calvin calls the Lord the *pastor ecclesiae*. He is the shepherd of the church, not only because he cares for and guides the faithful as he indeed does among all mortals, but also because he distinguishes them from the rest of the world by taking them under his fatherly protection.[60]

The real difference between believers and non-believers, though, rests in the acquaintance of Christians with reconciliation. The faithful know that the light of God's favor constantly shines upon them, even in the darkest times. They abide therefore in a father-child relationship, knowing that God as their heavenly Father will be propitious to them during hardship. The unfaithful however are not reconciled with God; hence they are not aware of the fatherly love of God, and they consequently do not know any tranquility in times of adversity. Calvin explains this paradox employing the terms "light" and "darkness." The light of God's grace is intended for those who are surrounded with darkness and know that God uses the darkness, but the ungodly on the other hand are blind in the midst of light.[61] By a variation on the famous motto of the city of Geneva (*post tenebras lux*), this view of God's providence suggests both *inter tenebras lux* as well as *per tenebras lux*. There is not only light amidst darkness; there is also light by means of the darkness when they stand in contrast to one another.

Calvin also portrays the distinction between general and particular providence with the respective designations of "outward" and "inward." Commenting on Psalm 90:16, he speaks about the particular dealings of

---

[58] Ps. 33:18 (*CO* 31, 333).

[59] "Nam specialiter Dei providentiam celebrat in regendis fidelibus," Ps. 73:1 (*CO* 31, 675).

[60] "...Deum vocari ecclesiae suae pastorem, non qualiter reliquos mortals promisque alit, sustinet ac gubernat: sed quia eam a toto mundo distinxit, ut paterno sinu foveat," Ps. 95:7 (*CO* 32, 31).

[61] Ps. 112:3 (*CO* 32, 173-4).

God with his children and the special attention that God shows for the church as distinct from God's care for the world's unbelieving inhabitants:

> He directs his work regarding the reprobate externally with his hidden providence, but he governs the believers internally by his Spirit.[62]

Furthermore, in his commentary on Psalm 9:4, Calvin poetically articulates the contradictions that find expression in these respective works of God.

> And certainly he alone is the one who governs the unadorned
> with his Spirit of wisdom, but on the contrary
> makes the cunning inept and strikes them with stupidity,
> who fills the effeminate and scared with gallantry
> and freezes the bold petrified with fear,
> who provides the vulnerable with new strength
> and paralyses the strong entirely,
> who helps up the unarmed with his own hands
> and hits the sword from the hands of the war-minded,
> who ultimately brings the fight to a noble or dreadful end
> exactly as he wills.[63]

The distinction between these two categories of people as it relates to God's providence embodies itself in the arena of human behavior as well. As long as things are going well, all people tend to still acknowledge that the world is governed by God, but the moment confusion arises from various kinds of disturbance, hardly any people remain persuaded of this truth.[64] The remarkable difference between the *filii Dei* and *profanes homines*[65] thus becomes evident. This distinction manifests itself in the responses of tranquility[66] among the first group and restlessness in the case of the second group. While non-believers are agitated in such troubled circumstances, believers are characterized by calmness.[67] All who do not have a true knowledge of God end up in a dismal state of fear and uncertainty that

---

[62] Ps. 90:16 (*CO* 31, 842).

[63] Ps. 9:4 (*CO* 31, 497-8)

[64] Ps. 11:4 (*CO* 31, 123).

[65] Ps. 26:3 (*CO* 31, 265).

[66] This notion of acquiring *tranquillitas* resembles the humanistic ideal that Erasmus contrasts to the strain and concern that the world causes. See John B. Payne, "Erasmus's influence on Zwingli and Bullinger" in *Biblical Interpretation in the Era of the Reformation*, ed. Richard A. Muller and John L. Thompson (Grand Rapids: Eerdmans, 1996) 67.

[67] "Notatur enim antithesis inter vagos et erraticos, imo violentos eorum motus, qui sorte sua non contenti sese temere proiiciunt, et piorum modestiam qui in Dei vocatione tranquilli resident," Ps. 131:2 (*CO* 32, 341).

induces people to search desperately all over as they in fact acquire tranquility nowhere.[68] Calvin contrasts this *misera inquietudo* with the *tranquillo animo* which is the share of those that possess an accurate theology.[69] It is evident that Calvin here speaks from the context of the sixteenth century and that he operates with the generally accepted conception of God. Thus, Calvin does not consider the possibility that there are people who, despite the fact that they lack "the true knowledge of God" in adversity, are yet no more panic-stricken than those who do possess a believer's knowledge of providence.

Believers know God's providence and they may therefore, confiding serenely in God's word, anticipate a beneficial conclusion in situations of anxiety and distress. They are delighted in the knowledge of God's providence, Calvin writes, because without this knowledge they would be harassed by doubts and fears, being uncertain of whether the world is ruled by mere chance.[70] Consequently, believers need not act falsely in all kinds of ways in order to escape hardships. The knowledge that God rules the whole world also eliminates the necessity of avenging injustice for oneself. He who keeps God's providence in mind can instead resist to the temptation to retaliate against those who do evil.[71] Meanwhile, those who are ignorant of God's providence seek to remedy all perceived injustice through their own actions, and in the end they have no other objective than to overcome evil with evil.[72] This is the remarkable distinction between those "who are looking around" in search of help and those "that deem themselves secure in trusting God."[73] Whether those without the knowledge of the true God encounter distress or success, they do not take heed of divine providence and are therefore "seeing but not perceiving."[74] In fact, since they derive nothing from such experiences, their conduct is even more inexcusable. The righteous, however, are able to contemplate God's equity, kindness and wisdom with eyes that truly see and perceive the works of God's hand.

In Psalm 112:7 this distinction between those who understand providence and those who do not is related to the two responses of anxiety and reassurance. Calvin here observes that

---

[68] Ps. 16:5 (*CO* 31, 153).

[69] "...nempe sedato ac tranquillo animo se in uno Deo acquiscere..." Ps. 16:6 (*CO* 31, 154).

[70] Ps. 107:42 (*CO* 32, 144).

[71] "...fraenabit etiam omnem intemperiem, ne ad retaliandas iniurias prosiliant," Ps. 62:12 (*CO* 31, 592).

[72] "...quia tamen ignota est illis Dei providentia, raptantur huc et illuc...," Ps. 26:3 (*CO* 31, 265).

[73] Ps. 32:2 (CO 31, 317). See also Ps. 92:6 (CO 32, 11): "...circumspiciunt huc et illuc...eorum securitati qui in Deum recumbunt...."

[74] "...caecutiunt tamen videndo...," Ps. 107:42 (*CO* 32, 144).

...unlike the ungodly who tremble even at the slightest rumor, the righteous calmly and without trouble confide in God's paternal providence amidst all evil tidings that may reach them. The constant anxiety of unbelievers derives from the concept that, while God remains at ease in heaven, they are puppets in the hands of fortune on earth. Now it is no surprise then that they are thrown into confusion and their courage fails when they hear just the rustling of a leaf falling from a tree. The prophet confirms that the faithful are not burdened by similar uneasiness because they do not give heed to rumors, and fear does not prevent them from constantly invoking God.[75]

When people assume that God is at leisure (*otiosus*) and that humanity is left to the mercy of blind chance, it is no wonder that they are terrified by the slightest rumor.[76] However, there is nothing to be afraid of when you comprehend that the God who covers his own with the shadow of his wings is the very same God who governs the universe according to his will and simultaneously restrains the work of Satan and all the ungodly.[77] In contrast, though, the believer who loses sight of God's care will also be startled by even the rustling of a falling leaf![78]

Nevertheless, Calvin immediately adds, this does not suggest that believers will never experience fear in any way. The children of God may also be scared at the prospect of impending danger. For, if they were to have no concern whatsoever for the calamities of life, such indifference would not be the result of trust but of insensibility.[79] Instead, those who rely on God's providence are not free of all anxiety, but they can nevertheless pursue their course through life by entrusting themselves to God's disposal. As the Reformer puts it, "In a word, believers are not of iron, nor do they resemble solid blocks, but the trust they put in God lifts them above all anxieties."[80]

6. Distinctions in Special Providence

It is clear to all that God also makes distinctions when interacting with the believer. He does not manifest his favor equally or uniformly to all Christians. This view is not only presented by Calvin, but he also offers an

---

[75] Ps 112:7 (*CO* 32, 175).

[76] Ps. 62:12 (*CO* 31, 592). Cf. Ps. 112:7 (*CO* 32, 175).

[77] Ps. 62:12 (*CO* 31, 592).

[78] Ps. 121:8 (*CO* 32, 302).

[79] "...quia si nulla eos malorum cura tangeret, stuporis esset, non constantiae securitas," Ps. 112:7 (*CO* 32, 175).

[80] Ps. 112:7 (*CO* 32, 175).

explanation as to why this is so. In giving the reasons for God's dissimilar treatment of his children, Calvin utilizes the significant concept of *causa*.[81] He says that there are believers who need to be healed of a secret disease by way of hardship while others do not need such a remedy. In some cases God even puts the patience that he has previously conferred upon them to the test. Others, through their suffering, are set forth by God as examples to other believers. God thus has a particular purpose with each person, and such can only be sufficiently explained by his reasons which are often unknown to us. According to Calvin, though, God's common purpose is to humble all of his people, every single one without differentiation, by tokens of his anger so that all believers may be brought to repentance and conversion. They thus often stumble upon the same afflictions as non-believers in order to perceive to a greater extent how much they need the protection of God.[82] This also reflects Calvin's *theologia crucis* insofar as God imposes "crosses" of suffering to draw people unto himself.[83] God thus disciplines us by means of the cross to put our faith to the test.[84] He imposes the cross intending to exercise believers in faith, patience and expectancy.[85] This also explains why Calvin calls it "more than a mediocre comfort" when believers are exercised in persistence by God's providence.[86] Were it not for the consolation that chastisement leads to the furthering of our sanctification, our condition would indeed be miserable.[87] When Calvin observes that the true disciple, through a willingness to submissively bear the cross, distinguishes himself from the false, he offers the reader a *syllogismus practicus*.[88] Another explanation why God's children are not exempted from adversity is that it is not so much a punishment for sin as it is chastisement that prevents sin from strengthening its hold on them when they have committed a particular offense.[89] In this respect, suffering ought to be considered a blessing if one shares Calvin's logic.

The use of the concept of *causae*, however, does not indicate that Calvin here supposes a necessary causal relation between punishment and guilt,

---

[81] "Sunt enim multiplices causae cur non peraeque suum erga omnes pios favorem declaret Deus in mundo...," Ps. 37:25 (*CO* 31, 378).

[82] Ps. 23:4 (*CO* 31, 240).

[83] "...cruce servos suos exercet...," Ps. 92:6 (*CO* 32, 11).

[84] "...nos Deus cruce exercet...imo quum rebus adversis fidem examinat Deus," Ps. 23:4 (*CO* 31, 240).

[85] Ps. 79:5 (*CO* 31, 749).

[86] Ps. 28:2 (*CO* 31, 283).

[87] "Itaque miserrima esset sine hoc consolatio nastra conditio, beatos esse quos Deus cruce exercet," Ps. 94:12 (*CO* 32, 23).

[88] Ps. 94:12 (CO 32, 24). On Calvin's use of the *syllogismus practicus*, see: Joel R. Beeke, *The Quest for Full Assurance: the legacy of Calvin and his successors* (Edinburgh: Banner of Truth, 1999) 65-72.

[89] "...ne peccata in ipsis radices agant...," Ps. 34:17 (*CO* 31, 343).

although this is often the case given the providence of God and the adversity of man.[90] What God intends, rather, is to keep people's thoughts fixed upon an impending eternal life in heaven, and he does this by letting them experience how miserable life on earth really is. When a believer is subjected to adversity, it is of great importance to recall that it proceeds from God's hand because only then can one apprehend that misery is intended for our good.

> To summarize, the truth conveyed here is that although God castigates those who belong to him with chastisements of a severe description, he will ultimately crown them with joy and prosperity.[91]

Calvin notes that God deals with prosperity in much the same way. God promises temporal blessings to the faithful, but he confers these upon each person individually in so far as he considers it desirable in that particular case.[92] Some need much prosperity to be persuaded of God's favor towards them, but there may also be believers that, for this purpose, must be brought to poverty. Conceivably God seeks to help this last group to lift up their minds to that heavenly state in which God will recompense them for all that is now wanting in this transitory life.

According to Calvin, however, it is profoundly important not to reverse this form of "causality" such that, for example, every destitute believer would assume that he or she is thus too little fixed upon heaven. Against this erroneous reversal Calvin incisively warns in the exposition of Psalm 91:15:

> Indeed, if God affords to some his favor in granting wealth and other worldly conveniences, it does not consequently follow that the poor apparently are objects of divine displeasure. Soundness of physical health is a blessing from God, but on this account we may not conceive that he regards the weak and the failing with disapprobation.[93]

It is remarkable that when Calvin treats the topic of prosperity on his commentary, he more emphatically speaks of God's hand than when he speaks about human afflictions. Accordingly, on the one hand, he speaks of the glittering manifestation of God's blessings while, on the other hand, he uses the impersonal and passive form to refer to someone being pinched by

---

[90] See the discussion on sin and punishment below in the chapter "God the Judge."

[91] Ps. 66:10 (*CO* 31, 614).

[92] "Fateor inquam non frustra neque de nihilo promitti fidelibus copiam quae ad victum sufficiat: modo addatur exceptio quatenus scilicet expedire Deus noverit...," Ps. 37:25 (*CO* 31, 378-9).

[93] Ps. 91:15 (*CO* 32, 9).

poverty.[94] Calvin has an appreciable hesitation in attributing misery to God in the same respect as prosperity. Moreover, in this very same section he observes that there is no inconsistency within God when believers sometimes undergo the same punishments as those by which the Lord takes vengeance upon the ungodly. They must realize, Calvin writes, that their lot is not given them because they were living in an equally ungodly way, but they should simultaneously comprehend that it is only by mercy that they are spared from the punishment they do deserve. Here we come across Calvin's characteristic theodicy: human suffering emanates from God but he is not to be blamed.

Throughout his entire discussion of this theme, though, it clearly is not Calvin's intention to provide strict rules and perfectly consistent explanations for these difficult matters. Rather, he seeks to elucidate to the faithful that God always seeks the best for each believer. Calvin wants to comfort and admonish each individual Christian that God, even in bestowing afflictions upon us, still keeps our ultimate well-being in mind. Nevertheless, in other passages impediments are directly related to God's hand. Therefore Calvin grapples with the precise relationship between God and evil, and it is worth giving some special attention now to the various explanations which he offers.

7. God and Evil

The denunciation that human affairs are not regulated by "a blind wheel of fortune"[95] has the consequence for Calvin that evil is also explained by God's providence. Calvin denies the notion that God is the author of evil, but he still suggests that God navigates and directs evil since it came into the world on account of man's sin. In his commentary on the Psalms, he calls it the universal doctrine (*universalis doctrina*) that God makes use of Satan and the impious to execute his judgments. Hence he is not an instigator of sin, but he utilizes sin to the good.[96]

This notion entails that all disasters, shipwrecks, banishments,[97] infertility, diseases, and battles are to be considered as indications of God's displeasure. Such signs furthermore summon human beings before the divine throne of judgment owing to their sins.[98] A famine does not happen

---

[94] "Quodsi ad mendicitatem redigi contingat quempiam ex fidelibus...," Ps. 37:25 (*CO* 31, 379).

[95] "Docet primo res humanas non versari caeco fortunatae rotatu...," Ps. 107: introduction (*CO* 32, 135).

[96] Ps. 5:5 (*CO* 31, 68).

[97] Calvin's inclusion of banishment on this list may reflect his own biography. It is possible that he experienced his own forced sojourn abroad as a judgment by God because of his own offenses.

[98] Ps. 107: introduction (*CO* 32, 135).

by chance, and there is no other cause except this: God demonstrates his wrath in withdrawing his hand and taking away the means of support. Famine, pestilence and other scourges of God are obedient to him through his providential rule, and they are directed by him wherever it so pleases him.[99]

Therefore these tragedies are a confrontation with one's own guilt because, according to Calvin, all the afflictions we endure proceed from our transgressions and are the scourges of an irate God.[100] "To this principle we have to keep constantly: that all afflictions are God's rod. Thus there is no remedy elsewhere than his grace."[101] It should, however, be taken into account that in this case "grace" does not purport to be the salvific grace of acceptance in becoming a child of God. Rather it is the mercy that impels God to intercede through an act of deliverance or help. Hardships therefore do not imply that someone is not a child of God. These words of Calvin may nonetheless easily lead to the conclusion that disease and guilt, for example, are directly related. If somebody is not healed, regardless of prayer, it could indicate that he has not yet been sufficiently forgiven for a specific transgression. Indeed, as Calvin writes, "diseases neither come upon one by chance, nor are to be ascribed to natural causes alone, but they are God's messengers executing his commands."[102]

When commenting on Psalm 69:28, where David asks God to multiply the guilt of his rivals, Calvin again enters into a discussion of the relation between God's providence and evil. Does this mean that God is responsible for the accumulation of injustice and guilt? Calvin is aware that some try to avoid this consequence by speaking of God's consent and asserting that a particular form of the verb would allow for this interpretation. Calvin rejects this possibility though because, as he points out, everyone that is only minimally acquainted with the Hebrew language will have to admit that such an exposition does not fit. For Calvin it is not necessary at all to invent excuses on behalf of God. When he blinds the reprobate, it suffices for us to know that God has good and just reasons for doing so. Even when the deepest causes for their blindness lie hidden in the secret purposes of God, their conscience yet accuses them of their own guilt. Our task is not to justify God before men but to worship his high mysteries which surpass our understanding.[103] Here Calvin does not end up with a complete explanation, but we are only directed to God's *mysteria*. However, Calvin points nowhere to a change in the relation between sin and punishment since

---

[99] Ps. 105:16 (*CO* 32, 104).

[100] "Unde sequitur, mala omnia ex peccatis proficisci, quum sint irati Dei flagella," Ps. 89:47 (*CO* 31, 828).

[101] Ps. 107:10 (*CO* 32, 138).

[102] Ps. 107:20 (*CO* 32, 139-40).

[103] Ps. 69:28 (*CO* 31, 649).

Christ's incarnation. Perhaps this is a drawback of Calvin's emphasis on the *unity* of Old and New Testaments.[104]

The theme of God's relationship to evil within Calvin's writings is further illuminated by his comments on the *theologia crucis*. In this regard Psalm 105:25 asserts that God hardened the hearts of the Egyptians so that they started to hate his people. At first God saw to it that, through Joseph, Israel received a courteous treatment in Egypt, but afterwards God changed this hospitality to hostility. Through this transformation God purposed both the eventual exodus of Israel and the entry into the promised land. In this manner God attained the good by incorporating human evil into his redemptive plan in order "to bring forth light out of darkness."[105]

Calvin frequently refers to the cross by which God trains believers;[106] in such cases also God achieves his desired end (the faith and sanctification of Christians) through from the human perspective we may not see God's hand in the means (the chastisement and discipline of hardships). By exercising believers with tears and lamentations, God ignites a lamp in the believers to enable them to recognize his judgments more clearly.[107] The darkness of pain serves as a light for believers. Calvin states, "This is faith's true office—to see life in the midst of the darkness of death."[108]

Calvin offers a few explanations for the fact that God does not exempt believers from difficulty and suffering. He rejects the popular misunderstanding that people who are encountered by various impediments are being punished by God and consequently are not to be counted among the elect.[109] God can reverse the suffering of his children to become a blessing. The Bible teaches that God may have different reasons to impose affliction upon believers. Calvin suggests that he may want to exercise their patience,[110] or he may want to restrain them from their lusts of the flesh or to purify them. He may want to bring them to humility to make an example of them or to inspire them to ponder the heavenly life.[111] Satan, though, is the one behind those who trouble us, and behind him is God, who permits such events to exercise, discipline and purify us.[112] Another explanation Calvin offers is that God bestows upon us a cross to the extent that he may be able to reveal

---

[104] See for the unity of Old and New Testament the chapter "God the Speaking."
[105] Ps. 105:25 (*CO* 32, 109).
[106] "...dum cruce servos suos exercet...," Ps. 92:6 (*CO* 32, 11).
[107] Ps. 9:10 (*CO* 31, 100).
[108] Ps. 138:7 (*CO* 32, 375).
[109] Ps. 41:2 (*CO* 31, 418).
[110] "Deus vult suorum patientiam cruce experiri," Ps. 146:7 (*CO* 32, 424).
[111] Ps. 41:2 (*CO* 31, 418).
[112] "Esti enim, ubi nobis molesti sunt homines cum diabolo qui eos instigat nobis negotium est, ad Deum tamen ipsum conscendere necesse est, ut sciamus ab eo nos probari et examinari...," Ps. 44:13 (*CO* 31, 442).

himself more unmistakably to be our deliverer and defender.[113] Therefore the cross is always beneficial to us.[114]

Suffering is a "school" where the Lord teaches us, Calvin writes.[115] Meanwhile, though, faith and patience enable us to remain joyful in adversity,[116] whereby Calvin rejects the idea that suffering inevitably renders one overwhelmed by distress. For this reason he maintains that the one who estimates his affliction only by the feeling of pain it produces (and not noticing God's hand) does not differ at all from the beasts of the field.[117] At the same time, we can expect that God will lend a purely favorable ear to us when, in the spirit of meekness, we voluntarily submit ourselves to his corrections and bear the cross that he has laid upon us.[118] The only way to restrain bitterness and resentment, Calvin adds, is to take into consideration that we are not merely dealing with mortal men but with the righteous God, who will always maintain his own righteousness against all accusations.[119]

> Although the heavenly Father loves us in a most tender way, he uses a cross to keep us awake in order that we shall not indulge too much to the passions of the flesh.[120]

According to Calvin, God's providence displays itself most clearly when he delays his intervention on our behalf until the last moment. In order that his deliverance would appear even more extraordinary, God occasionally even withdraws all human assistance.[121] Sometimes God allows his children to come within the reach of death's power only to rescue them afterwards quite unexpectedly. It is, in fact, particularly characteristic of God's work to open up a way when there is altogether no alternative.[122] God's wait until the last moment conveys to believers that, "even in the midst of death, they may still hope for deliverance from his powerful and victorious hand."[123] Just as the believer threatens to succumb under the assault of his enemies, God displays his care and power. That is, Calvin says, "God's most appropriate time."[124] Hence believers must "give God's providence time to manifest

---

[113] Ps. 129: introduction (*CO* 32, 329).

[114] "...crux semper est nobis utilis," Ps. 125:3 (*CO* 32, 315).

[115] "...quam si Dominus nos in schola sua erudiat," Ps. 94:12 (*CO* 32, 23).

[116] Ps. 84:12 (*CO* 31, 785).

[117] Ps. 38:3 (*CO* 31, 387).

[118] Ps. 106:48 (*CO* 32, 135).

[119] Ps. 39:10 (*CO* 31, 402).

[120] Ps. 125:3 (*CO* 32, 315).

[121] Ps. 142:4 (*CO* 32, 398).

[122] "...sed in abyssos demersi, ad Dei manum spes nostros referamus, cuius proprium est viam per invia patefacere," Ps. 68:20 (*CO* 31, 629).

[123] Ps. 27:5 (*CO* 31, 274).

[124] Ps. 18:17 (*CO* 31,179).

itself,"[125] and thus they should not complain too soon during times of hardship.

Consequently, God preserves and protects his church in no ordinary way, but always delivers her in a manner that discloses his majesty in public; this often is effectuated in situations where all seems lost to the believers.[126]

Calvin elucidates God's work with a reference to the history of Joseph that is discussed in the exposition of Psalm 105. Considering the course of these events recorded in Genesis, it indeed seems as if God were asleep in heaven. However, from the conclusion of this history, it is evident that everything remained under his control. God was continuously at work, but he only discloses his delivering power at the exact moment when of Joseph is "expected just as much life as from one or another corpse."[127] Joseph endured many torments, escaping from one grave only to arrive in another. Calvin refers here to the well in which his brothers cast him and the prison in which Potiphar locked him away. God, though, delivered him when death threatened against him. For Calvin it is apparent that God's providence is more visibly demonstrated when he surmounts different obstacles than would be the case if he merely resolved things by a short or easy way before there was any doubt of the outcome.[128]

The sequence of the biblical narrative begins with Joseph being sent by God to Egypt. Only afterwards does a famine come to Israel, and subsequently Joseph realizes that a remedy had been presented by God's providence. In God's view, though, the sequence differs because he had prepared a remedy to save the household of Jacob through Joseph even before he afflicted the land with famine. While in the human point of view the deliverance of Israel appears later in the sequence of Joseph's story, in God's "sequence" this deliverance is the first and foremost event.[129]

After it had been decided to put Joseph to death, he was condemned to a less cruel death, namely, the well. From this grave he proceeded to a "grave" in Egypt. Who, Calvin asks, would have expected at the moment Joseph was doomed to death that he was to be the sustainer of the house of his father? People reflect on this history and attribute everything to "secondary causes" (*secundae causae*), to chance or to the deliberations of men, but very few trace them to the appointment of God. The selling of Joseph is here not interposed as a veil to hide God's providence, but rather

---

[125] Ps. 9:10 (*CO* 31, 100).

[126] Ps. 65:6 (*CO* 31, 607).

[127] Ps. 105:18 (*CO* 32, 106).

[128] "Sed providentia Dei superatis tot abstaculis, multo illustrare emergit quam si brevi et facili compendio totum negotium," Ps. 105:18 (*CO* 32, 106).

[129] "Recitat autem secundo loco quod temporis ordine prius est," Ps. 105:17 (*CO* 32, 105).

to disclose that, no matter what men may undertake, the course of matters is in God's hands. Nevertheless, people must remain responsible for their deeds. Joseph's brothers were guilty for their murderous scheme,[130] but God incorporated their wicked arrangements in his plan.

8. To Permit or to Determine?

In his commentary on Psalm 105 Calvin refers to the *mediatores*—those who search for an intermediate way between the confession that, on the one hand, God determines all things and the simultaneous belief in man's freedom on the other hand.[131] This middle way is distinguished, Calvin says, by the appeal to God's "permitting" of all things. In this view, God does not really do something although he makes allowance for it. Calvin cannot understand why anyone would defend this scheme given that Psalm 105:25 clearly asserts that it is God who hardened the hearts of the Egyptians. For Calvin the *claritas scripturae* is at stake here since, according to the intermediate view, the Holy Spirit says one thing while intending something else.[132]

Appealing to Augustine, Calvin declines to speak of God's permission of evil as if this would denote something different as God's will.

> Even matters that appear to us to be incongruous do not occur just because God permits them, but by his command and according to his counsel. For if our God is able to do everything he wants, why should he permit that to be done that he does not wish?[133]

For Calvin there are only two possibilities. Either God rules over all according to his will or everything occurs by chance, and the latter, as far as he is concerned, is impossible. God's nature is such that he can only permit that which is indeed according to his will. Consequently, Calvin explains how it is a rather straightforward conclusion to make:

> If we admit that God is invested with wisdom, that he superintends and governs the world that he has made, and that he does not overlook any part of it, it must follow that everything which takes place is done according to his will.[134]

---

[130] "...culpa in ipsis residet," Ps. 105:17 (*CO* 32, 106).

[131] Ps. 105:25 (*CO* 32, 109).

[132] "...quasi elinguis fuerit spiritus, ut aliud pro odio proferret," Ps. 105:25 (*CO* 32, 109).

[133] Ps. 115:3 (*CO* 32, 184).

[134] Ps. 115:3 (*CO* 32, 184).

Nor does God have a kind of unconscious will whereby he somehow merely sustains a particular course of matters. Calvin asserts that "if he wills something, then an apparent decision lies behind it, and he also has a good reason for that."[135]

A rather conspicuous question, then, is whether his opinion eventually leads to the conclusion that God approves of sin. Calvin does not flippantly disregard this question, but the way in which he characterizes those who raise this question already depicts something of his answer.

> Even though they are filthy dogs, they will not with their barking either succeed to turn the prophet here into a liar or to take the government of the world out of God's hands. If nothing occurs without the counsel and decree of God, then it seems that he does not disapprove of sin. He has, however, his own hidden and (to us) unknown causes why he permits that which perverse men do; and yet this is not done because he approves of their corrupt inclinations.[136]

Calvin perceives that this answer may seem illogical and so he provides an illustration of his thought. Appealing to history, he selects an event which exemplifies how industrious God's hand was in the destruction of Jerusalem prior to the Babylonian exile.

> It was God's will that Jerusalem should be destroyed. The Chaldeans also desired the same but because of a different reason. Now, even though he frequently calls the Babylonians his stipendiary soldiers and says that they were stirred up by him (Is. 5:26), yes, farther even that they were "the sword in his hand," yet we would not therefore say that they were his allies, inasmuch their object was very different. In the destruction of Jerusalem God's justice would be displayed, but the Chaldeans would be justly censured for their lust, covetousness and brutality. Hence, although everything that takes place in the world is according to God's will, he does not want any evil. For however incomprehensible his counsel (*consilium*) may be to us, still it is always based on the best of reasons.[137]

This citation manifests again something of Calvin's struggle with this theme. The key word in the illustration here is "incomprehensible." The Reformer attempts to solve the issue, but he eventually ends up with the conclusion that it is incomprehensible. It relates to God's decree, which

[135] Ps. 135:6 (*CO* 32, 359).
[136] Ps. 115:3 (*CO* 32, 184).
[137] Ps 115:3 (CO 32, 185). On the role of the enemies of God's people in the execution of God's will, see also Calvin's exposition of Ps. 137:8 (*CO* 32, 371-2).

Calvin says "resembles a deep abyss," and thus we cannot reach it with our understanding. Commenting on Psalm 135:6, he also asserts that it is not for us to inquire why God's will contradicts our will in particular cases because his will is in fact hidden to us.[138] Calvin speaks critically about the presumption of the *docta ignorantia* since he regards the acknowledgment of our ignorance as being much more learned than the acumen of those who assess God's works in terms of their own comprehension. When, however, Calvin himself does not give preference to these *docta ignorantia*, he ends up having problems. It is noticeable in his exposition of Psalm 141, where David asks of God not to incline his heart to any evil thing. An obvious question at this point is how God could incline the heart of a human being to evil? According to Calvin,

> We must not consider it inept if God inclines our hearts to the evil because these are in his hands to turn them the way he wants to. Not that he himself prompts them to evil desires, but....[139]

It is here where we expect the statement to continue with a solution to the issue, but Calvin unexpectedly (and without respect to grammatical conventions!) changes course, no longer speaking about "our hearts" but instead speaking about "the reprobate." He thus continues

> ...Not that he himself prompts them to evil desires, but, as he surrenders and effectually gives over the reprobate according to his secret judgments to the tyranny of Satan, which is without question an effective surrender, it is properly said that he blinds and hardens them. The blame of their atrocities rests with men themselves, and the lust which is in them.

Thus Calvin shifts the argument from David's prayer for the believer to God's guilty verdict towards the wicked and unbelieving. He effectively seems to evade the question that he himself raised as to whether or not it is absurd that God would incline a human being to evil.

Even when it seems as if Calvin wants to escape the potential risks in addressing this issue, he does not refrain from giving a clarification of the inexplicable. In his exposition of Psalm 92 he discusses the question of why God tolerates the slander of the ungodly while the faithful, on the other hand, suffer so much. For us it is indeed intolerable that God could subject his own people to the injustice and violence of the wicked while they continue uninterrupted in their ways of deceit and burglary. Calvin at the

---

[138] Ps. 135:6 (*CO* 32, 359).
[139] Ps. 141:1 ff. (*CO* 32, 393).

outset does not give an elucidation, but instead he points to the sheer majesty and incomprehensibility of God. However, in concluding the passage, he observes that we must not rage against God when he does not follow the terms of our wishes "because God has, for the better trial of our obedience, elevated his mysterious judgments far beyond the reach of our conceptions."[140] The intention here is not to present a rational explanation of suffering, but rather an exposition why God provides no answers to our queries. Calvin adheres to the conviction that although God's will is hidden to us, it indeed is the fountain of all justice, and therefore this hidden will is to be regarded with utmost reverence.[141] Calvin points out that even when God makes use of evil we still have to keep in mind that God is just. This knowledge must restrain believers against the temptation of breaking out against his judgments. Calvin realizes that it may be very difficult indeed when God's will for us seems to be most severe and harsh. God nonetheless is far from being cruel because he tempers his judgments with clemency.[142]

The best explanation for why Calvin refers to God's "determination" instead of his mere "permission" is that Calvin fears that leaving room for even a part of man's will being beyond the grasp of God would be disastrous as far as ethics is concerned. He who does not want to undermine the very foundation of *pietas* must keep to the principle that nothing takes place without God's consent.[143]

9. Providence and Pastorate

God's providence manifests itself in the human experiences of both prosperity and affliction, but behind God's superintendence over his creatures, Calvin says, he always has a clear intention. Prosperity as a gesture of mercy compels those who experience God's favor to glorify him. Calvin writes, "God feeds and maintains his people in this world with no other purpose than that they may praise him with their entire conduct in life."[144] Adversity, on the other hand, is described by the Reformer as a token of God's displeasure intended to humble people before God.[145] Beyond merely preventing distress among believers, God's governance accomplishes the deliverance of people after they have been subdued by the cross.[146] If he wants to display his goodness, Calvin notes, he can provide rain that irrigates the land and its vegetation, but when he wants to punish

---

[140] Ps. 92:6 (*CO* 32, 12).
[141] "Ac si abscondita nobis est eius voluntas, eam tamen…," Ps. 135:6 (*CO* 32, 359).
[142] Ps. 145:17 (*CO* 32, 418).
[143] Ps. 135:6 (*CO* 32, 359).
[144] Ps. 146:1 (*CO* 32, 421).
[145] Ps. 107: introduction (CO 32, 135).
[146] "…sed ubi nos diu cruce domuerit, tandem succurrat," Ps. 9:19 (*CO* 31, 106).

the sins of the people he can also turn the rain to hail and tempest so that the vegetation are entirely devastated.[147]

According to Calvin, this twofold aim explains many of the apparent mysteries of human experience, such as why God does not rescue all men alike during shipwrecks. In one passage of his Psalms commentary Calvin tells the story of a mocker, an "ancient joker," who entered a pagan temple.[148] When this man noticed the tablets that the merchants had displayed there as memorials of their having survived various shipwrecks, he asked where the plaques were which commemorated those in similar situations who instead drowned while calling upon the gods. This kind of mockery presents no threat at all to Calvin's view of divine providence. In reality all people deserve to undergo such a judgment, but God nevertheless spares a few that he might be praised by them. Therefore, says Calvin, the real question is why men are retained at all during a shipwreck when some do drown. Calvin's point of departure always remains the fact that all men are sinful and have no justification to complain to God if he should, for instance, just let them drown in the case of a shipwreck. His justice is revealed in the drowning, and his kindness in the deliverance. There are no contradictions in God, and therefore his clemency is never in disagreement with his justice.[149] Those who are saved in such a case have not been spared because of their faith but because it was the purpose of God's providence that now they should praise him. As will be discussed more comprehensively in the chapter below on "God, the Father," Calvin provides similar reasoning to exonerate God from the charge of injustice in predestination unto eternal salvation because election is just a part of God's providence.

Hence God has through his providence his honor in view because "his power and glory are not only revealed in the creation of the world but also in the guiding thereof."[150] Elsewhere Calvin declares that God intercedes to deliver us in order that we should celebrate his goodness.[151]

With his reflections on God's providence, Calvin aims to accomplish two results. First, as stated, he seeks to defend God's honor. Second, Calvin intends to build up the believer's trust and peace of mind since "nothing is more effective to increase our faith than the knowledge of God's providence."[152] Bearing this in mind, Calvin remarks that it is a hundred

---

[147] Ps. 148:7 (*CO* 32, 435).

[148] "...dicterium illud scurrae veteris...," Ps. 107:6 (CO 32, 137).

[149] "...qui sic est misericors ut simul tamen exerceat sua iudicia," Ps. 107:6 (*CO* 32, 137).

[150] Ps. 8:1 (*CO* 31, 88).

[151] Ps. 71:22 (*CO* 31, 662).

[152] Ps. 107:42 (*CO* 32, 144).

times more probable that the order of nature will be overturned than that God will withdraw his hand from his people.[153]

Calvin is aware of the questions that may arise from this assertion. According to the Reformer it is not very difficult to acknowledge that God cares for everything that occurs in the world. The difficulty surfaces, though, the moment this doctrine is applied to concrete everyday situations However, a believer only benefits from the confession of God's providential care when the general confession has been put in this concrete form,[154] which is why Calvin so fiercely speaks against those that deny the providence of God. "Those who aim to subvert the doctrine of the providence even a little deprive God's children of their true contentment and harass their souls with wretched unrest."[155] Here again theology proper is at stake since one's way of living is determined by his or her image of God. He who supposes that God does not care about the earth may live his own life untroubled, but he will lose his nerve when distress comes into sight. In contrast, the one who holds on to God's providence knows that even in the most awful anxiety and distress he is protected by God's hand.[156] It is a double confirmation of our faith when we know that the devil and the ungodly can only operate within the room that God grants them, and not only the hands of the ungodly but also their hearts are bound to God's rule.[157] However, God's children need special grace to resist the temptation of questioning God's providence when their lives are shaken.[158]

In addition to this knowledge of God's providence, Calvin notes that the practical use of this doctrine must be anchored in an understanding of God's power and mercy as well. The knowledge that God provides for everything and upholds all things by his providence remains useless unless man also appreciates that God is powerful. The mere knowledge of a powerful God is insufficient, though, because one may then become afraid of him. God's power is as essential to his character as his clemency, and it must always be borne in mind that he is as mighty as he is merciful.[159]

The pastoral concern behind Calvin's doctrine of God's providence finds particularly expression in his exposition of Psalm 37. In this Psalm David reflects on the question of why the ungodly are so often better situated than the faithful. According to Calvin it even seems sometimes as though the more boldly a man despises God, the more happily he seems to live, while those that live with God often suffer greatly. The faithful thus

---

[153] Ps. 27:10 (*CO* 31, 277).
[154] Ps. 10:14 (*CO* 31, 117).
[155] Ps. 107:42 (*CO* 32, 114).
[156] Ps. 10:6 (*CO* 31, 113).
[157] Ps. 105:25 (*CO* 32, 109).
[158] Ps. 73: introduction (*CO* 31, 674).
[159] Ps. 62:12 (*CO* 31, 591).

see things strangely confused in this world.[160] Does not God differentiate between the good and the wicked? This paradox, though, has a second level of irony to Calvin in that the prosperity of the ungodly is simultaneously their misfortune because they are living with the thought that their happiness is eternal when it is actually accursed. The faithful know that their calamities will come to an end through God's intervention and that it is their prosperity that, even in the midst of such adversity, God takes care of them. Calvin depicts this as a paradox which causes our human nature to cower.[161] Faith however appreciates that man experiences prosperity only when he is reconciled with God.[162]

Calvin regards it as consolatory knowledge that God is the author of calamity (*calamitatum auctorem*) because he is indeed the one from whom relief can be sought and in whom distress can be brought to an end. The same hand which smites is the hand that can save.[163]

Calvin warns his readers to be cautious in dealing with suffering. Satan may try to extinguish the foundation of a believer's faith through harsh and thoughtless verdicts of people.[164] He who speaks of suffering without discretion plunges those that suffer into the deepest abyss.[165]

10. *Labyrinth*

According to Calvin, one can only live with the paradox mentioned above when one holds to the conviction that God guides and rules all things. He who turns away from the biblical notion of God's providence will first stagger and then fall under the chance events and anxieties of life in a chaotic world. As Calvin expresses it, one plunges into an "abyss" of confusion without providence.[166] In the same place Calvin speaks of that "horrible labyrinth" in which man labors and from which he can not escape unless he focuses on the providence of God.[167] Slightly changing Calvin's image, it seems that he who deliberately wants to stay out of God's field of vision remains trapped in a labyrinth.[168] For Calvin, "abyss" and "labyrinth"

---

[160] "...res videant mire confuses...," Ps. 37: introduction (*CO* 31, 365).

[161] "Hoc quidem paradoxon est, a quo abhorret carnis sensus," Ps. 37: introduction (*CO* 31, 365).

[162] ...non aliter nobis bene esse sine quatenus proptius est Deus...," Ps. 37:5 (*CO* 31, 368).

[163] Ps. 44:11 (*CO* 31, 441). Idem Ps. 88:7 (*CO* 31, 808).

[164] Ps. 41:2 (*CO* 31, 419).

[165] "...eos demergimus infra omnes abyssos," Ps. 41:2 (*CO* 31, 418).

[166] "...quasi in abyssum se demergent," Ps. 37:5 (*CO* 31, 368).

[167] "...ex horribili...labyrintho...," Ps. 37:5 (*CO* 31, 368).

[168] Ps. 62:9 (*CO* 31, 589).

are concepts that denote the most extreme experiences of anguish;[169] therefore, when facing these realities, only trust in God's providence offers any comfort. Providence does not do away with the experience of the abyss and the labyrinth, but it does prevent one from utterly plunging into the abyss, and it directs the way out of the labyrinth. The relationship between God, Satan and mankind strikes us as a labyrinth because our thoughts cannot ascend to the heights of God. In reality, however, we are assured by Calvin that "there is no labyrinth"[170] because for God the matter is completely transparent.

Calvin offers the same conclusion when he says that the one who denies providence brings hell to earth: "for there does not exist a more awful torment than to be constantly racked with anxiety."[171] In Calvin's mind, however, hell does not designate corporal torments, but instead it implies the spiritual agonies of anxiety and doubt.[172] It is hell to be ignorant of the providential God. In contrast to this notion of hell, then, is Calvin's view of heaven: that to which faith must ascend in order to perceive things as they really are. The believer's confidence in God's providence therefore brings heaven to earth while the denial of God's providence brings the hell to earth. If we extend this to Calvin's concepts of *ordo* and *labyrinthus*, we can interpret him as asserting that the world is in tangles and that this confusion brings one into the labyrinth unless he regains the rehabilitated '*ordo*' in Christ. Calvin expresses the same with a distinction between light and darkness. We must climb through faith into heaven, as it were, in order to find there the light that we need for the hope of salvation amidst the darkness of this world.[173] If we have that light, we subsequently see that the *abyssus* of God's providence exceeds the depth of the *abyssus* of the wickedness of men,[174] and this indicates that all the crimes of the world cannot withstand God's government.

The attitude of one that holds on to God's providence will reflect both calmness and balance. Calvin appeals to a concept from classical philosophy which expresses this well:

---

[169] Bouwsma, *Calvin*, analyses Calvin in terms of these two concepts and concludes *inter alia* that Calvin was an anxious person. For a recent, very comprehensive critique on Bouwsma, see R. A. Muller, *Unaccommodated*, 79-98.

[170] "...nullus esset labyrinthus," Ps. 105:25 (*CO* 32, 109).

[171] "Proinde qui hanc doctrinae partem evertere conantur...inferos in hoc mundo fabricant," Ps. 107:42 (*CO* 32, 144).

[172] Cf. *Inst.* II.16.10, where Christ's descent into hell in the Apostles' Creed is also explained in terms of the spiritual agony that Christ suffered.

[173] Ps. 11:4 (*CO* 31, 123).

[174] "...nempe quantumvis magan scelerum abyssus inter homines exundet, terramque obruat, maiorem tamen esse providentiae Dei abyssum, ut iuste omnia dispenset ac temperet," Ps. 36:6 (*CO* 31, 362).

> We know that serenity of mind is justly reckoned the chief point of a happy life, that is, that we live serenely because we are reconciled with God, and his fatherly favor shines in our hearts.[175]

Calvin derives the concept of *euthumia* from the Greek philosopher Democritus. Calvin comprehends this concept as synonymous to Seneca's notion of *tranquillitas*. The translation of "tranquility," though, does not sufficiently reflect what these philosophers (and therefore Calvin, as well) really intended. It has to do with the experience of inward peace and balance that one can accomplish especially by keeping within bounds.[176] Calvin, however, links this classical idea of the way of living to the theology of the Reformation. He is of opinion that when one devoutly seeks serenity in what God has revealed in his word, that person is also capable of receiving the *mysteria* without disputation.[177] Calvin contrasts the state of complete confusion on earth with the quiet state of God in heaven and then says that faith can only endure in the chaos of this world by fixing itself upon this God.[178] The certainty that God guides such affairs offers, amidst confusion and turmoil, "the permanent heritage of a blessed life."[179] As a matter of fact this faith saves only through the hidden activity of God's Spirit.[180] This attitude is characterized by David in Psalm 62:7 as "being silent before God." This is the *doctrina* that we endure patiently and in a restrained way all the things that actually should disturb us. Calvin here uses the word *moderare*, by which he proclaims that what is meant here is an attitude that requires effort. *Moderare* can be translated as "observing moderation" and "restrain;" thus it is evident that Calvin is describing an attitude of faith that calls for effort. Based on both his readers' experiences and his own, Calvin knows that there is nothing more difficult for man amidst all the turbulences of this world than to merely remain calm.[181] When no imminent danger is threatening a person, belief is no effort at all, but when your soul stumbles upon everything that occurs in the world and when

---

[175] Ps. 119:165 (*CO* 32, 289).

[176] Calvin gives this exposition of *euthumia* in his commentary on Seneca's *De Clementia*. See *Calvin's Commentary on Seneca's De Clementia*, ed. Ford Lewis Battles and André Malan Hugo (Leiden, 1969), 60-1. See also Sharples' *Stoics*, 93, who translates *euthumia* in Democritus as possessing "good spirit."

[177] Ps. 105:25 (*CO* 32, 109).

[178] Ps. 28:5 (*CO* 31, 284).

[179] "Haec autem vera est beatae vitae stabilitas, ubi persuasi sumus divinitus eam gubernari," Ps. 61:8 (*CO* 31, 584).

[180] "...arcana spiritus sui consolatione fulcit, ne rebus adversis succumbant," Ps. 94:12 (*CO* 32, 24).

[181] "...quia nihil difficultuis quam homines, dum circumaguntur in mundo, manere sedatis et compositis animis, nec ullo perturbatione quatefieri," Ps. 37:3 (*CO* 31, 366).

your tranquility of mind is utterly disturbed, then it will be disclosed to what extent you have believed that God is mighty.[182]

One of the perpetual struggles of the believer is that against impatience. Impatience is the consequence of an erroneous theology because God's deeds are thereby measured according to our standards of time and existence. However, it is absurd to confine God to the fixed limits of time.[183] People who themselves pass away like a shadow must not be so audacious as to pull God from his eternity into our experience of time and subjugate him to the fluctuations of this changing world.[184] Impatience is eliminated only when believers focus their thoughts on God's eternity.

Tranquility in the knowledge of God's providence cannot be attained without the effort required to struggle against one's own flesh.[185] To reach this personal state of "being silent" before God, Calvin says, we must be "instructed in the Lord's school."[186] According to the Reformer, this is an attitude that can be learned, and it did, in fact, become a distinguishing mark of later generations of Reformed believers. The outlook of "no complaining but rather enduring" was characteristic in both the faith and the view of life of many generations of Calvinists. Far from being mere passivity or even fatalism, Calvin's notion of faith in God's providence is an active acceptance of God's way with man and world. Therefore, patience is not a stoic posture of letting everything overwhelm oneself, but instead it signifies a cheerful submission to God based upon a comprehensive reliance on his grace.[187] It concerns the combination of *resignatio* and *expectatio* whereby one leaves the course of events and its occurrence to God while at the same time he or she awaits to see whether God will allot either prosperity or adversity.[188]

The above mentioned difficulty of struggling with God's providence forms a sharp contrast with God's power (as evidenced by his laughter at the strenuous efforts of his adversaries—see Ps. 37:13). In Calvin's mind, this ought to incite man to obedience. His *theologia crucis* leads him to

---

[182] Ps. 46:2 (*CO* 31, 366).

[183] "...temporum angustiis...," Ps. 10:16 (*CO* 31, 118).

[184] "...quia hoc mundo eum ab aeterno solio detractum variis mundi inclinationibus subiiciunt," Ps. 55:20 (*CO* 31, 543).

[185] "...non sine molestia et sudore carnis," Ps. 37:7 (*CO* 31, 370).

[186] "...non aliter fieri quam si Dominus nos in schola erudiat," Ps. 94:12 (*CO* 32, 23).

[187] Ps. 94:12 (*CO* 32, 24). *Idem* Ps. 30:12 (*CO* 31, 299): "...ne stoicam duritiem fingamus in sanctis, quae omnem doloris sensum iis ademerit..."

[188] "Itaque vias suas in Deum devolvit qui actionum suarum eventum eius arbitrio resignans, et patienter exspectans utramque fortunam, curas quibus angitur...," Ps. 37:5 (*CO* 31, 368).

conclude that sometimes we must weep even during God's laughter.[189] He says that our tears are a result of our obedience to God's calling, and therefore they serve as a confirmation of this obedience as well. The tears of the faithful over their impediments—in contrast to the apparent joy and prosperity of the ungodly—are met with divine approval while God laughs at the schemes of the wicked. Our tears emanate from how we experience things; God's laughter from how things are in reality. Calvin also suggests that God himself derives benefit from the faithful having to await his aid for a spell of time. He writes, "If he does not keep the faithful for a short time in suspense, then it could not be said that it is his prerogative to save the afflicted."[190]

At the conclusion of his exposition of this psalm, Calvin summarizes one last time God's intention in the disclosure of his providence, anchoring our hope and confidence in the very nature of God:

> The sum of the whole is that, whatever may happen, the righteous will indeed be saved because they are in the hand of God and can never be forgotten by him. This ought to be particularly noticed that those who are greatly afflicted may be sustained by the assurance that the salvation which they expect from God is infallibly certain because God is eternal and governs the world by his power.[191]

11. Conclusion

The *providentia Dei* can be regarded as the most significant theme in Calvin's commentary on the Psalms. The question that Calvin and his fellow believers ask is how the God of the Bible relates himself to the difficulties they encounter so as to preserve faith in this God. Calvin answers the question by presenting God as continuously involved in every single aspect of world affairs. The activity of God in every part of his creation then receives so much emphasis that Calvin almost makes God responsible for evil as well. In his attempt to escape this implication, though, he establishes too close of a causal relation between individual suffering and personal sin. Calvin ends up with this suggestion because of his desire to offer believers a causal explanation. However, it is essential for our appreciation of this impulse to recognize that Calvin's explanation here emanates from his pastoral intentions.

---

[189] "...discamus patienter flere in Dei risu, ut lacrymae nostrae sint obedientia sacrificium," Ps. 37:12 (*CO* 31, 372).

[190] Ps. 18:28 (*CO* 31, 184).

[191] Ps. 37:39 (*CO* 31, 385).

5

God the Speaking

In the chapter on "God the Creator" we looked into Calvin's statements about God's revelation in nature. There we made the observation that Calvin ascribes more value to God's revelation in Scripture. The psalms prompt Calvin to elaborate on various aspects of the revealed word of God. Furthermore, as God's revelation is given over the course of history, we will also discuss in this chapter Calvin's doctrine of the progression from the Old to the New Testament.

1. The Word

For Calvin the word is equivalent to God's promises,[1] and therefore the emphasis is more on the preached word than on the written word in the Bible. God comes to us in the word, and only then may we expect anything from him.[2] In his word God gives a friendly invitation to come to him.[3] Since it is in the word that God comes to us with the promise of well-being and salvation, we also have the hope of God's salvation in no other way than by looking to the word.[4] God has revealed his goodness in the word, and so we must also seek certainty of his goodness towards us in the word.[5] Likewise, he who trusts in the word of God never has to doubt his help.[6] In contrast, the one who derives no encouragement from the word will in fact be dead.[7] Yet, if we give ourselves to mediation on the word, we will live even though we

---

[1] Ps. 119:49 (*CO* 32, 235). On the relationship between Word and promise, see W. H. Neuser, "Theologie des Wortes: Schrift, Verheissung und Evangelium bei Calvin" in *Calvinus Theologus: Die Referate des Europäischen Kongresses für Calvin-forschung*, ed. W. H. Neuser (Neukirchen-Vluyn: Neukirchener Verlag, 1976), 17-37.
[2] Ps. 119:65 (*CO* 32, 243).
[3] Ps. 119:149 (*CO* 32, 282).
[4] Ps. 119:81 (*CO* 32, 250).
[5] Ps. 119:149 (*CO* 32, 282).
[6] Ps. 119:85 (*CO* 32, 252).
[7] "…nisi animum recipiat ex Dei verbo, se fore exanimem," Ps. 119:49 (*CO* 32, 235).

find ourselves right in the midst of death.[8] In the word one can find comfort from all sorrows,[9] and the word is the best weapon by which we can stand firm against our enemies.[10] In the word, Calvin says, God has revealed the light of the heavenly life. Accordingly, its purpose is to give us a light which shows us the way, cutting through the thick darkness and the heresies with which Satan surrounds the human race until we have reached the heavenly heritage.[11] The word is to Calvin "the doctrine of piety which is a treasury of eternal salvation."[12]

The word is actually a little piece of heaven on earth; Calvin says that "although it lives on earth, making its way to our ears and living in our hearts, it still retains its celestial nature since it comes down to us in such a way that it is not subject to earthly changes."[13] The word is therefore the only constant factor in this world as it is not tied to any boundary or limit.[14] The word actually frees us, Calvin says, from the confinement of this world.[15] In light of this world's turbulence, the word is the only fixed point. It is also the only eternal thing in the midst of that which is temporal. Indeed, the word of God "stands fast for eternity."[16] Calvin goes so far as to suggest that the word's immutability is the most important foundation to our faith. Without this we could not be offered a certain hope of eternal salvation as God does give us in his word.[17] Without reference to the Bible, statements about faith are insipid in content and impotent in their ability to elicit the praise of God. This is why, Calvin summarizes, true piety is found exclusively in the foundation of God's revealed word.[18]

The word is more effective and better suited for our instruction than any revelation to our sight could be.[19] For this reason the psalmist says that the heavens *speak* of God's glory and not that the heavens allow us to *see* God's

---

[8] "Quare si probe meditemur verbum Domini, etiam in media morte vivemus…," Ps. 119:49 (*CO* 32, 236).

[9] Ps. 119:76 (*CO* 32, 247).

[10] Ps. 119:41 (*CO* 32, 232).

[11] Ps. 147:19 (*CO* 32, 431).

[12] "…pietatis doctrina, quae aeternae salutis thesaurus est," Ps. 147:19 (*CO* 32, 431).

[13] Ps. 119:92 (*CO* 32, 255).

[14] Ps. 119:96 (*CO* 32, 256).

[15] "Restat ut hanc amplitudinem concipiant animi nostri: quod fiet ubi se in angustiis mundi huius coniicere desierint," Ps. 119:96 (*CO* 32, 256).

[16] Ps. 119:152 (*CO* 32, 283).

[17] Ps. 119:152 (*CO* 32, 283).

[18] Ps. 29:9 (*CO* 31, 290).

[19] "…sed quia sensus melius excitat sonorae vocis praedicatio, vel certius saltem ac maiore cum profectu docet, quam simplex conspectus cui nulla coniuncta est admonitio…," Ps. 19:1 (*CO* 31, 195).

glory. Sight alone is insufficient for the knowledge of God without the revealed word. We need the word, Calvin says, in order that we might recognize the countless signs of God's favor. The word, for example, makes it clear that those things which are going well in our lives are blessings from God.[20] Calvin opposes the charge that the word of scripture is too obscure as it is claimed by Rome.[21] Thereby he turns the taunt of Rome—that amongst the Reformed every uneducated layperson reads the Bible—into a sign of God's blessing.[22] Calvin interpreted the Reformation as the result of the power of God's word. The fact that in such a short time so many people could be brought under the dominion of Christ was "solely due to the voice of the gospel, and this happened in spite of the opposition of the whole world."[23] Yet the word does not work mechanically. Here again though Calvin guards against necessarily connecting God with something external. God can bring it about that, although his word is present, someone doesn't know at all what to do with it. In such times, all of Scripture seems to be turned upside down and no matter how much one may long for that word, it doesn't affect you one bit.[24]

Although Calvin attributes the authorship of the Bible to the Holy Spirit inasmuch as he is the one who moved David's tongue,[25] there are several finer points which need to be observed about Calvin's doctrine of scripture as it appears in his commentary on the Psalter. First, this does not mean that Calvin ignores the human authors. For example, he has no problem in saying that David wrote things down at times with a special intention.[26] Secondly, Calvin states that the author of Hebrews quotes Psalm 8 (in chapter 2) because the concepts of "lowering" and "adorning" occur there. Apparently he is more concerned with the terms than with the meaning of these words. Furthermore, when Calvin turns to Psalm 88:6 and the line that God no longer thinks of those who are in the grave, he indicates that the human author here has let himself go, being so overwhelmed by his cares that he did not express himself as thoughtfully as he ought to have done.[27] Calvin even states that the light of faith has been momentarily dimmed although it

[20] Ps. 60:8 (*CO* 31, 577).
[21] Ps. 119:105 (*CO* 32, 260).
[22] "Rideant vero papistae, ut faciunt, quod scripturam promiscue ab omnibus legi volumus…," Ps. 119:130 (*CO* 32, 273).
[23] Ps. 110:3 (*CO* 32, 163).
[24] Ps. 77:8 (*CO* 31, 714).
[25] "…spiritus sanctus, qui Davidis linguam direxit…," Ps. 8:1 (*CO* 31, 88).
[26] Ps. 29:1 (*CO* 31, 287).
[27] Ps. 88:6 (*CO* 31, 807).

afterwards reappears. A little bit later in his interpretation of the same psalm Calvin says once again that the author is going too far.[28] These remarks confirm that Calvin had a very organic view of the inspiration of the scriptures:[29] the Spirit teaches us by David's mouth.[30] The Spirit also chooses a particular means of expression in order to reach this goal. For instance, the Psalms sing of God's power so that all fear may be removed from people.[31]

Calvin is convinced that David knows about the future calling of the gentiles,[32] which is why he can say that all gentiles will kneel before God. Because David understands that to Jewish ears it would sound like "an offensive novelty" that gentiles would worship together with the children of Abraham, David chooses to tone the message down by observing that the gentiles have also been created by God. On the basis of this reminder it is more natural to believe that the gentiles will in the end also worship God together with the Jews. Calvin again shows here his conviction that the Bible writers arrange in their own way that which the Spirit has inspired, David's poetry being just one case of this practice.

Calvin makes a striking comparison in order to indicate that our thoughts must always be tested against the touchstone of God's authoritative word. He likens those who do not do this to those "who derive their knowledge only from commentaries and do not have the book itself in front of them."[33] Looking at the papacy one can see what happens if tradition is made to rule over the word, and so Calvin accordingly rejects the idea that whatever is old must also be good.[34] In fact, he calls it foolish to act as if that which the forefathers said and did amounts to a kind of law that we must imitate. If this were so sins would continue to be passed on while in many instances he thinks it would be much better that their example not be followed at all.[35]

2. Word and Spirit

For John Calvin there is a close connection between the operation of the word of God and the Spirit of God, and throughout his commentary on the

---

[28] "...excusari tamen non potest excessus...," Ps. 88:11 (*CO* 31, 809).

[29] For an overview of the discussion about Calvin's doctrine of inspiration, see Stefan Scheld, *Media Salutis: Zur Heilsvermittlung bei Calvin* (Wiesbaden: Steiner, 1989), 60-5.

[30] Ps. 18:21 (*CO* 31, 180).

[31] Ps. 68:2 (*CO* 31, 620).

[32] "Nec vero Davidem latebat futura gentium vocatio...," Ps. 86:9 (*CO* 31, 794).

[33] Ps. 119:11 (*CO* 32, 219).

[34] "...et vetustas semper aliquam reverentiam sibi vendicat...," Ps. 95:9 (*CO* 31, 34).

[35] Ps. 78:8 (*CO* 31, 725).

Psalter he notes how this is affirmed in the words of the psalmists. For example, this connection is apparent when he says that the word is sufficient for Christ to bring his enemies to obedience, but Calvin describes this taking place through "the Spirit of his mouth."[36] Likewise, the word is presented to all people alike, but one only comes to a conviction of its truth when additionally one's mind is illumined by the Holy Spirit.[37] By this Calvin does not mean to say that the word only has power when the Spirit accompanies it but that the power of the word is only experienced by those who are indwelt by the Spirit. And yet the knowledge of God's word precedes the experiential knowledge of grace. There is no experience without the word.[38] "For if God wants to show himself to us as the present God (as people usually put it), he must first be sought in the word."[39] The scriptural word therefore does lead to experience. Calvin is not trying to underestimate the experience of faith. Faith comes from the word and rests upon the word, but it nonetheless derives much support from experience. Word and faith do not rest on experience, but the *experientia* does confirm the word and faith.[40] So also must God by his Spirit inwardly seal the assurance given by his word. The Spirit illumines our minds in such a way that we see the truth of God's salvation in the word as in a mirror.[41] This also applies to those who preach the word. No one can minister the word of God adequately if he has not first experienced the word firsthand. The doctrine of the gospel is not transferable by the lips if God has not first revealed it to the heart.[42]

The connection between the word and the Spirit enables us through God's word to also speak and witness on our own. The Holy Spirit connects the word of God that gives hope, with our word in order to confess the hope.[43] We do not, however, receive the Spirit of God so that we may then proceed "to despise the external word and to be carried away by all sorts of spiritual experiences."[44] Calvin thus rejects the notion of the *fanatici*, who reckon that

---

[36] "Respondeo pro armis omnibus spiritum oris sui ei sufficere...," Ps. 2:9 (*CO* 31, 48).

[37] Ps. 119:64 (*CO* 32, 242).

[38] An analysis of Calvin's *Commentary* on the Psalms which gives special attention to the relationship between Word and experience is found in W. Balke, "The Word of God and *Experientia* according to Calvin," in *Calvinus Ecclesiae Doctor*, ed. W. H. Neuser (Kampen: Kok, 1980), 19-31.

[39] Ps. 27:9 (*CO* 31, 676).

[40] "...non vulgaris tamen verbi et fidei confirmatio est ipsa experientia...," Ps. 43:3 (*CO* 31, 435).

[41] Ps. 119:152 (*CO* 32, 283).

[42] Ps. 91:1 (*CO* 32, 2).

[43] "...verbo spei adiungit verbum confessionis," Ps. 119:41 (*CO* 32, 233).

[44] Ps. 119:17 (*CO* 32, 222).

one can be spiritual only when one rejects the external word.[45] The fanatics instead relegate the word to a position that is inferior to their hidden revelations.[46] They reckon that a true believer does not need the word any more.[47] Submission to the word of God, however, prevents us from following our own flights of fancy.[48] The external doctrine must be coupled with the grace of the Spirit.[49] Or, as Calvin also says, the work of the preachers must be made effectual, if it does not want to be useless.[50] "The word falls upon our ears in vain unless the Spirit of God effectively pierces our hearts."[51] When God sets his word before us, he simultaneously teaches us inwardly. It is not sufficient that the word only sound in our ears if God does not at the same time also illumine our mind by the Spirit of knowledge.[52] His law must be heard, but the Spirit must in turn bring people to compliance, and God does not do one without the other. The Spirit does not release one from the word, but precisely causes compliance with that word.[53]

3. Word and Sacrament

The Psalms hardly give Calvin an occasion to speak of the sacraments. He does indeed call the cup of salvation from Psalm 116 "a symbol of deliverance," for instance, but in his exposition upon this verse he does not elaborate on the Lord's Supper.[54] The fullest discussion of the sacraments in the Psalms commentary comes in Calvin's elaboration on the external means that God gave to Israel so that they could better trust in his promises. The ark of the covenant, for example, is described as a pledge given to the faithful so that they may trust in the promise.[55] Calvin also calls it a sign that helps them to rightly honor God in a spiritual way.[56] The ark also functions as a sign of

---

[45] Ps. 119:17 (*CO* 32, 222).
[46] Ps. 119:133 (*CO* 32, 275).
[47] Ps. 119:171 (*CO* 32, 293).
[48] Ps. 119:171 (*CO* 32, 292).
[49] "...sed externam doctrinam cum spiritus gratia coniunxisse...," Ps. 119:133 (*CO* 32, 275).
[50] "...inutilis est doctorum opera donec efficax reddatur...," Ps. 119:171 (*CO* 32, 292).
[51] Ps. 119:133 (*CO* 32, 275).
[52] Ps. 119:171 (*CO* 32, 292).
[53] Ps. 119:171 (*CO* 32, 293).
[54] Ps. 116:13 (*CO* 32, 198).
[55] Ps. 68:35 (*CO* 31, 636).
[56] "...symbolum...quo potius adiuvarentur ad spiritualem Dei cultum," Ps. 106:19 (*CO* 32, 124).

God's presence with his people.[57] Through the ark God descends to his people in order that they may get to know him more closely, but the intention is also that the ark should lift *our* attention upward to God so that *we* would not be left with a mere earthly impression of him.[58] Calvin compares the commemorative meals, by which Israel offered thanks, to the Lord's Supper. He notes that these meals brought about a renewal of the spiritual life, but even in those days it was applicable only to those that partook in order to praise God in their hearts. Since the Lord's Supper points to the same spiritual promises with greater clarity, Calvin mentions it as the foremost of those meals renewing the spiritual life,[59] but then also it is only effectual in those who participate because they sincerely seek the Lord.

In the interpretation of Psalm 51:9 Calvin does look extensively into the meaning of the sacrament. When David asks whether God wants to purify him with hyssop, the psalmist is aware that this has to do with purification of the heart. Nevertheless man also needs the external sign of purification. Here Calvin turns to consider the Lord's Supper. Only by the blood of Christ is there reconciliation, Calvin says. Yet, because we humans want to see tangible evidence of this grace and even hold it in our hands, our conscience comes to rest only when we have used the outward signs.[60] It is notable here how strongly Calvin connects the visible signs with grace, even speaking of wanting to hold that grace in one's hands. The sinner who wishes to receive grace must direct his eye at the sacrifice of Christ and, for the confirmation of his faith, at the Lord's Supper and baptism.[61] One of Calvin's criticisms of the mass is that Christ there is robbed of his honor since it appears as if it is the priest that provides for reconciliation between God and man.[62]

By instituting sacraments God accommodates himself to the weakness of the people for whom his word is not enough.[63] The weakness of our flesh prevents us from reaching into heaven, and therefore God makes it visible in outward signs that he is near to us.[64] The purpose, accordingly, is that the

---

[57] Ps. 9:12 (*CO* 31, 102).

[58] Ps. 20:7 (*CO* 31, 210).

[59] "...multo uberius hodie haec vis se proferet in sacra Christi coena...," Ps. 22:27 (*CO* 31, 234).

[60] "...quia tamen nec oculis perspicitur, nec manibus palpatur spiritualis gratia, non possumus nisi externis signis adiuti, tranquillis animis statuere," Ps. 51:9 (*CO* 31, 515-6).

[61] "...deinde sacram coenam et baptismum in fidei suae confirmationem advocet...," Ps. 51:9 (*CO* 31, 518).

[62] Ps. 110:4 (*CO* 32, 165).

[63] "...non satis fuit a verbo Dei pendere fidelis...," Ps. 9:12 (*CO* 31, 102).

[64] Ps. 20:3 (*CO* 31, 208).

signs must help to direct our attention to God and to honor him in a spiritual way. Essentially, therefore, the sacraments are means that help us to rest upon the promises of God. This trust must remain, however, even when the sacraments temporarily are not used, but this will then only be the case with those who have not superstitiously attached themselves to the sacraments. Thus we should often contemplate "the hidden communion between Christ and his members" for our spiritual edification, and not merely reserve this essential doctrine to the celebration of the Lord's Supper.[65] Should a tyrannical power, for example, take the Lord's Supper from us for a time, this must not have the result that faith be diverted from a confidence in God's promises spoken to us as well as visibly manifested in the sacraments.

4. Hermeneutics

Calvin is careful that he does not prematurely look for Christological meaning in the Old Testament.[66] In fact, he warns against violating the text by directly relating it to Christ lest the Jews have proper grounds for their charge "that it is our aim by means of sophistry to connect things with Christ that do not directly relate to Him."[67] Thus Calvin rejects a Christological exegesis of such passages as Psalm 87:4. The reading that here the psalmist speaks about Christ (through whom those people who used to be strangers and enemies toward one another now want to be reckoned as residents of Jerusalem) is dismissed by Calvin as untenable albeit clever.[68] The meaning is simply that people are willing to give up their own nationality to be added into the citizenship of Jerusalem. Similarly, in his exposition of Psalm 88:6

---

[65] Ps. 63:3 (*CO* 31, 694).

[66] On Calvin's interpretation of the Old Testament, see W. de Greef, *Calvijn en het Oude Testament* (Groningen: T. Bolland, 1984) and David L. Puckett, *John Calvin's Exegesis of the Old Testament* (Louisville: Westminster John Knox Press, 1995). According to Richard Muller it may be assumed that Calvin's warning must be seen as a reaction to the well-known commentary on the Psalms by Faber Stapulensis where "Christ is taken to be the sole reference of the text, and David disappears entirely as a focus of meaning." See Richard A. Muller, "The Hermeneutic of Promise and Fulfillment in Calvin's Exegesis of the Old Testament Prophecies of the Kingdom," in *The Bible in the Sixteenth Century*, ed. David C. Steinmetz (Durham: Duke University Press, 1990), 77.

[67] Ps. 72:1 (*CO* 31, 664).

[68] "Quod offerunt Christiani, quamquam propter argutiam primo intuitu plausibile est, nihil tamen habet solidi…," Ps. 87:4 (*CO* 31, 802).

Calvin discards the Christological interpretation of St. Augustine as clever, but not in correspondence with the author's intention.[69]

Nevertheless he asserts that the texts of the Old Testament by themselves emphatically refer to Christ. The hermeneutical key that Calvin uses for the Christological interpretation of the text is this: *that which did not come to fulfillment in the time of the Old Testament must indeed refer to Christ.*[70] If an utterance does not fit with the historical situation, then it is a prophecy of Christ.[71] This key then opens a door to an interpretation by Calvin that is hardly distinct from the christocentric exegesis of Luther. When in Psalm 72:10 David foretells that all kings of the world will bow before Solomon, it is clear from the course of Solomon's history that this refers to Christ. The prophecy of Psalm 2:8, "Ask of me and I will give peoples to be your inheritance," cannot refer to David, and therefore it also applies to Christ.[72] The way in which Calvin performs such exegesis is illustrated well by these texts. When David speaks of his son Solomon, his mention of "all kings" indicates that the Spirit is lifting David above his own situation and is making him speak of the spiritual monarchy of Christ. Furthermore, from this it follows that "we" have not received the hope of eternal life by mere chance since in this text it is clear that God already had us in mind in the Old Testament. We can even deduce from this text that in the church there is room for monarchs. Calvin interprets the text this way in order to give support and comfort from this passage to his readers and his audience when a literal reading of the text does not explicitly do so.

Other passages in Calvin's Psalms commentary reveal the same pattern of biblical interpretation. When the author of Psalm 47 calls God the King over all the earth, it is indeed clear "from the context of these words" that here the reign of Christ is meant.[73] When in Psalm 89 there is talk of an eternal throne, it can only refer to Christ.[74] This also applies in Psalm 96:9 when the entire world is called upon to worship God despite the fact that in the Old Testament only Israel can do so.[75] On Psalm 110 Calvin observes that even if

---

[69] Ps. 88:6 (*CO* 31, 807).

[70] Ps. 72:10 (*CO* 31, 669). See also Calvin's introduction to Psalm 97 (*CO* 32, 42). De Greef calls Calvin's principle "a little whiff of rationalism in his exegesis" ("een rationalistisch trekje in zijn exegese") in his *Oude Testament*, 91.

[71] Ps. 149:7 (*CO* 32, 439).

[72] Ps. 2:8 (*CO* 31, 47).

[73] Ps. 47:2 (*CO* 31, 467).

[74] Ps. 89:31 (*CO* 31, 822).

[75] "Unde colligimus Psalmum hunc ad regnum Christi referri: quia donec patefactus fuit mundo, non alibi quam in Iudaea invocari potuit eius nomen...," Ps. 96: introduction (*CO* 32, 361).

Christ himself had not said in Matthew 22:42-44 that this psalm is about him the psalm would still not allow any other interpretation. The psalm is shouting out, as it were, that this is the only possible interpretation.[76] Calvin is of the opinion that in a discussion with Jews it could be proven by clear arguments that this song of praise is about nobody if not the mediator.

In interpreting all of the scriptures, one must take into account the fact that God adapts himself to people through his speech. In Calvin's thought the concept of "accommodation" hence plays a rather significant role.[77] David does not speak about creation in scientific terminology, but in his speech he adapts himself to the ordinary people.[78] When the Scriptures address such matters as physics, one should keep in mind that God describes things in such a way that they may be understood by ordinary people.[79] When the Bible speaks of the sun and the moon as the two great lights, this also is an adaptation of God to the readers. There are, of course, planets that are greater than the moon (Calvin mentions Saturn as an example), but the moon is more noticeable since it is nearer to the observer on earth. "Nor was it the intention of the Holy Spirit to teach astronomy."[80] The Spirit wanted to communicate in such a way that even the simplest could understand. The Holy Spirit would rather prattle like a little child, Calvin says, than speak in such a complicated way that ordinary people are excluded.[81] David realizes that ordinary people would not understand if he were to go and speak of the mysteries of astronomy, and therefore he speaks of the universe in everyday terms.[82] Had he been speaking to scientists he would have used other words, but as it is he adapts himself to simple and uneducated people.[83] The extreme form of God's *accommodatio*, Calvin notes, is evident in Psalm 78:65 when he compares himself to a drunken man waking up from his inebriation. This,

[76] "Psalmus ipse clamat se non aliam expositionem admittere," Ps. 110: introduction (*CO* 32, 159).

[77] See David F. Wright, "Calvin's Accommodating God," in *Calvinus Sincerioris Religionis Vindex: Calvin as Protector of the Purer Religion*, Sixteenth Century Essays & Studies, ed. Wilhelm H. Neuser and Brian G. Armstrong, Vol. XXXVI (Kirksville, Mo: Sixteenth Century Journal Publishers 1997), 3-19.

[78] "...non disputat philosophicae David...sed populariter loquens, ad rudium captum se accommodat...," Ps. 24:2 (*CO* 31, 244).

[79] "...ut se accommodent ad rudissimi cuiusque captum...," Ps. 148:3 (*CO* 32, 433).

[80] Ps. 136:7 (*CO* 32, 365).

[81] "...maluit spiritus sanctus quodammodo balbutire, quam discendi viam praecludere plebiis et indoctis," Ps. 136:7 (*CO* 32, 365).

[82] Ps. 19:4 (*CO* 31, 198).

[83] "...sed rudissimis quibusque se accommodans...," Ps. 19:4 (*CO* 31, 198).

Calvin quickly adds, is no adaptation to the people's simplicity, but rather to their obtuseness.[84]

Calvin explains that the Spirit has to choose between two extremes. When God expresses himself too simply in accommodating himself to our level, his way of speaking is looked down upon. Should he speak on a higher level, though, people use this as an excuse for their ignorance, saying they cannot understand it. The Holy Spirit combats these two possibilities however by speaking in such a way that everyone can understand it, provided that people are willing to learn.[85]

5. The Relationship between Old and New Testaments

Calvin emphasizes the unity of the Old and the New Testaments so that between the times before and after the incarnation of Christ the difference is more a matter of degree than substance.[86] The unity of the covenant receives so much emphasis that history, including the salvation history o Jesus, threatens to evaporate. The coming of Christ means that "the times have been renewed."[87] According to Calvin the period which has lasted since the coming of Christ may be designated as "the renewal of the church."[88] The coming of Christ is therefore not the beginning of the church but the beginning of a new era in the church.[89]

Calvin finds difference as well as similarity in the two testaments by means of the "anagogue."[90] He does not use this word in the sense of the medieval fourfold interpretation of scriptures wherein the anagogical sense gives the meaning of a text for the future, but rather Calvin describes "anagogue" as a comparative application of the text.[91] When Psalm 81 says

---

[84] "...quia accommodatur ad populi stuporem," Ps. 78:65 (*CO* 31, 742).

[85] "...si modo placidam docilitatem et serium proficiendi studium afferant," Ps. 78:3 (*CO* 31, 722).

[86] On the relationship of Old and New Testament see De Greef, *Oude Testament*, 93-154; and Hans Heinrich Wolf, *Die Einheit des Bundes: Das Verhältnis von Altem und Neuem Testament bei Calvin* (Neukirchen: Verlag der Buchhandlung des Erziehungsvereins, 1958).

[87] "Nunc, postquam adventu suo saeculum renovavit...," Ps. 48:8 (*CO* 31, 477).

[88] Ps. 48:11 (*CO* 31, 480).

[89] Ps. 96:7 (*CO* 32, 39).

[90] "Nunc ab illis ad nos anagoge tenenda est...," Ps. 81:7 (*CO* 31, 761).

[91] See Parker, *Commentaries*, 72-4. According to Parker "anagogue" in Calvin's thought functions as "a transference or application of a Biblical person or event to some theological truth," 72.

that God has freed his people from the burden of carrying stones in Egypt, after Christ this psalm means that God has freed us from the burden of the tyranny of Satan. For indicating the difference between the Old to the New Testaments Calvin uses various concepts and classifications such as "shadow" and "reality;" "childhood" and "adulthood;" and "less" versus "more."

Shadow/Reality[92]

With the coming of Christ a new era has commenced, and that also has the consequence that what is said in the Old Testament of Jerusalem is now connected "with the spiritual Jerusalem which is spread over the whole world."[93] The outward glory of Jerusalem has now been replaced by the spiritual wealth of the church. Just as Jerusalem was encircled with walls and towers under the shadowy time of the law, now the church has been adorned with spiritual gifts since the coming of Christ.[94] The kingdom of David and his successors is a shadow which points to the reality of the kingdom of Christ.[95] "By using the temporary kingdom as a type," Calvin writes, "a far better rule is described—a kingdom which does indeed give full joy and complete bliss to the church."[96] Elsewhere he suggests that the kingdom of Christ begins with the kingdom of David since David's reign lays the foundation for that of Christ.[97] The two kingdoms and their respective kings thus relate to each other as shadow and reality. There are even many similar experiences in the paths walked by each king, including for each, Calvin notes, a hidden beginning and later an open rejection.[98]

Another correspondence between shadow and reality is seen in the temple, which is the image in the Old Testament administration which keeps our focus on the priesthood of Christ, and the palace then means his monarchy.[99] The return from the exile is, according to Calvin, related to the

---

[92] Parker gives an analysis of this pair of concepts as it is used in the *Institutes* and Calvin's commentaries—Parker, *Commentaries*, 56-62. See also de Greef, *Oude Testament*, 136-41.

[93] Ps. 48:8 (*CO* 31, 477).

[94] Ps. 48:11 (*CO* 31, 480).

[95] Ps. 21:4 (*CO* 31, 214).

[96] Ps. 20:1 (*CO* 31, 207).

[97] Ps. 118:25 (*CO* 32, 210).

[98] "Arcana fuit David electio...Eadem regni Christi fuerunt exordia...," Ps. 118:25 (*CO* 32, 210).

[99] Ps. 112:4 (*CO* 32, 305).

kingdom of Christ as a prophecy of that kingdom.[100] The land was given to the people to hold in their possession until the coming of Christ since it is a foreshadow and an image of the heavenly fatherland.[101] Meanwhile Calvin does not consider it a disaster that no reunification of the Jews into a single land of their own ever took place since now they have found a much more fortunate reunification. In the body of Christ, he continues, they are reunited with one another as well as with the gentiles who believe. They are no longer in one physical land, but instead they constitute one church that is spread over the whole world and yet is one through the spiritual bond of faith.[102]

The dynamic of shadow and reality in scripture indicates not only difference but similarity as well. When the shadows of the law disappear, Calvin says, "spiritual truth remains for us."[103] Spiritual truth was thus also there under the law, and it entails that God must be praised in those circumstances as well. If this were not also the purpose of the outward ceremonies of the Old Testament, they would have been "a useless display." The essence and purpose of "shadow" and "reality" are therefore the same, but they do differ according to the way in which each operates. Canaan is a "pledge of the heavenly inheritance."[104] However, God shows his favor by earthly blessings[105] after Christ as well as before. This means that regardless of what he means by these "blessings," Calvin can not be charged with merely spiritualizing the text into matters of salvation.

Childhood / Adulthood

Another way of describing the difference between the two testaments is the analogy of differing ages. In the Old Testament the church finds herself in her childhood, but upon the coming of Christ her adulthood has commenced.[106] The sacrifices of the Old Testament are therefore "children's lessons for beginners"[107] which God had assigned in order to prepare the people in this epoch for something else—namely, the sacrifice of Christ.

---

[100] "…quia restitutio in patriam, cum regno Christi annexa erat…," Ps. 85: introduction (*CO* 31, 785).
[101] "…coelestis patriae fuisse symbolum…," Ps. 69:35 (*CO* 31, 653).
[102] Ps. 106:47 (*CO* 32, 134-5).
[103] Ps. 66:15 (*CO* 31, 615).
[104] Ps. 106:24 (*CO* 32, 126).
[105] Ps. 128:3 (*CO* 32, 328).
[106] "Quod si tam austera fuerunt pueritia rudimenta, nisi hodie, postquam in virilem aetatem Christi advenu adolevit ecclesia…." Ps. 129:2 (*CO* 32, 331).
[107] "…pueritia rudimenta…," Ps. 40:8 (*CO* 31, 413).

Earthly blessings also function as early lessons intended to teach us to seek that which is higher.[108] According to Calvin, such musical instruments also belong with the first years of learning.[109] After Christ, however, the church does not need these teaching tools any more. The functioning of the law, as well, belongs to the childhood years. When compared with the situation in the New Testament, the church under the old covenant found herself under the authority of the law as a pedagogue,[110] the slave that used to watch over the children and that accompanied them to and from school.[111] All of these remarks reflect Calvin's understanding of the movement from the Old Testament to the New as a change from childhood to adulthood.

Less/More

Calvin also describes the difference between the two dispensations with the categories of "less" and "more." In Christ God has revealed himself even *more* clearly, for instance, as our shepherd.[112] Calvin explains that the evidences of God's love towards us, even when it comes to living here on earth, are clearer after Christ than during the time of the Old Testament. In the old dispensation the knowledge of God was also more limited with the result that people were less able to see him in his exaltation.[113] Furthermore, the promise of God now is no longer limited to merely one people. The distinction between a particular ethnic group of people and the rest is gone, "so that the message of the gospel by which God reconciles himself with the world now comes to all people."[114] In the covenant God reveals himself as Father first to Israel and "subsequently more clearly (*clarior*) through the gospel that has given us the Spirit of adoption more abundantly (*uberior*)."[115]

The time of the Old Testament, by comparison with the New, is somewhat less civilized,[116] and in his revelation God adapts himself to the

---

[108] "...quia talibus rudimentis altius tunc deduci oportuit," Ps. 147:2 (*CO* 32, 430).

[109] "...ad tempus paedagogiae...," Ps. 149:2 (*CO* 32, 438).

[110] "...instar paedagogi veterem populum serviliter prae nobis regeret...," Ps. 26:8 (*CO* 31, 268).

[111] On the law as pedagogue, see Parker, *Commentaries*, 63-9.

[112] "...nobis luculentius quam olim patribus sub lege pastorem exhibuit...," Ps. 23:4 (*CO* 31, 240).

[113] "Sicuti enim prius obscurior erat eius notitia, sic minus conspicua fuit exaltatio," Ps. 97:9 (*CO* 32, 46).

[114] Ps. 81:12 (*CO* 31, 765).

[115] Ps. 67:3 (*CO* 31, 618).

[116] "...pro temporis ruditate...," Ps. 105:4 (*CO* 32, 99).

needs of each period. The Bible writer, for example, makes use of the customs of his time when he threatens as a divine curse that the remembrance of the sinner would be eradicated. One would expect, says Calvin, that it would be more applicable as a curse for someone's name to be erased from heaven. However, spiritual punishments had in this time not been as clearly revealed, "since the fullness of time wherein the complete revelation took place, had not yet come."[117] The same type of accommodation is also evident in the blessings. When a man is wished a fertile wife as a sign of God's blessing, the criticism could be made that this shows a rather earthly preoccupation. One needs to keep in mind however that he is speaking with those who are still under the law.[118]

Whereas in the Old Testament the presence of God is to be sought particularly in the tabernacle and the temple, "we now have at our disposal a much more confident way of coming to God,[119] since that which had formerly been only foreshadowed in the images of the law is now revealed to us in Christ. (By "the images of the law" Calvin means, for instance, such figures as the ark.) Whereas God says in the Old Testament that he lives in Zion, now it is known with more clarity that he is present everywhere Christian believers worship him purely in accordance with the word.[120] The way in which Calvin verbalizes this difference creates the impression that before the coming of Christ the people had to go to God while after Christ the case is that God comes to the people.

The difference also carries various applications by which present believers can be exhorted given the time in which they live. If David, though living "under the shadowy cult of the law"[121] and far away from the temple, could remain standing by means of prayer, how much more should the same be true for us, for whom the blood of Christ has opened a way and to whom God presents such a friendly invitation to fellowship. New Testament believers additionally ought to have more trust in God and more assurance of his aid. If the temple was a sign of God's presence to Israel which gave

---

[117] "...quia nondum advenerat maturum plenae revelationis tempus," Ps. 109:13 (*CO* 32, 152).

[118] Ps. 128:3 (*CO* 32, 328).

[119] Ps. 3:5 (*CO* 31, 55). Unlike the English (Parker Society) translation "a much easier way" and the German (Weber) translation "einen freieren Zugang," I prefer "confident" (Dutch: "vertrouwelijk") as a translation of *familiaris*. "Confident" better captures that it has to do with the *quality* of the way. Moreover, Calvin frequently uses the word *familiariter* when addressing the confidence which believers ought to have in approach their heavenly Father.

[120] Ps. 9:12 (*CO* 31, 102).

[121] Ps. 61:1 (*CO* 31, 581).

reason for trusting in him, how much more ought the church today reflect such trust now that Christ has come to bind us even closer to God.[122] The same also applies to the worship of God. If David praised God in his own day because God had saved him from death, how much more ought we, "who by the grace of Christ have been snatched from an even deeper abyss of death."[123] In the biblical accounts, David's life was prolonged just a little while, "but we have been brought from hell to heaven."[124] God required obedience from Israel as a sign of their gratitude for such deliverance. Calvin notes that such grateful obedience applies to us believers in Christ much more.[125]

6. Conclusion

For Calvin the vital aspect to God's revelation in the word is that through the word God really is present in this world. Nevertheless Calvin does not so bind God to the revealed word such that an identification of God with the Bible could be mistakenly made. We have also seen how Calvin's discussion of *accommodatio* has an apologetic character whereby he avoids the discussion on what can in fact be said about God if, in his speech, he so strongly adapts himself to humans. Calvin's emphasis on the unity between the Old and the New Testaments is meant to lead to making the differences between the two less significant. By denoting the relationship between the Old and the New Testament as "less" versus "more," the question arises as to the value of Christ's coming. When Calvin says that Christ has come "to bind us even closer to his Father,"[126] the question might be raised as to whether Calvin's theology does not perhaps make the meaning of the incarnation, death and resurrection of Christ something merely relative given how much carries over for Calvin from the old system into the new.

---

[122] Ps. 48:9 (*CO* 31, 478).
[123] "...ex altiore mortis abysso...," Ps. 86:12 (*CO* 31, 796).
[124] Ps. 86:12 (*CO* 31, 796).
[125] "...multo sanctior est nostra obligatio quam veteris populi," Ps. 81:7 (*CO* 31, 761).
[126] Ps. 48:9 (*CO* 31, 478).

6

God the King

The theme of the kingdom or kingship of God is repeated over and over again in the Psalms. Calvin applies this kingship to God's rule over this world at large, but his expositional work in the Psalter is considerably more directed towards the consequences of this kingship for the life of the believer. For this reason the present chapter will examine Calvin's use of the Psalms in describing the Christian's position in the world. At the same time, though, we will consider what Calvin says about the relation between the kingship of God and the rule of secular governments.

1. The Rule of God

In Calvin's thought, the rule of God or his supremacy refers particularly to his protection and order. Where God is ruling, there is order.[1] The Bible makes it clear that God is ruling for the sake of our salvation. If we were only conscious of God's reign for his transcendence and heavenly power, then the knowledge of the distance between him and us would drive away all our comfort at his rule.[2] However, since God's power and his justice are always in balance, his rule is no tyranny.[3]

God's rule is usually invisible, and thus he chooses hidden means to save those who are his.[4] For example, when the wicked rise up to persecute the church, one might doubt whether God still cares.[5] It is also a temptation to doubt God's rule when one does not see his judgment carried out against visible injustice.[6] Calvin thus mentions a "temptation of the eyes" by which we are lead to hallucinations.[7] The Holy Spirit, he says, must then raise us up to a higher level than that of our eyes in order to let us see that God indeed rules.[8] Calvin illustrates this with the metaphor of watchtowers which enable us to see at a greater distance than from our normal earthbound perspective.

---

[1] Ps. 145:10 (*CO* 32, 416).

[2] Ps. 146:10 (*CO* 32, 425).

[3] "...nefas esse imaginari tyrannicum in Deo imperium: quia perpetuus consensus sit inter potentam eius et rectitudinem." *Ibid.*

[4] Ps. 99:4 (*CO* 32, 50).

[5] Ps. 5:5 (*CO* 31, 65).

[6] Ps. 10:12 (*CO* 31, 115).

[7] "...oculis tentatio, nobis festinatio hallucinandi...," Ps. 37:37 (*CO* 32, 50).

[8] Ps. 49:2 (*CO* 31, 482).

Accordingly, we should not judge God's rule too hastily, but we ought rather to grant him time to restore to order the confused state of things.[9]

God's ways in governing are invisible to us, and they are also somewhat playful considering the ease with which he overcomes earthly obstacles. This is evident, for example, when the Lord defeats Pharaoh with an army of frogs instead of soldiers.[10] Calvin's discussion about God's dominion can thus be characterized as a kind of theodicy with a pastoral intention. This interpretation of God's acts in the context of his kingly rule is meant to answer the questions of the believers and to comfort them.

2. The Angels

In this section we treat Calvin's portrayal of the position and function of angels throughout the Psalter.[11] In brief, Calvin describes angels as servants of the King and executors of his decisions. They dwell around God like satellites around the sun and are continuously prepared to obey his commands.[12] Angels, therefore, are "heavenly spirits endowed with divine glory."[13] To the extent that they are heavenly powers, they can be called divine.[14] In them, Calvin says, something divine is shining.[15] They are the conveyors of God's glory in the sense that God, through the angels, shines upon the world with his glory.[16] Calvin's high estimation of the position of the angels is evident when he speaks, for instance, about maintaining a good conscience in the face of God and in the face of the angels who as heavenly spectators are viewing our activities.[17] However, God gave them such a place that they do not interfere with his glory.[18] They do not have a share in God's being. Although their glory is more magnificent than the splendor of the other creatures, it is not so great that it could obscure the splendor of God in any way. Calvin warns against the diabolical superstition which seeks to disproportionately raise the status of angels in relation to God. For such a promotion in status there is no good reason, Calvin suggests, since the Bible says that angels tremble before God's majesty.[19] We would do the angels

---

[9] "...dandumque Deo esse tempus quo res confusas in ordinem restituat," Ps. 37:37 (*CO* 31, 385).

[10] "...quia ludendo id praestabit quoties volet," Ps. 105:29 (*CO* 32, 111).

[11] On the historical and theological background to Calvin's reflection on angels, see especially Schreiner, *Theater*, 39-53. Cf. also Faber, *Symphonie*, 220-3.

[12] Ps. 89:7 (*CO* 31, 814).

[13] Ps. 89:7 (*CO* 31, 814).

[14] Ps. 135:5 (*CO* 32, 358-9).

[15] "...in quibus relucet aliqua deitatis particula...," Ps. 97:7 (*CO* 32, 45).

[16] "...quia Deus per angelos irradiat totum mundum...," Ps. 96:4 (*CO* 32, 38).

[17] "...quia sibi probe conscii sunt coram Deo et angelis, et coelesti theatro abunde sunt contenti...," Ps. 119:5 (*CO* 32, 217).

[18] Ps. 135:5 (*CO* 32, 358-9).

[19] Ps. 89:7 (*CO* 31, 814).

wrong if we were to grant them the same majesty as God.[20] On the contrary, there is an immense distance between God's majesty and the angels; God would have the right (*suo iure*) to condemn them just like condemned humans if he had not also shown the angels his fatherly care and descended to them in order to take care of them.[21]

It is the task of the angels to praise God. This is the highest end of their existence.[22] They also have other tasks, though. Calvin says that God uses angels, for example, to show the wind the way.[23] Even though God has established a certain order in nature, sometimes he uses angels to assure that particular commands are accomplished.[24] God also involves his angels to carry out his judgments about the rejected. Calvin remarks that there are some who find it inappropriate that angels, being mere servants of grace and salvation, are mustered to punish unbelievers. Calvin, however, is not astonished about this because angels can only guard over believers when they are prepared to fight for them, and angels can only help believers by resisting their enemies according to God's purposes.[25]

In speaking about the deployment of angels God is most obliging towards us. Calvin points out that it ought to greatly strengthen our faith to know that God has innumerable angels to his disposal who can hasten to help at any desired moment.[26] By the mention of his angelic servants God accommodates our weak faith in his promises, for it would be sufficient only to know that God cares for his church, but he mentions the angels for our benefit.[27]

Angels are deployed by God particularly for the rescue and protection of believers. Calvin has no problem in admitting this, but he cautions against the danger of angels receiving so much attention that justice is not done to the fact that God is the one who saves.[28] The angels are given to us as servants and protectors,[29] and they are keen on guarding over our lives because they know it is the task God has assigned to them.[30] Furthermore, they are consciously involved with events on earth and pleased about the salvation of the church.[31] Angels keep a watchful eye on every moment of our lives, but

---

[20] Ps. 96:4 (*CO* 32, 38).

[21] Ps. 113:5 (*CO* 32, 178).

[22] Ps. 103:19 (*CO* 32, 83).

[23] Ps. 18:11 (*CO* 31, 176).

[24] Ps. 78:44 (*CO* 31, 737).

[25] Ps. 35:4 (*CO* 31, 348).

[26] Ps. 34:8 (*CO* 31, 339).

[27] "...pro modulo ruditatis nostrae...," Ps. 34:8 (*CO* 31, 339).

[28] Ps. 18:17 (*CO* 31, 178).

[29] "...sed quam nobis dati sunt ministri et custodes, ad opus esse paratos," Ps. 103:21 (*CO* 32, 83).

[30] Ps. 34:8 (*CO* 31, 339).

[31] "...angelos...quibus in salute ecclesiae communis est laetitia et gratulatio," Ps. 89:6 (*CO* 31, 814).

anyone who lives frivolously or walks down another path than the one which God wills need not expect help from them.[32] Yet this does not mean that Calvin likes the notion of individual persons having a guardian angel to watch over them; Calvin thinks this is too *limited* a picture of our angelic help. God does not appoint *one* angel, says Calvin, but he orders a whole *army* of angels to watch over the salvation of every single believer.[33] The Bible says that angels (he draws attention to the plural form) encircle the believer. This is indeed a consolation, for in like manner as we have countless enemies, we also have countless more guardians. Calvin's critics on this concept of a guardian angel therefore encounter both a biblical and a pastoral argument: why be satisfied with either none or perhaps only one angel when man needs much more help from God and he indeed receives it through this army if heavenly servants? At the same time, though, Calvin points out that we should not try to investigate how precisely angels do their work. It is sufficient to know that they are appointed to serve us.[34] Incidentally, Calvin points out that we are indebted to the work of Christ for the fact that they serve us, for because of the fall angels did not have anything to do with us,[35] but it is Christ who reconciled the angels to us.

The evidence from his commentary on the Psalms therefore confirms the opinion that Calvin grants a more important place to the angels than it is often noticed by Calvin scholars.[36] However, Christ alone has conciliated the angels to us.[37]

3. *Chaos* and *Tranquillitas*: Calvin's Experience of Reality

The confession of God's kingship certainly does not lead to the conclusion by Calvin that the life of the believer will elapse in undisturbed peace and harmony. He writes that

> our situation in this world brings along with it so much trouble and the trouble is so diverse that almost no day passes without sorrow and pain. Yes, in every moment so much can happen that one simply cannot do anything else than to be constantly afraid and restless. In every direction which one looks he is encircled by a labyrinth of dangers.[38]

---

[32] Ps. 91:11 (*CO* 32, 6).
[33] "...nec modo singulis assignat unum angelum, sed coelestes suos exercitus de salute cuiusque fidelium iubet esse sollicitos," Ps. 91:11 (*CO* 32, 5).
[34] Ps. 91:11 (*CO* 32, 5-6).
[35] "...et illi nobiscum nihil habent negoti," Ps. 91:11 (*CO* 32, 6).
[36] "Certainly, angels appear in his writings far more frequently than much of the secondary literature indicates," Schreiner, *Theater*, 52.
[37] "Solus ergo Christus est, qui sublato dissidio angelos nobis conciliat...," Ps. 91:11 (*CO* 32, 6).
[38] Ps. 30:6 (*CO* 31, 295).

The way in which Calvin describes the daily reality of life in the world does not at all fit the image of someone who is fulfilling his station in life in peace and quiet (a stereotype which sometimes seems to be associated with the name of the Genevan Reformer). These statements by Calvin should therefore be carefully consulted if one wants to comprehend this man and his theology. Calvin's experience of life on earth is clear in his exposition of Psalm 102. There God is described as sitting peacefully on his heavenly chair without any change or movement. However, Calvin writes that this indicates what a great contrast there is with our "fragile and insignificant situation which hardly enables us to remain standing for one moment."[39] The holy serenity which is enjoyed by God reveals clearly that our life is nothing more than a plaything before him.[40] There is also something of an "element of playing" which one finds in Calvin's discussion of the way that God brings a large amount of suspense into human lives. It seems as if God has set out a circuit and that one can reach the finish without accidents when God's word is taken as guide "...since God sets traps everywhere, digging pitfalls, putting up hurdles on our way, and letting us finally arrive in the end at the abyss."[41] It is perhaps going too far to say that Calvin here criticizes God's way of acting, but he certainly is at least troubled as he seeks to understand God's rule from the perspective of these common experiences.

Consequently, we should not expect that God's reign is compatible with human logic. As he puts it, "his dominion is unknown to us."[42] Calvin himself experiences an immense distance between God's position of power and the vulnerability of human life. "We people are just like dry grass; we could perish at any moment. Death is very close; yes, it is as if we are actually living already in the grave."[43] Twice in the Psalms commentary Calvin says that our lives hang from just a silk thread because we are surrounded by a thousand deaths.[44] In fact, these dangers face us from the moment of our birth: "the leaving of the mother's womb is the entrance into a thousand deaths."[45] This imminent threat of death could not be expressed more pointedly by Calvin. "We have innumerable deaths constantly facing us, and there are many examples of change to awaken us to fear and worry."[46] Furthermore, we are always but a hair's breadth from our death.[47] Thus Calvin knows that death can at times keep us in such a grip that we cannot

---

[39] Ps. 102:13 (*CO* 32, 66).
[40] "...melius apparet vitam nostram merum esse ludibrium," Ps. 102:13 (*CO* 32, 66).
[41] Ps. 119:44 (*CO* 32, 234).
[42] Ps. 118:25 (*CO* 32, 212).
[43] Ps. 102:13 (*CO* 32, 66).
[44] Ps. 31:5 (*CO* 31, 302), and Ps. 10:6 (*CO* 31, 113): "...vitam suam de filo pendere...."
[45] "Imo exitus ab utero, ingressus est in mille mortus," Ps. 71:5 (*CO* 31, 656).
[46] Ps. 30:6 (*CO* 31, 296).
[47] "...tantum unius horae spatio a morte distare," Ps. 107:1 (*CO* 32, 136).

find a spark of life any more.[48] Calvin even appeals to the risks in nature, pointing out that when you enter a bush without knowing your way you can quickly become the victim of lions or wolves, which were apparently a familiar danger to those in sixteenth century Europe.[49]

Calvin does not speak about the reality of death though without mentioning the hope of God's deliverance from it. Various deaths surround us, and every moment a new danger threatens us.[50] Against such "countless deaths," however, there is fortunately also "the countless ways by which God saves."[51] Following a metaphor which he sees in Psalm 90, Calvin compares life to a circle. God puts us in this life, and when our "circuit" is completed, we return unto him, that is, he takes us again to himself. This circuit is small, though, and thus it takes but a little time to finish it.[52] Hence it is so splendid that God would take his servants at the end of their circuit to be with him. Calvin does not point to the brevity of human life out of scorn for our earthly existence. Rather, he exposes the folly of those who imagine they will live for some two thousand years. Unbelievers are not looking any further than the duration of the world, and so they measure the length of their life with that of fellow men. The believer, however, compares his or her life with God's eternity, allowing him or her to realize the shortness of life in comparison with an eternal future in union with God. Calvin's aim here is to warn against complete absorption with this life and forgetting eternity.[53]

According to Calvin our life is so short that it does not merely *pass* by, it *flies* by.[54] We are hardly born before we already have to die.[55] Even before people come to old age, "even in the very bloom of youth, they are involved in many troubles and cannot escape the worries, annoyances, sorrows, fears, illnesses, inconveniences and anxieties to which this mortal life is subjected. For that matter, this applies for the whole course of life."[56] Apparently Calvin speaks out of his own life experience since he adds, "And assuredly, when someone examines the situation of our life from the cradle to the grave, he finds burdens and difficulties at every stage."[57]

Wherever we look we see despair, the decay is inside of us, and we are nothing more than the reflection of death. Is not everything which happens

---

[48] Ps. 69:4 (*CO* 31, 638).
[49] Ps. 107:1 (*CO* 32, 136).
[50] Ps. 34:8 (*CO* 31, 338).
[51] Ps 68:20 (*CO* 31, 629).
[52] "...quod brevis quaedam versatio sit in qua celeriter gyrum implemus...," Ps. 90:3 (*CO* 31, 834).
[53] Ps. 90:3 (*CO* 31, 834-5).
[54] Ps. 102:26 (*CO* 32, 73).
[55] "...qui vixdum nati morimur?" Ps. 102:26 (*CO* 32, 73).
[56] Ps. 90:10 (*CO* 31, 838).
[57] Ps. 90:10 (*CO* 31, 838).

on earth a prelude to ruin?[58] The dangers are so great that we would go to rack and ruin if God's hand were not to protect us.[59] Christians live in this world as those among wolves.[60] Elsewhere, Calvin says our life is like a ship on a stormy sea.[61] The path of life is twisting (*flectuosus*) and unsteady (*multiplex*), and on it we are harassed continuously by various storms.[62]

Calvin's experience of reality is best expressed with his own words when he speaks of "a complete confusion."[63] In his opinion the "whole world is in a complete confusion and all parts of it are being thrown as it were to and fro."[64] This confusion is no cause for panic, though, since at the center of the world which turns around like a wheel,[65] there is the firmness (*firmitas*) of the kingdom of Christ. This fact also explains the trials experienced by Christians, who, though trusting in the kingship of Christ, might feel that they live amidst utter confusion. As long as the Judge is in heaven, it remains chaos on earth.[66] Believers are commonly subject to abuse and accusation. In this context Calvin compares the triumphs of unbelievers with the exuberance of robbers in the wilderness who can rejoice in their success because they know they are far away from judicial authority.[67]

In his exegesis of Psalm 119:30 the reader finds a more existential side to Calvin. With approval the Reformer cites an old saying which compares the course of a person's life to the crossroads of two different paths. This is an appropriate metaphor, he adds, because of the great significance in our choices from moment to moment. These decisions introduce threats as well as possibilities: "...as soon as we have undertaken anything, we are pulled in all directions and our thoughts are mixed within us as if we were being swept along in a stream."[68]

Calvin cannot imagine that people living in this chaos would not trust in God. One must be filled with a "devilish pride," according to Calvin, to think that he will fare better than the rest of humanity.[69] As for believers, although they are encircled by "turbulent movements," they enjoy an "inherent

---

[58] "...praeludium interitus?" Ps. 102:26 (*CO* 32, 73).
[59] Ps. 17:5 (*CO* 31, 162).
[60] "Caeterum quia fideles in hoc mundo semper inter lipos versantur...," Ps. 103:6 (*CO* 32, 77). Cf. Ps. 34:8 (*CO* 31, 338).
[61] Ps. 10:6 (*CO* 31, 113).
[62] Ps. 91:11 (*CO* 32, 6).
[63] "...in hac tam confusa perturbatione...," Ps. 25:13 (*CO* 31, 258). Cf. also Ps. 12:1 (*CO* 31, 126): "...confusi status..."; and Ps. 37: introduction (*CO* 31, 365): "...res videant mire confusas...."
[64] Ps. 30:7 (*CO* 31, 296).
[65] "Quamvis enim tenquam in rota volvatur mundus...," Ps. 21:8 (*CO* 31, 216).
[66] "...res in mundo miscentur...," Ps. 1:5 (*CO* 31, 40).
[67] Ps. 1:5 (*CO* 31, 40).
[68] Ps. 119:30 (*CO* 32, 227).
[69] "...diabolica superbia fascinatos esse...," Ps. 30:6 (*CO* 31, 296).

calmness (*interior tranquillitas*) which has more value than a hundred lives."[70] On this matter Calvin detects a partial similarity between the teaching of the Psalms and that of the philosophers. The philosophers rightly emphasize the vulnerability of life. However, on the most essential point, the Bible challenges philosophy by asserting that God's providence rules this world and that man finds a solid hold only in this fact.[71] Hence Calvin's basis for inherent calmness lies outside of man whereas the philosophers ultimately seek this hope within man. Only believers can maintain a true *composita mens*, that ideal of the classical philosophy,[72] in this turbulent life since they know that their actual aim in life, "eternal salvation,"[73] is reached through death. Therefore Calvin says that we must "live purely and steadily in this world as we glorify and fear God."[74]

Calvin points to an antithesis between the restless, hectic joy of this world and the peace with which believers are content because they know that they receive everything from the hand of God.[75] With the assurance of God's care, this latter group can know calm whether in times of pleasure or suffering. Christians can thus accept God's purposes "with joy and calmness and patience."[76] This ideal attitude of one who knows how to restrain his *passiones* Calvin finds in David.[77] He adds, though, that it is only possible to adopt David's disposition when one first has been "wrapped with the person of Christ."[78] Therefore in his discussion of the *composita mens* Calvin connects the humanistic ideal with the theology of the Reformation.

4. The Christian as Pilgrim and Soldier

The contrast between the fixed order and tranquility of heaven and the turbulence and disorder on earth has the consequence, Calvin says, that Christians living under the kingship of Christ constantly stumble amidst chaos. In interpreting this statement, though, one has to remember that the reading public in his day consisted mainly of refugees seeking protection from the religious persecution taking place in their home countries. Calvin then attempts to explain their circumstances in order to make them more tolerable.

---

[70] Ps. 37:29 (*CO* 31, 381).

[71] "...longe differe huius Psalmi doctrinam a praeceptis philosophicis...," Ps. 49:15 (*CO* 31, 489).

[72] See Sharples, *Stoics*, 82-115.

[73] Ps. 90:12 (*CO* 31, 840).

[74] Ps. 34:1 (*CO* 31, 334). Cf. Ps. 34:10 (*CO* 31, 340): "...quitus et placidus inter homines absque ulla noxa versabitur...."

[75] Ps. 37:4 (*CO* 31, 367-8).

[76] Ps. 25:13 (*CO* 31, 259).

[77] "...composcat turbidas animi sui passiones...," Ps. 69:2 (*CO* 31, 647).

[78] "Denique, ut veri simus imitatores Davidis, primum induere Christi personam necesse est...," Ps. 69:23 (*CO* 31, 647).

The reason and the basis for this particular way of life for the Christian is his communion with Christ. A Christian ought to bear the abuse to which he is subjected without protest lest he dishonor his Lord who also was persecuted. "Since Christ...did not hesitate to expose himself to every species of reproach for the maintenance of his Father's glory, how base and shameful will it be for us to shrink from a similar lot."[79] The fact that God the judge remains in heaven for the time being means that injustice can rule temporarily and Christians have to endure the injustice. This is an aspect of Calvin's *theologia crucis*: our life here on earth is marked by all the difficulties which God lays upon us on our pilgrimage.[80] We do already possess the heavenly life but only "in hope," and this explains the concealment.[81]

The certainty of the heavenly life and the certainty of Christ's second coming make the Christian a *pilgrim*, a foreigner on this earth.[82] Christians therefore have to remain convinced that "on this earth they are only journeying so that they focus themselves in hope and patience on a better life."[83] The uniting of believers to Christ means "that they forget their own people and their father's home" because they have become children of God and children of the church.[84] In this new existence, Calvin writes, the church becomes our new fatherland. God also uses these most humble of earthly circumstances for his good purposes since the person with whom everything is physically or materially well would be concerned less with God.[85] Perhaps here we find the roots of a Calvinistic distrust toward outward luxury and prosperity which could threaten one's pilgrim identity.

This theme of the believer as a pilgrim reveals a peculiar mixture of the biblical material with Calvin's own personal experience. He himself was, of course, a foreigner in a foreign country, a pilgrim who out of sheer necessity had to dwell outside his homeland of France. His writings therefore reflect the seamless movement from his own pilgrimage to the exposition of scripture: "It is in any case certain that the children of God, wherever they live, always have been pilgrims in this world."[86] Moreover, Calvin picks up

---

[79] Ps. 69:10 (*CO* 31, 642).

[80] "Der Wanderer zur Vollkommenheit zieht seine Straße unter dem Zeichen des Kreuzes." See W. Kolfhaus, *Vom christlichen Leben nach Calvin* (Neukirchen: Kreis Moers, Buchhandlung des Erziehungsvereins, 1949), 188.

[81] "...in mundo peregrinamur ... nunc abscondita sit in terris vita nostra," Ps. 89:47 (*CO* 31, 829). Cf. also "...quia salus nostra quae in spe reposita est, palam conspicua nobis esse non potest," Ps. 118:17 (*CO* 32, 207).

[82] "Nam quum fideles quamdiu peregrinantur in mundo...," Ps. 37: introduction (*CO* 31, 365).

[83] Ps. 4:6 (*CO* 31, 63).

[84] Ps. 87:5 (*CO* 31, 803). This was indeed a reality for many of Calvin's readership.

[85] Ps. 4:7 (*CO* 31, 63).

[86] Ps. 137:4 (*CO* 32, 369).

on this theme in David's life, and so he again seeks to apply it to the entirety of the church. When David compares his situation to that of a locust, "skipping" from one place to a next, Calvin gathers that the psalm pictures here an image of the whole church, "that we should not be surprised when God arouses us from our lethargy" by keeping us also at flight.[87] In light of the promise that God's children will inherit the land, Calvin cannot avoid the qualification that the promise is not always fulfilled so clearly. Often believers have to wander about like gypsies, not receiving a permanent residence from God.[88] This interpretation is applicable to the larger part of Calvin's congregation, which is perhaps the reason why Calvin immediately makes this pastoral observation. God so prevents us from feeling at home here that we forget our heavenly citizenship.[89]

The ever-present disorder which results in this fallen world brings the temptation of not obeying God's law but rather just living in the service of sin. Reflecting on the first psalm, Calvin states that the first step to blessedness is avoiding undesirable contact with the ungodly.[90] From the use of the word *consuetudo* it is apparent that this is not a matter of completely withdrawing from the world, but rather Calvin warns against forming close, intimate friendships with the wicked. Calvin thinks it is clear from the words of the poet that it is impossible to totally withdraw oneself from the world. When the poet speaks in the first verse about "walk[ing] in the counsel," he implies such sins which are not public yet; "sit[ting] in the seat," though, points to sins which have become habitual.

Other passages in Calvin's commentary also suggest that he strongly identified with those texts of the Psalter which highlight the mistreatment of the godly. When Calvin writes that nothing is more bitter than being unjustly condemned,[91] he probably alludes to his own experience. Similarly Calvin seems to relate to David, who stood alone against the public opinion when it opposed him. By appealing to the precedent of David, Calvin positively applies the scriptural text to the common calling of every Christian, who must be prepared to stand alone in forsaking the world in order to live in dependence on God.[92] In his comments on Psalm 119:69 Calvin again indicts those "arrogant" unbelievers with whom he's had firsthand contact—"the prominent who are inflated with trust on their honor and wealth."[93]

---

[87] Ps. 109:23 (*CO* 32, 156).

[88] "...quia et peregrinos in ea vagari oportet," Ps. 37:9 (*CO* 31, 371).

[89] "...atqui nisi instabiles huc et illuc feramur, obrepit coeli ac aeternae haereditatis oblivio," Ps. 37:9 (*CO* 31, 371).

[90] "...renuntiare impiorum consuetidini...," Ps. 1:1 (*CO* 31, 37).

[91] "Nam quum nihil sit acerbius quam nos immerito damnari...," Ps. 4:2 (*CO* 31, 58).

[92] See Ps. 35:1 (*CO* 31, 346).

[93] Ps. 119:69 (*CO* 32, 245).

Naturally, any false accusations against the Christian do bring a certain amount of loneliness, but he or she should be content with the certainty that God is a heavenly judge and that he knows who is innocent. It is important to bear in mind this relation with God in heaven, for to him we can appeal in our righteousness, whereby it does not imply righteousness in respect of God but justice in respect to the psalmist's enemies.[94] Not until the day of Christ's return will our innocence come to light, and in the meantime the Christian can expect that accusations and defamation will remain.[95] This mistreatment is the common experience of the righteous; therefore Calvin recommends a realistic expectation of such trouble. If David was not safeguarded against it, how will we escape it?[96] The one who loves himself and wants only his own advantage seeks to take immediate revenge in such situations. Yet Calvin cautions that it is better to restrain this impulse and rather follow the guidance of the Spirit. By suppressing these emotions we make room in our prayers for the grace of God "since it can happen that he who hates us terribly today may tomorrow become our friend."[97]

One further observation should be made about Calvin's comments on persecution and unjust accusations. When our conscience is clear, he notes, these attacks actually increase our confidence and boldness. After all, these attacks are directed against the word of God and true piety, thus they serve as proof that we belong to God. Calvin knows how to interpret the negative experience of defamation pastorally in order to strengthen the faith of believers through a practical syllogism for persecution.

Calvin also speaks of the Christian's life on earth as that of a *soldier*. Our life, he says, is a continuous active military service.[98] God exercises us in this service to prevent that "we would seek true peace in this world."[99] Moreover, it is "a tough military service" which God uses to exercise our faith; because of the war Satan is waging against us, there is little opportunity for pleasure.[100] Believers despise the troubles of this life and are ready at every moment to enter into the struggle for which they are destined and by which they will be wounded.[101] They therefore should not let misfortune confuse them "since the situation is simply that they have to struggle on this earth."[102]

---

[94] Ps. 4:2 (*CO* 31, 58).

[95] "Ita filiis Dei ambulandum est per infamiam et bonam famam, et patienter ferendae calumniae, donec eorum innocentiam Deus e coelo asserat," Ps. 35:11 (*CO* 31, 351).

[96] Ps. 119:22 (*CO* 32, 224).

[97] Ps. 109:5-6 (*CO* 32, 149).

[98] Ps. 94:12 (*CO* 32, 23).

[99] Ps. 147:6 (*CO* 32, 427).

[100] Ps. 42:2 (*CO* 31, 427).

[101] "...in ea militia, ad quam se norunt destinatos...," Ps. 30:7 (*CO* 31, 296).

[102] Ps. 119:153 (*CO* 32, 283).

5. Obedience: The Place of the Law

How should the Christian "pilgrim" or "soldier" here on earth live his or her everyday life? The single concept which best summarizes Calvin's response to this question that of *obedience*.

In his comments upon Psalm 81:9 Calvin states that obedience is the beginning of all true worship of God.[103] With such statements as this, it is not entirely surprising that Calvin's theology has been characterized as rather legalistic.[104] Given the many places where Calvin states that the purpose of life is to *serve*,[105] he can give the impression of advocating a religion of duty. For example, Calvin interprets the biblical expression "the fear of the Lord" as conscientiously living according to the law of God. Moreover, for Calvin *pietas* and *studium legis* are synonymous since the only way to honor God is to be obedient to his word.[106] In this context Calvin speaks about having "love for the law."[107] This love, he argues, is a sign that one is a child of God because love is the work of the Spirit.[108] However, for Calvin true service to God begins at an even more foundational level with faith since we must trust in him and give him all of the honor.[109] He writes, "Faith is the root of all piety since faith teaches us to hope for and desire every blessing from God, and it transforms us to yield obedience to him."[110] The concept of piety receives a practical role in Calvin's thought. He exhorts believers that "the only way to honor God appropriately is to strive to be of service to his holy servants,"[111] by which Calvin implies a love shown to fellow-believers. This service must also be extended to the unbelievers, though, because God makes himself an example to us in his kindness towards all, even the unworthy.[112]

However, our sanctification is no effort to be charted and accomplished through man alone. Personal holiness begins by following God.[113] The evaluation that Calvin (as opposed, for instance, to Luther) holds to a

---

[103] "Sed interea simul admonet, principium veri cultus incipere ad obedientia," Ps. 81:9 (*CO* 31, 763).

[104] In his book on Calvin's concept of the law Hesselink discusses the literature in which Calvin was "dismissed as a 'law-teacher.'" I. John Hesselink, *Calvin's Concept of the Law* (Allison Park, Pa: Pickwick Publications Allison Park, 1992), 1. See also Kolfhaus, *Vom christlichen Leben*, 115-69.

[105] "...esse vivendi finem ut Deum colam...," Ps. 81:11 (*CO* 31, 784).

[106] Ps. 1:1 (*CO* 31, 39).

[107] "Ex hoc legis amore fluit...," Ps. 1:1 (*CO* 31, 39).

[108] Ps. 119:159 (*CO* 32, 286).

[109] "...legitimum Dei cultum a fide incipere...," Ps. 78:7 (*CO* 31, 724).

[110] Ps. 78:21 (*CO* 31, 729).

[111] Ps. 16:3 (*CO* 31, 150).

[112] "Hic ergo legitimus est Dei cultus, quum homines inter se mutuo sunt benefici," Ps. 16:3 (*CO* 31, 150).

[113] "...non alium esse recte vivendi modum, quam ubi praeit, nos vero sequimur...," Ps. 86:11 (*CO* 31, 795).

legalistic conception of sanctification is surely not correct.[114] On the contrary, the Christian's freedom consists in being ruled by the Spirit of God.[115] Thus, grace brings *docilitas*, the willingness to learn. In fact, Calvin distinguishes between the first grace of conversion and the second grace of *docilitas*. This consequent grace is the sanctification which Calvin refers to as obedience, but it nonetheless remains an aspect of grace.[116] He who follows his own way, though, errs and is inevitably caught in the tyranny of Satan.

In Calvin's thought the law also has the function of showing man his sinfulness. The Reformer proceeds on the assumption that anyone who compares his life to God's law discovers that he cannot count on any reward from God, neither for his deeds nor his thoughts; thus he must seek his refuge in the grace of God. It does not suffice to merely ascertain what the law requires. We also must appreciate how far short we fall in light of the requirements of the law.[117] The law causes us to recoil at our sins.[118]

The notion of the law as a teacher about our sins is not developed in Calvin's *Commentary* on the Psalter nearly as much as he explicates the notion of the law as a guide for our lives. The latter concept is expressed so strongly that it sometimes seems as if the knowledge of the law stands on an equal level as the knowledge of the gospel. Calvin indeed speaks highly of the law. The law is a gift of God's grace, he says.[119] Only the law teaches what is truly correct whereas nothing but "confused" and "twisted" thoughts emanate from the heart of man.[120] Furthermore, the law contains perfect and absolute wisdom.[121] The law also enlightens reason[122] and gives life to the soul.[123] The law is the guide which directs us out from the "horrible labyrinths" in which we end up when we follow our own way.[124] The law is delightful, Calvin declares, and its sweetness attracts us to God and a good life.[125] In the law God reveals himself more intimately than in the creation.[126]

---

[114] "Das neue Leben ist letzlich ein Leben nicht 'im Imperativ' sondern 'im Indikativ' nach dem gemeinsamen Überzeugung der beiden großen Führer der Reformation," Kolfhaus, *Vom christlichen Leben*, 169.

[115] "Haec vero unica est piorum libertas, gubernari a Dei spiritu...," Ps. 119:133 (*CO* 32, 275).

[116] "Hic de secunda gratia loquitur, quam Deus erga fideles exserit, postquam subacti ad iugum ferendum, obedienter eius imperio se submittunt," Ps. 25:9 (*CO* 31, 255).

[117] Ps. 19:12 (*CO* 31, 204).

[118] "...perculsus eruperit in hanc vocem," Ps. 19:12 (*CO* 31, 204).

[119] Ps. 19: introduction (*CO* 31, 194).

[120] Ps. 119:113 (*CO* 32, 264).

[121] Ps. 19:7 (*CO* 31, 200).

[122] Ps. 103:7 (*CO* 32, 78).

[123] "...sic etiam lex vita sit animae," Ps. 19:7 (*CO* 31, 200).

[124] Ps. 119:105 (*CO* 32, 259).

[125] Ps. 119:15 (*CO* 32, 220).

[126] Ps. 19: introduction (*CO* 31, 194).

Nowhere else can one know God more clearly than in his law since he reveals in his law that he is merciful.[127]

Calvin emphatically explains that "under the term *law* he [the psalmist] not only means the rule of living righteously or the Ten Commandments but he also comprehends the covenant by which God had distinguished that people from the rest of the world and the whole doctrine of Moses...."[128] The law, according to Calvin, is "the entirely body of doctrine in which true religion and piety consists."[129] It is the entirety of the covenant of salvation.[130] It is not limited merely to demands, but it invites us to the hope of eternal salvation and opens up the door to real happiness.[131] The law contains both free adoption and all the promises which are connected to it.[132] The law actually ratifies the covenant in laying down the covenant as a fixed and eternal arrangement.[133]

6. Paul contra David regarding the Law

In the course of the Psalms commentary Calvin addresses the question of how David can speak so positively about the law while the apostle Paul apparently arrives at quite the opposite conclusion. He asks, "How can one harmonize the law restoring the souls of men with the law at the same time being a deadly and pernicious letter? The law rejoices men's hearts, but it creates terrible fear? It enlightens the eyes, and yet it sets a veil before our minds and excludes the light within?"[134] Calvin answers this hypothetical objection by noting that one must first consider that David does not speak merely about the naked regulations of the law but about the entirety of the covenant. This implies that he connects such precepts with the promises of salvation. David speaks of the law as the whole of its teachings, and the most important part of this is about the covenant of grace. If the law merely consisted of regulations, it would be deadly, but it also entails our merciful adoption as children.[135] This apparent conflict is further explained by Calvin's christological reading of the Psalms: David speaks about Christ, who is the real substance of the covenant. Paul is speaking of people who have misused the law by loosening it from the grace and the Spirit of Christ. The apostle

---

[127] "...quia nusquam clarius vel familiarius exprimitur Dei natura," Ps. 145:8 (*CO* 32, 414).

[128] Ps. 19:7 (*CO* 32, 222).

[129] "...totum illud doctrinae corpus ex quo constat vera religio et pietas," Ps. 19:7 (*CO* 31, 199).

[130] Ps. 119:168 (*CO* 32, 290).

[131] Ps. 119:142 (*CO* 32, 279).

[132] Ps. 119:142 (*CO* 32, 279).

[133] Ps. 111:9 (*CO* 32, 170).

[134] Ps. 19:8 (*CO* 31, 201).

[135] Ps. 119:103 (*CO* 32, 258).

therefore only speaks about the letter of the law and implies that the law without the Spirit of Christ does not arouse to life but actually brings death. Without Christ our flesh remains rebellious and resists the law ever more, and thus apart from Christ the law leads to slavery and terror.[136] When Paul contrasts the law with the gospel, he is only concerned with the regulations and the threats of the law when viewed apart from the grace of Christ and the covenant of salvation.[137] Therefore Calvin writes,

> If we separate the law from the hope of remission and from the Spirit of Christ, instead of tasting the law to be sweet as honey we rather find in it such bitterness as to kill our wretched souls.[138]

David and Paul appear to disagree because they are looking at the law from two different vantage points. Reconciling their views, however, is rather simple. Paul indicates what the law brings when it is loosened from the promise of grace. David on the other hand can praise the law since he equates it with the covenant, including Christ and the gospel.[139] Calvin accordingly warns elsewhere against separating the law from God's covenant by regarding it as mere regulations when the law in fact is intended by the Holy Spirit to refer to the promises which are found in Christ.[140] The law itself does not have the power to bring man to God, but he uses it nevertheless as his instrument in "restoring our souls."[141] In its function which is common to all men, the law is dead, and it does nothing more than beat the air in its impotence to produce true holiness.[142] Therefore inward peace is not obtained through slavish obedience to the external rule of the law but only by faith. The law has no "sweetness" to make it desirable, Calvin says, unless we know God as our Father and our heart is at rest through the assurance of our eternal salvation.[143] If the law had not revealed the grace of God, it would not in any way be so attractive to us.[144] The regulations alone would frighten a person, and therefore faith and the knowledge of God as Father are necessary to obey the law. In complete agreement with Luther, Calvin says that only he

---

[136] Ps. 19:8 (*CO* 31, 201).
[137] "Paulus legem evangelio comparans tantum attingit praecepta cum minis," Ps. 119:103 (*CO* 32, 258).
[138] Ps. 19:10 (*CO* 31, 203).
[139] Ps. 19:8 (*CO* 31, 201).
[140] "...non semper nuda praecepta arripi debere...," Ps. 111:9 (*CO* 32, 170).
[141] Ps. 19:7 (*CO* 31, 200).
[142] "...doctrina legis, quia tamen per se mortua est, et nihil aliud quam aërem verberat," Ps. 40:8 (*CO* 31, 412).
[143] Ps. 119:165 (*CO* 32, 289-90).
[144] "Et certe non potuit tam suavis et amabilis esse legis doctrina, quia percipiat quid rectum sit, nisi etiam praeponeret gratuitum Dei favorem," Ps. 119:168 (*CO* 32, 291).

who knows God as Father is able to handle the law appropriately.[145] Thus Calvin can point to the joy and gratitude which is generated by a knowledge of the law.[146] This connection of joy and thanksgiving to the law demonstrates that Calvin's thought lacks the legalistic character in which it is sometimes portrayed.[147]

7. Joy and Being a Pilgrim

Given his rather sober outlook on the hardships facing a Christian, does Calvin save any place for the enjoyment of life during this pilgrim existence on earth? In conformity with Calvin's view of the ideal life, this question can be answered with a reserved affirmation.[148] He says that it is the war-like situation in which the Christian lives which renders such little opportunity for joy.[149] However, he warns against despising this life since, in spite of everything, it still remains a special blessing from God.[150] Calvin points to the example in Psalm 104 that, although man has water to drink according to his needs, God has additionally given wine to make us cheerful (though it must not become a means for extravagance!).[151] Likewise rich people must learn to soberly handle their abundance lest the spiritual food of heaven loses its appeal to them.[152] For the gifts they receive they ought to acknowledge the Giver. Those who have more than others must acquire modesty and so live as if they had about as much as others. By nature man is given towards excess, yet Calvin says that the God who gives prosperity will also give his Spirit to restrain the flesh so that prosperity is appropriately used.[153] Calvin notes that

---

[145] Ps. 119:159 (*CO* 32, 286). Regarding the German Reformer, see Paul Althaus, *Die Theologie Martin Luthers* (Gütersloh: Gütersloher Verlagshaus, 1980), 218-38.

[146] Ps. 103:7 (*CO* 32, 78).

[147] The conclusion of Blaser's analysis of Calvin's sermons on Psalm 119 is that Calvin wants to be here nothing else than "...der kompromißlose Theologe des Evangeliums, der Zeuge der reinen Gnade Gottes in Christus." See Emil Blaser, "Vom Gesetz in Calvins Predigten über den 119. Psalm," in *Das Wort sie sollen lassen stahn: Festschrift für Professor D. Albert Schädelin* (Bern, 1950), 77.

[148] Engammare and Oberman have indicated that Calvin is not so absolute in the rejection of happiness and joy as has often has been alleged. See Max Engammare, "Plaisir des mets, plaisir des mots: Irdische Freude bei Calvin," in *Calvinus Vindex*, 189-208; and Heiko A. Oberman, "The Pursuit of Happiness: Calvin between Humanism and Reformation," in *Humanity and Divinity in Renaissance and Reformation: Essays in Honor of Charles Trinkaus*, ed. J. O'Malley (Leiden: E. J. Brill, 1993), 251-83.

[149] Ps. 42:4 (*CO* 31, 427).

[150] Ps. 49:21 (*CO* 31, 494).

[151] "...vino licere uti, non modo ad necessitatem sed ad laetitiam, sed haec laetitia sobrie temperanda est," Ps. 104:15 (*CO* 32, 91).

[152] Ps. 22:29 (*CO* 31, 236).

[153] "Dominus etiam dum fideles locupletat, simul lascivos carnis cupiditates restringit continentiae spiritu," Ps. 23:5 (*CO* 31, 241).

this does not mean that one may not take pleasure from his wealth, but the boundary between whole-hearted enjoyment on the one hand and excessive luxury on the other hand should not be crossed. Calvin characterizes dissatisfaction with one's situation and the desire for more than is necessary as despising God. Man must therefore attempt to moderate his longings or desires because when the flesh does not know such restraint it will not any longer be content with plain bread.[154]

From Calvin's point of view, moderation serves a clear purpose because people can so easily become fixed upon the gifts of God that they forget God himself. Yet moderation, meanwhile, entails both true joy and thankfulness "since for the believer there can be no joy without a feeling of thankfulness towards God."[155] A sense of enjoyment is also strengthened through receiving such earthly gifts in the conviction that God is our father. Wealth and prosperity then may clearly be seen as blessings of God, and for this reason a believer may also enjoy them.[156] Calvin notes that care for one's body or appearance should not be neglected, but he cautions that this work be kept within moderate bounds.[157] In the delights of the body the fatherly love of God is revealed. However, believers taste the love of the Father in such physical and earthly matters without being satisfied by them. The highest enjoyment instead consists in knowing "that God's hand is stretched out to govern us, that we live under his shadow, and that he guards over us with his providence."[158] Hence the Calvinistic emphasis on moderation arises out of concern that one would seek true joy somewhere else than in God himself.

The Christian's life is also hindered by the influence of his surroundings. When we let the chaos of this world influence us, "we have to take care not to howl with the wolves."[159] He explains,

> It is easy to act well when we are among the good. But if wicked men threaten us, if one man opposes us fiercely and another one robs us, if a third one deceives us in all possible ways and a fourth one assaults us with slander, then it is difficult for us to persevere in integrity, and we rather tend to howl with the wolves. Additionally, they are allowed this impertinence without the fear of punishment, a powerful instrument in shaking our faith. When God turns a blind eye, he seems as if he gives us over to them as prey.[160]

[154] Ps. 78:18 (*CO* 31, 729).
[155] Ps. 118:15 (*CO* 32, 206).
[156] Ps. 144:15 (*CO* 32, 412).
[157] Ps. 85:13 (*CO* 31, 790).
[158] Ps. 23:1 (*CO* 31, 238).
[159] Ps. 12:1 (*CO* 31, 127).
[160] Ps. 119:157 (*CO* 32, 285).

If one sees around him that everybody only cares for and enriches himself through fraud and theft without a moment's hesitation, he feels within the temptation to act in the same way. Jealousy over the prosperity of others can thus lead a man to even excuse himself of such an evil by reasoning that he needs those things on which he wants to get his hands.[161]

8. The King and the Kings

According to Calvin there is room in the church for kings and other authorities.[162] And neither the psalmist nor the Reformer insists that they get rid of their swords and crowns before they are allowed into the church. What is important, Calvin says, is that they kneel before Christ even with all of their dignity and power.[163] All authorities are established by God and are his representatives on earth.[164] In fact, commenting upon Psalm 82:1, Calvin argues that the "assembly of God" is the rather lofty name given to the world's political order.[165] The reason for this is that God's glory shines precisely there where the people are proficiently governed.[166] In typical fashion, Calvin distinguishes between the inward and the outward aspects, and he states that both should be in harmony with each other. In his opinion, it is only those who admit that they govern on behalf of God and who reflect this knowledge in their policies that have the right to govern. Those on the other hand who think that they owe their authority to luck, the entitlement of inheritance or their own efforts have no legitimate calling.[167] Yet Calvin stops short of the implication that one does not have to obey a government or an authority which does not recognize God.

Yet, Calvin takes the above mentioned viewpoint as an occasion to give his criticism of earthly authorities. It is only through the grace of God that they can remain within the bounds of what is right and fair. This means, in Calvin's opinion, that authorities who are not ruled by the heavenly Spirit of righteousness will reign in tyranny and robbery.[168] Calvin does not have a particularly high opinion of monarchs and other rulers since he notices how often they grow arrogant in their power by forgetting that they received it

---

[161] Ps. 34:10 (*CO* 31, 339-40). Cf. Ps. 37:3 (*CO* 31, 366). "Altera tentatio sequitur, quia eos titillat exemplum, ut scelerum societate se involvant."

[162] "...in ecclesia et grege Christi esse regibus locum...," Ps. 72:11 (*CO* 31, 669).

[163] Ps. 72:11 (*CO* 31, 669).

[164] Ps. 110:1 (*CO* 32, 160).

[165] "...ordinem politicum appellat coetum Dei...," Ps. 82:1 (*CO* 31, 768).

[166] "...dum legitima gubernatio inter mortales viget."Ps. 82:1 (*CO* 31, 768).

[167] "...ideoque ipsorum respectu ut plurimum legitima non est vocation," Ps. 110:1 (*CO* 32, 160).

[168] "...quia ubi non praeest e coelo spiritus rectitudinis, omne imperium in tyrannidem et latrocinium vertitur," Ps. 72:4 (*CO* 31, 665-6).

from God, and these monarchs are rarely moved by God's majesty.[169] Many authorities believe that the world exists only for their sakes. In their unscrupulous pursuit of more power, they seek to be praised and flattered.[170] They also do not put God at the center, even when they are ready to admit the ultimate source of their power, they still practically exclude God from the assembly, neither associating themselves with him nor submitting to his laws.[171] Indeed God does not receive any place in their assembly.[172] Calvin does not think it is incidental that in his psalms David calls upon kings by name to act with wisdom as "they do not let themselves be easily tamed. In addition they are so swollen with arrogance about their own vain wisdom that it hinders them from learning what is really right."[173]

We know from experience, says Calvin, that almost all kings are drunk from their own glory and therefore are extremely arrogant.[174] They are so busy with their own pleasure that they are blind to their duties regarding their subjects. Every day these tyrants invent something new in order to burden and oppress their people.[175] Most rulers therefore do not have the general interest in mind so much as their own advantage, and, as a consequence, they suppress their subjects.[176]

In spite of this judgment against tyrannical authorities, Calvin maintains trust that one can live in society due to his belief that God cares for the political order because the general welfare depends on it.[177] The existence of this order is inextricably tied to the upholding of justice. A good authority can be recognized by his protection for the rights of the poor and oppressed.[178] In fact, this is the end to which authorities are appointed since the poor and oppressed rely upon the help of others. This help is only possible if an authority is free from greed, ambition and other vices.[179] Authorities must stand up for the poor and distressed precisely for the reason that this group easily becomes the prey of the wealthy. Authorities are thus the "protectors" of the poor.[180] Their power and stateliness, however, make most authorities

---

[169] Ps. 29 (*CO* 31, 287).

[170] Ps. 82:1 (*CO* 31, 768).

[171] "...Deum a coetu suo procul expellant...," Ps. 82:1 (*CO* 31, 768).

[172] "...quod Deo locum in coetu suo non relinquunt," Ps. 82:1 (*CO* 31, 768).

[173] Ps. 2:10 (*CO* 31, 49).

[174] Ps. 101:2 (*CO* 32, 56).

[175] "...novas artes quotidie excudunt onerandis et gravandis subditis...," Ps. 101:2 (*CO* 32, 57).

[176] Ps. 72:12 (*CO* 31, 669).

[177] "...peculiari tamen modo curam suam extendere ad tuendam ordinem politicum unde pendet communis omnium salus," Ps. 144:9 (*CO* 32, 410).

[178] Ps. 82:3 (*CO* 31, 769).

[179] Ps. 82:3 (*CO* 31, 770).

[180] "...se tutores pauperibus esse datos...," Ps. 82:3 (*CO* 31, 770).

blind to the needs of the poor, and all too often they adopt an attitude that it is beneath their dignity to offer such care.[181] This oppression calls out loud,[182] Calvin says, and authorities therefore have to act boldly concerning the protection of the poor and the weak.[183] Calvin judges that poor people are the most exposed to injustice and violence. They are also the first victims when the law is not justly enforced since it is always the law of the strongest which prevails in such situations.[184]

The Psalms often depict the image of the ideal ruler, Calvin explains. The king is the protector of law and fairness; he is humane and merciful and stands up for the most despised.[185] Kings also have to be just and pure in their personal lives if they want to be able to carry out the duties of their office most virtuously.[186] Psalm 102, for example, is the real *Fürstenspiegel*, and in his exposition of this text Calvin once again sets forth all of the previously mentioned qualities pertaining to a good monarch. What is new, though, is his remark that a good monarch should only elect honest people for the various offices which must be filled. Appointments should be done carefully; otherwise the population loses any benefit from having a good monarch.[187]

The good monarch, of course, does act against injustice, but only according to his office as a ruling authority. When David receives permission to retaliate against injustice in the biblical story, he does not act as an individual person but as the king who has been granted this particular competence from God.[188] When one considers the historical context in which Calvin was writing, it is not surprising that more than once he makes this distinction between David as individual person and as king.[189] He who avenges injustice as private person tramples God's law underfoot. Calvin believes that everyone should stay within the boundaries of his own calling.[190] As he puts it in one place, our hands are bound.[191] It is thus better to seek refuge with God and to expect help and salvation from his protection than it is to enter into a struggle for justice in your own strength, which will always prove to be insufficient.[192] It is better to endure tyranny with patience than to upset the

---

[181] Ps. 72:12 (*CO* 31, 669).
[182] "...satis clamat oppressio...," Ps. 82:3 (*CO* 31, 770).
[183] Ps. 72:4 (*CO* 31, 666).
[184] Ps. 72:4 (*CO* 31, 665).
[185] Ps. 72:12 (*CO* 31, 669).
[186] Ps. 101:3 (*CO* 32, 57).
[187] Ps. 101:6 (*CO* 32, 59).
[188] "Neque enim privatus homo erat, sed pro regia potestate, iudicium quod exsequutus est divinitus ei iniunctum erat," Ps. 18:48 (*CO* 31, 192).
[189] Ps. 101:5 (*CO* 32, 58); Ps. 149:7 (*CO* 32, 439).
[190] Ps. 101:5 (*CO* 32, 58).
[191] "...nobis manus sunt ligatae," Ps. 41:10 (*CO* 31, 423).
[192] Ps. 83:3 (*CO* 31, 774).

social order with an uprising.[193] Believers are only armed with the sword of prayer, and through this channel they can petition God whether he wants to act as judge.[194] The believer does not bear the sword, and an appeal by the believer (in the psalm, David) for personal retaliation against evil is not valid apart from one holding a civil office. In punishing the wicked, David does not act as a private person but as a king who was appointed to his royal office by God. Moreover, David does not take revenge on his enemies out of a sinful or fleshly motivation, but he acts in judgment because of the responsibilities of the office to which he was called by God to punish his enemies appropriately for their rebellion.[195] Precisely because it is God's task to take revenge against the wicked, this duty is not ours. This especially serves as a reminder to us when the fleshly desire for revenge overwhelms us.[196] Meanwhile, civil authorities can appeal to God's calling in punishing wickedness only when they let the Spirit guide them rather than their tempestuous flesh.[197]

9. Conclusion

For Calvin the kingship of God proclaimed in the Psalter carries very practical implications for the life of a believer who is called thereby to service and obedience. In this respect humans have the same calling as the angels. (Incidentally, the position which Calvin ascribes to the angels is more substantial than one might generally assume from the Reformer.) By connecting our obedience to the law with our status through the doctrine of adoption, Calvin avoids a strictly legalistic approach to faith. Calvin's humanism is also evident *inter alia* in his emphasis upon the Christian's identity as a pilgrim and in his pursuit of inward peace. Although our knowledge about Calvin's experience of reality does not prove that he ought to be characterized as an anxious person, it does reflect that anxiety was an essential element in Calvin's emotional life.

---

[193] "Itaque discamus queti manere, quamvis tyrannice potestate sibi divinitus commissa abutantur principes, ne tumultuando legitimum ordinem turbemus," Ps. 119:161 (*CO* 32, 288).

[194] Ps. 41:10 (*CO* 31, 423).

[195] "...sed pro ratione officii poenam hostibus denuntiare quam meriti sunt," Ps. 41:11 (*CO* 31, 423).

[196] "...carnis libido...," Ps. 8:16 (*CO* 31, 87).

[197] "...modo tamen rite composito spiritus zelo ageretur, non carnis impetus," Ps. 18:48 (*CO* 31, 192).

7

God the Judge

1. God's Righteousness

In the Psalms much is said about justice and righteousness, wrath and retribution. When these themes appear, the psalmist's cry to God to act as judge usually receives particular emphasis, along with the assurance that God is the punisher of sin. As a Reformed theologian, Calvin depicts God through his interpretation of such passages as a judge who inspires awe without striking terror. The question may be asked, though, whether Calvin succeeds in this attempt. This chapter will provide an overview of Calvin's portrayal of God as the heavenly judge through his commentary upon the Psalter.

Calvin interprets the righteousness of God as his faithfulness and mercy whereby he protects believers.[1] God's righteousness, he states, "is his continual protection by which he watches over his own and the goodness by which he comforts them."[2] Just as in Luther's thought,[3] Calvin's notion of the righteousness of God does not mean the righteousness God demands of us but the righteousness he give to us. A difference, though, is that Luther connects God's righteousness more with his forgiveness while Calvin's emphasis is on God's faithfulness to the covenant. In his interpretation of Psalm 71:16, Calvin again explains God's righteousness as faithfulness, and he explicitly rejects the exegesis of St. Augustine who repeatedly offers this verse as evidence against the merit of works. In doing so, Calvin argues, Augustine forces upon the text a different meaning than it actually has.[4] God's righteousness is not the fact that he gives to each his due. It is rather the faithfulness he shows toward his own by protecting them and setting

---

[1] Ps. 5:9 (*CO* 31, 69). See also Ps. 7:18 (*CO* 31, 87): "Iustitia Dei hoc loco pro fide accipitur quam servis suis praestat in tuenda eorum vita...."
[2] Ps. 40:11 (*CO* 31, 414); cf. Ps. 48:10 (*CO* 31, 479).
[3] For Luther's conception of righteousness, see Althaus, *Theologie*, 195-202.
[4] "...in alienum sensum torqueri verba Davidis...," Ps. 71:16 (*CO* 31, 659).

them free,[5] and it "is a proof of his goodness, grace and faithfulness as it has already been said elsewhere."[6] Thus, the righteousness of God is not to be associated with human merit, but, Calvin again states, "by the righteousness of God we mean his goodness which leads him to defend his people."[7]

This righteousness of God in his protection and his faithfulness demands a similar righteousness on the part of believers. Here Calvin thinks especially of the need for social justice, and he makes a few observations about this in the Psalms commentary.[8] Since the widow, the orphan, and the refugee are so defenseless, God commands Christians to protect and look after them in particular.[9] The one who treats them unjustly thereby sins against God since he desires extra care and protection for these groups. Calvin explicitly mentions children as those who particularly need to be protected from all kinds of harm because of their total vulnerability. Injustice towards the defenseless, though, summons God's wrath.[10] Calvin warns that God turns a deaf ear to the prayers of those who ignore the cries of the poor and the oppressed.[11] We must stand up for those who are suffering injustice since nothing is more miserable, Calvin thinks, than living in this world without order and justice.[12]

The protective righteousness of God manifests itself in his punitive justice toward the enemies of God's people. In fact, Calvin remarks that it is part of God's proper duty to govern the peoples.[13] This should be kept in mind by the faithful at all times, especially during periods of distress and trouble. Because God cannot forsake his duty, this offers the individual believer a lasting comfort, because the burden of suffering injustice individually is much harder than enduring it collectively. According to Calvin's exegesis, God will avenge the sins committed against his people and

---

[5]   Ps. 71:14 (*CO* 31, 658); See also Ps. 103:17 (*CO* 32, 82): "Deus ergo iustus est: non quia unumquemque remunerat prout dignus fuerit, sed quia fideliter cum suis agit, eos manu sua protegendo."

[6]   Ps. 98:1 (*CO* 32, 48).

[7]   Ps. 143:1 (*CO* 32, 400).

[8]   The limited attention accorded to social justice may be explained in the fact that the commentary is especially focused on God. On Calvin's activity in the social realm, see Jeannine E. Olson, *Calvin and Social Welfare: Deacons and the Bourse Française* (Selinsgrove, PA: Susquehanna University Press 1989).

[9]   "...quia eo plus merentur humanitatis et misericordiae, quo magis obnoxii sunt iniuriis," Ps. 94:5 (*CO* 32, 20).

[10] "Itaque magis in se provocant iram Dei qui crudeliter in illos insurgunt," Ps. 94:5 (*CO* 32, 20).

[11] Ps. 18:42 (*CO* 31, 189).

[12] Ps. 97:1 (*CO* 32, 43).

[13] "...proprium esse Dei munus iudicare populos," Ps. 7:9 (*CO* 31, 83).

will reveal himself as the protector of his church.[14] For it is not in keeping with God's nature to leave sin unpunished.[15] If God does not leave the wicked nations to go unpunished, nor will any individuals be able to claim immunity before God.[16] His very nature guarantees such judgment according to his justice. God's judgment against these enemies is also an expression of his immense love toward the faithful.[17] God's response to injustice strikes both duty and gladness in the faithful.[18] Besides this joy Calvin also considers one great difficulty which can arise from the knowledge that God is judge: the more the faithful are persuaded of divine judgment the greater their disappointment can be when God does not seem to hear their prayers.[19]

Nevertheless God does not delay all punishment for sin until the end, but occasionally, even in this present age, he intervenes in history. He does this to make his wrath known and to instill fear in the unconverted.[20] Thus his judgment is not merely a matter of the future. He also exercises his judgment daily, Calvin writes, in making a distinction between the righteous and the wicked.[21] Furthermore, God continues to punish transgressions, yet he does this in secret.[22] Hence, when David says in Psalm 7:12 that God carries out his judgment daily, Calvin observes that there is not much of this which we in fact see each day. However, according to Calvin, he who goes to the trouble of truly opening his eyes sees that God never lets a day pass without distinguishing between the just and the unfaithful.[23] What we see is a world in disarray,[24] and therefore we must raise our eyes to appraise things from the perspective of God's rule. God's judgments are indeed visible, but we do not see them.[25] Furthermore, we forget them soon, and therefore "we need to be brought daily into the theater where we are compelled to perceive God's hand."[26] Every day God must, so to speak, raise the curtain so that believers may be convinced of what is actually taking place and who is ruling. Calvin

---

[14] Ps. 5:5 (*CO* 31, 68).
[15] Ps. 5:5 (*CO* 31, 68).
[16] Ps. 94:10 (*CO* 32, 22).
[17] "...immensum erga nos Dei amorem," Ps. 74:3 (*CO* 31, 693).
[18] Ps. 52:8 (*CO* 31, 528).
[19] Ps. 73:21 (*CO* 31, 685).
[20] Ps. 2:12 (*CO* 31, 51).
[21] Ps. 1:5 (*CO* 31, 41).
[22] Ps. 37:34 (*CO* 31, 384).
[23] "...imo nullus dies praeterit, quo non certis documentis probet, quae permista sunt in mundo, a se discerni...," Ps. 7:12 (*CO* 31, 85).
[24] "...rebus in mundo confusis...," Ps. 7:12 (*CO* 31, 85).
[25] Ps. 119:52 (*CO* 32, 236).
[26] Ps. 59:12 (*CO* 31, 570).

notes that God carries out his judgments quite gradually rather than all at once. He does this, the Reformer suggests, because we would too quickly forget if God were to save us from our enemies all in an instant. Since God gives such rescue and help but occasionally, his judgments are this way better engraved upon our hearts.[27]

Calvin does handle one objection which some will voice against his argument that God's judgments bring comfort. They say that comfort clashes with the nature of judgment since judgment intends to frighten people. The Christian's response to such detractors, though, is clear to Calvin: God's judgments only serve to frighten people insofar as fear is required for the mortification of the flesh.[28] The ultimate intention, meanwhile, is the gladness (*felicitas*) of God's people. Therefore, the judgment of God has a medicinal purpose for the faithful.

2. Sin, Guilt and Punishment

God has to act as a judge because there is sin in this fallen world, and every sin, including those against one's neighbor, is a sin ultimately committed against God. Calvin points out that he who realizes this truth "needs no other accusers anymore because God then counts for a thousand accusers."[29] Sin has brought it about that God and man are estranged from each other.[30] Furthermore, our sins are like a wall between us and God so that God neither hears our prayer nor reaches out to help us. Without being reconciled to God on account of our sins then there can be neither prayer nor any other fellowship with God.[31]

Calvin often speaks about conscience as the element in our constitution which corresponds with God's judgment.[32] The conscience of man, he says, is the organ by which God's judgment may be known. According to Calvin there is through conscience a natural and general recognition that no one is perfect and that every person needs forgiveness.[33] Conscience derives this

---

[27] Ps. 59:12 (*CO* 31, 570).

[28] "...iudiciis Dei terreri fideles quatenus illis ad carnis suae mortificationum expedit," Ps. 119:52 (*CO* 32, 237).

[29] Ps. 51:6 (*CO* 31, 511).

[30] "...alienatio quae ex peccato sequuta est...," Ps. 33:12 (*CO* 31, 330).

[31] Ps. 25:7 (*CO* 31, 253).

[32] "Nam eos ad tribunal Dei citando, retrahit ad propriae conscientiae examen," Ps. 94:11 (*CO* 32, 23).

[33] "Hanc igitur confessionem profanis quoque hominibus extorquet ipsa natura...," Ps. 32:1 (*CO* 31, 314).

knowledge from the realization that God is the judge. However, it is possible for one's conscience to fall asleep for a time as with David in his adultery with Bathsheba. Afterwards, though, God does awake the conscience again.[34] Calvin calls it a paradox that in difficult times it is innocence, and not revenge, which is the best guard against injustice and a stricken conscience. It is only the one who commits no injustice of his own who may call on God with a clear conscience.[35] A good conscience has value only when one seeks refuge in God,[36] and at the same time one's conscience must be clear in order to ask for help from God.[37] When someone's conscience is pure he may then call upon God's judgment and vindication, even though the whole world may be coming down upon him.[38] Thus David learns amidst many false accusations to content himself with his own good conscience.[39]

The most insidious sin, for Calvin, is pride (*superbia*). "Pride," he says, "is the mother of all injustice," since pride wickedly elevates one's self-regard and so leads to contempt for one's neighbors.[40] Pride despises both God and one's neighbor, and from this attitude comes forth sin. Therefore, it is a proper designation for the unregenerate to call them "the proud."[41]

Sin initiates a chain reaction insofar as God has created everything in an orderly cohesive structure, but through the perversion of this order by sin, there is an eradication of the knowledge of God, a demise of honesty and human kindness, and an inability to make any distinction between good and evil.[42] Sin disturbs God's *ordo*, and this means that sin changes both the honor of God and the salvation of men in their opposites.

When, as in the psalmist's portrait of the fool, God is finally removed from his throne and dismissed from his duty as the judge, godlessness has reached its pinnacle. Man's way of life then becomes so depraved that all decency and humanity in human dealings vanishes.[43] Calvin's message is clear: a view of life in which God is no longer the sovereign king nor the

---

[34] Ps. 51: 1 (*CO* 31, 508).

[35] Ps. 34:10 (*CO* 31, 340).

[36] Ps. 35:11 (*CO* 31, 351).

[37] Ps. 54:3 (*CO* 31, 532).

[38] "Nos vero discamus, Davidis exemplo, quamvis totus mundus surdus sit, in bonam conscientiam recumbere, atque ita provocare ad Dei tribunal," Ps. 58:2 (*CO* 31, 559).

[39] Ps. 41:9 (*CO* 31, 422).

[40] Ps. 10:2 (*CO* 31, 109).

[41] "Designat autem proprio nomine incredulos, dum superbos vocat," Ps. 119:51 (*CO* 32, 236).

[42] "...nempe quia ordinem perverterint, ut nullum maneat iusti ac iniusti discrimen, nulla honesti cura, nullum humanitatis studium," Ps. 14:1 (*CO* 31, 136).

[43] Ps. 14:1 (*CO* 31, 137).

judge who punishes will initially lead to the demise of all true theology, and thereafter it will result in an inhumane society of unchecked wickedness.

Sin is the cause of all misery; therefore when misfortunes occur, Calvin says, we must ascertain whether there are particular sins that have given God a cause to chastise us. If upon such reflection we find there is such a sin to be confessed before God, we must not ignore it, lest we act like an "unskillful physician" who upon diagnosing a disease merely treats the symptoms while doing nothing at all about the source of the ailment.[44] However, if a person is able to determine the cause of some adversity, Calvin explains that he or she may then identify the sin provoking God's displeasure. This corresponds to our greatest need before God—not to be freed from our troubles, but to be forgiven of our sins.[45] Calvin associates the experience of suffering with the realization of one's actual sinful condition before God, and this greatly increases the sorrow in our suffering. Nothing touches us deeper, he writes, than the awareness of God's hostile towards us.[46]

Man's guilt before God is not a matter of merely one or two sins, but of *countless* sins. This perverseness (*pravitas*), Calvin notes, "not only robs us of God's blessing, but changes life into death."[47] Calvin characterizes David's position in facing the multitude of his sins as that of a person who finds himself in a labyrinth.[48] Furthermore, the person who honestly evaluates their life according to the perfection demanded by God's law will admit that he or she deserves to be lost a thousand times.[49] Calvin therefore advises that we set our lives next to God's law so that it may be apparent that we can expect no reward at all, and thus we may be compelled to seek our refuge only in God's grace.[50] As we have seen in Calvin's thought, the knowledge of oneself and the knowledge of God are again connected. The knowledge of sin brings one before God as the judge in order that he or she may call upon God as savior.

Calvin's identification of David with every believer leads him to make a close connection between sin and punishment. For example, Calvin writes as if every believer were guilty of adultery and murder when, based on David's words about God's punishment of sins, he makes applications that apply to

---

[44] Ps. 25:7 (*CO* 31, 253).
[45] Ps. 39:9 (*CO* 31, 401).
[46] Ps. 102:11 (*CO* 32, 65).
[47] Ps. 19:12 (*CO* 31, 204).
[48] Ps. 19:12 (*CO* 31, 204).
[49] Ps. 130:3 (*CO* 32, 334).
[50] Ps. 19:12 (*CO* 31, 204).

each and every believer. In commenting on Psalm 3, where the subject is the rebellion of Absalom, Calvin states that David recognizes the rebellion is a punishment for his sins of adultery and murder, and then the Reformer proceeds to apply this confession to every believer. When God chastises us by means of malicious people, Calvin says, we must first of all determine why God is doing this since we never suffer anything which we do not deserve.[51] Even if God may have different purposes when he gives one a cross to bear, Calvin offers the general rule that every time there is affliction we must first examine our conscience and beg God's forgiveness.[52] This relationship between sin, guilt and punishment has accordingly been preserved for several centuries now as an expression of Calvinist spirituality.

Calvin's view on the relationship between sin and punishment stands out most clearly in his interpretation of Psalm 6:2-3 ("O Lord, do not rebuke me in your anger..."). There he says that adversity must not bring one to indignation, but to humility. Indeed, one derives no benefit at all in difficulty if he does not relate it to his own sins and the punishing hand of God. Calvin estimates that "scarcely one out of a hundred takes note of the hand that strikes"[53] because people prefer to ask why they suffer than acknowledge in themselves the blame and in their sins the cause. David, however, shows a different attitude in recognizing God as a just judge. At the same time, though, he fears the wrath of God and pleads for a fatherly punishment.[54] In a similar way Calvin deals with the problem of enemies. There are enemies of God, and he makes use of them to punish the faithful. However, he ensures that the faithful ultimately remain safe under God's protection.[55]

3. Punishment as Medicine

Calvin tries throughout, though, to set God's judicial punishment in the context of his fatherly relationship to believers. When God punishes his children, he always makes his grace and love apparent: "Not only does he mitigate their punishment, but by spicing the punishment with comfort, he even makes it pleasant."[56] God's chastisements are temporary, and this gives

---

[51] "...nihil scilicet nos perpeti, quod non promeriti simus...," Ps. 3:1 (*CO* 31, 52).

[52] Ps. 25:18 (*CO* 31, 261).

[53] Ps. 6:2 (*CO* 31, 73).

[54] "Nam irae et furori tacite opponitur paterna et levis castigatio...," Ps. 6:2 (*CO* 31, 74).

[55] Ps. 3:1 (*CO* 31, 52).

[56] Ps. 39:11 (*CO* 31, 403).

the faithful confidence that after the passage of time the trouble will turn into joy.[57] Calvin responds to the question of why chastisements can then last so long with the example of a physician's treatment. When a patient is somewhat healthier, he explains, the doctor does not all of the sudden end the treatments. If he were to withhold the medicine from the patient at this point and allow him to once more eat anything desired, it would only be injurious to the patient. Likewise, God also continues with our chastisement because we simply do not between one day and the next completely heal from our sins.[58] It is thus for our own good that punishments continue for longer than we would like, and at the same time it is also our fault that it carries on for so long. Chastisements are medicine, and that is how the faithful should also view them.[59] It must be understood, though, Calvin says, that God is not actually mad at us because his chastisements are intended as "medicines," that is, for our healing rather than our punishment.[60] This healing consists in adopting once again a correct attitude before God. In short, God punishes us in order to humble us.[61]

On this point, Calvin addresses the distorted Roman Catholic theology which holds that chastisements from God are a retribution for sin—a view leading to the system of reparations.[62] God does not seek retribution, rebukes Calvin, but only healing. Forgiveness requires that no more punishment will follow. Calvin also emphatically rejects "the fiction of the sophists,"[63] that God may indeed forgive the transgression but the punishment for the transgression still stands.[64] The Bible however provides no grounds at all for this notion. On the contrary God makes known on every page that forgiveness means the termination of all punishment.

Calvin thereby frees divine chastisement from the purely judicial sphere by relating it to God's fatherly care. He writes, "This is the true and also the only comfort: that even though God chastises us, he does not forget his mercy."[65] The reason that God punishes us is not that he doesn't want us

---

[57] Ps. 85:6 (*CO* 31, 787).

[58] Ps. 85:9 (*CO* 31, 788).

[59] Ps. 89:31 (*CO* 31, 823).

[60] Ps. 74:1 (*CO* 31, 692).

[61] "Quia autem hunc finem in poenis sumendis Deo propositum esse scimus, ut nos humiliet…," Ps. 6:3 (*CO* 31, 75).

[62] Ps. 89:31 (*CO* 31, 823).

[63] Ps. 85:3 (*CO* 31, 786). By "sophists" Calvin throughout his writings means the Parisian theologians. See Richard A. Muller, "Scholasticism in Calvin: A Question of Relation and Disjunction," in Muller, *Unaccommodated*, 39-61.

[64] In the *Institutes* III.4.29 Calvin looks into this question more extensively.

[65] Ps. 86:14 (*CO* 31, 797).

anymore, but, quite the opposite, it is because of his concern for our salvation. His fatherly expression of punishment is not a sign of rejection but of care.[66]

The identification between David and every believer, mentioned above, prevents Calvin from offering an explanation for the experience of believers because the problem of suffering seems to be no real problem for him. The reason lies in Calvin's view of God. It is assumed to be impossible that God would do believers any harm, and therefore suffering must be a reaction to our sins and necessarily a reaction that benefits us.[67] Calvin thus has no choice but to attribute adversity to the hand of God because he wants in all situations to prevent adversity from being ascribed to blind chance, that impossible situation in which events bypass God's power and control.

4. The Wrath of God

Discussions of God's wrath in Calvin's thought have a certain ambivalence. On the one hand Calvin calls speaking about God's wrath an inappropriate (*improprie*) way of saying, because God's wrath is always mingled with his grace—a truth especially evident when he withdraws his hand of chastisement and shows his favor again.[68] In God's anger, Calvin says, he does not stop being a father.[69] Moreover, properly speaking, God is never angry with his elect.[70] The Spirit however uses the word "wrath" not because God is truly wrathful but because this is the concept which calls forth from us humans the proper response of guilt. The Spirit thus uses a concept that befits our flesh.[71] Calvin's concept of *accommodatio* is relevant here in that something familiar to human experience is said of God that in actuality is not true of God. Wrath is a manifestation of emotion which implies a change in the state of mind, and this, of course, is not fitting to God's nature.[72] When Calvin speaks about God's discontent, he observes that God cannot fall prey to emotions.[73] Calvin's God is therefore not without feelings, but he has feelings that are not in conflict with his immutability, and the Reformer is careful to avoid any implication that God is subject to change. God is unchangeable, but he "wears a human mask" in order that we may feel the

---

[66] Ps. 79:10 (*CO* 31, 752).
[67] Ps. 143:2 (*CO* 32, 400).
[68] Ps. 6:2 (*CO* 31, 74).
[69] Ps. 74:9 (*CO* 31, 695).
[70] "Etsi enim, proprie loquendo, non irascitur Deus electis suis," Ps. 74:1 (*CO* 31, 692).
[71] "...ad sensum carnis," Ps. 74:1 (*CO* 31, 692).
[72] "Et quanquam nullum iracundiae motum patitur Deus...," Ps. 74:1 (*CO* 31, 692).
[73] "...non quod in eum cadant eiusmodi passiones...," Ps. 104:31 (*CO* 32, 97).

severity of his wrath.[74] The angry God is not the true God. God is by his nature merciful and reconciliatory and his strictness is only happenstance.[75] When God is angry and exercises retribution he speaks differently than he usually does, and Calvin notes that he even takes on a different disposition.[76] God's nature is inclined toward forgiveness, and thereby he attracts us to himself.[77] Even when God is angry, he does not lay aside his fatherly love.[78]

At the same time, though, Calvin speaks about the wrath of God as the cause of all misfortune without any fear of contradiction.[79] The wrath of Christ will come over us, he says, when we decline his friendly invitation. The gospel is like the breath of life, but the grace of Christ is a source of terror when people resist it.[80] The greatest spiritual anguish is experienced when "the sinner senses that he is dealing with the judge whose wrath and strictness encompass, besides eternal death, countless other deaths as well."[81] Calvin's writings here give the impression that he speaks from experience as, for example, when he says that the realization of God's wrath can overwhelm us with an immense terror and can stop our mouths from all praise of God.[82] Humans are not able to fathom how dreadful the wrath of God is.[83] Moreover, it is true to say that we do not know the joy of reconciliation if we have not properly felt the greatness of God's wrath.[84] The wrath of God brings the faithful to admit that they are nothing before God so that they subject themselves to him.[85] Calvin thus writes, "for the holy, nothing is more to be trembled at (*horribile*) than the judgment of God."[86] Furthermore, believers fear the judgments of God because they know that he does not sit in heaven for nothing, but he rules in heaven as a judge.[87] Besides, they know that God treats his children more strictly than he treats the ungodly.[88] It is

---

[74] "...inducere cogitur hominis personam...," Ps. 106:23 (*CO* 32, 125).

[75] "...scriptura naturaliter clementem et propitium praedicans, quasi accidentale esse significat si quando severus ac rigidus est," Ps. 86:14 (*CO* 31, 797).

[76] "...et quasi alienam personam induere," Ps. 18:26 (*CO* 31, 183).

[77] "...sicuti natura ad beneficentium propensus est...," Ps. 107:43 (*CO* 32, 145).

[78] Ps. 89:3 (*CO* 31, 812).

[79] "Quia vero calamitatum omnium causa et origo est ira Dei...," Ps. 85:5 (*CO* 31, 786).

[80] "...haec gratia in terrorem vertetur...," Ps. 45:7 (*CO* 31, 453).

[81] Ps. 32:4 (*CO* 31, 318).

[82] "Quare nihil mirum si ira Dei, quae nos terrore absorbet, laudes eius exstinguere dicatur," Ps. 6:6 (*CO* 31, 76).

[83] "...quam horribilis sit ira Dei," Ps. 90:11 (*CO* 31, 839).

[84] Ps. 32:3 (*CO* 31, 318).

[85] Ps. 90:11 (*CO* 31, 839).

[86] Ps. 88:7 (*CO* 31, 808).

[87] Ps. 10:5 (*CO* 31, 112).

[88] Ps. 90:11 (*CO* 31, 838).

thus also the faithful who are deeply affected by God's wrath, and their concern over it increases in proportion to their devotion.[89]

Among the unfaithful, in contrast, there is no reaction to God's wrath, even when God shakes the heavens and the earth inside out, but the godly tremble as soon as God merely moves his finger.[90] And yet the wrath of God is destined for the wicked and not for God's children,[91] even if the latter are more frightened by the reality of the wrath.[92] Accordingly, Calvin writes that the faithful fear God's wrath despite the fact that such wrath will not strike them, but among the unfaithful it is precisely the other way around. We might say that only believers experience God's wrath since they alone know and fear the Lord. On the unfaithful the wrath of God makes no impression.[93]

The reality of God's wrath is thus threatened by an overly optimistic view of man, and the danger in the notion that man yet has much good in him is that the wrath of God will then be ignored. This notion of human goodness, Calvin charges, has already been instilled by Satan in the papists, the Turks and the Jews.[94] If the radical degeneracy of man is denied in Christian anthropology, Calvin reasons, it leads to a decidedly different theology.

In all of these passages, Calvin's struggle with the biblical concept of divine wrath is perceptible. Following the biblical text Calvin must account for God's wrath and punishment, but he tries nevertheless to view this in light of God's fatherly grace. Herein lies Calvin's criticism of Rome: she makes people scared of God by representing him only as the judge, but the biblical picture of God meanwhile invites us to come to him.[95] Calvin himself repeatedly insists that the wrath of God does not fit well with his nature, yet it is a reality. In order to resolve this matter, he urges believers not to apply these words about God's wrath to themselves but rather to acknowledge that such words are intended in truth for the ungodly.[96]

5. The Function of Penance

When difficulties arise from God's punishment of sins, penance as the confession of sins is the solution. According to Calvin, when there is

---

[89] Ps. 6:7 (*CO* 31, 77).
[90] "...sed Deo vel minimum digitum movente, statim contremiscunt," Ps. 90:11 (*CO* 31, 839).
[91] Ps. 6:3 (*CO* 31, 74).
[92] "...ira Dei quae nos terrore absorbet...," Ps. 6:6 (*CO* 31, 76).
[93] Ps. 90:11 (*CO* 31, 839).
[94] Ps. 32:1 (*CO* 31, 315).
[95] Ps. 145:8 (*CO* 32, 414).
[96] Ps. 2:12 (*CO* 31, 51).

misfortune we ought to seek the blame within ourselves so that we may at once ask God's forgiveness for our guilt and consequently obtain it. We are, after all, only well when we are reconciled with God, and this means that "a multitude of afflictions will remain as long as he does not forgive us our sins."[97] Our self-abasement opens the door for God's mercy—that is, his proper work in helping and saving.[98] Such self-abasement, of course, does not come easily to people. In the case of David we find no easy prayer for forgiveness, but there is clear mention of his sincere remorse and penance. David writes that his guilt torments him. With reference to this, Calvin concludes that reconciliation with God is only possible "when our own conscience wounds, depresses and persecutes us all the while until God reconciles himself with us."[99] To receive forgiveness, not only a confession of one's guilt is required, but also a careful examination of the character of the transgression.[100] Calvin's emphasis on a genuine and precise contrition is certainly a reaction to an externalized penance and a routine forgiveness that follows automatically from the confession.

Proceeding from these observations Calvin looks into "the difficult issue"[101] of the relationship between penance and grace, a matter which must indeed be discussed when David states that a broken heart pleases the Lord. According to Calvin, this text should not be taken as proof that a person's repentance makes God gracious towards the sinner. Repentance is a component of faith, and thus it does not precede faith. He writes, "Faith is not separable from the humility that David is speaking of."[102] The broken heart of which the psalmist speaks has no thought of merit and so it does nothing but prostrate itself before God's grace, pleading for his forgiveness. David does not divorce penance from faith, nor does he subtly bring all sorts of distinctions into his penance,[103] but he merely points out that grace is only obtained by calling upon God's mercy.

Calvin also includes other criticisms of the papal doctrine of penance. The decree of the Lateran Council (1215) that each and every believer must confess his or her sins every year[104] is incorrect, argues Calvin, since no one

---

[97] Ps. 6:2 (*CO* 31, 74).

[98] Ps. 6:3 (*CO* 31, 75).

[99] Ps. 51:5 (*CO* 31, 510).

[100] "...sed rigidum et formidabile examen habere de peccatis nostris...," Ps. 51:5 (*CO* 31, 510).

[101] Ps. 51:19 (*CO* 31, 522).

[102] Ps. 51:19 (*CO* 31, 522).

[103] "...nec fidem disiungit, nec subtiliter numerat singulas poenitentiae partes...," Ps. 51:19 (*CO* 31, 523).

[104] H. Denzinger, *Enchiridion Symbolorum*, 29th ed. (Freiburg: Herder, 1953), 204-5.

is able to determine the true nature and scope of his or her own sins. Not only is it *foolish* to demand this from people, but Calvin also notes that it lacks pastoral concern in asserting that God only forgives those sins which have been confessed. In this way one might fall into despair because of the uncertainty as to whether one has noticed and confessed all sins.[105] For Calvin, the Roman Catholics reveal here both a wrong anthropology and a wrong theology. Rome overestimates man's abilities and underestimates God's gracious nature. Calvin therefore calls the *"facere quod in se est"* an absurd notion because, even if somebody were to do what he could, he would still not comply with God's requirement. Man's sinfulness is far greater than we think, but so is the grace of God.

6. The Terror of God

In his commentary on the Psalms Calvin discusses at some length the various fears which are common to all people, and he directs the reader's attention in particular to the terror of God and his judgment. For Calvin there is scarcely a difference between the terror of God and that which is understood by "the fear of the Lord" in the Bible as for example in Proverbs 1:7. In the introduction to Psalm 22, then, he mentions in quick succession some of the concepts which constitute such terror: anguish (*angustias*), despair (*desperato*), and the abyss of afflictions (*tentationum abysso*).[106] Calvin is clearly speaking here of those who know what it is to tremble before eternal death. This trembling comes over people, he says, when they realize both the extent of their sins and the reality of God's wrath.[107]

Calvin goes to great lengths to rid the faithful from such a terror of God. The holiness and majesty of God, he says, are not described in order to frighten us, there being nothing more beautiful and pleasant in fact than to seek God's countenance, but they are made known to promote the humility by which we may rightly and earnestly honor God.[108] Furthermore, reverence for God and the awareness of divine judgment effectively save us from being ruled by the fire of our lusts.[109] The knowledge that one does not mean anything and is unworthy must also not deter him or her from seeking to please God, Calvin explains, since God invites precisely those who are worthless.[110] Because all people are naturally arrogant, it is necessary that

---

[105] "…desperatione obrui…," Ps. 19:12 (*CO* 31, 205).
[106] Ps. 22: introduction (*CO* 31, 219).
[107] Ps. 6:7 (*CO* 31, 77).
[108] Ps. 96:9 (*CO* 32, 40).
[109] Ps. 86:14 (*CO* 31, 797).
[110] Ps. 115:12 (*CO* 32, 189).

they all be struck with a proper terror of God,[111] yet only in the faithful does it lead to humility. Among the rejected it only produces temporary shame, and soon their arrogance returns. One might mistakenly conclude then that God brings the elect to obedience by means of *fear*, but this is far from an accurate way of describing God's work.[112] There is no divine coercion bringing individuals to humility before God, the Reformer writes, but rather this happens voluntarily because God makes their hearts receptive and willing. By this argumentation Calvin dismisses any notion of an involuntary obedience to God.

Additionally, Calvin addresses how God sometimes instills fear in humanity in order to evoke awe at his works. For example, God may use bad weather.[113] When there is such a severe storm that trees are uprooted and houses are flattened, this is a display of God's power intended to frighten us.[114] Calvin links bad weather to God's wrath even when the biblical text on which he is commenting does not make the connection.[115] The believer needs only to sense the slightest sign of God's wrath, "and he is not merely frightened but completely enveloped in the shadows of death."[116] The faithful, he says, fear nothing more than the judgment of God.[117] God therefore uses this fear to shape us since we are compelled by our terror to seek the grace of God.

One might say as Calvin does that our fear is the beginning of our love.[118] Thus, we must pay close attention to God's judgments so that in our fright we manifest true penance.[119] Divine judgment on the heathen, may therefore fill the faithful with great fear.[120] The sin nature, along with its resulting thoughts and actions, ensures that nothing else remains but a terror of God.[121] This is equally true for the one who is born again since in him as well every deed is mingled with sin.

When God's children have sinned, it is the fear of God which brings them to repentance.[122] As its positive side, this repentance entails personal

---

[111] "...necesse est promiscue omnibus a Deo terrorem incuti...," Ps. 9:21 (*CO* 31, 108).

[112] "...proprie non dicitur eos metu cogere," Ps. 9:21 (*CO* 31, 107).

[113] Ps. 68:32 (*CO* 31, 636).

[114] "...trepidandum est sub istis Dei flagellis," Ps. 104:3 (*CO* 32, 85).

[115] Ps. 148:7 (*CO* 32, 435).

[116] Ps. 6:9 (*CO* 31, 78).

[117] "...quia sanctis nihil magis horribile est Dei iudicio," Ps. 88:7 (*CO* 31, 808).

[118] "...timor amoris initium...," Ps. 119:120 (*CO* 32, 268).

[119] Ps. 119:120 (*CO* 32, 268).

[120] Ps. 69:23 (*CO* 31, 647).

[121] "Certi nihil praeter anxiam trepidationem illis restabit," Ps. 32:1 (*CO* 31, 315).

[122] "...ad resispiscentiam eos sollicitat Dei timor," Ps. 28:3 (*CO* 31, 282).

sanctification. Calvin notes that he who realizes that God judges how he lives will make sure that his conscience is clear.[123] In this way the certainty of judgment stimulates one to Christian living, and God trains us through the realization of his wrath.[124] Yet his intention is not for us to become frightened but that we might pray for forgiveness. Because he wants people to enjoy his forgiveness, it is first necessary that they realize his wrath lest they think they do not need forgiveness. After all, only the realization of God's wrath will bring one to ask forgiveness.[125] The most important thing for Calvin then is not a person's terror of God but rather a terror of God's just judgment.

Regarding all other terror (which does *not* have to do with one's relationship to God) Calvin has much less to say. He mentions that a believer need not have any terror, but he does not say that the believer will necessarily avoid all terror. David, for example, was not made of iron, and various setbacks brought him great anguish.[126] Therefore, when David says in the twenty-third Psalm that he fears no evil, this does not mean that he *knows* no terror, but instead it means that the nearness of the Lord will help him to conquer his fear. God's presence with us, he says, does not mean that we do not know terror any more.[127] Terrors arise from the fact that people burden themselves too much with their lives and give too little thought to the fact that God will protect them.[128] He who remains mindful of God's promises, though, will be able to go fearlessly about his way.[129] Still, because of the weakness of his flesh, a believer will never reach the point where he or she is completely free of fear.[130] These faithful ones, of whom Calvin is thinking, are by no means perfected Christians who withstand every doubt and trouble, but rather they are people who know terrors and difficulties as well as every other person, and this includes Calvin himself.

7. The Second Coming of Christ

In his commentary on the Psalms Calvin does not speak much about "the last things," and it is true in general that the Reformer gives a much less

---

[123] Ps. 10:3 (*CO* 31, 110).
[124] "...irae suae sensu nos Deus exercuerit," Ps. 32:3 (*CO* 31, 318).
[125] Ps. 32:1 (*CO* 31, 314).
[126] "..., neque enim ferreus fuit David quin res adversae eum in miseras anxietates coniicerent," Ps. 4:2 (*CO* 31, 59).
[127] "...neque enim Dei praesentiam requireret timoris vacuitas," Ps. 23:4 (*CO* 31, 240).
[128] Ps. 27:1 (*CO* 31, 271).
[129] "...intrepidi ambulare in viis nostris," Ps. 4:4 (*CO* 31, 61).
[130] Ps. 27:1 (*CO* 31, 271).

prominent role to eschatology in his treatment of this biblical book.[131] This follows Calvin's conviction that the joy of faith must not be limited to the heavenly life after one's death. Though not in its perfection, this joy is to be experienced to a large degree here in this earthly life.[132]

Calvin's view of the present and the future is characterized by the theme that, although the life of the faithful is currently shrouded in darkness, the coming of the Lord will be for believers like the break of morning in which the elect and the outcast will awaken. The faithful will arise from their sluggishness and lethargy (even here Calvin does not neglect to point out the weakness of the faithful!), and they will see both Christ who is the "sun of righteousness" and the fullness of life which is in him. The unfaithful who are now completely blind, however, "will arise from their indifference and start a new life that they have never known before."[133]

With regard to this matter as well, Calvin is not overly concerned with detailed descriptions and explanations so much as the question of what the second coming means for the faithful. Calvin considers it essential, for instance, to keep the second coming in view as part of the Christian faith because there is so much in this life that keeps us from thinking about the future, and meanwhile there are many who openly deny a future life. Calvin describes how the faithful must arm themselves with the word of God which says that after the "night" of this world a new "morning" will come, ushering us into our eternal and true life.[134] Elsewhere, Calvin sympathetically reflects on the reasons why the faithful are not always focused on the future life. Cares and fears can so occupy a person that he or she simply stops thinking about it. Calvin rebukes those who think it absurd that the faithful do not know how to find their way directly to heaven when they end up in difficulty. It is, after all, a fact, according to Calvin, that often there are thick clouds between us and heaven, obscuring our view of glory. Everyone who has had to cope with God's judgments or life's afflictions knows that the spiritual life is not always as it is supposed to be. This does not mean, however, that there is no faith anymore. Rather, notes Calvin, "There is somewhat of a difference between the weakening and the complete disappearance of faith."[135]

---

[131] For a comparison of Calvin's eschatology with that of Roman Catholic theology, see: Raimund Lülsdorf, *Die Zukunft Jesu Christi: Calvins Eschatologie und ihre katholische Sicht* (Paderborn: Bonifatius, 1996).

[132] Ps. 17:15 (*CO* 31, 168).

[133] Ps. 49:15 (*CO* 31, 489).

[134] "...exoriturum subito novum mane, quod faciem verae et aeternae vitae nobis restituet," Ps. 49:15 (*CO* 31, 490).

[135] Ps. 89:47 (*CO* 31, 829).

Calvin's remarks about last things are characterized by an element of solace. For the faithful, despite all the adversity faced in this life, there is a happy ending "because for us a heavenly inheritance awaits."[136] At this time the faithful will finally be freed from all dangers and cares and they will come to rest.[137] Remembrance of the life to come is not an evasion or escape from living here on earth. Instead, he who has tasted God's grace and the heavenly life is able here on earth to endure such chastisements.[138]

The *meditatio futurae vitae* thus serves those living on earth here in the present. One's outlook on the future is necessary in order to endure as a Christian in the current confusion.[139] In this respect the discussion of judgment has a pastoral intention since "we know how immense the cruelty of the faithless is and how easily our faith would expire because of it if the knowledge of God's judgment did not help us to get back up."[140] There is comfort in the certainty that the outcome does not lie in the hands of the mockers but in God's hands.[141]

As it was already observed in the earlier chapter on "God the Creator," Calvin consistently relates the second coming of Christ to God's restoration of order in the world.[142] As he states it in another context as well, God's intervention as ruler entails his restoration of order.[143] In Calvin's thought there is thus no preoccupation with personal salvation to the exclusion of any concern with the restoration of all of reality. Rather, he writes that God will put an end to the great confusion and will restore the original order.[144] Furthermore he instructs his readers to pray for the second coming: "Prayer must be made to God to restore order in the world and to regain his supremacy."[145] While Christ's second coming is apparently taking much time and it may seem as if God is asleep, in actual God is only postponing his judgment until a fitting moment.[146] "We must patiently await the day of the

---

[136] Ps. 49:15 (*CO* 31, 489).

[137] "...sed daturus sit tranquillum statum," Ps. 55:23 (*CO* 31, 545).

[138] "Ita quisquis ad vitae coelestis meditationem erectus erit, nunquam afflictionibus, licet continuis, succumbet," Ps. 30:6 (*CO* 31, 295).

[139] Ps. 37:1 (*CO* 31, 365).

[140] Ps. 21:9 (*CO* 31, 217).

[141] Ps. 9:16 (*CO* 31, 105).

[142] Ps. 49:2 (*CO* 31, 481).

[143] "...qua Deus ubi visum est, res turbatas in ordinem restituit," Ps. 9:18 (*CO* 31, 106).

[144] "...post confusam perturbationem Deus tandem res in legitimum ordinem componet...Rebus autem in verum ordinem restitutis," Ps. 94:15 (*CO* 32, 25-6). See also Ps. 1:5 (*CO* 31, 41): "...statum mundi ad rectam normam componere."

[145] Ps. 82:8 (*CO* 31, 772).

[146] Ps. 73:16 (*CO* 31, 682).

final revelation," Calvin writes, "when Christ will separate the sheep from the goats."[147]

8. Death and Eternal Life

That the faithful remain living even after the death of the body is assured, argues Calvin, through God's divine nature, especially his immutability. "The faithful are born again from imperishable seed and will survive death because God always remains the same."[148] God will thus save our lives even from death itself since, when one dies the Lord will keep him or her from being destroyed.[149] Calvin claims that the grace of God would be grossly underestimated if he were able to take care of us only in life.[150] Appealing to scripture he asserts that "death for God's servants does not mean destruction, and they are not wiped out when they depart from this world, but they keep on existing."[151] Although it seems that our soul disappears when it leaves the body, in fact "it is gathered in God's bosom in such a way that it is faithfully preserved there until the day of resurrection."[152] Consequently it is a serious heresy to believe that everything just ends upon death.[153] On the contrary, God protects us throughout our lives and then finally takes us to be with him.

Therefore the faithful have no need to fear death, Calvin writes, since death is the destruction of the flesh but not of the soul.[154] Indeed he says that the one who truly trusts in God scorns death.[155] This is something which only those who direct themselves toward Christ can do. David already knew that Christ would rise from the dead, and from this he derives the assurance that he himself will also be resurrected. However, we share in this imperishability only if we have become subject to what is perishable. This means that the fullness of life that is in Christ, our head, filters down the members of his body "only in drops."[156] By this Calvin means that through justification the

---

[147] Ps. 1:5 (*CO* 31, 41).

[148] Ps. 102:29 (*CO* 32, 74).

[149] "...ut ab interitu vindicet in ipsa morte...," Ps. 31:5 (*CO* 31, 303).

[150] Ps. 16:11 (*CO* 31, 157).

[151] Ps. 25:13 (*CO* 31, 259).

[152] Ps. 49:16 (*CO* 31, 491).

[153] Ps. 88:11 (*CO* 31, 809).

[154] "...quae licet carnis sit interitus, animas tamen non exstinguit," Ps. 31:5 (*CO* 31, 303).

[155] "Unde sequitur, neminem vere Deo fidere, nisi qui salutem sibi a Deo promissam ita apprehendit ut mortem despiciat," Ps. 16:10 (*CO* 31, 156).

[156] Ps. 16:10 (*CO* 31, 157).

faithful do not also directly begin to participate in the resurrection and the glorification of Christ. The faithful will first have to make their way through death and the grave. In the burial of people God does indeed want something to be evident of the resurrection on the last day,[157] and therefore it is entirely grievous when circumstances prevent the faithful from being buried. Burial is an aid to the living,[158] suggesting something almost sacramental for Calvin, but it is not absolutely required. Faith looks toward immortality even without an actual burial.

The continued existence of the faithful after this life, Calvin asserts, does not mean that there is form of communion amongst the dead where they praise God together.[159] Here the Reformer is not referring to the status of the dead but to communication between those deceased. As far as any communication with God is concerned there is the troubling statement in Psalm 88:6 that God no longer remembers those who are in the grave. Calvin solves this matter by interpreting that here the author has let go of himself, being so overwhelmed by his cares that he does not express himself as thoughtfully as he should.[160] Calvin even speculates that the light of faith may have been momentarily dimmed in the author of the psalm.[161]

When David says that in death there is no consideration of God, this is no proof that the dead are aware of nothing. David here points out in prayer to God that a dead David has no opportunity anymore to praise God among the living. Meanwhile, God's consideration will be considerable if it is God who keeps him alive.[162] Calvin emphatically rejects the interpretation of those who conclude from this verse that the dead no longer feel or realize anything.[163] Death does indeed put an end to our praise of God,[164] but that does not imply that "when the souls of the faithful have discarded their bodies" they no longer have any knowledge of God or any sentiment towards him.[165]

---

[157] "Porro quum in hominem sepultura Deus aliquod testimonium exstare voluerit ultimae resurrectionis," Ps. 79:1 (*CO* 31, 747).

[158] "...media adminicula...," Ps. 79:1 (*CO* 31, 748).

[159] "...non est autem talis inter mortuos communicatio et societas, ut mutuo laudes Dei inter se concinant...," Ps. 115:17 (*CO* 32, 192).

[160] See in connection with this notable solution the chapter "God the Speaking."

[161] "...quia suffocatur erat lumen fidei, quod statim emicuit...," Ps. 88:6 (*CO* 31, 807).

[162] Ps. 6:6 (*CO* 31, 76).

[163] However, as Schreiner notes, "Calvin's opponents in his attacks on the doctrines of soul-sleep and soul-death are hard to identify," *Theater*, 60.

[164] Death is mentioned as the end of one's praise to God also in Calvin's comments upon Ps. 30:10 (*CO* 31, 298) and Ps. 88:11 (*CO* 31, 809).

[165] Ps. 6:6 (*CO* 31, 76).

Calvin describes how even after death we continue existing before him. Those who no longer exist bodily are yet kept safe in his embrace.[166] This formulation begs the question though as to the way in which deceased believers continue existing—a question which is not answered by Calvin's observation that although the faithful are indeed resting in the grave they are nevertheless in hope in heaven.[167] The faithful do descend into the grave, but they do so with the hope that they will also once again emerge. To questions about the mode of existence for the faithful after death, Calvin's commentary on the Psalms gives no answer. He does address, however, another question which is often asked. According to Calvin, there is no wine in heaven nor will other means of living be found there since these are matters which are only required for this earthly life.[168]

Calvin states that there is a clear difference between the faithful and the unfaithful where their eternal existence is concerned.[169] It is noteworthy that, while saying that believers have eternal life with God, in the commentary on the Psalter Calvin says nothing about the continued existence of the unfaithful. Also he says is that there is such a continued existence for the unfaithful, but he offers no details about the end which awaits the godless. There is only a single instance where he speaks of hell as the eternal fire that has been prepared for the outcast, hell being the place into which Christ will throw his enemies.[170] In a different passage, he does not go any further than to say that those who reject Christ will have to deal with the majesty of God.[171] He also dismisses as too harsh the common interpretation he has encountered that, in Christ's victory over his enemies, so much blood will flow that it will form a stream from which Christ will drink.[172] He states that it is sufficient to know that the end will result in the damnation of the unfaithful and that their lives here on earth have been of no consequence.[173] He often points out the contrast between the faithful, who find themselves in an abyss of adversity but also come out of it again, and the unfaithful, who

---

[166] "…in suo sinu et custodia qui videntur secundum carnem exstincti," Ps. 9:13 (*CO* 31, 103).

[167] "…quin potius in sepulchro reconditi, spe tamen in coelo habitant," Ps. 9:18 (*CO* 31, 106).

[168] Ps. 115:16 (*CO* 32, 190).

[169] Ps. 16:11 (*CO* 31, 157).

[170] "…aeternae gehennae quae reprobis parata est…," Ps. 21:9 (*CO* 31, 217).

[171] Ps. 97:1 (*CO* 32, 44).

[172] "Verum hunc nimis dure, meo iudicio, exponunt multi interpretes…," Ps. 110:7 (*CO* 32, 166).

[173] "…quum eorum vita nihil sit," Ps. 73:16 (*CO* 31, 683).

ultimately find themselves in eternal ruin.[174] The blame for their destruction lies within themselves, Calvin declares, since God's vengeance is a response to their depravity.[175] God hates transgressions, and therefore he casts out those who commit them.[176] He who does not voluntarily honor God now will in the end be forced by God to humble himself before God.[177] When God approaches us in a friendly manner and we do not respect him or receive him in sincerity, destruction awaits us.

Calvin sets forth the cities of Jerusalem and Nazareth as illustrations of God's judgment. The desolate state in which these cities find themselves in Calvin's time is "a showcase of God's wrath."[178] These cities prove that it is not sufficient to have God in one's midst if one does not also receive him in faith. Christ grew up in Nazareth, and he lived and preached in Jerusalem, yet both cities were nevertheless ruined.

Calvin thus devotes relatively little attention to the end which awaits the godless. His primary concern is not the question of how the wicked perish but rather how the faithful persist when it seems as though God does not concern himself with the things which are done to his children.[179] This is precisely why he points out that it is God's duty to reject the godless and not our duty.[180]

It is however the duty of the faithful to warn the godless. Calvin interprets Psalm 21:9 ("Your hand will find all your enemies...") as a prophecy of Christ's final judgment. The purpose in speaking so clearly about the horror of the judgment is to wake up those people who mock God's judgments. Since Christ is the one who carries out the judgment, believers themselves should not take up the sword, but they should instead patiently bear their cross.[181] Though it is Christ who will judge and his judgment is terrifying, Calvin reminds his readers that this truth is not in opposition with Bible passages which say that Jesus is gentle. A shepherd is, after all, kind to his flock, but he takes energetic action against both wolves and thieves.[182]

---

[174] Ps. 55:24 (*CO* 31, 546).

[175] Ps. 37:20 (*CO* 31, 376).

[176] "...cuius officium est improbos omnes perdere, quia odio habet omne scelus," Ps. 5:5 (*CO* 31, 68).

[177] Ps. 66:3 (*CO* 31, 611).

[178] Ps. 78:59 (*CO* 31, 741).

[179] Ps. 21:9 (*CO* 31, 217).

[180] Ps. 5:5 (*CO* 31, 68).

[181] Ps. 21:9 (*CO* 31, 217).

[182] Ps. 110:7 (*CO* 32, 166).

9. Conclusion

While John Calvin consistently depicts God in his Psalms commentary as a heavenly Father who is close at hand to care for us and save us, his efforts to console his readers present him with some challenges when he must interpret passages in the Psalter about God's wrath and judgment. These difficulties reveal some ambivalence in speaking about God's wrath, which is on the one hand an undeniable reality while on the other hand it is something that does not actually fit in with God. Calvin's treatment of the terror of God well illustrates this ambivalence. Calvin also connects God's role as judge with his eschatological action, which is a restoration of the original order. Even if Calvin speaks very little on the topic of last things in this commentary, his interpretation of Psalm 150:6, the concluding verse in the Psalter, does end on the note of eschatology. Together with the Jews we praise God here on earth, he writes, "…until we are gathered in the heavenly kingdom where together with the elect angels we will sing an eternal hallelujah."[183]

---

[183] Ps. 150:6 (*CO* 32, 442).

8

God the Hidden

God's *being God* implies amongst other things that his nature as well as his comings and goings are in part hidden. This hiddenness, Calvin says, can bring the believer to the point of desperation so that doubts about God's care or even an intense terror of God can, as fierce temptations, torment a person, afflicting his or her faith.

In past Calvin scholarship, hardly any attention has been paid to what Calvin says about the *hiddenness* of God.[1] A possible reason for this may be that a God who is hidden and intentionally keeps himself hidden does not fit in with standard interpretations of Calvin's theology. This tendency to ignore the explicit statements about divine hiddenness in favor of more "comfortable" theological language is evident in the popular English translation of Calvin's commentary on the Psalms which was originally published in 1845 by the Calvin Translation Society. Whenever this concept of hiddenness is mentioned in the text, James Anderson generally translates the passage as if Calvin is speaking about the mere *semblance* of God's hiddenness. Meanwhile Calvin himself does not say this hiddenness only "seems" to be the case, but he speaks precisely about the *reality* of God's hiddenness.[2] It is thus apparent that the supposed distinction on this topic between Calvin and Luther (all scholars acknowledging the latter alone to have spoken more about God's hiddenness) does not really exist despite the widespread assertion of this contrast in the literature.[3] Calvin's commentary

---

[1] A notable exception is the study by Brian Gerrish, "'To the Unknown God': Luther and Calvin on the Hiddenness of God," in *The Old Protestantism and the New: Essays on the Reformation Heritage* (Chicago: University of Chicago Press, 1982), 131-49.

[2] For example, consider Anderson's rendering of "...qui utcunque opem suam ad tempus occultet..." from Ps. 135:13 (*CO* 32, 361) as "...though God may seem to have overlooked and deserted us...." in *Commentary on the Book of Psalms by John Calvin*, Vol. V, trans. James Anderson (Edinburgh, 1845), 178. Cf.: "...although God may seem to dissemble for a time...," Vol. V, 124, as translation of "quamvis ad tempus dissimulet Deus...," Ps. 129:3 (*CO* 32, 331).

[3] Gerrish writes, "Surprisingly, however, there is no such body of literature on what Calvin thought about God's hiddenness." See "To the Unknown God," 141.

on the Psalms makes it clear in any case that on this point he is Luther's student, regardless of the differences in emphases which lie between them or the relative brevity of the Genevan Reformer on this matter.

A closer look at the topic in his writings shows that Calvin speaks about the hiddenness of God in three ways. First of all, God is hidden in part because we as human beings simply cannot know God exhaustively. Here the hiddenness is connected with our *humanity*. Secondly, we also obscure God through our sin, creating a kind of smoke screen between him and ourselves. Here the hiddenness is due to our *being sinners*. Lastly, and most importantly, God's hiddenness is the result when God deliberately conceals himself from us. Here hiddenness originates in God's *being God*. It is this last explanation for God's hiddenness that creates the greatest difficulty, and therefore it also receives the greater part of Calvin's attention. For each of these three "types" of hiddenness Calvin discusses the causes and then shows a way to deal with the hiddenness of God. Each type has its own cause and requires its own approach.

Because the first two types of hiddenness which have to do with being human and being sinners are very closely related, being distinguished but not separated from one another in Calvin's thought, they are here discussed together as well. Therefore, this chapter begins with an appraisal of such a *passive* hiddenness of God whereby God is hidden to sinful humanity, and following this we will turn to consider his *active* hiddenness—the third type.

1. God's Passive Hiddenness

In the paragraph above on Calvin's anthropology we noted that man as a created being is limited in his knowledge and insight. This limitation is particularly evident when it comes to the assessment of God's actions. Much of God's work and his nature remains hidden to humans because it simply is not visible to them.[4] Thus Psalm 9:18 speaks of the hidden work of God's hand which can invisibly oppose the enemies of God's people. This hiddenness is not attributed to sin nor to any deliberate concealment by God, but it is simply explained by the fact that people cannot perceive God's actions. The believer merely knows that God's hand is involved, and that is enough.[5]

---

[4] "Si de essentia eius agitur, habitat certe lucem inaccessam," Ps. 104:1 (*CO* 32, 85).
[5] Ps. 9:18 (*CO* 31, 106).

Calvin expresses this fact quite memorably in his interpretation of Psalm 39:11 where God is compared to a moth. He remarks that this simile seems rather absurd at first because of the vast disparity between such a tiny little bug and the infinite majesty of God. Yet, according to Calvin, the psalmist's is a very fitting comparison. Just as a moth eats away at garments until the clothing is ruined without anyone having noticed, God's curse likewise takes its course with the godless although God's work remains invisible.[6] The hiddenness described here clearly has to do with our humanity since God's work is evident, but we do not see it.

This deficient understanding can however lead to mistaken or unfounded conclusions. For example, it may seem to us as though God were deaf, clearly an inaccurate impression which only arises because people judge situations from their limited perspective while they are blind to God's ways. As Calvin famously points out, God adapts himself to people, but people in dealing with God do not adapt to him. If our conclusions are merely based on considerations of the "flesh," Calvin suggests, we lose the proper perspective on God. Fleshly reasoning assumes that since God does not answer our petitions directly he is deaf to our prayers.[7] Another typically human argument explains misfortune as God's being far away (as in Psalm 6:4), and if God's help is not immediate, it assumes that he must have forgotten us (as in Psalm 13:2). It is also this fleshly reasoning which concludes during personal hardship that God makes no distinction between righteous and unfaithful people.[8] The mistake common to such examples of erroneous thought is measuring God's works by human norms, and thus people quickly lose heart or even become despondent when they call on him and he does not directly answer through immediate intervention. These people who do not understand God or his ways deduce from this that he is not listening to them, but they judge by earthly criteria and so jump to false conclusions.[9]

According to Calvin, these experiences and the false conclusions we draw from them greatly affect our interaction with God. We see this specifically in David's prayer when he asks God to let his face shine on him. One can only offer up such a prayer if experiences are going to determine your view of God. In the commentary over this psalm, Calvin writes:

---

[6] "…occulta eius maledictione…," Ps. 39:11 (*CO* 31, 403).

[7] "…ex sensu carnis dicit propheta eum esse surdum ad preces," Ps. 80:5 (*CO* 31, 755).

[8] Ps. 125:4 (*CO* 32, 315): "Et certe quia in afflictionum tenebris non perspicitur Dei auxilium, quin potius videtur coram Deo nullum esse iustorum et impiorum discrimen."

[9] Ps. 9:13 (*CO* 31, 103).

As we have previously said and will also observe later on in other places, this way of speaking comes from a human feeling which commonly occurs: people reckon that God is not looking after them when he does not make it very obvious that he in fact does take care of them. After all, adversities obscure God's countenance just as clouds obscure the brightness of the sun. This is why David asks God to help him immediately that God may thus make it evident that David has been reconciled with him and that he is favorably inclined toward David. In the darkness of adversity this is not so easily recognizable. There are two ways one could speak of God's countenance shining on us: either he opens his eyes in order to proceed in giving us care or he lets us see his favor. Yet these two are closely connected with each other. Yes, the one even depends on the other. However, in the first way of speaking we ascribe to God a mutability that actually does not suit him. The second way denotes that it is our eyes and not God's eyes which are closed and worn-out anytime it seems as if he has no concern for our misery.[10]

Another possible cause for the impression that God has concealed himself is our forgetfulness. It was this way in which the people of Israel came to doubt God's presence and care while in the desert, charging that God had thus far always kept himself hidden. The people jumped to the conclusion of God's hiddenness because they had forgotten his revelation through the liberation from Egypt, and therefore Calvin calls this lapse of memory an accusation against God.[11]

We can also deceive ourselves into thinking that God is absence by so exaggerating our cares and troubles that he, practically speaking, just disappears into the background. To clarify what he means Calvin uses the metaphor of making a mountain out of a molehill.

As soon as even just a single affliction befalls us, we instantly make a mountain out of a molehill. Yes, we suddenly fabricate heights so steep that we start thinking God's hand can no longer reach us.[12]

Although we have thus far described these two kinds as quite different phenomena, there is nevertheless a clear connection between the case when

---

[10] Ps. 31:16 (*CO* 31, 308).

[11] "...ubi dubitant de eius praesentia ac si ante fuisset absconditas, perversa oblivio crimen auget," Ps. 95:9 (*CO* 32, 34).

[12] Ps. 71:19 (*CO* 31, 661).

God is hidden to us and when God actively conceals himself. Indeed Calvin himself observes in his commentary on Psalm 43:2 that adversities function like clouds which obscure the face of God to us, but a little bit further on he states that all misfortunes occur when God withdraws the signs of his fatherly love from us, and this is the same things as his hiding his countenance from us.[13] The effect of misfortune is that *God is hidden to us*, but the cause of misfortune is that *God hides himself*. This brings us to the remaining kind of hiddenness—the active hiddenness of God.

2. God's Active Hiddenness

The other variety of God's hiddenness neither arises from our being human nor from our being sinners, but it results from the will of God, who sometimes rather actively hides himself. It is well known that Luther, especially during his early period through 1525, spoke much about this hiddenness of God.[14] However, it is also a theme in Calvin's theological writings even if it has hardly been noticed in Calvin research. Given Calvin's style of writing, this topic is not as prominent as in Luther's early works, but this does not make it any less present.

There are multiple locations where Calvin describes the reality of God's hiddenness. He says that God can hide his countenance from us until he appears to be our enemy.[15] In several instances in the Psalm commentary Calvin uses the image of "clouds behind which God's countenance goes into hiding." For example, he explains one passage which refers to the light of God's countenance by saying that "in a certain sense he 'clouds over' his face when he lets misery befall us."[16] Therefore misfortune is quite clearly both the cause and the effect when God hides his face from us. God also covers up his countenance with clouds when he deprives us of delight in his word. According to Calvin it often happens that God conceals himself from us in this way when the word is no longer to our liking.[17] Other times God delays the fulfillment of his promises so that it seems as if those who are his

---

[13] Ps. 43:2 (*CO* 31, 434).

[14] See Helmut Bandt, *Luthers Lehre vom verborgenen Gott* (Berlin: Evangelische Verlagsanstalt, 1958). Also cf. Althaus, *Theologie*, 238-48.

[15] "...quamvis ad tempus faciem suam occultet Deus, imo speciem alienationis praebeat...," Ps. 80:15 (*CO* 31, 757).

[16] Ps. 44:4 (*CO* 31, 438).

[17] "Saepe autem contingit ipsis quoque obnubilari in hac parte Dei faciem, dum genuino verbi sui gustu eos privat," Ps. 119:135 (*CO* 32, 276).

are forced to wander around for a time.[18] The mention of "wandering around" reminds one of sheep, one of Calvin's favorite metaphors for believers. Both sheep that are temporarily without their shepherd and sheep that are destined for the slaughterhouse due to various hostilities are illustrations of believers who proceed without the light of God's face.[19] However, just as real as God's hiddenness during such "wandering" is his—however hidden—protection against hostilities.

In these situations when God is hidden, it seems as if God makes no distinction between the faithful and unbelievers but instead treats everyone the same. Calvin challenges this notion, though, by asserting that God hides his righteousness from our view. When he does not hurry directly to our aid, the Reformer writes, a layer of clouds comes between him and us, between God's care and our experience of his care,

> ...and these clouds keep out the light of God's fairness, and by this, in a sense, judgment and justice are torn from each other.[20]

There will come a day, however, when God will eliminate this hiddenness, when his fairness and righteousness will once again be clearly visible and everything will be restored to its proper order.[21] It is therefore important to keep sight of this outcome since in the end it will be apparent that, although God allows both the good and the bad to face similar perils for a time, the outcome for each group is different.[22] Calvin uses Latin terms such as *promiscue (mixed)* and *confuse (confusing)* to indicate how God's actions may appear to us while at the same time implying that God himself will enable us see that the reality is different. God's hiddenness and disorder are linked together in Calvin's thought just as God's presence and order are related.

This last connection may also be the reason why Calvin has so much difficulty with the reality of God's hiddenness. This is not surprising with a man who is so attached to order and who fears chaos so much. For Calvin the contrast of order and disorder hangs together with the difference between

---

[18] Ps. 13:3 (*CO* 31, 133).

[19] "...fideles...oves sint mactationi destinatae, prope tamen esse eorum salutem, quae occulta Dei custodia protegitur...," Ps. 119:155 (*CO* 32, 284).

[20] Ps. 94:15 (*CO* 32, 26).

[21] "Rebus autem in verum ordinem restituis...," Ps. 94:15 (*CO* 32, 26).

[22] "Nam quum promiscue in discrimen coniiciat bonos et malos, diverso exitu tandem probat se non confuse miscere paleam tritico, quia suos separatim colligit," Ps. 17:7 (*CO* 31, 162).

God's presence and his hiddenness. When God conceals himself this world immediately finds itself in a bewildering darkness, but order is restored as soon as he lets his countenance be seen once more.[23] Calvin hides his difficulty with the hiddenness of God by pointing out that the hidden God is not the real God. At Psalm 90:16 Calvin observes that when God withdraws himself from the congregation he takes on a role foreign to his nature and presents himself differently than he actually is since his actual work is undoubtedly the protection of the church.[24] In order to give expression to those actions which are uncharacteristic of God, Calvin makes repeated use of the qualification "for a while" (*ad tempus*).[25] God hides himself only temporarily since his office is of one who is present with help and protection.

God can also conceal himself in the ordinary things of life, which are the means he uses in providence. Calvin points this out in discussing Psalm 98:1, which says that the right hand of God has brought the people to victory. The Reformer here contrasts God's "hand" with God's ordinary means in helping his people. Ordinary means detract nothing from God's might, he states, yet they do slightly conceal it. Thus Calvin speaks of the shrouds in which God's might is wrapped and consequently hidden. Nevertheless, sometimes God acts personally in an expressly recognizable way, but generally he hides his might in the means that he uses.[26] Calvin expresses a similar idea when he turns to Psalm 94:16. Here as well he says that most of the time God's help comes by way of other people, unfortunately resulting in recipients who are often slow to notice that it is God's grace which had provided the help.[27]

Elsewhere, Calvin points out that God can also hide himself from his people as an expression of his wrath. He compares God to a king who is angry with his people and therefore secludes himself in a secret place.[28] It may be that

---

[23] "Nam hic primum tacita comparatio est inter statum bene ordinatum, ubi Deus suo iudicio restituet quae nunc confusa sunt, et turbulentam caliginem, quae tacente Deo faciemque suam occultante mundum occupat," Ps. 18:15 (*CO* 31, 167).

[24] "Quia Deus ecclesiam suam deserens, quodammodo *alienam personam* induit, scite Moses *proprium eius opus* nominat protectionis gratiam...," Ps. 90:16 (*CO* 31, 840). Italics added.

[25] E.g.: "ad tempus dissimulet," Ps. 1:5 (*CO* 31, 41); "ad tempus discurrem," Ps. 13:3 (*CO* 31, 133); "ad tempus faciem subducat," Ps. 18:15 (*CO* 31, 167); "ad tempus subtrahat," Ps. 25:6 (*CO* 31, 252); "ad tempus occultet," Ps. 80:15 (*CO* 31, 757); "ad tempus dissimulat," Ps. 110:5 (*CO* 32, 165); "ad tempus dissimulet," Ps. 129:3 (*CO* 32, 331); and "ad tempus occultet," Ps. 135:13 (*CO* 32, 361).

[26] Ps. 98:1 (*CO* 32, 48).

[27] Ps. 94:16 (*CO* 32, 27).

[28] Ps. 18:11 (*CO* 31, 176).

the wrath of God mentioned here not only affects his people but the whole world. Accordingly, when God sees that piety in the world is waning, he retracts his hand or prevents us from noticing it anymore.[29] Here it is apparent that it is God's being and office to be gracious due, for to Calvin his countenance is equivalent to his grace. See, for example, his comments on Psalm 74:9, a psalm which Calvin assumes to have originated during the exile in Babylon. The author acknowledges that the exile is a just punishment for the sins of the people, but at the same time he laments the fact that this punishment lasts so long. The people find themselves in great darkness since God has hidden his countenance and is withholding every sign of his grace from them. The way in which Calvin here connects God's countenance being hidden with punishment and wrath makes it clear that God's countenance is an expression of his grace.[30] God is gracious by his very nature. Therefore, if he wants to show his wrath, he must do this by temporarily hiding himself.

At the same time, however, God's punishment is an expression of his love and care since God's actions in punishment mean that he carries his people in his heart and is still involved with them. What is much more shocking is when God goes completely silent:

> When God hides himself and keeps quiet to the point where he does not even administer the medicine of punishment anymore, that is the worst sort of punishment that could hit us, and it is the sign of a dreadfully hopeless state of affairs. After all, for as long as he rebukes us, brings us before his seat of justice, and frightens us by his judgment, he is thereby at the same time inviting us to penance. However, when he sees that all his effort is in vain and his reprimands are of no help, then by remaining silent he declares that he has given up his care for our well-being.[31]

According to Calvin, therefore, God's hiddenness can have the result that God in effect lets go of us and hands us over to the guidance of Satan.

3. The Hiddenness of Man

The fact that God hides himself to people does not entail that we are similarly hidden to him, yet this is sometimes the experience of believers. For

---

[29] Ps. 99:8 (*CO* 32, 53).

[30] "Atqui potius queruntur fideles ablata sibi esse signa gratiae, quod Deus faciem suam quodammodo absconderit," Ps. 74:9 (*CO* 31, 695).

[31] Ps. 81:14 (*CO* 31, 764-765).

example, David laments in Psalm 10:1 that God is so far away and that he seems to have no regard for the needs of his people. Is God so far away that he cannot see our need? Calvin offers a solution to this difficulty by interpreting David's lament in light of the anthropomorphic speech about God in the Bible.[32] When the psalmist complains that God is far away and thus cannot have any eye for our troubles, Calvin asserts that we are dealing with a non literal way of speaking about God since he is always there and nothing is hidden to him. God allows us merely to speak with him as we would speak with each other. We must realize though that, despite this way of speaking, we may not draw any conclusions about the nature of God. We speak based upon what we experiences in some situation, and then it may seem as if God is far away. Calvin therefore does not deny the hiddenness of God, nor does he interpret the hiddenness as merely an appearance, but he rejects the extrapolation whereby we are also hidden to God. It would oppose God's nature for something to be hidden from him. Moreover, Calvin shrewdly observes, David himself was aware that his words did not match the facts

> ...because, although he laments the fact that God is far away, David is nonetheless quite sure that God is close at hand since otherwise he would surely not call upon him.[33]

This duality of that which is experienced and that which is believed is also found in Psalm 59:5, where David calls on God to look upon his plight. Here Calvin asserts that "The sensation of the flesh mixes itself with the doctrine of faith."[34] When faced with all sorts of injustices, believers experience it as if God were holding his eyes closed. However, David's acknowledgement in these words that God can see clarifies the knowledge of faith that nothing is hidden to God.[35]

Calvin always warns against judging the heavenly situation through our earthly experiences.[36] In other words, he rejects a theology "from below" which seeks to understand God from the viewpoint of experience or history.

---

[32] "Improprie tamen et per anthropopathiam Deum in loco remoto stare dicit...," Ps. 10:1 (*CO* 31, 108).

[33] Ps. 10:1 (*CO* 31, 108).

[34] "Porro quum dicit vide, sensum carnis permiscet doctrinae fidei...," Ps. 59:5 (*CO* 31, 566).

[35] "...fide agnoscit nihil eius providentiae esse absconditum," Ps. 59:5 (*CO* 31, 566).

[36] "...verbi Dei constantiam ex statu terreno minime aestimandam esse, quia subinde fluctuat, et instar umbrae effluit...," Ps. 119:89 (*CO* 32, 253).

Calvin states that the *coelesti prudentia* is required in order to avoid the *carnis sensus*.[37] The danger of making one's experience the norm is exposed when David shouts out that God lives after the LORD gave him victory. Calvin thinks it wise not to draw from these words of David any conclusions about God's nature but only sees this pronouncement as an utterance revealing the way in which David experienced God. After all, he reasons, the same often happens with us: we say God lives when he reveals his might to us very clearly, but "as soon as he conceals his might from us, we lose not only the feeling that he lives but also the knowledge thereof."[38]

4. *Theologia Crucis*

Based upon what he says about the hiddenness of God as well as his description of the Christian life, it is clear that Calvin holds to a *theologia crucis*. It is characteristic of the theology of the cross that reality is manifested in its opposite just as the victory of Christ over death shrouded itself in the crucifixion. According to this logic, God hides the purpose of his actions by doing the opposite of what he has in mind. For example, God can deprive us of all his gifts in order thereby to give us back our trust in him. God gives by taking away. Calvin describes this as

> …quite definitely a wonderful and unbelievable (*incredibilis*) way of working, that by hiding his countenance and covering us in darkness, as it were, God illuminates the eyes of his servant, eyes that saw completely nothing when there was bright light.[39]

Since we are often blind to God precisely when his countenance shines friendly upon us, we should not be surprised that God sometimes hides his countenance to the end that we should start noticing him again.

Closely related to this *theologia crucis* is the distinction between "*coram Deo*" and "*coram mundo*." During a time in which God hides his help and delays his rescue the world may take the faithful to be poor and miserable, and by earthly measures they indeed are. However, from God's viewpoint they are enormously fortunate because in his fatherly grace they have received the greatest possible blessing. Likewise, tearful eyes can provide a

---

[37]   Ps. 94:12 (*CO* 32, 23).
[38]   "…evanescit etiam ex animis sensus ac notitia vitae eius," Ps. 18:47 (*CO* 31, 192).
[39]   Ps. 30:8 (*CO* 31, 297).

better view of God's judgments, as Calvin gleans from Psalm 9:10. When God becomes silent in times of stress,[40] it brings about great afflictions in his people, but God is delaying his help in order to train his people

> ...with tears and supplications. In this way he ignites a light so that the people get a better view of his judgments.[41]

The intent of this hidden action is God's purpose to make it clear to his children without others noticing that he is helping them. According to Calvin it is sometimes even the case that God hides himself during his saving action, pretending to be weak while he is all the while at work with a powerful hand.[42]

There is another apparent contradiction in Psalm 96. Calvin describes it as very noteworthy that the author elaborately and unperturbedly calls upon the entire world to sing praises to the LORD in a time when Israel finds herself in a great struggle with the hordes of idols among her contemporaries. The peoples in Asia, Europe and Africa may worship Jupiter, but the author shouts out that Israel's God is superior to all gods, declaring it while this God has stuck himself in Judea which is nothing but a dark little corner.[43]

When Calvin speaks of the hiddenness of God, he thus always immediately follows it with an explanation. God never simply does something for no particular reason; all his actions serve some purpose. By appending an explanation Calvin correlates God and man. He describes how God can hide himself in order to teach us something, as, for instance, he might hide himself in wrath in order to bring us to repentance. Thus, as the Reformer interprets the significance of God being hidden, he always tries to identify how God's goodness shines through. Yet, sometimes God hides himself and his grace because, if he were always to intervene directly, we would not know any misfortune, and then we would cling too dearly to this life.[44]

As he comments through the text of Psalm 9, Calvin brings another possible reason for God's silence to the fore. While it can sometimes seem as

---

[40] "...censerie coram mundo pauperus et miseros...silente Deo...," Ps. 9:10 (*CO* 31, 100).

[41] Ps. 9:10 (*CO* 31, 100).

[42] "Saepe enim occulte et sub specie infirmitatis Deus fideles suos liberat, ut sentiant quidem ipsi se manu eius fuisse ereptus, hoc autem aliis non sit perinde cognitum...," Ps. 118:15 (*CO* 32, 206).

[43] "Verus enim Deus in Iudaea, quasi in obscuro recessu, latebat," Ps. 96:4 (*CO* 32, 38).

[44] Ps. 9:13 (*CO* 31, 103).

if God is not concerned by our oppression, Calvin suggests that God wants to lead us to pray for these things. In other words, he only wants to put his hand into action after we've asked him for it. From our perspective, though, it seems like he only remembers us when we pray to him.[45]

Another reason for his hiddenness is God's desire to test whether we will remain obedient to him even when he allows his people to be persecuted and his name to be blasphemed. To put our obedience to the test he conceals his judicial intervention, and it certainly goes beyond our understanding.[46] In addressing Psalm 116:7, Calvin again brings the idea of testing under consideration since the psalmist calls on himself to trust in God once again. Calvin adds that there would remain little room for either faith or the power of the promise if believers were only to rest in God during times when he clearly reveals himself as savior. In contrast, it is an essential evidence of faith that one remains confident in God's grace even when God hides his favor.[47] Encouraging humility can be God's design in this hiddenness. He may therefore hide his help from us for a while until he sees that we have sufficiently humbled ourselves before him. At that moment, though, he will reveal his help plainly.[48]

Therefore, nowhere do we find Calvin ending the discussion with only a reaffirmation of God's mystery since an explanation for his hiddenness is always offered. These explanations by Calvin have a strongly apologetic character because he is obviously concerned to defend God's *being God*.

The active hiddenness of God can also have a completely different effect: not in God hiding himself, but in him hiding the faithful. In connection with Psalm 83:3 Calvin emphatically rejects the interpretation of those who suppose that here "God's hidden" means that we cannot see or experience God's care, much as it is described in Colossians 3:3. Calvin considers this interpretation forced and contrary to the verse's context and meaning in the psalm. Instead, this text affirms that God hides us in the shadow of his wings.[49] He does not withdraw himself from our eyes, but rather he withdraws us from the eyes of the enemy. Calvin underscores this reality at Psalm 91:1, where he speaks quite pleonastically about "the hidden who are

---

[45] Ps. 9:18 (*CO* 31, 106).

[46] "...quia Deus, ut obsequium nostrum probet, arcana sua iudicia longe supra captum attolit," Ps. 92:6 (*CO* 32, 12).

[47] Ps. 116:7 (*CO* 32, 194).

[48] "...cruce et miseriis suos humiliat Deus...ad tempus faciem ab illis suam subducat...," Ps. 18:15 (*CO* 31, 167).

[49] Ps. 83:3 (*CO* 31, 774).

hidden under God's protection."[50] Although Calvin's use of pleonasm does not seem consistent with his well-known aspiration for *brevitas et perspicuitas*, his word choice here accentuates his pastoral intention in speaking of God's hiddenness.

5. Pastoral Care and Hiddenness

Calvin, of course, has great pastoral interests in the implications of God's hiddenness. He realizes that nothing is more difficult than to honor God at the moment in which he hides himself from us.[51] As one example, in his interpretation of Psalm 73:10-11, Calvin devotes considerable attention to the afflictions which one may suffer when God does not let himself be seen for a time. Believers may even struggle with the question whether God is indeed there. While it is true that in their questioning and mourning they do not go as far as unbelievers, there is still quite a remarkable continuity:

> David here tells us that even the faithful start faltering. Not that they are bursting into a similar blasphemy, but nevertheless they indeed cannot immediately contain themselves when it looks as if God has stopped performing his duty.[52]

In light of these realities, Calvin has a ready answer for those who protest God's ways when he emphasizes that God nevertheless has a positive result in mind when he hides himself, a pattern which we could label "the pedagogic character of God's hiddenness." Calvin also responds to the trials which accompany God's hiddenness by reminding his readers of the providence of God. It is God's office to protect and care for his own, and his being God implies that he will never relinquish this office. God is never *otiosus*, and therefore even when he hides himself he cannot stop exercising his providence. According to Calvin this has the consequence that

> ...we can be sure that, although he does not directly come to the aid of those who are oppressed, he nonetheless never gives up his care for them. And we need to be particularly clear that when he hides himself,

---

[50] "...eos qui absconditi latent sub Dei custodia...," Ps. 91:1 (*CO* 32, 1).

[51] "Quia autem nihil magis difficile est quam tribuere Deo hunc honorem, ut ab eo pendeamus quum se procul occultat, vel auxilium suum differt," Ps. 27:14 (*CO* 31, 279-80).

[52] Ps. 73:10-11 (*CO* 31, 680).

he does not forsake his duties but is testing their patience, and so we can calmly wait for the good outcome.[53]

Just how much God's being God helps us through the temporary hiddenness of God is apparent in Psalm 25:6 where David cries out for God to remember him. On this text Calvin remarks that God is merciful by nature, and therefore though he may temporarily hide himself by taking his hand from us he still cannot betray himself. He simply cannot empty himself of his mercy. It is so fixed, according to Calvin, that God could no sooner divorce himself from his merciful attachments than from the very eternity of his being.[54] Only when people know this God and his providence are they able "to bear their cross patiently when God hides himself for a time while enemies are ranting and rampaging. After all, God knows when the time is right and the precise moment for vengeance has arrived."[55]

6. Faith and Hiddenness

Calvin suggests that the hiddenness of God corresponds to the distance between heaven and earth. There is nothing short of a chasm between heaven and earth, between darkness and light, between experience and fact, and between what is seen and what is real. The only means of bridging this chasm is to climb up into heaven (despite the distance the believer experiences between God and himself) to see from there the actual state of affairs. In this matter Calvin speaks of "penetrating into heaven."[56]

Calvin says that only a faith that does not let itself be determined by experience but instead by the knowledge of God knows how to bridge the chasm. Faith is able to break through the clouds and to see God's hidden righteousness.[57] With the eyes of faith one can reach through to God's grace, even if it is hidden,[58] since faith enables one to overcome the judgment of the flesh.[59] Though there are clouds which hide God from us, faith functions as

---

[53] Ps. 9:10 (*CO* 31, 100). See also Ps. 12:8 (*CO* 31, 131): "Quod si occulta erit Dei custodia, patienter exspectent fideles donec exsurgat Deus."

[54] Ps. 25:6 (*CO* 31, 253).

[55] Ps. 110:5 (*CO* 32, 165).

[56] "...penetrare in coelum...," Ps. 80:5 (*CO* 31, 755).

[57] "Fide quidem in rebus confusis iustitiam Dei licet absconditum, apprehendere nos decet...," Ps. 94:15 (*CO* 32, 26).

[58] "Simul, tamen, praeeunte fidei luce usque ad Dei gratiam (quamvis esset abscondita) mentis oculis penetravit," Ps. 13:2 (*CO* 31, 132).

[59] "...fide se altius attoli, ut praeter carnis iudicium," Ps. 13:2 (*CO* 31, 132).

the wings with which one can ascend above the clouds until we arrive at a place of rest. At this height God's countenance becomes visible once more and one can now see how things actually fit together.[60] It may indeed be difficult to trust in God when he keeps himself hidden, but it is possible, and it is also the only way to get through these afflictions.

> Nothing is more difficult in moments when God holds himself hidden and delays his help than to still give him the honor that we trust in him. For this reason David exhorts himself to gather his strength as if to say that, when fear creeps up on you, when affliction opposes your faith, when the sensations of the flesh throw you this way and that way, then be sure that you do not succumb to it but work through it with untiring strength of spirit.[61]

Because one is always influenced by experiences and the "sensations of the flesh," faith continually finds itself in tension. On the one hand faith knows how to climb up so that it is sure of God's presence, but on the other hand there are afflictions arising from experiences by which the "fleshly" judgment determines whether God is there or not.[62] Faith lives with the paradox of experience and fact, where God is experienced as far away and yet he is addressed as close at hand. Living with this paradox is possible provided that faith directs itself to God's promises by which it can "see" what is invisible. Thus, based on Psalm 102:16, Calvin observes,

> Though amidst adversities God's might is hidden to the faithful, they nevertheless have it in view with the eyes of faith and in the mirror of his promises.[63]

Faith is therefore not left to its own devices, but it can cling to God's promises. "This is the way in which we are to seek him because, even if he hides his might from us, we must find our rest in his promises which are not hidden."[64] Where this is concerned, believers in the New Testament have a more certain foundation than those under the old covenant. In the Old

---

[60] "...alis fiduciae se attolit in serenam tranquillitatem, in qua res legitimo suo ordine compositas videat," Ps. 18:15 (*CO* 31, 167).

[61] Ps. 27:14 (*CO* 31, 280).

[62] "...ab effectis metiri solemus Dei praesentiam vel absentiam," Ps. 69:19 (*CO* 31, 645).

[63] Ps. 102:16 (*CO* 32, 69).

[64] Ps. 119:123 (*CO* 32, 269).

Testament, when God had withdrawn himself because of the sins of the people and the people were living in the darkness of God's absence, the prophets were the ones who came to remind them of God's promises of grace and salvation. These messengers of comfort were repeatedly needed once again, and therefore the lament is so profound when in Psalm 74:9 it says that there is no prophet anymore. To the church of the New Testament however it has been confirmed once and for all now that Christ has come that God cares for his people and is gracious to them. Now it is no longer necessary that the faithful be reminded of the mere promise of liberation since in Christ the promise has been fulfilled, and now the hiddenness of God is easier to bear.[65] As the promise of redemption has been fulfilled, it is easier to remain directed towards the promise of God's saving presence.

In Calvin's thought faith directs itself to the promises given by the *Deus absconditus*, but through these very promises God shows himself to be the *Deus revelatus*.

7. Conclusion

The hiddenness of God is a very real theme in the theology of John Calvin, and it is a theme which ought to be investigated more closely. What Calvin says about it arises from his search for answers to the question of how God interacts with this world and with the faithful in particular. On this topic as well, Calvin seeks to provide pastoral explanations for the sufferings that believers undergo. When in some cases Calvin presents the hiddenness of God as a kind of explanation, he is able to remind believers of the promises of God which are distinctively not hidden but revealed quite clearly. This connection between the hiddenness of God and the revealed promises of God shows a strong correlation between Calvin's commentary and the way in which Luther approaches this same problematic issue.

---

[65] Ps. 74:9 (*CO* 31, 696).

9

God the Holy One

1. Sanctification and Justification

The relationship between justification and sanctification in Calvin's theology can be described as follows: sanctification manifests justification, though justification precedes sanctification. Therefore, justification is the cause and sanctification the effect, but since sanctification is more visible, scripture often mentions it in the first place. For instance, Calvin points out that David gauges a man's piety towards God from his attitude towards his neighbor.[1] Furthermore, the fear of the Lord and obedience to the law are inseparable,[2] and he who wants to be counted among the children of God must prove it by a pure life.[3] This means, Calvin says, that only those who serve God in purity may come to him.[4] Sanctification, however, is not the basis for justification but merely its manifestation. Likewise, obedience to the second table of the law indicates whether the first table is also kept, "for if someone treats his neighbors with righteousness and equity, he thereby shows that he actually fears God."[5] Yet, Calvin adjoins to this statement a warning that we never conclude that we may ignore God just as long as we give to our fellow men their due.

The value of the believer's good works depends upon the gracious remission of sins. God accepts us in spite of our imperfections. Not a single good work *per se* is found as perfect by God, and so any reward given stems purely from his goodness. Calvin notes that the biblical promises that good works will be rewarded are not intended to negate the grace of God but rather to stimulate believers in their zeal for piety and justice.[6] The reward which God gives to a person for a righteous life serves as an encouragement to persist in such righteousness. Indeed, Calvin suggests, it

---

[1]   Ps. 24:4 (*CO* 31, 246).

[2]   "...quia res sunt individuae timor Dei et legis observatio...," Ps. 128:1 (*CO* 32, 327).

[3]   Ps. 15:1 (*CO* 31, 143).

[4]   "Summa tamen est, non patere ad Deum accessum nisi puris eius cultoribus," Ps. 15:1 (*CO* 31, 144).

[5]   Ps. 15:2 (*CO* 31, 144).

[6]   "...ad studium pietatis et iustitiae...," Ps. 62:12 (*CO* 31, 593).

is impossible for God to disappoint those who truly worship him because it is his proper office to reward righteousness.[7]

Calvin treats the relationship between faith and good works while commenting on Psalm 106:31 and the deed of Phinehas, Aaron's grandson (Num. 25:1-18), whose actions were "imputed to him for righteousness." The explanation is not so difficult, the Reformer thinks, because what is true of Phinehas is true of all believers. "God imputes the works of the faithful to them for righteousness—not because of the intrinsic value of their works, but because of his grace."[8] We receive righteousness not by works but through faith; yet this righteousness through faith casts its rays upon our works. Every man lacks righteousness until God reconciles such a man to himself by the blood of Christ. Faith is the way by which the pardon for sins is received. Therefore, there is no justification by works, but only through faith; and yet, as God confers righteousness upon us, he freely bestows it also upon our works.

When it is said therefore that a deed is imputed to us for righteousness, this "righteousness" is simply a title which does not indicate any corresponding merit in the person.[9] Calvin says that the righteousness by works is subordinate to the righteousness through faith.[10] Calvin's argument here reveals traces of a "double justification" which is also present in his exposition of Psalm 5:13. God receives us into his favor by not counting our sins against us. Therefore he accepts our zeal to glorify him for perfect righteousness.[11]

2. *Tertius Usus Legis*

Love for God is visible through our obedience his commandments; meanwhile true obedience can only exist when love moves us to do his commandments.[12] Thus Calvin states the reciprocal relationship between love and obedience in the believer. Accordingly, obedience to the law is insufficient when it is but a slavish, loveless obedience. Calvin writes, "A man cannot be regarded as a true observer of the law until he reaches the point where delight in the law renders obedience agreeable to him."[13] Hence, he is emphatic and passionate throughout the Psalms commentary in correlating love and the law. He pleads, "We must strenuously seek to

---

[7] "...quia proprium eius est beneficiis iustitiam suam testari," Ps. 24:5 (*CO* 31, 247).
[8] Ps. 106:31 (*CO* 32, 128-9).
[9] "...titulum, non dignitas...," Ps. 106:31 (*CO* 32, 128-9).
[10] "Huic vero iustitiae subalterna est (ut loquuntur) operum iustitia," Ps. 106:31 (*CO* 32, 128-129).
[11] "...rectum studium pro iustitia perfectione illis fert acceptum," Ps. 5:13 (*CO* 31, 72).
[12] Ps. 119:132 (*CO* 32, 274).
[13] Ps. 112:1 (*CO* 32, 172).

cleanse our hearts in order that love of the law may reign in them."[14] Furthermore, love for the law and hate for deceit are also inseparably connected, which demonstrates how the inner attitude towards the law is decisive.[15] Simply to respect the law will not lead to its obedience, for no one will gladly follow it unless he has tasted its pleasantries. God, of course, does not demand slavish obedience, but, as Calvin notes, "He wants us to come to him cheerfully."[16] As for rightly keeping the law, Calvin shows that delight in the law and the blessing of the law do not depend on perfect obedience, but instead on upright obedience. This cheerful and upright obedience to the law is caused by the certainty of the remission of our sins when we fail to obey it.[17]

The first step towards obedience consists in the mortification of the flesh. Since no men are by nature inclined to mortify their flesh, God uses afflictions (some of them being quite severe) to tame our flesh and to bring us to a sense of duty.[18] The means for accomplishing this vary in each situation. In some cases he humbles by poverty, in others by shame. Even disease and domestic trouble can be his ordained means in promoting mortification. However, we must reap the fruits of these afflictions lest we be ungrateful.[19] Therefore Calvin says:

> The chief virtue of the faithful is their bearing of the cross and the mortification by which they calmly submit themselves to God.[20]

In Calvin's view the believer never rises above the status of *simul iustus et peccator*. This is evident in Psalm 19 where a man regenerated by the Spirit yet laments the burden of his sins.[21] Therefore, sanctification itself is not a human endeavor for, if God were not to restrain us, our hearts would return to their own natural inclinations in despising God. Calvin's description of the regenerate man's struggle against sin explains that a believer is *declared* righteous without actually *becoming* righteous. Sanctification is the internal struggle to tame the carnal inclinations which

---

[14] Ps. 119:162 (*CO* 32, 288).

[15] "...legis amor et fraudis odium res sunt coniunctae...," Ps. 119:162 (*CO* 32, 288).

[16] "Nam fieri quidem poterit ut tangatur quispiam aliquo reverentiae sensu: sed nemo alacriter legem sequitur nisi qui hanc sauvitatem conceperit," Ps. 119:103 (*CO* 32, 258).

[17] Ps. 119:1 (*CO* 32, 215-6).

[18] Ps. 119:67 (*CO* 32, 244).

[19] "Nos vero nimis ingrati summus, nisi fructus hic quem ex castigationibus percipimus...," Ps.119:67 (*CO* 32, 244).

[20] Ps. 119:166 (*CO* 32, 290).

[21] Ps. 19:12 (*CO* 31, 206).

rule us by nature. It is a fight with one's self.[22] Yet it is indeed possible to progress in sanctification. The progress is especially marked by a growing fear for the Lord and a simultaneous growing hatred for sin.[23] The more someone progresses in sanctification throughout life, the more he or she realizes the distance by which he or she has fallen short of the righteousness of God, and all that is left is to trust in God's mercy.[24]

Calvin's most frequent warnings are those against hypocrisy. The most important aspect of righteousness, he says, is to hate deceit, and consequently in our zeal we must pursue uprightness above all else.[25] Although the conscience ought to be sufficient to guide one in such righteousness, even it needs an external rule in order to be trustworthy. Conscience is not a reliable guide because Satan can beguile us to such extent that we do not even perceive the worst sins.[26]

Calvin places sanctification in the context of personal thankfulness for salvation. Knowing that we are unable, God does not demand that we propitiate our own sin, but he does accept from us our true gratitude. Therefore the faithful need not try to liberate themselves. Calvin notes that our heavenly adoption should stimulate us to imitate God in doing good to all.[27] However, when we realize what God has given to us, the thanksgiving and praise which he primarily commands in return are not much at all.[28] This concerns not only the sacrifice of our tongues but of our whole lives and even all that we possess.[29] The only response to his mercy which God asks is thankfulness which expresses itself in praise and commemoration of his bounty.[30] This is also the final aim of salvation. God redeems us in order that we may glorify him.[31] The end of redemption is the salvation of his people and, through it, the glory of God.[32]

According to Calvin there is no better rule of life (*vivendi regula*) than "to be content with the lot which God has given, not trying to fashion one's own happiness but only considering what he [God] calls us to, neither longing for or aspiring to prestige but remaining content with one's

---

22 "…cum proprio ingenio strenue luctati simus…," Ps.119:103 (*CO* 32, 258).
23 Ps. 119:104 (*CO* 32, 259).
24 Ps. 32:1 (*CO* 31,317).
25 "Primum iustitiae caput est odium fraudis ac detestatio: sequitur nihil integritate esse praestantius," Ps. 119:162 (*CO* 32, 288).
26 Ps. 19:12 (*CO* 31, 204).
27 Ps. 30:5 (*CO* 31, 204).
28 Ps. 116:13 (*CO* 32, 198).
29 Ps. 116:13 (*CO* 32, 198).
30 Ps. 6:6 (*CO* 31, 76). Cf. Ps. 35:18 (*CO* 31, 354).
31 Ps. 40:3 (*CO* 31, 406).
32 Ps. 135:8-10 (*CO* 32, 360).

situation."[33] He who prefers another rule of life, Calvin notes, will end in a labyrinth.[34] This rule has been followed by generations of Calvinists and according to the nature of monastic rules, it could be said that the "Calvinistic order" has faithfully kept this *regula Calvini*.

Meanwhile, the Protestant Reformer denounces the opinion that success belongs to those who have managed their worldly interests well, often to the detriment of the simple.[35] This does not mean that Calvin scorns an industrious life. On the contrary, the word of God nowhere censures hard work or planning, and faithfulness towards one's duty is a praiseworthy virtue. Thus, it is not the will of God that we should sit idly with folded arms but that we should instead use our talents. Calvin grounds this ethos of diligence in creation. Indeed, the pains of labor stem mainly from the curse of sin, but even if we had remained in the original sinless state, we would have labored just as Adam's charge proves.[36]

Yet, in spite of all our exertions to this end, we still depend upon God's blessing. This does not mean that he who works hard is blessed; it means instead that even hard work is fruitless without God's blessing. The promise of God's blessing can stimulate us to diligence, but this blessing is no mere reward.[37] Challenging a well-known hypothesis, Calvin's commentary on the Psalms disproves the idea that he was the father of capitalism.[38]

Calvin clearly denounces the secular attitude common to his era and ours which aspires after "the good life (*beatam vitam*) in idleness, pleasure, and wealth."[39] This rejection should not surprising to us since, just as Calvin believes that God cannot be idle, the same applies to mankind which bears God's image. Diligence should never seek as a final end merely to enjoy of the fruits of one's labors; for Calvin, the purpose of industry is service.

Consequently Calvin favors a positive attitude towards the Sabbath. The Sabbath, of course, belongs to the shadows of the law, yet it is an image of new spiritual life which rests from our works while God works in us.[40] This separate day, therefore, was not given to be inactive, but to praise

---

[33] Ps. 131:1 (*CO* 32, 339).

[34] "...necesse est in labyrintho vagari," Ps. 131:1 (*CO* 32, 340).

[35] Ps. 119:34 (*CO* 32, 229).

[36] Ps. 127:1 (*CO* 32, 321).

[37] "...accedat promissio, ut certa spe alacriter officio fungantur," Ps. 127:2 (*CO* 32, 323).

[38] Biéler presents a critical exposition of the authors who see a close relation between Calvinism and capitalism. See André Biéler, *La pensée économique et sociale de Calvin* (Genève: Librairie de l'universite, 1961) 477-514.

[39] Ps. 128:2 (*CO* 32, 327).

[40] "...ut Deo in nobis operante feriemur ab operibus nostris," Ps. 95:11 (*CO* 32, 36).

God and to think about his works. Daily toil prohibits us from giving due attention to this during the other days of the week. Calvin represents this as an anthropological problem: because our minds are so inconstant we are easily distracted from many things, including God.[41] Hence we must have one day free to direct ourselves wholly to him.

Another characteristic of the ethics in Calvin's commentary on the Psalter is its orientation towards the well-being of our fellowmen. This is especially evident in Calvin's exposition of Psalm 15:5 which addresses whether or not interest should be charged for loans ("...who does not put out his money at interest," RSV).[42] Here Calvin decries the way in which his contemporaries amassed money for themselves through interest on loans. While interest as such is not wrong, Calvin warns against the great danger of exploiting the needs of a neighbor. Among those who earn an income in this way, Calvin says, it is scarcely possible to find one man who is not an extortionist peddling a dishonorable gain. Calvin regards it as odious and shameful that, while everyone else earns their money by hard work, bankers simply sit back and receive a tribute from the labor of others.[43] It is not the rich, therefore, but the poor who suffer under interest, and it is not without cause that God (in Leviticus 25:35-36) has forbidden his people from charging interest while commanding them to help the poor. God's law was intended to prevent the oppression of the poor, and thus its purpose is to support them. However, Calvin believes that receiving a gain from charging interest is perfectly lawful when it does not injure anyone. The standard on this ethical matter is the measure to which the neighbor is served or injured. The command to care for one's neighbor is rooted in man's creation and renewal in the image of God. "For there is nothing in which we are more like God than in being bountiful."[44]

Apart from the rule of love for one's neighbor, Calvin gives no other rules. God's blessing is on him who abstains from injustice, fulfills his humanitarian duties, and exerts himself in doing toward his neighbors that which is good.[45] Both the confusion and troubles in society, and the widespread loss of any peace of mind, Calvin attributes to self-seeking behavior which has no regard for one's neighbor. Calvin also condemns the unbridled desire for gain through plundering others. A Christian, in

---

[41] "...ut lubricae sunt mentes nostrae, si distrahantur huc et illuc, facile alienantur a Deo," Ps. 92:1 (*CO* 32, 10).

[42] Ps. 15:5 (*CO* 31, 147-8).

[43] "...solos trapezitas sedendo vectigal ex omnium labore colligere," Ps. 15:5 (*CO* 31, 148).

[44] Ps. 30:5 (*CO* 31, 294). For Calvin's ideas about interest and usury, see Biéler's *Pensée*, 453-76.

[45] Ps. 37:27 (*CO* 31, 380).

contrast, must realize that he or she does not live for self-promotion through convenience and advantage, but a believer is instead obliged to promote the benefit of the community.[46]

3. An Anthropological Problem: *Simul Peccator*

The problem of sanctification, as Calvin describes it, is "the tardiness of our understanding" and "the inflexibility of our heart."[47] Therefore, we must pray for an understanding directed towards the law and for a docile (*docile*) and obedient heart.[48] The course of sanctification is not only obstructed by Satan, who ceaselessly attacks us, but also by our own tardiness from "internal impediments."[49]

Sanctification is of great concern to the man who knows his weakness, who feels himself threatened by Satan, and who remains conscious of his dependence upon God. In the Psalms commentary, Calvin describes the uncertainty experienced by those in the course of sanctification, saying, "The way is so slippery, the feet so weak, and our thoughts so prone to go astray on innumerable wrong paths."[50] Therefore, he concludes, the faithful are never self-satisfied, "for they perceive how far they are still removed from perfection."[51]

Because of man's weakness in the face of temptation, Calvin warns against overly intimate relationships with unbelievers. Sometimes a "divorce" from the wicked is necessary, he says, to attain communion with God.[52] Since man is inclined to follow the bad rather than the good, we must take great care not to be affected by the unfaithful with whom we interact.[53] By adopting us God has separated us from the wicked, a reality which has several applications. In particular, Calvin warns against the worshipping of images, something to which everybody is inclined.[54]

Calvin categorically rejects the ideal of holiness held out by the "fanatics" (Calvin's term) who espouse a "devilish perfection."[55] As it renders the forgiveness of sins totally superfluous, he considers this idea of

---

[46] "...sed quoad suppetet facultas, in commune prodesse cupiant...," Ps. 137:27 (*CO* 31, 380).

[47] "...mentis nostrae tarditas...," Ps. 119:5 (*CO* 32, 216).

[48] Ps. 119:5 (*CO* 32, 216).

[49] "...impedimentis intus summus constricti...," Ps. 119:60 (*CO* 32, 240).

[50] Ps. 119:101 (*CO* 32, 258).

[51] Ps. 15:4 (*CO* 31, 145).

[52] "...divortium fecit cum hominibus, ut se ad Deum colligeret," Ps. 119:115 (*CO* 32, 265).

[53] "...quia ad mala exempla nimium propensi summus...," Ps. 106:35 (*CO* 32, 130).

[54] "...ad quam unumquemque suum ingenium inclinat...," Ps. 106:35 (*CO* 32, 131).

[55] Ps. 106:6 (*CO* 32, 118).

perfect righteousness to be in reality contempt for God.[56] This idea, of course, totally contradicts one of Calvin's assumptions about the believer in this world—that he is *simul iustus et peccator*. He whom God adopts is not thereby also delivered from the sins of the flesh at the same time. The enthusiasts on the other hand believe (Calvin would say *dream*) that the incorporation into the body of Christ entails the end of everything corrupt in us. Is it true, exclaims Calvin, that we can so change our nature as to become perfect like the angels? As this is not so, Calvin advises his readers to speedily depart from such a "devilish figment" towards "the asylum of forgiveness."[57]

Calvin also denounces the position of those who seem to be more temperate than the "fanatics" by speaking so much about regeneration as if to say that the kingdom of Christ consists only in sanctification.[58]

4. The Purpose of the Liturgy

The worship service as service unto God should be regarded as the highest form or "primary means" of sanctification, for Calvin offers the following as the purpose of worship: to praise God, to confess faith and grow in it, to advance in one's knowledge of the word, to confess and experience the unity of faith, and to commemorate God's blessings.[59] According to Calvin then the purpose of worship is not to come to faith but to grow in faith.[60]

In one passage of the commentary, Calvin notes that the purpose of every element in the worship service is "to magnify God's goodness in acknowledging his benefits."[61] Moreover, we worship God when we submit ourselves to his word and use the sacraments faithfully.[62] To this end, our life on earth is a school for practical instruction on the adoration of God, and its purpose is that we should progress in God's school.[63] The curriculum in this school consists mainly in worship.[64] The end of public thanksgiving likewise consists in the glory of God and the salvation of man. For Calvin, the primary purpose of the believing congregation is "to exercise themselves in various ways in the service (*cultus*) of God and to

---

[56] Ps. 143:2 (*CO* 32, 401).

[57] Ps. 89:31 (*CO* 31, 822).

[58] "Magnifice regenerationem extollunt, ac si in puritate vitae consisteret totum Christi regnum," Ps. 143:2 (*CO* 32, 401).

[59] Ps. 81:2 (*CO* 31, 760).

[60] Ps. 84:6 (*CO* 31, 781).

[61] Ps. 26:7 (*CO* 31, 268); "...quia in hunc maxime finem aguntur sacri conventus, ut Deo laudem sacrificent sui cultores...," Ps. 11:1 (*CO* 31, 167).

[62] Ps. 132:7 (*CO* 32, 345).

[63] "...hic sit vivendi finis ut proficiant in schola Dei...," Ps. 119:35 (*CO* 32, 229).

[64] Ps. 84:2 (*CO* 31, 781).

incite each other to this service."[65] In the worship service, the attention of the congregation is always directed anew towards the grace of the covenant. Calvin even stresses the individual's importance for the community in like manner by saying that "David will glorify the names of God in the congregation in order that his brothers should be encouraged to do the same."[66] Sensing anew the covenantal benefits, the faith of the congregation as well as the glory of God will steadily increase.[67]

The reason for praising God is that his benefits are thereby proclaimed anew. Essential for Calvin in the service is the interchange of word and adoration, of *doctrina* and *laudatio*. Without proclamation the liturgy would be a mere outward ritual.[68] On the other hand, ceremonies and customs are only profitable when they imprint the pure truth of God upon us. Therefore, customs which do not conform to the word of God do not promote piety but rather spoil it. The cognitive element in the church service is obvious, but it is knowledge that helps to promote the glory of God through words and deeds. The cognitive element is even central to Calvin's analysis of singing. He warns that singing without contemplation of the words inevitably degenerates into a kind of ritualistic superstition. It is essential to contemplate the meaning while singing and to then concentrate upon it, otherwise the name of God, instead of being praised, is desecrated by howling.[69]

The liturgy functions as a staircase which elevates us to God.[70] God does not command us to ascend into heaven, but, because of our weakness, he descends to us.[71] Having no wings, people are left to use the staircase of liturgy to ascend to God.[72] In the church service, Calvin argues, God supplies us with the means to desire and love him even more.[73] The aim of the church service then is to elevate us, as far as the weakness of our flesh permits it, toward him who graciously descends to us.[74] "For what is the

---

[65] Ps. 22:23 (*CO* 31, 231).

[66] Ps. 22:24 (*CO* 31, 232).

[67] Ps. 81:2 (*CO* 31, 760).

[68] "...dum extincta doctrinae luce, externo tantum cultu defungitur populus," Ps. 81:2 (*CO* 31, 760).

[69] "Requiritur ergo ad legitimum psallendi ritum scientia, ne vano clamore nomen dei profanetur," Ps. 47:6 (*CO* 31, 470).

[70] See comments by Erasmus in *Desiderii Erasmi Roterodami Opera omnia emendolivra et auctiora* (Lugduri Batavorum, 1703-1706; Reprint, Hildesheim, 1961-1962) V 28E. Henceforth, abbreviated as LB.

[71] Ps. 42:2 (*CO* 31, 426).

[72] Ps. 42:2 (*CO* 31, 426); Cf. Ps. 132:7: "...non cogimur sine adiumentis illuc usque evolare...," (*CO* 32, 345).

[73] "...quae illic offert Deus adiumenta ad suum usum accomodant, ac utilitas ista desiderium et amorem in eorum cordibus accendit," Ps. 26:8 (*CO* 31, 268).

[74] "...nos pro carnis nostrae infirmitate pietatis exercitiis sursum ad Deum attoli," Ps. 24:7 (*CO* 31, 248).

purpose of the preaching of the word, the sacraments, the assembling of the saints, and of the whole external constitution of the church but that we may be united with God?"[75] Already in the Old Testament, Calvin points out, the temple cult served to strengthen faith.[76] This still holds, although the congregation of the New Testament now needs fewer elements and instruments. However, the word still remains essential. If the voice of God, inciting us towards faith and piety, is no longer heard in the congregation, then it is futile to assemble.[77]

In view of the fact that believers do need these external means, Calvin urges that they should not neglect the meetings of the congregation where they encourage each other to worship God and to glorify him.[78] Under the reign of Christ all the faithful, even those of the lowest social class, have become Levites; thus Scripture exhorts all to praise God mutually.[79] The faithful, being pilgrims on earth, have a need for holy assemblies, and therefore God has prescribed them. Calvin denies the notion of those who believe they can cope without such assemblies because they themselves have the ability to ascend to heaven.[80] Furthermore, Calvin concurs with Erasmus that those who view ceremonies not as a means to an end but as an end in themselves have fallen into superstition.[81] Ceremonies, he says, are simply external means which guide us to enjoy of the heavenly fruit.[82] When we despise the preaching of the word and the sacraments, though, we should not marvel should God withdraw himself from us.[83]

5. The Church Service as Celestial Theater

One of the essential aspects in Calvin's notion of liturgy is that heaven and earth are *connected* in the church service through God's presence with his gathered people. Since God is invisible, he presents the sanctuary as the symbol of his presence.[84] In fact, he calls the assembly of the congregation a "celestial theater" to which the presence of angels adds splendor.[85] Furthermore, the word, the sacraments, prayer, and everything else in the

---

[75] Ps. 24:7 (*CO* 31, 248).
[76] "Aedificium ad fidei confirmationem…," Ps. 24:7 (*CO* 31, 248).
[77] Ps. 81:9 (*CO* 31, 762).
[78] Ps. 52:10 (*CO* 31, 529).
[79] Ps. 113:1 (*CO* 32, 177).
[80] Ps. 84:2 (*CO* 31, 780).
[81] See *Desiderii Erasmi Roterodami Opera Omnia* (Leiden 1703-1706) (LB) V 32F.
[82] "Bona sanctuarii vocanda externa adminicula commendat, quae nos ad bonorum coelestium fruitionem deducunt," Ps. 65:5 (*CO* 31, 606).
[83] Ps. 24:8 (*CO* 31, 249).
[84] Ps. 96:6 (*CO* 32, 39).
[85] "…quia sacer conventus quasi coeleste theatrum est…," Ps. 138:1 (*CO* 32, 372).

service are all mirrors in which God manifests himself to us.[86] As long as we abide in the world we are far from God because in the world there is a great distance between faith and sight. He who wants to "see" God then must come to church, to the sanctuary of God, where he is "seen" in the word and sacraments.[87]

Therefore it is so impressive and important that God shows himself in the church service and there comes so close to us. On this account, Calvin rejects the mystical approach. We cannot ascend to God, and indeed we have no need to do so, for in the church service he descends to us and we can see him. On our own we are too feeble to ascend to him; consequently we need external signs of his presence through which we might perceive something of the invisible God.[88] It is the Holy Spirit, he insists, who elevates us to heaven *by means of* these external aids.[89]

Calvin holds that God's presence in the congregation promotes confidence among believers because public worship strengthens faith and the experience of God's closeness stimulates prayer.[90] Yet he has no clear idea on how this presence of God ought to be imagined concretely. As a proof of his love, God descends to us, moving his habitation from heaven to earth in order to abide among his people.[91] However, we cannot say that God "sits" somewhere or "dwells" in a certain place. The psalmist's expression that "God sits among the cherubs" only serves to teach us that he is not far away, Calvin says. Additionally, calling the temple God's "footstool" is nothing but the stammering of the Holy Spirit as he aids our weakness.[92]

Concerning liturgical matters Calvin also looks for the *via media*, seeking to neither underestimate nor overestimate the external aids. On the one hand, he wants to avoid "the pernicious superstition" that God is confined to the temple. On the other hand, he denies that "the church is using the external symbols in vain."[93] In this way Calvin comes to a sort of liturgical *extra-Calvinisticum*. God is not bound to the ceremonies of the church service, but he uses them to our profit because of our weakness.[94] In

---

[86]   Ps. 27:4 (*CO* 31, 274).

[87]   Ps. 27:8 (*CO* 31, 276).

[88]   Ps. 96:6 (*CO* 32, 39).

[89]   "...ut nos a terrennis elementis in coelum evehat," Ps. 132:7 (*CO* 32, 345).

[90]   Ps. 74:2 (*CO* 31, 692). Cf. Ps. 74:5 (*CO* 31, 694): "...ut sciamus non fuisse illic comprehensam eius essentiam, sed virtute sua in templo habitasse, quo maiore fiducia illic a populo invocaretur."

[91]   "...quod se quodammodo extenuat ut ad eos descendat, sedemque et domocilium sibi deligat in terra, ut habitet in medio ipsorum," Ps. 80:2 (*CO* 31, 754).

[92]   "...quam utiliter balbutiat spiritus sanctus pro infirmitatis nostrae captu...," Ps. 132:7 (*CO* 32, 345).

[93]   Ps. 132:7 (*CO* 32, 345).

[94]   "...hoc infirmitatis suae adminiculum...," Ps. 28:2 (*CO* 31, 281).

a similar way, God's majesty and power are not confined in the Old Testament to the ark, "yet the ark is no empty symbol of God's presence."[95] Therefore, we have to use the symbols of God's presence without putting our trust in them as such.[96]

A wrong usage of ceremonies stems from a wrong theology—that is, a wrong image of God. For instance, he who holds that God needs sacrifices disregards the difference between God, who is self-sufficient, and man, who, among other things, needs nourishment. Calvin utilizes the term "*autarkia*" to express the total independence and self-sufficiency of God.[97]

The whole liturgy is a senseless game[98] when God is not worshiped spiritually and the external ceremonies are not directed to the most important offering, which is the praise of God. In the Psalms commentary, Calvin describes the coldness and tardiness which often characterizes the spiritual lives of people, especially in matters of worship. Although everyone who goes to church knows that he or she is created to glorify God, yet nothing of this is seen in every day life.[99] Calvin denounces those who ostentatiously attend the church service, "creating the impression [that they] burn with ardent zeal," but in reality they only seek to demonstrate to others how much they perform their religious duties towards God.[100]

Liturgy concerns the heart of man, for it is the attitude of the heart which determines whether God is indeed praised. He can only be praised by those with tranquil and cheerful hearts, persons reconciled with God and hoping for eternal blessedness.[101] From those who worship him God expects not only ceremonies but, above all, true and cordial love.[102] Calvin fears the danger to which, in his view, both the Jews and the Papists have succumbed by heartlessly observing the ceremonies with the presumption that they thereby satisfy God in merely going through the rites.[103] The Reformer observes that "man is naturally inclined to outward rites without faith and purity of heart."[104] By stating this, Calvin bids farewell to the age

---

[95] Ps. 47:6 (*CO* 31, 469).
[96] Ps. 132:7 (*CO* 32, 345).
[97] Ps. 50:9 (*CO* 31, 500).
[98] "...ludicrum et nihili...," Ps. 134:1 (*CO* 32, 355).
[99] Ps. 113:1 (*CO* 32, 177).
[100] Ps. 84:2 (*CO* 31, 780).
[101] Ps. 67:4 (*CO* 31, 618).
[102] Ps. 40:7 (*CO* 31, 410).
[103] "Ita Iudaeis proclive fuit legis figuras temere arripere, ac si earum observatione Deum rite placerent...," Ps. 50:1 (*CO* 31, 495).
[104] Ps. 50:1 (*CO* 31, 495).

old idea that our acts in worship have intrinsic value by their mere performance.[105]

Calvin, of course, also expects that the heart which worships God aright will also be the source for a Christian believer's good works. He writes, "It would be insufficient to extol his grace without practical piety."[106]

6. Liturgy of the Old and New Testament

Calvin's conception of the relation between Old and New Testaments is also reflected in the liturgy, where some differences and similarities are brought to light. He notes how previously God had burdened the Israelites with the ceremonies which suited the church at that time; now, however, the church of the New Testament is set free from these additional ceremonies. "Essentially," he explains, "it concerns the same cult with the only difference in the outward form."[107] Regarding the inward and spiritual character of true worship, Calvin points to a basic continuity since the prophets of the Old Testament depicted such inward service to God by means of the symbols employed during their time.[108] The Old Testament was thus also concerned with worship which originates in the heart. Calvin pictures the Old Testament times as "infantile" over against the time of "ripeness" inaugurated by the New Testament.[109] Those who live after the advent of Christ do not any longer need the childish aids of the Old Testament, and this explains why worship in the present is simpler than in the times of Israel though it remains essentially the same.[110]

The temple which stood during the Old Testament was richly ornamented, yet even at that time its greatest excellence was the presence of God.[111] When Christ came as the reality to which such former "shadows" pointed, the purpose for this visible symbol expired, and therefore Calvin reminds us that we should not be amazed that the temple is no longer visible upon mount Zion. Because of Christ, a true temple now extends across the whole world.[112] Erasmus may have seen the world as a great monastery; but

---

[105] Angenendt describes the development towards the idea of a "rituellen Selbstwirksam-keit," in which "die Intention des Menschen nicht mehr den Ausschlag gab," Angenendt, *Religiosität*, 380.

[106] Ps. 105:44 (*CO* 32, 115).

[107] Ps. 50:14 (*CO* 31, 502).

[108] Ps. 69:7 (*CO* 31, 640).

[109] Ps. 92:1 (*CO* 32, 11).

[110] "...nobis cum vero post Christi adventum adolevimus, simplicius agit: in ipso interim nulla mutatio," Ps. 50:14 (*CO* 31, 502).

[111] Ps. 24:7 (*CO* 31, 248).

[112] "...cuius amplitudo totum orbem occupat," Ps. 24:7 (*CO* 31, 248).

Calvin sees it as a temple.[113] As God is omnipresent, he can be worshiped everywhere. While the temple and the ark have vanished, they are replaced by the word and sacraments. Meanwhile, though, the benefit in being united to God by these means has remained the same.[114] David himself had already drawn the distinction between true spiritual service of God and the initial aids for advancing piety and faith in believers.[115] The primary concern for Calvin is to foster the spiritual worship to God, and since God was no less a spirit during the dispensation of the Old Testament as during the New, it follows that Israel's offerings and ceremonies were also intended for their spiritual significance.[116] Consequently, the aim of a church service in the present is the same as it was under the law—to praise God.[117] Calvin mentions the differences as follows: formerly the temple was the symbol of God's presence; now it is Christ who has descended in order to lift us up to God. The one who intends to draw near unto God once had to go to the temple, but now he or she should go to Christ.[118]

Concerning his use of musical instruments, David is not the example given for us to imitate according to Calvin. Rather, in the Reformer's interpretation, David uses the harp in bringing praise to the Lord as an additional typological aspect to worship in the Old Testament. He explains that instruments in the worship service belong to the puerile phase of the church as part of the "pedagogy" of the law.[119] They were aids employed by God before the coming of Christ to move the faithful of the Old Testament to even greater zeal as they praise him.[120] Like other elements of worship during the old dispensation, instruments should be counted among the "shadows" which God used during the times before Christ. However useful they may have been as a help for "the old people" of Israel, Calvin asserts that musical instruments as such were not essential to true worship then, and he implies that this is even truer for the Christian church today.[121]

According to Calvin the human voice exceeds all soulless instruments by far. While acknowledging that music is indeed apt to touch the human heart, his fear of contaminating the praise of God overrules this

---

[113] See Kohls' interpretation of Erasmus and the "Mönchtum in der Welt" in Ernst-Wilhelm Kohls, *Die Theologie des Erasmus*, vol. I (Basel: F. Reinhardt, 1966), 30-2.

[114] "...quatenus tamen communis nobis ratio est cum patribus...," Ps. 24:8 (*CO* 31, 249).

[115] Ps. 40:7 (*CO* 31, 411).

[116] "Atqui non coepit demum esse spiritus quum abrogavit caeremonias legales," Ps. 50:14 (*CO* 31, 502).

[117] Ps. 81:2 (*CO* 31, 760).

[118] Ps. 28:2 (*CO* 31, 281).

[119] "...pars fuerit legalis paedagogiae...," Ps. 33:2 (*CO* 31, 325).

[120] Ps. 81:2 (*CO* 31, 760).

[121] Ps. 92:4 (*CO* 32, 11).

concession.[122] He fears that, by using musical instruments, the correct balance would be disturbed between the joy caused by music and the joy due to the praise of God.[123] It should quickly be added though that Calvin has no objections about playing on musical instruments at home. However, when elsewhere quoting from 1 Corinthians 14:13 where the apostle says that God should only be praised in a known tongue, he takes this occasion to reject the use of any instruments in the church.[124] Musical instruments belong to the phase during which the church was still under a pedagogue.[125] They were peculiar to the infancy of the church, he notes, being useful to lift the hearts of God's people.[126] They were necessary at that time to lead men away from all kinds of sinful pleasures to a sensible and pious joy.[127] Therefore, God employed music (though it lacks inherent sacred value) to attain his sacred aim. Calvin's reservations about music stem from his notion of God, who, unlike men, does not feel such delight through music.[128] Men may be stirred by music, but this is not the case with God who has no need for instruments despite having given such simple aids to help and stimulate Israel in honoring him.

As Calvin explains, the adoption of something peculiar to God's people of the old covenant would be a misguided way of following them.[129] In fact, it would not be *following* so much as *imitating*[130]—something to which Rome is inclined, sneers the Reformer.[131] It would be absurd, for instance, if women were to play upon the drum today.[132] Since the outward rituals have been abolished by Christ's offering, it could only be a stupid superstition to reintroduce them.[133] Through a similar line of argument Calvin solves the question of dancing. In Psalm 30:12 the poet praises God because he has turned lamenting into dancing. Calvin though doubts that this refers to secular dancing as much as it signifies "an elegant and holy expression of joy."[134]

---

[122] "...musicam ad excitandos hominum animos plurimum valere...," Ps.33:2 (*CO* 31, 325).

[123] "...ne a Dei laudibus suam laetitiam separent...," Ps. 33:2 (*CO* 31, 325).

[124] Ps. 71:22 (*CO* 31, 662).

[125] "Musica instrumenta quorum meminit, ad tempus paedadogiae pertinent...," Ps. 149:2 (*CO* 32, 438).

[126] Ps. 24:7 (*CO* 31, 248).

[127] Ps. 150:3 (*CO* 32, 442).

[128] Ps. 92:1 (*CO* 32, 11).

[129] "...ne stulta aemulatione in usum nostrum trahamus quod proprium fuit veteri populo," Ps. 149:2 (*CO* 32, 438).

[130] "...non esse patrum imitatores, sed simias...," Ps. 92:1 (*CO* 32, 11).

[131] "Unde apparet papistas hoc ad se transferendo, simias fuisse," Ps. 81:2 (*CO* 31, 760).

[132] Ps. 68:26 (*CO* 31, 631).

[133] "Nunc vero plus quam stupida est eorum superstitio...," Ps. 69:31 (*CO* 31, 651).

[134] "... gravis et sancta professio laetitia...," Ps. 30:12 (*CO* 31,299). The combination of "gravis" with "laetitia" indicates that something is amiss.

Calvin regards images not as ornaments but as a pollution of the church. Moreover, we do not live any more in the age of the tabernacle and temple. Yet Calvin concedes that churches should exhibit a distinct beauty to impress the faithful and stimulate them to corporate worship.[135]

7. Conclusion

In discussing sanctification in the Psalter, Calvin is still more concerned with God's deeds than man's actions. Theologically, sanctification is not the human reaction to justification but God's work in man as part of justification. Moreover, the end of sanctification is not the believer's progress but rather the result of this progress—the glory of the God who sanctifies, and this correlation between growth in faith and the glory of God is indicative of Calvin's thoughts about liturgy. Calvin's trouble with external matters like musical instruments results from this combination and from his opinion that the liturgy of the New Testament is a purification of a similar liturgy in the Old Testament.

[135] Ps. 27:4 (*CO* 31, 274).

10

God the God of the Covenant

According to John Calvin, man can only reach the purpose for which he was created, living to the honor of God and to the salvation of man, if he remains in the relations in which God has put him.[1] Of these several relationships, the *covenant* is the most important.[2] Since Calvin holds prayer to be the means by which partners in the covenant communicate with each other, prayer is discussed in this chapter. Furthermore ecclesiology belongs in this discussion since Calvin considers the church to be a community of the covenant, an idea rooted in his view on the relationship between Old Testament Israel and the church of the New Testament.

In recent years ecclesiastical and theological discussions about the precise similarities and differences between the covenant and election have dominated much of the research done on this theme.[3] In contrast, this chapter attempts insofar as it is possible to let Calvin speak for himself on this topic, leaving most of the above-mentioned discussions aside for now.

1. God and Man in Relation

God created man in relation and it's according to the nature of the community which mankind forms that each person stands within all kinds of relational bonds. Because God puts humanity in such interpersonal relations, "the Holy Spirit condemns everyone who breaks these holy, natural bonds."[4] Upon this assumption, Calvin calls it the characteristic work of Satan to break these ordained relations, leaving man on his own. After all, the one

---

[1] For the relational position of man, see J. L. Witte, S.J., *Het Probleem Individu-gemeenschap in Calvijns Geloofsnorm*, 2 vol. (Franeker: Wever, 1949).

[2] The research on the doctrine of the covenant according to Calvin is limited. Graaf-land presents in his own analysis of Calvin's view on the covenant a review of the state of research: C. Graafland, *Van Calvijn tot Comrie: Oorsprong en ontwikkeling van de leer van het verbond in het Gereformeerd Protestantisme*, 2 vol. (Zoetermeer: Boekencentrum, 1992), 71-82.

[3] In the Dutch speaking context, examples include P. J. Richel's *Het kerkbegrip van Calvijn* (Franeker: Wever, 1942) and W. H. van der Vegt, *Verbond en verkiezing bij Calvijn* (n. p.).

[4] "Interea sciamus damnari a spiritu sancto eos omnes qui sacra naturae foedera violant quibus erant inter se devincti," Ps. 55:13 (*CO* 31, 540).

who abandons these relationships cannot meet the law's fundamental demand to serve God and other people.

Of all these ordained relationships, the one established by faith is the holiest.[5] This relation occurs within the framework of the covenant of grace, and the covenant, meanwhile, is the way in which election takes place. "Consequently," Calvin writes, "if the cause or the origin of the covenant is sought, man arrives at the election of God."[6] In the covenant, God shows that he wants to be a father for his people.[7] It also constitutes the holy unity between God and the children of Abraham.[8] The covenant furthermore overcomes the gap between the inconceivably splendid God and us,[9] and it means that God is present among his people.[10] The most important part of the covenant however is reconciliation with God.[11] The promise held out to man in the covenant is a heavenly inheritance,[12] but the purpose of the covenant is to advance the glory of God.[13]

God is willing to enter into a covenant with man, but he does so upon conditions which are equal for both sides.[14] This arrangement is not a business contract, but instead, as he calls it, a "spiritual covenant."[15] Nor does this covenant last only a few days or a short period of time since it is an eternal covenant.[16] Calvin suggests that the origin of the covenant lies in the legislation on Mount Sinai: "From Sinai the law has come and out of this source the covenant of grace streams to us."[17] In the covenant God promises everlasting grace and protection of his people.[18] The gracious character of the covenant is evident from the fact that God promises us a reward although he does not owe it to us. He states,

> In the covenant of adoption the gracious pardon of sins is included, upon which depends the granting of righteousness. Thus a reward is

---

[5] "Sacratissimum autem est pietatis foedus," Ps. 55:13 (*CO* 31, 540).

[6] Ps. 89:4 (*CO* 31, 813).

[7] Ps. 67:3 (*CO* 31, 618).

[8] "...vinculum esse sacrae unionis..." Ps. 68:18 (*CO* 31, 627).

[9] Ps. 146:10 (*CO* 32, 425). Cf. also Ps. 68:18 (*CO* 31, 627).

[10] Ps. 24:1 (*CO* 31, 243-4).

[11] "...praecipuum aeterni foederis caput...de gratuita reconciliatione...," Ps. 143:2 (*CO* 32, 401).

[12] "...foedus quod ad spem usque aeternae haereditatis patebat...," Ps. 105:11 (*CO* 32, 101).

[13] "Praecipuum deinde foederis caput, et fere summam totam proponit, ut solus ipse emineat," Ps. 81:9 (*CO* 31, 763).

[14] Ps. 81:12 (*CO* 31, 764).

[15] Ps. 105:1 (*CO* 32, 98).

[16] Ps. 80:9 (*CO* 31, 756).

[17] Ps. 9:12 (*CO* 31, 102).

[18] Ps. 19:16 (*CO* 31, 177).

paid for the works of the believers—a reward which is actually not deserved.[19]

Only the grace of God enables us to speak about reward and retribution, for our works are purified through grace, and then God can reward them.[20] Calvin adds that speaking of God's promises does not suggest any darkening of his grace as if speaking about God's commitments could somehow detract from grace.[21] On the other hand, remission of sins does not nullify the covenant since remission is entailed as a condition of the covenant. Without the promises of God which we find in the word, "we have no right to imagine something of his grace or to presumptuously attach our hope to something which he does not promise."[22] For Calvin, the word and the promise are factually identical.[23] Thus God would also be merciful towards believers when they do not meet his demands since the remission of sins is part of the covenant.[24]

God enters into covenant with only part of humanity.[25] Even from before their births these people are heirs of the covenant because it originates among the patriarchs with whom God entered into a covenant. In this relationship in which God's choice precedes everything, the covenant partners are holy. Consequently, this holiness is neither rooted in nature nor does it rest in behavior, but it is objective because of God's choice.[26]

2. Promise and Obligation

Calvin's theology deals with a real mutual relationship in the covenant since man participates in it as a full partner. This bilateral aspect to the covenant is emphasized by Calvin when he says, "We should not be afraid that God will disappoint us if we remain in the covenant."[27] Assenting in faith to God's promises is understood by Calvin as "living sincerely and in service."[28] The believer's personal faith is thus expressed in deeds, especially in living a holy life of service.

This raises the question, however, as to whether the fulfillment of God's covenant promise depends upon us keeping our promises. Calvin writes, "The conditions to which God has committed himself create the impression

---

[19] Ps 19:11 (*CO* 31, 204).
[20] Ps. 18:21 (*CO* 31, 180).
[21] Ps. 102:14 (*CO* 32, 67).
[22] Ps. 89:4 (*CO* 31, 813).
[23] See, for instance, Ps. 130:5 (*CO* 32, 336).
[24] "...quia coniuncta est cum foedere peccatorum remissio," Ps. 89:31 (*CO* 31, 823).
[25] "...cum exigua hominum parte...," Ps. 24:1 (*CO* 31, 243).
[26] Ps. 105:6 (*CO* 32, 100).
[27] Ps. 25:10 (*CO* 31, 256).
[28] Ps. 15:1 (*CO* 31, 143).

that the covenant of God will only be valid if the people fulfill it faithfully. Hence the effect of the promised grace would depend on their obedience."[29] Calvin proceeds however to mention a few arguments which answer the question negatively because the certainty of God's promises does not hang upon human obedience. In the first place, he points to the fact that the covenant finds its origin exclusively in the initiative of God; thus God has committed himself unconditionally and voluntarily.[30] Since God's initiative lies behind both the covenant and the obligations in it, believers can have greater assurance that it will be kept. After all, if God were to keep his promises only because he owes us something or because we deserve what he has promised, our part would necessarily bring some uncertainty into the covenant.[31] In the second place, history illustrates clearly that the people's disobedience cannot deter the fulfillment of God's promises. Christ has come in spite of Israel's disobedience.

However, God maintains the right to punish disobedience. As an example of divine punishment within the covenant, Calvin mentions the Babylonian captivity and the related fall of Israel's monarchy. God had promised that David would always have a descendant on the throne. Did God therefore break his covenant through the banishment to Babylon?[32] After the return from captivity, Israel remained without king. Did God again somehow set aside the covenant? No, rather God illustrated to Israel at that time how seriously he considers the demands of the covenant. At the same time, though, he shows in the coming of King Jesus that he has not broken his covenant and that he fulfills his promise.[33] According to Calvin then our disobedience cannot nullify the covenant, but it can be a reason for God to inflict punishment as stipulated by the covenant's demands.

Calvin also knows about children in the covenant who do not follow in the faithful paths of their parents. Many are born to believing parents and yet never manifest the same faith.[34] Thus Calvin notes that faith is not automatically inherited from believing parents; faith is a personal matter. The general doctrine of the church remains cold until one appropriates it in the sure conviction that he or she is a child of God.[35] Calvin remarks, "We are

---

[29] Ps. 132:12 (*CO* 32, 348).
[30] Ps. 132:12 (*CO* 32, 348).
[31] Ps. 119:155 (*CO* 32, 284-5).
[32] "...Deus foedus suum irritum facere...," Ps. 132:12 (*CO* 32, 348).
[33] Ps. 132:12 (*CO* 32, 349).
[34] "Semen et filios piorum intelligit non quoslibet, quia multi ex carne geniti sunt degeneres: sed qui a fide parentum non desiscunt," Ps. 102:29 (*CO* 32, 74).
[35] Ps. 92:10 (*CO* 32, 14). Cf. Ps. 119:76 (*CO* 32, 247): "...sed quod Deus toti ecclesiae promisit, pro fidei natura ad se accommodat."

rightly handling the promises whenever one applies that to himself which God presents to all in general."[36]

Calvin remarkably not only speaks about the lost humanity from which believers are saved. He also speaks about a humanity which is connected with Christ in a certain way, and yet among them there are some who break out of it because of their unbelief. In commenting upon Psalm 22:23, Calvin suggests that it is properly applied to all people that they are "brothers of Christ" in some way.[37] Unbelievers, however, destroy this bond with Christ by their disbelief; and thus they are, by their own guilt, rendered strangers to him. Since Christ has destroyed the wall between Jews and heathens, he proclaims that he wants to adopt the whole world and that he wants to be a brother to all peoples. Yet Calvin explains that only believers are his real brothers.[38]

God presents himself through his promises as though he voluntarily makes himself our debtor.[39] In actual he has obligated himself by a contract, and thus he is liable for these commitments.[40] God has committed himself to reward our obedience.[41] Man may point out to God that there is a covenant and that this covenant is eternal. If God wants to avoid that his faithfulness is slandered, then he must show that these promises have not been given in vain.[42] Through the covenant, our enemies are God's enemies, and this guarantees us his protection insofar as the covenant includes protection by God.[43] Meanwhile, God has an interest in keeping his promise, for if his people suffer harm, his majesty is also damaged because he has bound his name to his people.[44] Calvin calls it inappropriate that God would not keep his promises.[45] On biblical grounds, Calvin sharply rejects the "diabolical" idea of Servet that it is foolish to approach God with his own promises.[46] Rather, the covenant gives Israel the *right* to protection from God. Although this right is based on God's grace, it is still a right in the full sense based upon the nature of the covenant.[47] Again, through his discussion about the covenant, Calvin's commentary on the Psalms clearly illustrates that the Genevan Reformer follows the nominalists in speaking about God's free

---

[36] Ps. 49:16 (*CO* 31, 491).

[37] "...nobis fuisse cum Christo ius fraternae coniunctionis. Etsi autem competit hoc aliquatenus in totum genus humanum...," Ps. 22:23 (*CO* 31, 231).

[38] Ps. 22:23 (*CO* 31, 232).

[39] "...quasi voluntarium debitorem...," Ps. 119:58 (*CO* 32, 240).

[40] Ps. 143:8 (*CO* 32, 404).

[41] Ps. 19:11 (*CO* 31, 230).

[42] Ps. 115:2 (*CO* 32, 183).

[43] Ps. 146:10 (*CO* 32, 425).

[44] Ps. 83:3 (*CO* 31, 773).

[45] Ps. 80:9 (*CO* 31, 756).

[46] Ps. 74:19 (*CO* 31, 699).

[47] Ps. 68:35 (*CO* 31, 636).

obligation of himself to certain commitments.[48] It is by the power of the covenant that God does not constantly need a new reason to act as a savior and helper, but he always intervenes to prove both his faithfulness and the purposes of his covenant.[49] This is the reason, he says, why God continues to care for Israel despite her sins.

Meanwhile, though, in the covenant *believers* are also under an obligation *to God*. Despite emanating from the grace of God, the covenant asks for the approval of both sides. Calvin calls this bilateral aspect "the rule of the covenant" (*regula foederis*).[50] By virtue of this bilateral nature, God has the covenantal right to be honored by us.[51] For example, God's condition for the liberation of his people is that they must honor him at certain times for his grace.[52] Also, through the covenant, the grace of God and the piety of man are connected so that they conform to one another. As Calvin observes, man should not be surprised if God should consequently pull back his hand after the piety of people has diminished.[53] Both the legal character of the covenant and God's place in it lead Calvin to describe it as "a terrible injustice" when people do not trust God's promises.[54]

3. Covenant and Faith

Faith is by its very nature focused on the promises of the covenant.[55] Indeed, Calvin writes, "There is a mutual relationship between God's promises and our belief."[56] This relationship allows the believer to enter into discussion with God when it appears as if he has not kept his promises. Additionally, God's promises, he says, have to be activated in the sense that they require both meditation[57] and trust.[58]

When God's hand of chastisement is felt in our lives, the thought of the covenant gives one a grip on which to hold, for God has adopted us in the

---

[48] "[It is] not the Stoic but the longstanding medieval vocabulary of commitment that we encounter with Scotus and the nominalistic theologians as the *pactum Dei* to which God is bound *de potentia ordinate*." Heiko A. Oberman, *Sacrae Scripturae*, 121. See also Berndt Hamm, *Promissio, Pactum, Ordinatio: Freiheit und Selbstbindung Gottes in der scholastischen Gnadenlehre* (Tübingen: Mohr, 1977). Hamm points to the influence of Roman and Canonical Law on the terminology of the "Selbstbindung Gottes."

[49] Ps. 105:42 (*CO* 32, 114).

[50] Ps. 15:1 (*CO* 31, 143).

[51] "Quia autem in foederibus mutua est conventio...," Ps. 81:5 (*CO* 31, 760).

[52] Ps. 81:5 (*CO* 31, 761).

[53] Ps. 99:8 (*CO* 32, 53).

[54] Ps. 27:1 (*CO* 31, 271).

[55] Ps. 25:4 (*CO* 31, 252).

[56] Ps. 30:10 (*CO* 31, 298).

[57] Ps. 4: introduction (*CO* 31, 57).

[58] Ps. 13: introduction (*CO* 31, 131).

covenant as his children.[59] In this promise we see that God deals with us not as a judge but as a father. God's promise of the covenant is the key which opens the door to him. Just like Luther, Calvin points out that we should remind God of his own promises since this is the only way to receive God's favor. Calvin furthermore calls it a "comfortable" way since it does not require of us any exceptional feat.[60] At the same time, though, Calvin relates this to the hardships entailed in the *theologia crucis*, which affirms that "there is no place for the promises of God in shadow and peace but only in the fiercest struggle."[61] God's promises reveal their power only at that moment when it is necessary, and thus they give hope for life in the midst of death.[62] In times of ardent struggle and terrible fear it is God's promises which revive hope and serve as a shield against various types of temptation.[63] As a promise is "the mother of patience,"[64] so it is patience and hope which open the door to the fulfillment of God's promises. The promised grace cannot come to us if we do not trust in God's promises.[65] Finally, he notes, the only safeguard against inherent confusion and depression is to seek support in the promises of God.[66]

4. Old and New Covenant

Although Calvin begins with the assumption of the unity of the covenant before and after Christ, he does discuss some of the differences which are nevertheless evident. After Christ, for example, it is clearer that the covenant concerns the fatherhood of God as the Spirit of adoption is now poured out more abundantly.[67] In the New Covenant no other contents are added, but they are presented more clearly and more people are brought into the covenant. The coming of Christ also brings "a renewal of the church" in that the separation has ended and the heathen now share in the adoption as God's children.[68]

While the sacrifices of the Old Testament system were indeed offered before Christ's death on the cross, they did not have anything meritorious about them. Rather, these sacrifices were also grounded in Christ's atonement. In their sacrifices, Calvin describes, "The Jews were actually

---

[59] Ps. 74:1 (*CO* 31, 692).
[60] Calvin uses "*facilem.*" Ps. 27:7 (*CO* 31, 275-6).
[61] Ps. 37:14 (*CO* 31, 372).
[62] Ps. 3:1 (*CO* 31, 52). Cf. Ps. 13: introduction (*CO* 31, 131): "...inter mortis terrores certam vitae fiduciam ex Dei promissione concipit."
[63] Ps. 4: introduction (*CO* 31, 57).
[64] Ps. 130:5 (*CO* 32, 336).
[65] Ps. 48:9 (*CO* 31, 475).
[66] Ps. 42:6 (*CO* 31, 429).
[67] Ps. 67:3 (*CO* 31, 618).
[68] "...adoptionis consortes...," Ps. 96:7 (*CO* 32, 39).

borrowing from Christ a ransom which no mortal possesses."[69] Consequently man's role in the sacrifices of the Old Testament was just as passive as the role of those who live after Christ.[70]

Calvin also details how (even before the time of Christ) heaven is the ultimate objective of the covenant. Canaan, though, is a pledge of this ultimate goal and it serves to encourage the people to keep their attention directed towards the heavenly inheritance.[71] "The promises of the law were spiritual,"[72] he writes, again reflecting the lack of essential differences between the Old and New Covenant in his theology. The *patres* furthermore knew that they were but pilgrims on the earth, on the way to the heavenly fatherland. They did not seek it in a life here on earth, but they lived on earth with their focus directed towards heaven.[73] Likewise, the believers of the Old Testament were directed to a better life than this life.[74]

Calvin's view holds that the covenant with Abraham is included in God's covenant with the church. There is *one* covenant which God "entered into from the beginning with the whole church."[75] As a consequence, for any local church and any particular church member at any point in history, they are necessarily part of the same covenant and belong to the same church. As Calvin remarks based on Psalm 89:4, there is only *one* covenant concerned. God did not enter into his covenant with David only but with the whole church; that even includes the church of the coming centuries.[76] The kingdom of David was erected to be a shadowy image "in which God shows the mediator to his church."[77]

Calvin builds upon the implications of this continuity when he suggests that the church should be comforted in difficult times by the benevolent deeds which God has done in times past.[78] Calvin's emphases on both the covenant's unity and its unchanging contents have a pastoral intention: the believers in his own day could be assured that God would be favorable towards them precisely because the promises apply towards all of Abraham's descendants.[79]

---

[69] Ps. 51:18 (*CO* 31, 522).

[70] "...adeoque sacrificia legis, hominum respectu, mere passiva erant," Ps. 51:18 (*CO* 31, 522).

[71] Ps. 105:11 (*CO* 32, 102).

[72] Ps. 49:16 (*CO* 31, 491).

[73] "...sed mentibus in coelum sublatis cucurisse per hunc mundum...," Ps. 49:16 (*CO* 31, 490).

[74] Ps. 49:15 (*CO* 31, 489).

[75] Ps. 15:1 (*CO* 31, 143).

[76] "...sed totum ecclesiae corpus in futuras aetatis respexit," Ps. 89:4 (*CO* 31, 813).

[77] Ps. 89:31 (*CO* 31, 832).

[78] Ps. 44:3 (*CO* 31, 438).

[79] "...posteri, ad quos promissae gratiae haereditas pertinet...," Ps. 46:8 (*CO* 31, 464).

5. Prayer as Covenant Communication

The contents of the promise are not available loose, and therefore the covenant demands communication between the partners in the covenant. This communication mainly takes place through prayer.[80] In the Bible prayer is often called the invocation of God as an indication of the whole of our worship to God.[81] According to Calvin prayer is the most important part of one's religious life.[82] Without prayer, faith is indeed dead since prayer is both the demonstration of the Spirit of adoption in God's children (the Spirit being the one who incites us to prayer[83]) and a reflection that we accept God's promises as firm and binding.[84] Calvin reasons that faith cannot exist without prayer: "…for without prayer faith would be without deeds and life."[85] To be active in experiencing and strengthening faith believers will find great encouragement in prayer.[86] Meditation on God's promises through the covenant only makes sense when it results in prayer.[87] Furthermore, through personal prayer, the sincerity of belief is apparent.[88] For Calvin, prayer activates the covenant in the sense that the Spirit (who accepts the person) and the believer (who accepts the promises of God) there meet each other, reflecting that the covenant deals with two parties in relationship. Calvin describes the contact between both partners of the covenant as *"familiariter,"* a term which suggests a child speaking with his father.[89] This contact, though, is most threatened when prayer is neglected. The remedy for this is to regularly address God in prayer as "my God."[90] This *familiaritas* also carries the implication that the believer can be as he or she is when speaking to God and that it is not so bad when we do not know exactly how to say something in prayer. Calvin suggests that God even *prefers* it when we stammer in

---

[80] For a comprehensive survey of Calvin's view on the meaning, content and practice of prayer, see Hans Scholl, *Der Dienst des Gebetes nach Johannes Calvin* (Zürich: Zwingli Verlag, 1968). Cf. Hesselink, *Catechism*, 129-39 and Kolfhaus, *Leben*, 453-81.

[81] "…per synecdochen…" Ps. 14:4 (*CO* 31, 139).

[82] "Caeterum Dei invocatio, quia praecipuum est pietatis exercitium…," Ps. 14:4 (*CO* 31, 139).

[83] Ps 17:1 (*CO* 31, 159).

[84] Ps. 145:18 (*CO* 32, 418).

[85] Ps. 119:58 (*CO* 32, 239).

[86] Ps. 109:21 (*CO* 32, 155).

[87] "Et certe nisi nos ad precandum sollicitet promissionum Dei meditatio, ad nos sustinendos impar erit," Ps. 42:7 (*CO* 31, 430).

[88] "Ergo ex precibus cognoscitur fidei veritas, sicuti bonitas arboris ex fructu," Ps. 22:5 (*CO* 31, 224).

[89] Ps. 10:13 (*CO* 31, 116).

[90] "Deum quoque vocando regem suum et Deum suum, quia acrius se ad bene sperandum incitavit: discamus haec elogia in similem aptare usum, nempe ut Deum nobis familiarem reddamus…," Ps. 5:2 (*CO* 31, 66).

speaking to him rather than use the most splendid rhetoric,[91] a remarkable statement for someone who was devoted to pure and clear formulations!

For the readers of his Psalms commentary Calvin points to the promises of the covenant. He says, for example, that the basis of prayers for help is nothing but the fact that "God has adopted us in his merciful election as his people."[92] God's promise also invites us to prayer,[93] and it is our certainty in resting upon God's promises which leads to prayer.[94] God promises that he will be favorable towards believers when they pray. Furthermore, the promise is a particular privilege since God invites believers to himself with this promise.[95] This is also the promise that we do not have to be afraid of God and that no one prays to him in vain. The door, Calvin says, is open to everyone.[96] We must first know and trust this promise before we can appropriately come to God. On this topic, Calvin again takes the opportunity to criticize Roman Catholic doctrine whereby, according to him, people always pray to God in fear and doubt due to their uncertainty of grace. Over and against this, Calvin praises "the unimaginable privilege" that a believer continually possesses in being able to approach God freely.[97]

Although Calvin can certainly sympathize with the fears of believers, knowing many of them himself, he wants to make it clear that despite life's uncertainties there is no reason to be afraid when approaching God in prayer:

> So often as we pray to God many doubts steal upon us; consequently we either approach God with a trembling heart, we stop praying, being discouraged and deathly afraid, or our faith fails through fear. For this reason David declares that God hears without exception all who call upon him.[98]

Calvin describes how even in our prayer God accommodates himself to us. In his exposition of Psalm 44:23, for example, the call to awaken God from his sleep provides an occasion for Calvin to reflect more deeply upon this *accommodatio*. The Reformer likens this verse to mere "babbling" (*balbutire*) by the believer, whether in connection with speech directed to God (namely, prayer) or in speech about him. God tolerates this type of speech only if we do not think that God really does not take notice of us any

---

[91] "...verum haec balbuties Dei gratior est quam omnes quantumvis nitidae ac splendidae rhetorum figurae," Ps. 5:5 (*CO* 31, 67).
[92] Ps. 74:19 (*CO* 31, 699).
[93] Ps. 50:14 (*CO* 31, 502).
[94] Ps. 36:13 (*CO* 31, 364).
[95] Ps. 145:18 (*CO* 32, 418).
[96] "...aperta est ianua, ut certatim omnes ad eum confluant," Ps. 65:2 (*CO* 31, 603).
[97] Ps. 65:2 (*CO* 31, 603).
[98] Ps. 145:18 (*CO* 32, 418).

more. Such a prayer, of course, is corrupted by mistaken notions of God's nature, but God's grace forgives these sins and gives us room to say the things in such a way.[99] Hence, though such a prayer is wrong, God nevertheless forgives and permits it according to the remarkable conclusion of Calvin's argument: God allows us to deal with him in prayer "*familiariter.*"[100] In concrete terms, this means *inter alia* the permission to urge him to haste in prayer, provided that believers know to be moderate in this petition as they subject themselves to his will.[101] Since the aim of our life is to know God as our Father and to enjoy his fatherly benevolence, we may urge him in our prayer to make haste so long as it is within certain bounds of piety.[102] God gives us the freedom to pray in this way, but he will not let himself be rushed.[103]

In the Psalter, Calvin observes that God gives us quite a bit of latitude concerning how we are to pray. This freedom is particularly apparent whenever the question of suffering is in view. For instance, in Psalm 110 David asks why God keeps himself at such a distance. David then calls upon God to answer him and pleads that he may not have to wait such a long time before receiving help. However, David does this without doing injury to God's honor. Calvin interprets this struggle with God's ways not as a reproach to God but instead as an encouragement for him who prays that he would be confident through this manner of speech that God will hear him. The boundary for this kind of prayerful lament is when our complaint about suffering becomes an actual reproach of God.[104] Calvin uses the word "*licentia*" to speak of the room God grants to believers. God gives man a license to complain.

> Of course it would not be worthy of his majesty for us to nag like spoiled children if he himself had not granted us permission. Therefore I use the word "license" intentionally in order that those weak in faith who are afraid to approach God might also know that he invites them gently so that nothing would hinder them from approaching God as if they were in his presence like a child at home.[105]

---

[99] "...sciamus eius indulgentia abstergi vitium hoc, ne preces nostras contaminet," Ps. 44:24 (*CO* 31, 448).

[100] "...verum ut curas suas et dolores familiariter reiiciat in eius sinum, ut nobis permittit secum familiariter agere," Ps. 89:39 (*CO* 31, 826). See also Ps. 119:58 (*CO* 32, 239).

[101] Ps. 89:47 (*CO* 31, 829).

[102] "...ut Deum suis precibus ad festinationem incitent," Ps. 89:47 (*CO* 31, 829).

[103] Ps. 40:14 (*CO* 31, 416).

[104] Ps. 10:1 (*CO* 31, 108-9).

[105] Ps. 102:3 (*CO* 32, 63).

By his inspired description of prayer throughout the Psalter, the Holy Spirit also accommodates himself to human capacities by speaking in a way which we can understand.[106] This accommodation is apparent, for example, when David, in the course of prayer, calls upon God to first look upon him in order that he might see his need and consequently help him. In reality, however, these are two actions are carried out by God simultaneously.

6. Contents and Attitude of Prayer

The most important aspect of prayer is to seek the remission of sins, for only after such remission is the way opened for God to help us.[107] Likewise, guilt must be confessed in prayer in order to maintain communication with God. Through prayer, man appreciates both his failure to live according to the righteousness required by the covenant, and he is assured that there is only a reward for good deeds when sins are forgiven.[108] Thus, the believer's prayer is both offered up and heard based upon the sacrifice of Christ. For our prayers to be acceptable to God, Calvin says, they first have to be purified and sanctified by the blood of Christ.[109] In the Old Testament God connects approaching him in prayer with bringing him sacrifices, implying both that prayers on their own do not have any value and that they are heard only by God's grace through the sacrifice of the mediator.[110]

There is a correct order to our prayer, though, inasmuch as the believer ought to first pray for the church and only secondarily for himself. Prayer for the whole body precedes any prayer for a mere member of the body. As the reason for this sequence, Calvin explains that an individual believer's salvation is anchored in the salvation and welfare of the broader church.[111]

Through the course of his Psalms commentary Calvin offers a number of rules for our prayer. One rule is that the hope and focus should be totally turned towards God, for only when we direct our hope away from humans and earthly things do we give God the honor.[112] Another "*precandi regula*" is the injunction not to cease praying even when after a long time it seems futile to us.[113] A true believer, he notes, does not quit after only one prayer.[114] Furthermore Calvin gives the rule that man has to dispose of his own dignity

---

[106] "...spiritum sanctum precandi formas ad sensum nostrum data opera accommodare," Ps. 13:4 (*CO* 31, 133).

[107] Ps. 119:58 (*CO* 32, 240), Ps. 65:4 (*CO* 31, 604).

[108] "...quia sine gratuita remissione peccatorum nulla operum retributio speranda est," Ps. 25:11 (*CO* 31, 257).

[109] Ps. 20:4 (*CO* 31, 209).

[110] Ps. 119:108 (*CO* 32, 261).

[111] Ps. 122:6 (*CO* 32, 306).

[112] "...orandi regula...," Ps. 25:1 (*CO* 31, 250).

[113] Ps. 22:3 (*CO* 31, 222).

[114] Ps. 86:6 (*CO* 31, 793).

before he starts praying, for only then will he expect something of God's kindness.[115]

Next to these rules which primarily have to do with the content, Calvin also recommends a rule for the regularity of prayer. Just as Israel had fixed times in which to present the sacrifices, our weakness in faith suggests that we also should have specific times for prayer, both individually and corporately.[116] The best time to pray, says Calvin, is when you feel that God has flung you far away from him.[117] According to the Reformer, David here teaches us that "the more that misfortune depresses us, the more suitable the moment is to pray."[118]

The value of prayer, however, is not determined by its form but by the essential attitude of the one who prays. Calvin criticizes here a ritualized practice of prayer. Instead, one's inner attitude must reflect their certainty in faith. Indeed, prayer is only sincere when someone is sure about God's salvation.[119] There is no prayer without the certainty of faith, and so to pray while doubting is a wasted effort.[120] Elsewhere Calvin remarks that a prayer without hope is senseless.[121] Trust is the key which opens the door to the heart of God.[122]

Since our attitude is often reflected in our bodily posture, Calvin finds praying with raised hands a useful aid for prayer.[123] He is also rather favorable towards kneeling down for prayer since he considers it necessary that a thankful heart find expression in the position of the body. Believers therefore fulfill their duties well, he observes, "when they present themselves openly as a sacrifice to God by bending their knees or with some other [outward] sign."[124]

Calvin can understand those who make rather uncontrolled utterances in their prayer. These people "do not speak from a simple and peaceful mind," but by their words "the vehemence of their feelings" is heard.[125] Singleness of heart, he writes, is the only rhetorical element in prayer which is appreciated by God.[126]

---

[115] Ps. 115:1 (*CO* 32, 183).

[116] Ps. 55:17 (*CO* 31, 542).

[117] "...quum videri posset procul a Deo reiectus, sibi hoc maxime opportunum fuisse tempus orandi," Ps. 116:1 (*CO* 32, 193).

[118] Ps. 118:5 (*CO* 32, 203).

[119] Ps. 140:7 (*CO* 32, 388).

[120] "...dubitanter orando nihil aliud quam opera luditur," Ps. 140:13 (*CO* 32, 390).

[121] "...frivolas esse preces, quibus non est spes annexa...," Ps. 5:4 (*CO* 31, 67).

[122] Ps. 7:2 (*CO* 31, 80).

[123] Ps. 28:2 (*CO* 31, 281).

[124] Ps. 95:6 (*CO* 32, 30).

[125] Ps. 89:47 (*CO* 31, 829).

[126] "...quia tota rhetoricae nostrae gratia coram Deo mera est simplicitas," Ps. 17:1 (*CO* 31, 159).

7. The Benefit and Aim of Prayer

God could just as easily establish his kingdom without the prayers of believers, of course, but he instead wants to involve their prayers since it is the task of believers to advance God's honor.[127] This also applies to prayer for the coming of Christ's kingdom. Christ does not *need* our prayers, Calvin explains, but he demands them as proof of the faith of those who serve him.[128] Thus, prayer is not a *"medium salutis,"* but it is a *"medium honoris."*

The purpose of God hearing our prayer is to make it clear that God is the protector of their salvation.[129] At the same time, though, that is also the limit to prayer in the sense that God does not help when it is not really necessary. Consequently believers ought not to present their wishes to God at random, but they should be careful to avoid asking for more than what God has promised in his word.[130] Calvin states it as a rule of prayer that we must subject our requests to God's will as it is revealed to us in the word.[131] In Calvin's opinion the honor of God should also take priority in prayer. Hence to not pray would mean to deprive God of his honor since thereby one would not acknowledge his help in need nor recognize his care in prosperity.[132]

The question though is whether prayers can have an effect on the plans of God. Calvin's answer to this question amounts to the conclusion that God, by means of our prayers, does what he has planned all along to do. Calvin's insight into the matter concerns the relationship between God's promises and our prayers. Not our prayer but God's grace is the cause for his help, but this help comes via prayer since God has promised that he would help him who prays for it.[133]

For the believer herself, prayer has a clear purpose in Calvin's mind. While the feelings of the flesh create the impression that God keeps himself hidden in the darkness, prayer is necessary to show God's light again. Prayer therefore does not bring God back into the light, but it helps us to see that God has not been hidden.[134]

Calvin's view of God may seem to hinder his doing justice to the biblical data about prayer. Calvin asserts that prayer is not meant to bring about any change to God, "for it is not necessary to persuade God by arguments, but

---

[127] Ps. 118:25 (*CO* 32, 213).

[128] Ps. 72:15 (*CO* 31, 670).

[129] Ps. 145:18 (*CO* 32, 420).

[130] Ps. 145:18 (*CO* 32, 419-20).

[131] Ps. 7:7 (*CO* 31, 82).

[132] Ps. 17:1 (*CO* 31, 159).

[133] "...quia quum gratuita promissionibus annexae sint preces, harum effectus ex illis fluit," Ps. 102:18 (*CO* 32, 69).

[134] Ps. 94:1 (*CO* 32, 19).

God allows believers to communicate with him familiarly (*familiariter*) in order that they would lay down their worries."[135]

Beyond its theological dimension, prayer also has much more of a psychological dimension for Calvin. It gives people the opportunity to unburden their hearts.[136] As far as God is concerned, it is unnecessary that we remind him of our feelings and arguments because he knows them already. God gives us prayer in order that we might be relieved of our worries and that our confidence might be increased.[137] Calvin often speaks about how prayer can unburden man from the things which depress him.[138] God gives prayer to relieve us of our burdens, for through it we can pour out our hearts to God.[139] In our prayer God also allows us to express disappointment.[140] Through prayer Calvin even instructs the reader to "put your worries bit by bit on God."[141] There we lay down our troubles on God's lap.[142]

Since Calvin considers these psychological aspects in prayer, he runs the risk to lay the emphasis more on prayer's purpose for the believer than for God. He continuously reiterates that prayer is not meant to give God information as much as to give the one who prays the assurance that God is acquainted with his situation, even calling it the purpose of prayer.[143] Thus, the mention of the divine titles which illustrate God's greatness is not intended to flatter God but to encourage the person who prays.[144]

However, in Calvin's commentary we also find various indications that he thinks prayer does somehow *affect* God. When believers present their needs to him, it compels God to help them with his grace.[145] God hears the prayers of his people, and he never disappoints them when they call upon him.[146] It is against God's nature, in fact, to not hear and answer prayers.[147] Calvin says that God is inseparable (*inseparabile*) from the work of hearing and answering prayer. He is affected then when we remind him that our troubles concern his cause.[148] Therefore, we read in the commentary that David "provokes God's mercy" by his prayer.[149] Calvin furthermore admits

---

[135] Ps. 31:9 (*CO* 31, 305).

[136] Ps. 10:1 (*CO* 31, 109). Cf. Ps. 10:14 (*CO* 31, 117): "...exonerati...."

[137] Ps. 10:13 (*CO* 31, 116).

[138] Ps. 22:3 (*CO* 31, 223).

[139] Ps. 102:1 (*CO* 32, 61).

[140] Ps. 22:3 (*CO* 31, 223).

[141] Ps. 86:6 (*CO* 31, 793).

[142] Ps. 89:39 (*CO* 31, 826).

[143] "...hic tamen est precationis usus et finis...," Ps. 17:9 (*CO* 31, 163).

[144] Ps. 18:3 (*CO* 31, 17).

[145] Ps. 27:7 (*CO* 31, 275).

[146] Ps. 65:2 (*CO* 31, 603).

[147] "...quia eas repudiando Deus quodammmodo naturam suam exueret," Ps. 65:2 (*CO* 31, 603).

[148] Ps. 89:52 (*CO* 31, 831).

[149] Ps. 22:7 (*CO* 31, 224).

the influence of prayer when he says that "we should never cease praying since we know that we are lost if God were only to take away his grace for a moment!"[150] Calvin is also convinced that prayer can hasten God's involvement and can increase his hatred towards enemies.[151] When we pray we do not make an appeal to him in vain, for it is natural for God to help people in distress.[152] Prayer allows one to convince God when, for instance, he can be reminded that help given to one believer would be in the interest of all believers.[153] Hence prayer highlights a type of interaction with the believer: God permits us to incite him to haste, but the result is limited insofar as God will respond and help us in his own time.[154] Calvin says we also must give him time to hear our prayer.[155] In the temptations we face when God hides himself and leaves us waiting, prayer is the means we have to remain steadfast by calling upon God to show himself. Temptation ought to lead believers to prayer.[156] One can resist the enticement towards despair which springs from God's hiddenness only if prayer relies on the grace of God, for then God will certainly answer with grace.[157]

When we survey the entirety of Calvin's utterances about prayer, it is clear that this theme concerns both the honor of God and the salvation of man. For Calvin, prayer has a greater interest in honoring God than in changing him. As to the purpose for the believer, prayer has a *psychological* benefit in providing relief from his or her burdens. Yet, it still remains an open question whether Calvin's opinions are in conformity with the biblical view of God when, in his opinion, prayer is not so much about moving God to a responsive action so much as it is given to bring a believer to greater confidence.

8. The Church as Community of the Covenant

In the Psalms Calvin can find much which is applicable to the church because he understands the kingdom of David as foreshadowing the kingdom of Christ.[158] Along these lines, Calvin calls the reign of David and the other kings of Israel a *pledge* of the rule of Christ.[159] He appeals to the apostle Paul, who in Romans 3:13 refers to Psalm 5:10, seeing the church described in the

---

[150] Ps. 50:14 (*CO* 31, 502).

[151] Ps. 5:1 (*CO* 31, 70).

[152] Ps. 38:12 (*CO* 31, 392).

[153] Ps. 5:12 (*CO* 31, 71).

[154] Ps. 6:4 (*CO* 31, 75).

[155] "...dandum esse tempus Dei providentiae...," Ps. 10:1 (*CO* 31, 117).

[156] Ps. 25:6 (*CO* 31, 252-3).

[157] Ps. 80:15 (*CO* 31, 757).

[158] "Caterum hic typus vaticinium continet de futuro Christi regno...," Ps. 2: introduction (*CO* 31, 41).

[159] "...velut arrha quaedam veteri populo fuit aeterni regni...," Ps. 2:1 (*CO* 31, 43).

person of David.[160] Calvin therefore concludes of David "that he in his person represents Christ as well as the whole body of the church."[161] What is said about David then applies both to Christ and to all Christians.[162]

Calvin indicates that the church of his time was not in good shape. Without any protection by the authorities it simply lays out in the open as an easy prey for the enemies of the church. He remarks that the church was left in ruins in a big confusion,[163] and it was in a pathetic state of decline.[164] This had been the situation ever since the beginning of the Reformation, that moment, says Calvin, "in which the gospel began to appear."[165]

> For even though God has his temples here and there where he is purely worshipped, if we cast our eyes upon the whole world, we see that his holy temple is everywhere demolished in desolate ruins because his word is trampled and worship to him is defiled in countless abominations. Even small churches where God dwells are torn and scattered.[166]

Because of this situation Calvin supposes that all believers are longing for the restoration of the church[167] and that God will again gather all his elect back into one body of Christ "in order that the mutilated body of the church, which is still torn apart daily, will once more be restored in its integrity."[168] With the Reformation, a period which Calvin compares to the return from the Babylonian Captivity, God has begun to collect his church again.[169] For Calvin the spiritual unity of the believers cannot exist apart from the visible unity of the church.

God has entered into a holy relationship with the church.[170] As Calvin describes it, this bond is "a spiritual covenant through which God elects for

---

[160] "...sub Davidis persona nobis describi ecclesiam tam in Christo capite quam im membris," Ps. 5:10 (*CO* 31, 70).

[161] Ps. 109:1 (*CO* 32, 147).

[162] Ps. 120:2 (*CO* 32, 296).

[163] "...in tristi corruptissimi et prorsus confusi status...," Ps. 12:1 (*CO* 31, 126).

[164] "...in deploratis ecclesiae ruinis...," Ps. 14:1 (*CO* 31, 135).

[165] Ps. 123:3 (*CO* 32, 310).

[166] Ps. 102:15 (*CO* 32, 68).

[167] "...modo sincero fidei consensu simul adspirent ad restitutionem ecclesiae...," Ps. 102:18 (*CO* 32, 69). The mention of the impossibility of legitimate meetings indicates that Calvin is thinking particularly of the believers of France.

[168] Ps. 147:2 (*CO* 32, 427).

[169] Ps. 126:2 (*CO* 32, 318).

[170] "...vinculum sanctae coniunctionis...," Ps. 44:3 (*CO* 31, 438).

himself a church which leads a heavenly life on earth."[171] The origin of the church lies in the undeserved love of God.[172] Furthermore, God wants people on earth who praise him. Thus the aim of the church is the praise of God. The church also has the task of testifying to God's kindness.[173] Although it was originally the task of the entire human race to honor God, this role is now being fulfilled by the church. This is the reason for calling the church "a planting of God to his honor."[174] Calvin speaks more about the election of the church as a whole than about the election of individual believers; when he speaks about the individual's election, he always does so in the framework of the community of the church.

For the Reformer, the church is the community of the covenant in two distinct ways: as the place where the covenant with God takes shape in the communication between God and man, *and* as the place where the bond with other believers is formed based upon the covenant. The glory of the church is that God has entrusted the covenant of eternal life to the church; hence the heavenly splendor shines most brightly in her.[175]

The church is a theater where one can see God's glory.[176] Although the whole world is "the theater of God's kindness, wisdom, justice and power," Calvin mentions that in this theater the church is actually the part which illustrates it the best—like an orchestra.[177] The congregation of the church is the holy place which God has appointed for his praise since this praise originates from the experience of God's care.[178] The church is thus elected by God to be "the theater of his fatherly care."[179] Given this connection between the church and the praise of God, Calvin declares that the best way to see the increase of God's praise is to promote the growth of the church.[180] When there are more believers, there will be more praise to God!

Considering God's purposes for the church, Calvin notes that she can be absolutely sure of God's continuous protection.[181] In fact, this certainty can be found all the way back in God's work of creation as it is described in the

---

[171] Ps. 105:1 (*CO* 32, 98).

[172] "Et certe hic fons et origo est ecclesiae, nempe gratuitus Dei amor," Ps. 44:4 (*CO* 31, 439).

[173] "...Deum sibi consulto in hunc finem gratuita adoptione creare ecclesiam in mundo, ut nomen suum rite a legitimis testibus laudetur," Ps. 33:1 (*CO* 31, 324).

[174] Ps. 95:7 (*CO* 32, 31).

[175] "...quod foedus aeternae vitae in ecclesia sua deposuerit...," Ps. 93:5 (*CO* 31, 18).

[176] "...ecclesia insigne sit gloriae Dei theatrum...," Ps. 76:2 (*CO* 31, 706).

[177] "...mundus theatrum...pars tamen illustrior, instar orchestrae, est ecclesia...," Ps. 135:13 (*CO* 32, 361).

[178] Ps. 18:50 (*CO* 31, 193).

[179] "...ut theatrum esset paternae suae sollicitudinis." Ps. 68:8 (*CO* 31, 622).

[180] "...nunquam melius celebrari Dei nomen quam dum propagatur religio et crescit ecclesia...," Ps. 102:22 (*CO* 32, 71).

[181] Ps. 68:20 (*CO* 31, 629).

scriptures. God created the world so that there might be people who would acknowledge and praise God as their Father. Had God not saved the church, though, there would not have been such a people and the whole creation would have been rendered senseless.[182] God therefore must take care of the church lest he fail in his objective in creation. Calvin also addresses the certainty of the church's survival from the standpoint of grace. The fact that the church originates and exists through the grace of God (and not through any human work) guarantees her survival. Indeed, Calvin argues that the church is too precious for God to let its existence depend on the efforts of people.[183] Consequently, he is convinced that the church will never perish based upon his view on the character of God. Once God has decided to save the church, no power is able to prevent it. God takes the church to heart, and it is his nature to care for that which he loves.[184] Because God has created the church in order that there would be a people to honor him, the end of the church would mark the end of his kingship.[185] Here also it is clear how Calvin in a way ties God up to the creation and to the church through the mutual dependence between God and church.

The church's right for existence rests solely in the preaching of God's word. Calvin explains, "Only because of the preaching of the grace of God will the church never perish."[186] Calvin hereby offers the conclusion that the church has to make sure that the true teaching (doctrine) should be handed down well and thus taught well so that this teaching—and with that also *the church herself!*—would remain even after we pass away. Therefore, *"doctrina," "praedicatio"* and *"ecclesia"* cannot exist without each other. The church is only found where religion is pure, namely, where the gospel is purely proclaimed and God is purely served.[187]

The way that the Bible speaks about the church as a bride and Christ as a bridegroom also points to the covenantal character of the relationship between God and the church. Calvin's criticism on Rome is that men have forgotten the correct relation which is to exist between a bride and a bridegroom, and thus the bride has assumed an unbiblical power to make new rules. Although the church sits at the right hand of the king and it is even called a "mother," nowhere in the Bible is it stated that Christ has elevated the church so high that he thereby loses his own authority.[188] Undoubtedly the

---

[182] "...irrita erit mundi creatio...," Ps. 115:17 (*CO* 32, 192).

[183] Ps. 78:86 (*CO* 31, 745).

[184] "...quia Deo curo ecclesiae servandae...," Ps. 3:9 (*CO* 31, 57).

[185] "...ecclesia, cuius abolitione rex esse desineret," Ps. 135:13 (*CO* 32, 361).

[186] Ps. 22:31 (*CO* 31, 237).

[187] "...sed ubi viget pura religio, illic quaerendam esse ecclesiam," Ps. 122:8 (*CO* 32, 307).

[188] Ps. 45:11 (*CO* 31, 457).

commentary on the Psalms shows that the church holds a place of preeminent importance in Calvin's mind.

9. The Church as a *Corpus Mixtum*

As Calvin points out through his analysis of the Psalter, God calls unto sanctification all those whom he allows in his flock.[189] Only those who sanctify themselves in order to serve God have the right to come into his sanctuary. This rule applied for the tabernacle, and it still applies in his governance of the church.[190] Yet when Calvin states that the church of his time was infected with impious people just like Israel in the Old Testament, he does not call for disciplinary measures but for prayer. The church has to ask God, he says, whether he wants to deliver them from these people as he did at the time of Israel.[191]

Contrary to the ideal of the Anabaptists, who held that a church without sin is possible, Calvin states that we have to leave it to Christ to separate the sheep from the goats.[192] "It is not for us to purify the church, although we have to long for its purity."[193] Based upon the connection between David and both Christ and the church, Calvin insists that David's words in Psalm 18:47 (that revenge should be left to God) have direct bearing for the church on earth who also has little right to take revenge except towards those who stubbornly persist in their sins.[194] On the contrary, it is the task of the church to do good to her enemies and to pray for their salvation. Furthermore, the church devotes herself to the conversion of sinners until it is absolutely certain that there is no longer a hope for recovery. Accordingly, Calvin explicitly warns against taking disciplinary measures too soon.[195] We have to endure the evil insofar as it is a fact we cannot change until the time of Christ's purification. The church however must wait "until the heavenly judge separates the rejected from the elect."[196] This does not mean that we should be indifferent in this regard. As far as possible we should strive that all who confess the name of Christ also live according to his will and that the church of God should be purified as much as possible from all decay.[197] Yet when the church proves herself to have shortcomings while striving towards

---

[189] "Ergo quoscunque admittit Deus in gregem suum, ipsa adoptione ad sanctitatem vocat," Ps. 24:3 (*CO* 31, 245).

[190] "...ad perpetuum ecclesiae regimen accomodare oportet," Ps. 24:3 (*CO* 31, 245).

[191] "Rogandus tamen est Deus ut domum suam cito purget...," Ps. 10:16 (*CO* 31, 119).

[192] Ps. 10:16 (*CO* 31, 119).

[193] Ps. 22:26 (*CO* 31, 233).

[194] "Ecclesiae sub Christi auspicis militanti, non alia quam adversus obstinatos vindicta permittitur," Ps. 18:48 (*CO* 31, 193).

[195] "...ne ante tempus praecipites feramur," Ps. 18:48 (*CO* 31, 193).

[196] Ps. 79:6 (*CO* 31, 749).

[197] Ps. 10:16 (*CO* 31, 119).

holiness, this is no justification for then leaving the community of the church.[198]

On this subject Calvin mentions by name the Anabaptists, whom, because of their ideal of perfect purity in the church, Calvin categorizes with the Donatists, the Cathari and the Novatians.[199] It is clearly an error, he implies, to believe that one has to immediately withdraw from a church for fear of infection if ever the good is found to be mixed with evil. David, for instance, continues going to the temple even after he has called the community there a "meeting of unbelievers." He keeps on going since the temple is the place appointed by God where a person can "take part in holy matters."[200] After all, although the Israelites proved themselves unfaithful in terms of true piety, they still remain part of the church.[201]

Calvin remarks that there are even enemies of Christ inside the church. Although such people are externally members of the church, they are not reborn through the Spirit of God.[202] Not all who have a place in the temple, he observes, have this place legitimately.[203] They may come to church often, but their actual intention is to stay away from God as far as it is possible.[204] Calvin says they decorate themselves with the name "Israel" as if they are the most important people of the church, but deep down they belong to the Ishmaelites or Edomites.[205] This is nothing more than "playing Israelites."[206]

As Calvin surveys his contemporaries, he notes that there are many "hypocrites" resting in the bosom of the church, but such are Christians in name only.[207] By virtue of the covenant they do have a place in the temple, but as they do not agree with "the rule of the covenant," Calvin suggests that they actually do not belong there.[208] Although both the true children of God and these hypocrites are found in one church (as the wheat and the chaff, respectively), the difference lies in that believers remain steadfast and the others are blown away.[209] Furthermore, hypocrites can clearly be identified by their style of living since they do not strive towards righteousness and uprightness.[210] They who devote themselves to God, though, are the real,

---

[198] Ps. 26:5 (*CO* 31, 267).

[199] Ps. 26:5 (*CO* 31, 266).

[200] "...sacrorum participatio...," Ps. 26:5 (*CO* 31, 266).

[201] Ps. 80:17 (*CO* 31, 758).

[202] Ps. 5:10 (*CO* 31, 70).

[203] "...neque iure omnes locum in templo occupabant," Ps. 65:5 (*CO* 31, 606).

[204] Ps. 24:6 (*CO* 31, 247).

[205] Ps. 73:1 (*CO* 31, 675).

[206] "...larvatos Israelitas...," Ps. 73:1 (*CO* 31, 675).

[207] "...sicuti hodie plerique titulo tensus Christiani locum in ecclesiae gremio occupant," Ps. 10:16 (*CO* 31, 118).

[208] Ps. 15:1 (*CO* 31, 143).

[209] Ps. 52:10 (*CO* 31, 530).

[210] Ps. 15:1 (*CO* 31, 143).

spiritual children of Abraham.[211] They meekly serve the *"aequitas"* and accept the covenant in which God seeks to adopt us as his children in the sincere obedience of faith.[212] Thus, urges Calvin, it is not only a matter of concern that we dwell "in the church of God, but that we strive to be considered as her legitimate citizens."[213] In spite of the presence of hypocrites,[214] Calvin's reference to "we who are elected" indicates that this is not a separate group to which he addresses himself. Calvin of course knows that there is a difference, but he often speaks and preaches without differentiation when speaking of the church.

In his exposition of Psalm 18, however, the Reformer emphasizes that that God has to save the church from internal enemies (as well as external ones) although the psalm does not even mention them. Calvin here again makes use of the analogies between David, Christ, and the church. Christ also faces the hostility of his own fellow citizens. Moreover it is the church's experience throughout the ages to be afflicted by quarrels which are caused by the hypocrites in her midst. Calvin remarks, "We know how difficult it is to keep someone under control who is not accustomed to a yoke."[215] The Psalm itself does not saying anything about this, but it is indeed the experience which Calvin had in Geneva. Appealing to Bernard of Clairvaux, Calvin writes that these "internal enemies" cannot be evaded or driven away, but Satan infects the church through them as they are more vicious than the mere physical violence of "foreign" opponents.[216] For Calvin these enemies are the unfaithful brothers present in the church.[217]

The church is therefore a *corpus mixtum* of both permanent citizens who truly reside in God's kingdom and intruders temporarily among her. As a consequence, Calvin advises his readers that "when the temple of God is infected with many impurities, obstinacy and pride should not drive us to leave the church."[218] By "impurities," Calvin is referring to an unchristian style of life. As long as the doctrine and the liturgy remain pure, the unity of the church may not be broken due to sins committed by members of the church.[219] Calvin repudiates the Anabaptists here by name since they wrongly believe that a church without sin is possible here on earth. In contrast, he

---

[211] Ps. 73:1 (*CO* 31, 675).

[212] "...qui spiritu mansuetudinis praediti, aequitatem colunt cum fratribus, et oblatum ab ipso foedus adoptionis sincero fidei obsequio confirmant," Ps. 50:4 (*CO* 31, 497).

[213] Ps. 129:7 (*CO* 32, 333).

[214] "...hypocriti, qui degeneres erant Abrahae filii...," Ps. 115:11 (*CO* 32, 188).

[215] Ps. 18:44 (*CO* 31, 190).

[216] "...hostes domesticos...," Ps. 55:13 (*CO* 31, 540).

[217] "Sicuti hodie nulli importunius in nos insaniunt quam degeneres Christiani," Ps. 83:6 (*CO* 31, 776).

[218] Ps. 15:1 (*CO* 31, 143).

[219] "...hominum delictis non ita nos offendi convenit, ut propterea scindamus unitatem," Ps. 15:1 (*CO* 31, 143).

writes that a church can even be decayed until the largest part is constituted by hypocrites, but if there are yet some sincere believers, be they ever so small a portion, you may not withhold from them the name, "people of God."[220]

10. Christ and His Members

When Calvin's doctrine of the covenant between God and the church is related to individual church members, he holds that we do not become members of the church by natural birth but by being reborn.[221] Furthermore, Calvin declares that "we are reborn into the heavenly life in no other way than through the ministry of the church."[222] The significance of the church is emphasized when he says that a person becomes a child of God as well as of the church by being reborn.[223] Hence it is not possible to be a lone believer without a church. He writes,

> He who wants to be considered a child of God has to search for a place in the church in order to practice brotherly unity with other believers in this way.[224]

The bond between Christ as head and the church as his body is a constant refrain in Calvin's writings. Whereas Christ is the eternal priest who is continuously praying and pleading for us before God the Father, the church also has to unite herself in praying to God.[225] When the head prays, the body likewise prays. Indeed the prayer of the church is only heard and answered when Christ proceeds with his prayer. Additionally, through this connection, when the church is oppressed, Calvin asserts that the head of the church also experiences this as his own oppression.[226] This bond with Christ guarantees the unity of the church as well as her continual existence. As Christ is living in union with his members, forming but *one* church, this church will remain until the end of this world.[227] The bond with Christ also explains the richness of the church—a richness which Calvin thinks reflects the divine nature of Christ himself.[228] Likewise Calvin says that the church is the mirror in which the grace and justice of God become visible.[229]

---

[220] Ps. 50:4 (*CO* 31, 497).

[221] "...quia tamen ipse in ecclesiam transitus secunda est nativitas...."

[222] "...per ecclesiam ministerium...," Ps. 87:5 (*CO* 31, 803).

[223] "...tam Dei, quam ecclesiae filii esse incipiant...," Ps. 87:5 (*CO* 31, 803).

[224] Ps. 47:10 (*CO* 31, 471).

[225] Ps. 20:2 (*CO* 31, 208).

[226] Ps. 20:2 (*CO* 31, 208).

[227] Ps. 61:7 (*CO* 31, 583).

[228] Ps. 45:14 (*CO* 31, 458).

[229] "...ecclesia speculum est gratiae et iustitiae Dei...," Ps. 11:5 (*CO* 31, 168).

Christ brings salvation from the Father to the church. Yet our participation in salvation is only possible under two conditions, both hinging upon the relationship between Christ and the church. In the first place, it is necessary "that we are all bound in *one* body under one common head." Secondly, Calvin continues, it is necessary that "all of us also take care of one other, not only caring each one for himself."[230]

The individual member of the congregation should be there to serve the church. Calvin, in fact, goes so far as to say that the one "who does not put a care for the church above all other concerns is not worthy to be considered as a member of the church."[231] He also charges that it is "absolutely absurd" for separate members, though praying for their own welfare, to not pray for the whole body.[232] Calvin acknowledges the danger that believers might think particularly of themselves in situations of worry and distress such that their concern for the brothers and sisters decreases. Yet he insists that God uses these individual troubles "to direct our worries to the whole body of the church."[233] Someone in the midst of his own misery ought not to forget the entirety of the church since "the mutual communion which exists among believers requires that everyone is glad with the happiness of the other and that all are thankful for the salvation of each one separately."[234] Through the communion of the saints, everyone experiences the needs of all the others as his or her personal burden, taking it to God.[235] It is necessary then that the Holy Spirit be the one to bring us to pray for the salvation of the entire church since, by natural inclination, everybody takes very good care of his own matters, but there are few people who are touched by the troubles of the church.[236] Sometimes the nation of Israel needed to be directed again to the contents of the covenant; God then performed some special actions like the passage through the Red Sea. In the same way God might call his covenant with the whole church to remembrance with a blessing to just *one* member of the church so that "*one* redemption is an example and pledge of eternal salvation."[237]

The individual member is also an example for the community. Everyone who praises God, Calvin writes, also encourages the whole church to do the same.[238] Furthermore, every individual believer is called to share with others

---

[230] Ps. 20:10 (*CO* 31, 212).

[231] Ps. 102:4 (*CO* 32, 62).

[232] Ps. 128:5 (*CO* 32, 329).

[233] Ps. 14:7 (*CO* 31, 142).

[234] Ps. 22:25 (*CO* 31, 232).

[235] "...mutua inter sanctos societas postulat ut singuli publicis miseriis affecti, apud Deum uno consensu gemant," Ps. 25:22 (*CO* 31, 262).

[236] "...vix centesimus quisque ecclesiae malis, ut par est, afficitur...," Ps. 102:2 (*CO* 32, 62).

[237] Ps. 18:16 (*CO* 31, 177).

[238] Ps. 22:24 (*CO* 31, 232).

that which he has received personally from God. Calvin here seems to have in mind the knowledge of faith which comes from God, calling it "*doctrina*." In this context the term does not concern dogmas so much as "the knowledge which is in our heart," an experienced knowledge of God.[239] Calvin knows that God has not given everyone the same measure of faith.[240] Nevertheless the call remains for every believer to help others progress in the fear of God.[241]

The only way to serve God well is to serve our fellow believers. Since our good deeds cannot reach God anyway, he gives us instead other believers unto whom we can do good deeds. The one who wants to love God can do so by loving the believers.[242] Calvin even suggests that God has isolated the church from the world so that, as believers serve each other in the church, they might manifest there the characteristics which are not present outside of the church, namely justice, fairness and peace.[243]

Calvin also inquires into the role of love for the church. Love is present, he says, whenever people are satisfied with the glory of the spiritual kingdom of Christ as opposed to the glory of the world.[244] This love is furthermore of such a nature that, as the situation in the world worsens, we love the church all the more.[245] Even when the church lies in ruins, we then still love the heap of ruins.[246] The wicked, meanwhile, reveal themselves as those who are not interested in the welfare of the church since, as Calvin comments, "If the salvation of the brethren is precious to us, and if we have faith very much at heart, then we will try as much as we are able to see that nothing negative happens to the church."[247]

11. The Unity of the Church

"Unity is something invaluably good."[248] This assumption, expressed in his Psalms commentary, helps explain Calvin's efforts to restore the "*unitas ecclesiae*."[249] He there describes that the children of God must seek and serve

---

[239] Ps. 119:171 (*CO* 32, 293).

[240] "...quisque pro fidei suae mensurae...," Ps. 119:171 (*CO* 32, 293).

[241] "...ut aliis alios promoveant in timore Dei...," Ps. 119:63 (*CO* 32, 242).

[242] Ps. 16:3 (*CO* 31, 150).

[243] "...ut iustitiam et aequitatem inter nos colendo beata pace omnes fruamur," Ps. 94:12 (*CO* 32, 23).

[244] Ps. 87:7 (*CO* 31, 805).

[245] "Ergo quo tristior est ecclesiae desolatio, eo minus alienari nos oportet ab eius amore," Ps. 102:15 (*CO* 32, 68).

[246] "Sed nulla desolatio obstare debet, quominus amemus ecclesiae lapides et pulverem," Ps. 102:15 (*CO* 32, 68).

[247] Ps. 122:8 (*CO* 32, 309).

[248] Ps. 133:1 (*CO* 32, 353).

[249] See W. Nijenhuis, *Calvinus Oecumenicus: Calvijn en de eenheid der kerk in het licht van zijn briefwisseling* ('s-Gravenhage: M. Nijhoff, 1959).

the unity of the church, especially considering how the enemies of the church have come together forming their own pact.[250] Unity and harmony are necessary whenever the church wants to persist in this world, and this holy unity must be served and guarded with faith and love.[251] Since God has formed a church out if his desire to be honored and worshipped by the community of believers, "All children of God should tie themselves to each other by a brotherly bond in order to thereby honor their Father with unanimous love and devotion."[252] Thus, the Reformer holds that ecumenism serves the honor of God. The best sacrifice we can make to God, Calvin writes, is that we join the communion of all believers and hold on to this communion with "a brotherly benevolence."[253]

Consequently, Calvin warns against having a multitude of churches that tears apart the unity of the body of Christ.[254] There is only *one* bride of Christ, and that bride is the sum of all Christians in the world. For Calvin such unity does not exist in outward appearances or accidental circumstances. He writes, "The unity of the church consists in the fact that the people are wholly prepared to follow the word of God so that there is *one* flock and *one* pastor."[255] As there is discord through mutual hate and tensions, "we are still brothers because of the fact that everyone has a bond with God, but we cannot be considered as *one* since we are *de facto* loose pieces of one torn body."[256] The aim of ecclesiastical unity is that all would together subject themselves to God as his servants and then collectively honor him.[257] Yet, the motivation for reaching unity must proceed from the believer himself:

> As much as we are able, let us then devote ourselves to making room for brotherly harmony (*fraterna concordia*) so that God's blessing can remain among us. Let us desire to accept with outstretched arms those who hold a different view from ours unless they refuse to come back in the unity of faith, for if they do not want this we must bid them farewell.[258]

---

[250] Ps. 119:63 (*CO* 32, 242).

[251] "Caeterum admonet David non aliter stare incolumen ecclesiam nisi ubi viget consensus, et fide ac caritate coagmentatu santam unitatem colit," Ps. 122:3 (*CO* 32, 304).

[252] Ps. 16:3 (*CO* 31, 150).

[253] Ps. 16:3 (*CO* 31, 150).

[254] "Nam si plures fingantur ecclesiae, lacerabitur corporis Christi unitas," Ps. 45:11 (*CO* 31, 456).

[255] Ps. 47:10 (*CO* 31, 471).

[256] Ps. 133:1 (*CO* 32, 353).

[257] Ps. 133:2 (*CO* 32, 354).

[258] Ps. 133:2 (*CO* 32, 355).

Calvin thus urges every member of the church to strive for "the brotherly consensus which must exist among all the children of God," and he pleads for the acceptance of everyone who subjects himself to God in the community of the church.[259] Only those who stubbornly resist God ought to be denied brotherly communion.[260] This last group causes much sorrow, though, since everyone who has but a little bit of faith experiences much grief concerning those who turn themselves away from God. "We not only shed a few tears in our eyes, but a whole river [of tears]."[261]

As it has already been noted, there is no spiritual unity for Calvin without a visible unity. When we are indeed *one* in our belief in God the Father and in Christ, this unity must find expression in both the way of consensus and brotherly love.[262]

12. Church and Israel

Calvin often gives attention to the particular position of Israel in his biblical commentaries, and this issue again appears in his exegesis of the Psalms.[263] God cares for the whole world, Calvin affirms, but by virtue of the covenant he is especially the God of but one nation—Israel.[264] Likewise, God is the king of all nations, but he only resides in the one nation of his covenant.[265] The Jews themselves had nothing through which they stood nearer to God than the other nations, but by God's election of them as his nation he established a certain "holy connection" with Israel which was completely unknown among the surrounding peoples.[266] Thus God required of Israel a certain lifestyle by which they would differentiate themselves from the other nations in keeping with the holiness of God and of the covenant.

Calvin's hermeneutical presupposition informing this topic is the unity which exists between Old Testament Israel and the New Testament church. Thus, whenever he speaks about Israel in his commentaries he frequently appeals to the concept of "*ecclesia*."[267] Just as David speaks about God's

---

[259] Ps. 133:1 (*CO* 32, 353).

[260] Ps. 133:1 (*CO* 32, 354).

[261] Ps. 119:136 (*CO* 32, 277).

[262] Ps. 133:1 (*CO* 32, 354).

[263] Calvin's view of Israel has received only limited attention in the literature. For an overview of Calvin's thoughts see: De Greef, *Oude Testament*, 191-209, and the monograph by C. Graafland, *Het Vaste Verbond: Israël en het Oude Testament bij Calvijn en het Gereformeerd Protestantisme* (Amsterdam: Bolland, 1978).

[264] "...esse tamen peculiarem Deum uni populo...," Ps. 105:6 (*CO* 32, 100).

[265] Ps. 24:1 (*CO* 31, 243-4).

[266] "...sacrum aliquod coniuntionis vinculum...," Ps. 24:1 (*CO* 31, 243).

[267] Ps. 12:1 (*CO* 31, 126); Ps. 14:1 (*CO* 31, 135); Ps. 65: introduction (*CO* 31, 602).

nation, Calvin speaks about the church.[268] He also, for instance, calls Israel's deliverance from Egypt an "earlier deliverance of the church."[269]

The New Testament, though, brings some aspects of discontinuity with Israel. Calvin explains that God brings the deadly struggle with the uncircumcised nations to an end, breaking down the dividing wall between Jew and Gentile. Hence Christ is not the savior of *one* nation only.[270] He is instead the link between the old and the new church,[271] and only through the coming of Christ has the church become mature.[272] Calvin even argues that Christ, as a savior for people from all nations, "enters into a marriage" with the whole world just as a Jew could marry a wife from a far and heathen country.[273]

In describing the jewels which Christ presented to the church with his coming, Calvin notes in particular the blessing of the church's extension.[274] The following passage in his Psalms commentary describes the early growth of the church:

> True religion, which had previously been locked up within the boundaries of Judea, was spread over the whole world. People then started to call upon God in the different languages of all nations, though he had formerly been known by only one family. Then the world, which had been terribly torn into countless sects by superstition and misconceptions, melted together into a holy unity of faith. All people then strove to join the Jews although they beforehand had an aversion towards them. Kings and nations voluntarily yielded themselves in obedience to Christ. Wolves and lions became lambs. The gifts of the Spirit were poured out upon believers—gifts which far surpass all the glory, beauty and riches of this world. The body of the church was also wonderfully brought together from the most distant territories, increased and preserved, and the proclamation of the gospel took place within an incredibly short period of time while having great success.[275]

This radical change which Calvin traces means that the children of God will originate not only from the children of Abraham but also from the children of

---

[268] Ps. 3: introduction (*CO* 31, 52).

[269] "...antiqua ecclesiae redemptione...," Ps. 18:16 (*CO* 31, 178).

[270] Ps. 2:8 (*CO* 31, 47).

[271] "...Christum...qui medius fuit inter veterem et novam ecclesiam...," Ps. 45:17 (*CO* 31, 458).

[272] "...quia matura ecclesiae aetas Christi demum adventu completa fuit...," Ps. 102:24 (*CO* 32, 72).

[273] Ps. 45:11 (*CO* 31, 456). Calvin here would have Deut. 21:10-14 in mind.

[274] "...quam splendide Christus adventu suo ecclesiam ornaverit...," Ps. 87: introduction (*CO* 31, 799).

[275] Ps. 87: introduction (*CO* 31, 799).

Adam.[276] The Jews are not therefore excluded from the covenant with the coming of the gospel, but the heathen are added to it as they are planted in the lineage of Abraham. According to Calvin, "We are considered as children of God in no other way than by being grafted into Abraham and his offspring."[277] Israel was the body of the church, and Calvin asserts that we have been added to it.[278] The heathen nations are steadily becoming "one body with the elect nation."[279] Elsewhere, Calvin explains that the kingdom of Christ began in Israel and thereafter expanded to the heathens.[280] God first revealed himself as father to the Jews, which is why they are the firstborn. The heathen, though, are accepted into the house of Abraham, and through the promise made to Abraham the redemption of the whole world has emanated.[281]

The unique privilege which Abraham's descendants enjoy by having the presence of God in the tabernacle and temple is comparable, Calvin notes, to God's splendor when Christ comes upon all nations.[282] It is also remarkable that Calvin sees that privileged position in the fact that in Christ (who was after all a Jew) the heathen are subjected to Israel.[283] It is the delight of the Jews that they may be the fountain from which God waters the whole earth.[284] On the other hand, those Jews who reject Christ cut themselves loose from the covenant by their disbelief. In spite of the fact that most Jews have not accepted Christ, Israel's honor remains preserved.[285] Thus the church has not replaced Israel, but instead believers from among the Gentiles are being brought into the symphony of the Jews to sing God's praise together.[286]

Calvin treats the unity of Israel and the church from a pastoral perspective. He writes that the history of "the old church" (Israel, of course) should give believers of today the strength to remain patient.[287] As God helped Israel in past times of confusion, he will also help the church of today.[288] Calvin views the church's situation in his own times as analogous to that of Israel just after the captivity—a view which he probably derived from

---

[276] Ps. 45:11 (*CO* 31, 456).

[277] Ps. 47:10 (*CO* 31, 471).

[278] Ps. 110:2 (*CO* 32, 162).

[279] Ps. 69:9 (*CO* 32, 40).

[280] Ps. 118:1 (*CO* 32, 203).

[281] Ps. 98:3 (*CO* 32, 48).

[282] Ps. 47:4 (*CO* 31, 467).

[283] "...quo sensu dicantur populi subiecti esse Iudaeis," Ps. 47:4 (*CO* 31, 468).

[284] Ps. 97:8 (*CO* 32, 45).

[285] "...non obstitit maioris partis defectio, quin reliquiis maneret hic honor," Ps. 47:10 (*CO* 31, 471).

[286] "Atque hoc vaticinio nos in eandem symphoniam Iudaeis coniuncti fuimus, ut assiduis laudum sacrificiis colatur Deus inter nos...," Ps. 150:6 (*CO* 32, 442).

[287] "...veteri ecclesiae fato confirmabimur ad toerantiam...," Ps. 83:6 (*CO* 31, 775).

[288] "...si eadem sit sua conditio, quae olim fuit Davidiis," Ps. 12:1 (*CO* 31, 126).

Luther's *De Captivitate Babylonica*. After the Babylonian captivity only a small group of believers remained; for a long time the temple lacked its previous glory, and believers expected that there would never again be a period of such prosperity. However, a period of flourishing arrived with the coming of Christ. Calvin describes Christ's coming and the church of the first centuries as one unified time of prosperity [growth] and blessing, indeed, a golden age.[289] Afterward, though, a time of decay returned, and today the church again suffers under the sins of believers, the attacks of Satan, the cruelties of tyrants, and the slander of the world. As this desolate situation is identical with the previous one, Calvin suggests that there can be hope again for God's future. From Calvin's point of view, the prosperous period had not yet come, for the early Protestant church was still akin to the phase just after the captivity. Calvin likely has this in mind in his exposition of Psalm 80, stating that God has extinguished the destructive fire which we ignited. Here though Calvin describes how God raises up a people from the ashes who will call upon his name.[290]

However this correlation sometimes leads Calvin to evaluate the situation in his time as a precise parallel to the situation in Israel, seeing similarities which in reality do not exist. A closer examination of the sources, though, should lead historians to better insight into the events in Geneva in order to understand more clearly the relationship between Calvin's exegesis, the historical situation in Geneva, and Calvin's interpretation of the situation.[291]

13. *Ecclesia Militans*: Church between God and the Devil

The church faces opposition all the time and is never without enemies,[292] even "fierce enemies,"[293] who "oppose it severely and ruthlessly."[294] Furthermore, nobody can maintain the hope that the church will arrive in this world in a peaceful situation; for Satan will harass her with new enemies. God allows this, Calvin writes, in order to exercise and test our patience.[295] In being surrounded by enemies, the church is trained for military service.[296]

---

[289] "...praeclara et incomparabilis aurei illius saeculi conditio...," Ps. 87: introduction (*CO* 31, 799-800). Calvin here especially means the time before Constantine, saying for example that the glory of the church did not consist of gold and purple but of the blood of the martyrs. The church was spiritually wealthy but poor with regard to material possessions, and its honor lay hidden under the cross of Christ.

[290] "...ubi ignis a nobis accensus...," Ps. 80:17 (*CO* 31, 758).

[291] An important initiative into this kind of investigation has been done by William G. Naphy, *Calvin and the Consolidation of the Genevan Reformation* (Manchester: Manchester University Press, 1994).

[292] Ps. 21:9 (*CO* 31, 216).

[293] Ps. 86:22 (*CO* 31, 692).

[294] Ps. 46:7 (*CO* 31, 463).

[295] Ps. 68:31 (*CO* 31, 634).

[296] Ps. 110:2 (*CO* 32, 162).

God intends thereby to both humble his church and allow him the opportunity to reveal his strength.[297] God then can loosen Satan's reins in order to reveal his glory much better.[298] Through theses attacks, the church at once realizes her inability and experiences God's power. Calvin provides a more optimistic explanation however when he says that God exposes us to unjust persecution "in order that we might exult more joyfully that we are carrying the cross together with Christ and that we also might share with him in the resurrection."[299]

History teaches that the church has always suffered injustice, but it also recalls that the church has survived such ordeals very well.[300] Therefore history may be encouraging insofar as a view back on God's past deeds can provide courage for those in the present.[301] Calvin considers this one of the reasons to read the Psalms: "nothing is happening to us today which has not happened among God's church in earlier times."[302] Moreover, behind the events of history, a struggle is being contested between God and Satan. This struggle remains consistent through every phase of history: Satan attacks the church and then God reacts to save her. Since David is a type of Christ in the Psalter, he also is opposed by Satan.[303] Calvin insists that history is nothing but the chronology of the course of the gospel.[304] The church may live in this history between God and Satan, but God will win: "It is truly a divine wonder that the church, which is attacked so fiercely by Satan and innumerable enemies, is still preserved."[305]

Just as the return from captivity did not bring an end to suffering and struggles for Israel, so also will the church experience hardship even after the death, resurrection and ascension of Christ. Until the time of Christ's second coming, "we have to struggle under the cross."[306] This "defamation of the cross," as Calvin calls it, obscures the glory of the church before the eyes of the world (*coram mundo*).

The church will continue to know struggle "...for Christ can only obtain a peaceful kingdom by waging war."[307] Although the kingdom of Christ is a kingdom of peace and rest and although peace is presently entering this

---

[297] Ps. 48:4 (*CO* 31, 475).

[298] "Quia ergo Deus ut potentiam suam clarius illustret, laxat fraenum Satanae...," Ps. 118:25 (*CO* 32, 212).

[299] Ps. 44:23 (*CO* 31, 447).

[300] Ps. 129:1 (*CO* 32, 330).

[301] Ps. 4:2 (*CO* 31, 59).

[302] Ps. 10: introduction (*CO* 31, 108).

[303] "Porro quum gestaret Christi figuram non mirum est diaboli satellites tam atrociter in eum saevisse," Ps. 140:1 (*CO* 32, 387).

[304] "...evangeli cursum...," Ps. 2:1 (*CO* 31, 43).

[305] Ps. 73:15 (*CO* 31, 681).

[306] Ps. 44:1 (*CO* 31, 436).

[307] Ps. 18:38 (*CO* 31, 188).

world through Christ's reign, it cannot expand without turbulence because God's kingdom clashes with the evil of people in the world. Calvin gives this *"theologia crucis"* a rather pastoral spin by saying that the opposition which faces the church is no reason for panic. Instead it is the grounds for encouragement. In fact, uproar ought to be taken as a sign of the progress of Christ's kingdom.[308] A "theology from below" lurks here for Calvin. What we observe outwardly is a kingdom of Christ which is scattered, declining, and maimed. When Psalm 2 deals with the rule of Christ and the ruin of the wicked, we might be tempted to think the opposite is the case today. The iron scepter mentioned in the ninth verse is not in the hands of Christ but in the hands of the impious, who proceed to dash the church instead of being dashed.[309] An understanding that the church will always face hostility is an additional reason not to panic when a new type of attack appears.[310] Comfort for the struggling church emerges from the relationship she has with Christ. God acts in protection since he considers everyone who attacks the believers to be his own enemy.[311] The one who turns his hand against the church turns his hand against God.[312]

In his exposition of Psalm 83 Calvin speaks quite concretely about the pope as one who incites the whole world against "us" with a "diabolical rage."[313] Nowhere else in the Psalms commentary does the Reformer speak so severely about the pope and his hostility against the church. Calvin sees a clear parallel with the sufferings to which Christ was subjected on earth. He too was opposed by the official office holders of the church, and in the same way his body is also now opposed by the official servants who see themselves as the successors to Peter though in reality Calvin charges that they prove themselves to actually be the successors of Caiaphas.[314]

Although references to "us against the rest of the world"[315] imply a type of "Calvinistic isolationism," Calvin's Psalms commentary itself nowhere calls for a breach with the Roman Church. Calvin however points to the problems which people encounter when they live in a church where the light becomes darkness and the majesty of God is ridiculed.[316] He notes that even David

---

[308] Ps. 2:2 (*CO* 31, 43).

[309] "...imo sub ferreis eorum malleis ecclesia ainfirma testae similis est...," Ps. 2:9 (*CO* 31, 49).

[310] Ps. 66:10 (*CO* 31, 614).

[311] Ps. 68:22 (*CO* 31, 630); "...bellum cum Deo suscipere quicunque ecclesiam infestant...," Ps. 83:6 (*CO* 31, 775).

[312] "...pronuntiat Deus, quoties iniuste laedimur, se quoque violari...," Ps. 83:6 (*CO* 31, 775).

[313] "Videmus enim ut diabolica furore totam orbem in nos infalmmet papa," Ps. 83:6 (*CO* 31, 775).

[314] Ps. 118:25 (*CO* 32, 212).

[315] "Nam ut in nos conspiret totus mundus...," Ps. 83:6 (*CO* 31, 775).

[316] Ps. 120:2 (*CO* 32, 298).

became a foreigner in his own country, an experience which a believer may also find in the church.[317]

Calvin can apply the parallels between David, Christ, and the church in a positive direction as well. He mentions for instance that David was a fugitive who could hardly save his own life,[318] but then God reversed the roles at the end, and consequently David's enemies had to flee. The enemies of God's church will not share the experience of Julius Caesar, who is reported to have said after his easy conquest into Egypt that he came, saw and conquered. Instead, God's enemies will come, will stand stunned and will be defeated.[319]

God does not necessarily always protect the church in a visible way. Outwardly the church can even disappear so that it seems that the church is dead. Precisely at this moment though God "creates" it, as it were, once again.[320] According to Calvin this is typical of the way in which God acts, for just as God once created heaven and earth out of nothing (*ex nihilo*), it fits his *modus operandi* to also set up the church from the mere darkness of death.[321] Calvin seems to modify the well known motto "*post tenebras lux*" in order to affirm "*ex tenebris mortis ecclesia*" as well.

In the same way that the divinity of Christ was mostly hidden, his body (the church) also may remain hidden in some respects. Once again, Calvin relates this to the parallels between Christ and David, noting that the son of Jesse had been anointed as king at an early stage but his kingship remained hidden for a long time. This applies to the kingship of Christ as well.[322] The concealment of the church also lends itself to the warning against judging by mere outward appearances. The huge buildings and their impressive altars which belong to the papacy are in fact abhorrent to God and his angels while, in contrast, "the ruins of the true church are holy."[323]

14. *Ecclesia Ministrans*

The church is especially important for Calvin as she is the "mediator" of salvation.[324] God has entrusted the church with the covenant of eternal life. This means that people can only be reborn through the ministry of the

---

[317] "Et notandum est, quum in patria ageret, fuisse inquitinum...," Ps. 120:5 (*CO* 32, 297).

[318] "Profugus quidem ad tempus fuit David...," Ps. 18:38 (*CO* 31, 188).

[319] Ps. 48:4 (*CO* 31, 475).

[320] "...sed ubi mortua videtur, repente novam creari...," Ps. 102:19 (*CO* 32, 70).

[321] Ps. 102:19 (*CO* 32, 70).

[322] Ps. 118:25 (*CO* 32, 210).

[323] Ps. 102:15 (*CO* 32, 68).

[324] "Die Kirche nimmt eine zum Heil notwendige Vermittlungsfunktion wahr," Faber, *Symphonie*, 345. On the function of the church in the "Heilsvermittlung," see also Scheld, *Media*, 8-17.

church.[325] God also uses the church to bring the enjoyment of heavenly gifts through proclamation and worship. God can of course provide for the needs of believers directly from heaven, but he prefers to use the church as his instrument unto this end. Even though we may not put our trust in the doctrine or liturgy, we also dare not despise it.[326]

Christ confers his rule upon ecclesiastical office holders who are charged to *serve* and not to *reign* in his place. They exercise power because Christ has entrusted them with the gospel, "the scepter of his rule." In this way Christ subjugates the whole world through his servants. Meanwhile, the churches which we find in various countries form the princedoms of Christ.[327] Calvin's view of church office is consistent with the *"etiam extra"* theme in his theology. The title of the office holder alone gives no guarantee since the decisive element lies in how the office is filled. If the mere title were sufficient, Christ would have had to be silent when the priests rejected his teaching. Therefore it is still applicable today that "If we have to heed as a legitimate pastor everyone who is entrusted to ordained authority, Christ must be silent."[328] This also addresses Calvin's problem with the pope: it is not the papal institution itself which concerns the Reformer but the fact that the pope assigns himself to the place of God, making him the antichrist.[329] Calvin would not object to leaving the pope and the rest of the Roman clergy in their titles if only they would not show themselves as tyrants under the title of servants.[330] They indeed have the *"potestas,"* but they do not use it for edification but for demolition.

This clarifies Calvin's view that God uses the offices but he can also act without the offices. However, the office of a preacher is held very high. The aim of proclamation (preaching) is that people would lay down their pride and make themselves captive to Christ.[331] Following his ascension, this role of witnessing to Christ is taken over by the apostles, and thereafter their task is transferred to the *"doctores."* Yet it still remains Christ's own witness, and so, according to Calvin, the authority of the office is founded upon Christ's authority. The testimony of the preacher is the testimony of Christ, and when his words are spoken by others, it remains Christ's voice.[332] When the gospel

---

[325] "Et certe non aliter renascimur in coelestem vitam, quam per ecclesiae ministerium," Ps. 87:5 (*CO* 31, 803).

[326] Ps. 65:5 (*CO* 31, 606).

[327] Ps. 45:17 (*CO* 31, 459).

[328] Ps. 118:25 (*CO* 32, 211).

[329] "Neque enim Antichristus esset papa, nisi sederet in templo Dei," Ps. 118:19 (*CO* 32, 208).

[330] "...quatenus tamen ordinaria potestas penes eos residet, titulum illis concedere nihil obest...," Ps. 118:25 (*CO* 32, 211).

[331] Ps. 68:19 (*CO* 31, 628).

[332] "Atque hinc etiam melius sancitur evangelii autoritas, quia licet ab aliis publicetur, Christi tamen vocari non desinit," Ps. 2:7 (*CO* 31, 46).

is proclaimed by human beings, one should consider it as Christ speaking. Calvin calls it a benevolent deed that Christ himself invites us to salvation.[333] Moreover, the word which is spoken by a human is just as effective as when God himself spoke directly from heaven.[334] The inherent strength of the Spirit is connected to the external word when the preacher fulfills his task well and speaks only according to the word of God.[335] Therefore, Calvin ascribes a tremendous value to the *official* proclamation of the word, but he does not make the officeholder the "owner" of the word and Spirit.

15. Conclusion

In the theology of John Calvin as it is found in his Psalms commentary, God's covenant is found to play a much more important role than one would expect given the research thus far on this topic. Calvin's view on the unity of Old and New Testaments forms the foundation for this subject. The emphasis on the covenant's obligatory character is also significant, being applicable for man as well as for God. Calvin describes prayer as the communication which takes place between the partners of the covenant, but Calvin's view of God seems to prevent any real communication. The Reformer apparently gives a preference to logic over the biblical material which might suggest prayer's influence on God's actions. Calvin also argues for the central importance of the church in God's administration of the covenant since it is both the theatre of God's glory and an instrument which mediates salvation. Finally, we noted that the unity of the church between the Old and New Covenants enables Calvin to develop his doctrine of the church as both a "*corpus mixtum*" and an "*ecclesia militans.*"

---

[333] "...propria voce nos ad se comiter invitat," Ps. 2:7 (*CO* 31, 46).

[334] Ps. 105:31 (*CO* 32, 111).

[335] "...cum externa eius voce coniuncta est interior virtus spiritus," Ps. 105:31 (*CO* 32, 111).

11

God the Father

The purpose of election is God's fatherhood. In his Psalms commentary, Calvin writes that God takes us to be his children in order to comfort us in his bosom.[1] In his theology of the doctrine of God, the Reformer often returns to this idea again and again. By his frequent reference to the fatherhood of God it is evident that he views God first and foremost as a father, and this pattern justifies a separate chapter now devoted exclusively to this theme. Furthermore, as Calvin holds that the fatherhood of God is *the definitive purpose* of God's works of grace, this chapter is the last in this study. In Calvin's thought the relationship established by faith consists mainly in the father-child relationship which a believer has with God, and therefore Calvin's concept of faith also fits under this point.

1. The Way to Faith

Calvin describes the order of salvation when he says that God "frees me from the tyranny of the devil and adopts me to be his child, washes my impurity with the blood of Christ, renews me through the Holy Spirit, incorporates me into the body of his Son and leads me to the heavenly life."[2] However, Calvin offers no consistent chronological order for these operations.[3] Rather he just mentions all aspects of the transition from being lost to being righteous. Calvin does seem to have an *ordo salutis* though in the sense that the conviction of sin and repentance are necessary elements in the process of justification. God accepts in grace only those who repent of their sins. This

---

[1] Ps. 102:29 (*CO* 32, 73).
[2] Ps. 109:21 (*CO* 32, 155).
[3] Graafland presents as one conclusion of his investigation into this subject that it is not possible that "Calvins Theologie eine heilsordnungsartige Theologie zu nennen." See C. Graafland, "Hat Calvin einen ordo salutis gelehrt," in *Calvinus Ecclesiae Genevensis Custos*, ed. Wilhelm H. Neuser (New York: Lang, 1984), 221-44.

does not mean that forgiveness is to be earned by repentance, but repentance is nevertheless inseparably bound up with faith. For Calvin, repentance is a fruit of the Spirit and belongs with regeneration.[4] Therefore it is indicative of faith. Repentance and the confession of guilt are not prerequisites for grace, but they are indeed means by which one is reconciled to God.[5] Forgiveness of sin is not obtained without the conviction and the confession of sin.[6] Calvin states this in order to convey that the reception of grace is something one experiences consciously when one is conscious of the consequences of grace, namely, the forsaking of sin and the praising of God. He adds that God only wants to be a healer for those who humble themselves before him.[7] Self-abasement as the confession of one's sin is the first step toward reconciliation with God because he himself reveals that our misery moves him to be reconciliatory towards us.[8] Consequently, there is no true faith without both genuine repentance and the realization of guilt before God. "After all," Calvin interjects, "he who does not feel the disease will also reject the medicine."[9] Yet it is not sufficient that someone merely senses his own misery since he must also be convinced that he cannot save himself from it and that he must therefore ally himself with the one true God.[10]

The misery is that extreme distress which results as a sinner feels God's hand pressing heavily upon him or her, bringing the knowledge of a judge whose severity encompasses, besides eternal death, many other deaths as well.[11] According to Calvin it is even true to say that we shall never experience the true joy of faith if we have not felt the enormity of God's wrath amidst intense inner afflictions.[12] Yet, to recognize one's misery is not a prerequisite for justification as much as it is a component of it as one realizes God's work in him or her. God must reveal himself to us, and only then will one's own frailty be the cause to surrender oneself to him.[13]

---

[4] "…non quod poenitentia sibi veniam acquirant, sed quia a spiritu regenerationis divelli nunquam potest fides," Ps. 32:11 (*CO* 31, 323).
[5] Ps. 32:5 (*CO* 31, 320).
[6] Ps. 106:6 (*CO* 32, 118).
[7] Ps. 109:21 (*CO* 32, 155).
[8] Ps. 102:76 (*CO* 32, 73).
[9] Ps. 32:2 (*CO* 31, 317).
[10] Ps. 28:1 (*CO* 31, 281).
[11] Ps. 32:4 (*CO* 31, 318).
[12] Ps. 32:3 (*CO* 31, 318).
[13] Ps. 39:8 (*CO* 31, 401).

248

Because man is by nature spiritually dead and buried, coming to faith entails "a resurrection from the grave."[14] Concerning that moment at which someone attains faith, Calvin does not elaborate except to say that regeneration takes place through the word and the Spirit.[15] Furthermore, Calvin implies that God is the sole source of faith by comparing its origin in a person to God's action in creation. God makes us alive from the dead "just as it is completely his own pattern of work to create everything from nothing."[16] One might even say that for Calvin a believer is a *"creatio ex nihilo."* Only upon God's intervention can such a one "who is nothing start being something."[17]

2. The Primacy of Grace

Fundamental for the relationship between God and man is God's unconditional grace. Although Calvin gives no separate exposition of this topic, it functions as presupposition throughout his commentary. He briefly defines grace in one place as the love by which God enfolds his elect apart from them deserving it.[18] Equally concise is his remark that there is no middle ground between justification by works and justification by faith.[19] When he does speak about grace, his discussion is generally characterized by an effort to disprove possible theological errors relating to grace.

God not only brings us into the state of grace, Calvin writes, but he also keeps us therein. Along these lines, Calvin distinguishes between two kinds of mercy: one by which God brings us from death to life, and another by which he preserves us in that restored relationship with himself.[20] Calvin sharply denounces the notion of the Romanists that God only takes care of the first kind, leaving the second to man. He also challenges the Anabaptist notion that one can attain perfect righteousness in this life so that the second grace is no longer required. In both versions, he argues, God is relegated to the background while in fact God must always maintain the central place. This is one of the reasons why he brings attention to the daily forgiveness

---

[14] Ps. 103:4 (*CO* 32, 76).
[15] "...hominum multitudinem Christi spiritu et evangelio esse regenitum...," Ps. 110:3 (*CO* 32, 163).
[16] "...sicuti proprium munus eius est, ex nihilo omnia creare," Ps. 39:8 (CO 31, 401).
[17] Ps. 39:8 (*CO* 31, 401).
[18] Ps. 106:4 (*CO* 32, 116).
[19] "Atqui inter haec duo, quae scriptura inter se opponit, nihil est medium, Iustificari operibus et Iustificari fide," Ps. 143:2 (*CO* 32, 401).
[20] Ps. 103:11 (*CO* 32, 80).

that God gives.[21] Man cannot go for even a single day without God's grace. Calvin's criticism of Roman theology here alleges that it removes the blessing of forgiveness by saying that man must provide his own part. Not the effort of man but the forgiveness of God is the door to eternal life, Calvin affirms.[22] This is not to say that an individual's own responsibility disappears. God must turn the heart of people to him, but they themselves are guilty insofar as desire brings them to sin.[23] The connection between grace and personal responsibility is illustrated when Calvin says that "only they have access to God who serve him purely."[24]

In the Psalms commentary Calvin also describes the chasm which separates sinful man from a righteous God. Man's situation before God is such that, no matter how hard he tries, he can never produce a sufficient achievement before God. Our efforts can never raise us up to his height because there is nothing he needs from us and furthermore we have nothing with which we could honor him. God never owes us anything. Therefore whoever wants to come to him must set aside all self-confidence because whoever imagines that he or she has something passably good takes away an important aspect to God's glory. In Calvin's evaluation of the human situation, any contribution we would make towards our righteous standing before God takes away from the complete and sufficient goodness of God. Yet, when we honestly confess to him that we neither possess nor can earn anything on our own, "this humility before God is like a delightful perfume that will incline him to be merciful."[25] The emphasis in Calvin's thought is therefore not on man having nothing but on God having everything.

Because faith is a gift of God, Calvin can attribute value to it. Faith, he explains, reconciles one with God and sanctifies everything that is incomplete in a person, and this is how one becomes righteous before God.[26] In fact, such importance is even given to faith in Calvin's thought that God's actions might even appear to be dependent on man's faith. In Psalm 17:7 for example David describes God as the savior for those who seek shelter in him. Without addressing the potential question as to whether God's salvation *depends* on our seeking his shelter, Calvin elaborates on David's words, remarking that God takes upon himself the protection of everyone who trusts

---

[21] "...quotidiana venia...," Ps. 103:11 (*CO* 32, 80).
[22] Ps. 32:1 (*CO* 31, 316).
[23] Ps. 78:8 (*CO* 31, 725).
[24] Ps. 15:1 (*CO* 31, 144).
[25] Ps. 16:2 (*CO* 31, 150).
[26] Ps. 32:11 (*CO* 31, 323).

in him. This means that we do not invoke God as our protector in vain and that we do not have to doubt his help if our faith continues trusting in his grace.[27] Conversely, those who call upon God without believing in him reject his grace by their doubt.[28] The same connection may also be found in Calvin's interpretation of Psalm 37:19 where he states that our doubt obstructs God's generosity.

Calvin also describes the return to a proper relationship with God in terms of *reconciliation*, a concept meaning that God recognizes as his children those toward whom he should actually be hostile. The emphasis is not on our former enmity towards God but on God's former enmity towards us.[29] From the human point of view, we have lost our status as God's children through the fall into sin. For man then there is no other hope but that God would elect to adopt unworthy people once more to be his children.[30] Reconciliation with God is also the absolute prerequisite for a blessed life. A *beata vita* is only found in the state of being reconciled to God.[31] Additionally, Calvin describes it as ultimate bliss to be reconciled with God.[32] Reconciliation with God is also put forth as the source from which all of God's blessings come forth.[33] Man's problem is not disease, but sin; it is not suffering, but guilt. Therefore, there can only be bliss when there is reconciliation with God.[34] For a human being, to be reconciled with God is the most important of all things. One can suffer poverty and injustice, hunger and thirst, or innumerable other difficulties, Calvin writes, and yet be blissful if one has peace with God.[35] For Calvin the central issue is the relationship with God. It is essential, therefore, not that sin be forgiven, but rather that through this forgiveness things be right with God once again.[36]

---

[27] "...quia non frustra vocatur Deus sperantium servator, modo in eius gratiam recumbat fides nostra, minime timendum esse quin paratus sit ad opem nobis ferendam," Ps. 17:7 (*CO* 31, 163).

[28] Ps. 28:6 (*CO* 31, 285).

[29] "...quibus placatus esset Deus, ut pro filiis agnoscat, quibus merito inimicus esset," Ps. 32:1 (*CO* 31, 314).

[30] "...nec alia est felicitatis ianua, quam ut mero beneplacito indignos eligat," Ps. 33:12 (*CO* 31, 330).

[31] "...hoc summum et unicum esse beatae vitae caput, si Deus hominem abolito reatu sibi gratuito reconciliet," Ps. 32: introduction (*CO* 31, 314).

[32] Ps. 17:15 (*CO* 31, 167-8).

[33] Ps. 103:3 (*CO* 32, 75).

[34] Ps. 130:8 (*CO* 32, 338).

[35] Ps. 63:4 (*CO* 31, 595).

[36] Ps. 79:9 (*CO* 31, 751).

3. Faith, Assurance and Promise

In his commentary on the Psalms Calvin puts great emphasis on the assurance of faith. However, it pertains much less to the assurance of God's grace than to the assurance of God's care though these two are inseparably interconnected since God's grace evidences itself in God's care. Instead of asking the question whether someone is a child of God, Calvin is drawn to the question whether God is still caring for that child. Believers often notice that things may go well with the unbelievers in this world while they themselves encounter all sorts of trouble. This can cause their faith to falter. To prevent this they need the assurance that God will keep them from harm, but this assurance is only there because God is gracious towards them. God forgives their sins, and therefore he will also keep them safe. Grace and protection go inseparably together such that Calvin can say that the faithful "seek refuge in God's grace" when their troubles threaten to overcome them.[37]

The faithful can find this assurance by clinging to God's covenant promise that he will save those who are his.[38] Amidst situations of terror, torment and death, people persevere only by holding on to God's promises.[39] Calvin adds that the assurance of faith frees them from every terror and fear.[40] The fear of death and the grave arises from a lack of faith. Believers become frightened because they do not sufficiently entrust themselves to God,[41] even though Calvin recognizes that we have a natural terror of the violent aspect of death.[42] In the promise they find *"stabilitas"* although they experience *"instabilitas."*[43] The certainty of salvation thus rests assured in God, and therefore the faithful "drop the anchor of faith in heaven."[44] In this way faith is able to bring one up from the most profound depths to God.[45] In keeping with this view, Calvin points out that the psalmist in Psalm 85:8 says that he wants to go and hear what God *says*, not that he wants to see what God will *do*. He refers the faithful to God's mouth and not to God's hand

---

[37] Ps. 10:5 (*CO* 31, 113).
[38] Ps. 68:29 (*CO* 31, 633).
[39] Ps. 119:25 (*CO* 32, 225).
[40] Ps. 16:10 (*CO* 31, 156).
[41] Ps. 49:16 (*CO* 31, 491).
[42] "...violentiam mortem naturaliter magis horremus," Ps. 86:6 (*CO* 31, 807).
[43] Ps. 10:5 (*CO* 31, 113).
[44] Ps. 102:29 (*CO* 32, 74).
[45] Ps. 69:4 (*CO* 31, 638).

because the benevolent deeds of God proceed from God's promises.[46] This shows that Calvin finds great meaning in the divine operation of *"fides ex auditu"* just as Luther did.[47] Faith must always direct itself to God's speech.[48] Moreover, faith has nothing else on which to stand because "without the word of God we have not a single ground for believing that he is gracious."[49]

Faith's foundation in God's promise is especially clear precisely when God conceals the signs of his favor:

> After all, what room still remains for faith and what is then the power of the promises if believers could simply come to rest through God's open revelation of himself as a liberator to them?[50]

God's deeds can lead to doubt, but his speech cannot. Faith endures the test when amidst the greatest darkness it is able to let itself be guided by the light of God's promise.[51] This is, as Calvin describes it, "the distinctive characteristic of faith" that amidst terrors it finds rest and expects God and his help.[52] Nor does faith allow itself to be determined by what is visible since the Reformer says that faithful trust means "to await grace patiently even if it is concealed and to cling to his word even if it takes so long before any of that word can be discerned."[53] Faith knows how to link heaven with earth so that, as Calvin beautifully puts it, "in all the shipwrecks that befall us, we cast the anchor of our faith and of our prayers in heaven."[54]

The assurance that faith will prevail in all circumstances does not however mean to Calvin "that God's children can stand around laughing when in danger or that they should jokingly babble on about death, but rather that they ought to regard the help that God has promised them as much higher than all the dangers that could strike terror into them."[55] It is not true that believers do not know fear because they also have feelings. Calvin

---

[46] "...sed quoniam beneficia quibus ecclesiam prosequitar, ex promissionibus fluunt, os potius quam manum posuit," Ps. 85:9 (*CO* 31, 788).
[47] "Fides, quae ipsa ex auditu nascitum," Ps. 132:6 (*CO* 32, 344).
[48] "...ex ore Dei pendere debet fides," Ps. 89:4 (*CO* 31, 812).
[49] "...nihil nobis sine verbo Dei imaginari fas est de eius gratia," Ps. 89:4 (*CO* 31, 813).
[50] Ps. 116:7 (*CO* 32, 194).
[51] Ps. 71:14 (*CO* 31, 658).
[52] "...fidei proprium...," Ps. 25:4 (*CO* 31, 252).
[53] Ps. 52:11 (*CO* 31, 530).
[54] Ps. 88:7 (*CO* 31, 808).
[55] Ps. 46:4 (*CO* 31, 461).

writes, "There is, after all, a difference between insensibility and the peace of mind which comes from faith." Therefore, the faithful are not utterly overwhelmed by terror, but they always know how to restrain it.[56] To exemplify a believer's fear, Calvin points to the words of the psalmist David in Psalm 23. There, when David says that he fears no evil (verse 4), it does not mean that he knows no fear but that he knows he will conquer the fear by entrusting himself to God. To know that God is with oneself does not necessarily imply that one is not afraid.[57]

God's promise and God's word are one and the same; consequently, Calvin can say that the word leads to assurance precisely in those times when we notice nothing of God's might and grace. In such afflictions, only the word holds us upright.[58] In his interpretation of Psalm 56:11 Calvin points out the meaning of the word three times in succession.[59] Even more fundamentally, Calvin bases the assurance of faith in the nature of God: "It must be a certainty for us that the goodwill of God can never be exhausted and that his generosity never makes him poor." God does not change in his nature, and so, because his goodness belongs to his nature, he cannot strip himself of his goodness.[60] God's being God is thus the source of the hope for the faithful.

4. The Experience of Faith

Knowing God, trusting God, honoring God and believing in God are all virtually synonyms to Calvin. As he puts it, we seem to know God well only when we give him the honor that is due to him, and we cannot honor him better than by trusting in him.[61] The most important part of believing, however, is to love God. Calvin writes, "There is no better way to honor God

---

[56] Ps. 46:2 (*CO* 31, 461).

[57] "…neque enim Dei praesentiam requireret timoris vacuitas," Ps. 23:4 (*CO* 31, 240).

[58] "Multum ergo profecit qui inter tentationes unico Dei verbo fretus viriliter pergit in eius laude," Ps. 56:5 (*CO* 31, 549).

[59] "…verbo solidam gloriam tribuere…in eius tamen verbo quiescam…ut inter tentationes firmam gloriam retineant, nudo verbo contenti…," Ps. 56:11 (*CO* 31, 552).

[60] "…quia Deus naturam non mutat, nec bonitatem, quae praeditus est, potest exuere," Ps. 138:8 (*CO* 32, 376).

[61] "Interea tenendum est, tunc rite a nobis Deum cognosci, dum ei suum honorem tribuimus, nempe sit in eum recumbat nostra fiducia," Ps. 36:11 (*CO* 31, 364).

than to love him."[62] Moreover, the connection is established in his comment that *to believe* is to love God for his kindness towards us.[63] The attitude we ought to adopt towards God is best expressed in the word "respect," but insofar as he wants us to serve him with all our heart, there is no better offering than that we bind ourselves to God with "a bond of heartfelt and spontaneous love."[64] Therefore believers are mentioned in the scriptures as those who love God. Furthermore, the love of God is "the root of true piety" because from it arises the heartfelt longing to subject oneself to him.[65]

In contrast with the Roman Catholic concept of faith as *"fides implicita,"* Calvin states that faith must be experienced. "It is not sufficient that we are loved by God unless the experience of love also gets through to us."[66] This experience is the work of the Holy Spirit because, Calvin explains, God "floods our hearts with his Spirit and gladdens us with a sincere and certain joy."[67] God is also present on this earth with his might and grace, and that presence is experienced as well.[68] Calvin therefore finds the *"praesentia realis"* not so much in the sacrament but in the totality of the world's events. Along with pointing out the necessity of experience, Calvin emphatically warns that one ought not to take the experience of faith as the norm. When the experience of God's benevolent deeds is not linked to his word, they leave us unaffected. Conversely, the fact that God is benevolent only inspires us when we also experience the acts of benevolence.[69] Our heart comes back to life, as it were, through the word, particularly as this word is faithfully accepted.[70] Furthermore, agreement with the word is insufficient when the agreement of the heart is not added as well.[71] "The most important thing in serving God is sincerity of heart," Calvin writes. God accepts this sincerity of the heart as if the entire heart has been pure and perfect.[72]

---

[62] Ps. 18:2 (*CO* 31, 170).

[63] Ps. 5:12 (*CO* 31, 72).

[64] Ps 18:2 (*CO* 31, 170).

[65] Ps. 145:20 (*CO* 32, 420).

[66] Ps. 4:7 (*CO* 31, 63).

[67] Ps. 4:7 (*CO* 31, 63).

[68] "...sed ad sensibilem eius gratiam referri debet, quia experientia docebat, quamvis coelum et terram impleat eius maiestas, virtute et gratia suis esse praesentem," Ps. 135:15 (*CO* 32, 363).

[69] "...ubi tamen ad verbi testimonium accedit experientia, non vulgariter nos animat," Ps. 80:9 (*CO* 31, 756).

[70] Ps. 107:20 (*CO* 32, 140).

[71] Ps. 78:34 (*CO* 31, 733).

[72] Ps. 32:11 (*CO* 31, 323).

Along with his attention paid to the experience of faith throughout the Psalms commentary is Calvin's concern for the necessity of growing in faith. God does not give the gifts of the Spirit all at once, but he only gives them gradually, depending on what is best for each believer. In this way he leads the faithful to the "lasting perfection."[73] For Calvin, growth in faith is an increase in the practical knowledge of living with God. During this growth, the believer meanwhile diminishes in some sense because the more one trusts in God, the less one trusts in oneself.[74] This growth also involves the recognition that the goal is still far from reached. Calvin notes in one place, "Certainly the more someone makes progress in learning piety, the better he sees how far removed he still is from the goal."[75] Thus, one is able to test his or her own growth by determining whether the solace that comes from God's word overshadows the troubles that actually befall one until every melancholy (*tristitia*) disappears from one's heart.[76] For Calvin this means that growth arises through the increase of the knowledge of faith. He says that we have to learn in "the school of God"[77] throughout all of our lives to let go of vain thoughts in order to let the light of faith shine more brightly as one increases in spiritual wisdom. In this way piety and knowledge go together. In fact, the essence of piety consists firstly in awe and respect for God. Secondly, yet inseparably related to the first, Calvin holds that piety consists in "the knowledge of heavenly doctrine."[78]

5. The Joy of Faith

For John Calvin, joy is an essential ingredient of faith. It stems from God's word since in that word the promise of grace and care comes to us.[79] Though

---

[73] "…donec adducat ad solidem perfectionem," Ps. 65:5 (*CO* 31, 606). In *Institutes* III.17.15, Calvin clarifies that he understands "perfection" in the Augustinian sense: "Perfectam, inquit, sanctorum virtutem quum nominamus, ad ipsam perfectionem pertinet etiam imperfectionis tum in veritate tum in humilitate cognitio."

[74] Ps. 84:6 (*CO* 31, 782).

[75] Ps. 86:11 (CO 31, 795).

[76] Ps. 119:142 (*CO* 32, 279).

[77] "…in eius schola proficere…," Ps. 16:7 (*CO* 31, 155).

[78] "…discimus quae sit vera pietatis natura, timorem Dei vel reverentiam priore loco ponit: sed mox adiungit coelestis doctrinae scientiam, ut sciamus res esse coniunctos," Ps. 119:78 (*CO* 32, 249).

[79] "Hoc autem gaudium dicit auditu percipi, quia donec verbo Dei exhilaretur peccator ut animum colligat frustra alia solatia sibi accerset," Ps. 51:9 (*CO* 31, 516).

the Reformers are known for insisting that *"fides ex auditu,"* Calvin seems to think that *"gaudium ex auditu"* as well. Faith and joy cannot be separated.[80] As Calvin remarks, this joy is rooted in the experience of God's fatherly love.[81] Furthermore, true joy arises from the assurance of God's shelter.[82] To know that we live under the caring hand of God bestows not only serenity but also joy and mirth.[83] Therefore, the faithful rejoice because there is nothing more beautiful than to know that God is by one's side.[84] They can derive this great joy not only from their current circumstances, but also from the assurance that God will provide for salvation in the future. Calvin writes,

> Though we are not immune to sorrow, it is nonetheless necessary that a gladness of faith must rise above it making us to sing of the joy to come.[85]

Bound up with this eschatologically-oriented joy is also a soteriological interest since, as Calvin adds, "He who has God lacks not the slightest little thing for a truly blissful life."[86] One is only fortunate if he or she has been reconciled to God.[87] Consequently only the message of reconciliation brings joy, and there is not a single form of oppression which can take this joy away.

> Even though, for as long as they make their pilgrimage through this world, the faithful constantly struggle with misery and are plagued by all sorts of worries, hazards and burdens, it is sufficient for the easing of their sorrows merely to hear of joy; for the joy of the Spirit cannot be separated from faith.[88]

Calvin contrasts the gladness which arises from knowing that one has been truly reconciled to God with the unbridled elation of those who despise

---

[80] "...gaudium spiritus a fide est inseparabile...," Ps. 51:9 (*CO* 31, 516).

[81] Ps. 5:13 (*CO* 31, 72). Cf. Ps. 89:16 (*CO* 31, 816): "...qui laeti et hilares Deum agnoscant patrem."

[82] Ps. 5:12 (*CO* 31, 72).

[83] Ps. 16:9 (*CO* 31, 155). Cf. Ps. 16:9 (*CO* 31, 156): "Denique nemini placide gaudere contingit, nisi recumbere dedicit in unum Deum, suamque salutem in eius manu reponere...."

[84] "...quia nihil illis optabilius quam sentire propinquum sibi esse Deum," Ps. 68:4 (*CO* 31, 620).

[85] Ps. 13:6 (*CO* 31, 134).

[86] Ps. 16:6 (*CO* 31, 154).

[87] Ps. 80:4 (*CO* 31, 755).

[88] Ps. 51:9 (*CO* 31, 516).

God.[89] Nothing gives as much joy as a clear conscience because through it we know that our lives please God. Therefore the source of this gladness is faith because through faith there is reconciliation with God, and reconciliation renders the conscience clear.[90]

This connection between faith's joy and both eschatology and soteriology carries the inference that this joy is determined by what *has* happened (soteriology and reconciliation) as well as by what *will* happen (eschatology and the completion of salvation). The believer is thereby able in the present to remain standing with joy. Joy in the midst of adversity: this is Calvin's timely message for those who were either seeking asylum in Geneva or facing persecution in France.

6. The Struggle of Faith

Considering both the content of the Psalms and the experiences Calvin's reading audience had probably faced, it is not surprising that he devotes a significant amount of time in his commentary to the difficulty of believing. By his treatment of this topic, Calvin shows that he is not a mere unmoved mover for a staunch group of dogmatically attuned believers. He writes,

> Believers are not made of iron, nor do they know a stoic rigidity that numbs them to pain and sorrow, but in their inmost being they face a heavy struggle against gloom and fear.[91]

Here, of course, there is no disagreement with Luther. There is disagreement, though, over the nature of the inner conflict. Whereas in Luther's thought *"tentatio"* is more a matter of the relationship between a righteous God and the sinful believer, Calvin places the emphasis on the relation between God and the events in the world. Calvin also certainly knows about the difficulty of accepting grace. He observes that "Our hearts are frightened, and they falter because there is nothing more difficult for us than to come to realize that God is gracious."[92] Similarly, he mentions the yearning of the believer to be freed from the terrors of conscience.[93]

---

[89] Ps. 2:10 (*CO* 31, 50).
[90] Ps. 19:8 (*CO* 31, 200-1).
[91] Ps. 61:1 (*CO* 31, 581).
[92] Ps. 103:8 (*CO* 32, 78-9).
[93] "...e terroribus conscientiae...," Ps. 51:3 (*CO* 31, 509).

Yet most of Calvin's attention is devoted to the adversity that besets a believer in his life and in the world when it is hard to reconcile with the omnipotence and the providence of God. He strikingly articulates this adversity when he says that the believer always finds himself in the situation where "nothing is certain and nothing is sure." Furthermore, various questions assail him: "Why should I continue believing? What is there left for which I may still hope? Where can I still flee?"[94] This situation produces a state of mind that the Reformer frequently denotes as *"tristitia."*[95] This *tristitia*, however, becomes *"desperatio"* when one does not surrender his troubles to God but instead keeps them to himself. In so doing he becomes ever more tangled up from the inside.[96] The faithful can be so occupied by this melancholy that "the light of faith is extinguished in them."[97] If this were not enough, Calvin even states that God does not always console, and the invocation of his name may lead to disappointment.[98]

When dealing with the struggle of faith, Calvin frequently uses military terminology. This fits in with Calvin's view that life is "an ongoing military service."[99] He speaks, for instance, about the battle with oneself when hoping for something different from God than that which one actually sees from him.[100] In this "battle," Calvin guarantees victory. "Faith secures victory not in the first battle, but only after it has been trained with many setbacks, and in the end it emerges as the conqueror."[101]

The causes of this struggle of faith are twofold: the opposition that the believer encounters from the outside, and the failings of one's own faith. Calvin knows from experience that the weakness of our flesh can lead to a point where even the strongest believer scarcely escapes great anxiety when Satan opposes us.[102] Even though Satan's attacks combine well with the weakness of faith, nevertheless the two causes should be distinguished here for the sake of clarity. Therefore we shall begin by first examining the activities of Satan.

---

[94] Ps. 116:11 (*CO* 32, 197).
[95] Ps. 116:7 (*CO* 32, 195).
[96] Ps. 62:9 (*CO* 31, 589).
[97] Ps. 88:6 (*CO* 31, 807).
[98] Ps. 77:4 (*CO* 31, 712).
[99] "...in toto vitae cursu, qui in continua militia peragendus nobis est," Ps. 94:12 (*CO* 32, 23).
[100] Ps. 10:12 (*CO* 31, 115-6).
[101] Ps. 22:2 (*CO* 31, 221).
[102] "...a proprio experimento nobis petenda est," Ps. 119:43 (*CO* 32, 233).

7. Man between God and Satan[103]

In his commentary on the Psalms Calvin devotes much attention to the destructive efforts of Satan, whom he depicts as tormenting the faithful until the end of the world.[104] Calvin writes that, as soon as someone puts his trust in God, he or she must at once prepare for the attacks of Satan.[105] Every day he launches attacks on our faith, and this is why God must not only accept us to be his own, but he must also protect us in the faith relationship.[106] To be positioned between God and Satan should not surprise the faithful since such a position follows from their identification with Christ. Calvin describes in his commentary the bond which exists between Christ as the head and believers as his body. As the Son of God was Satan's target during Jesus' life on earth, Satan will certainly not spare the body of Christ now.[107]

Through his exposition of the Psalter, Calvin points out that it is at times tempting to develop a "theology from beneath" in the sense that we are inclined to draw conclusions about God's attitude and actions based on earthly events and experiences. Satan makes use of such a theology, and he exploits our feelings. For example, when we sense nothing of God's benevolent deeds, we conclude that he must have forgotten us.[108] By this example Calvin alerts us to the danger of establishing too close a connection between our faith and feelings. This temptation arises from our sinful flesh. Calvin writes, "The flesh knows only a God who is either conciliatory or hostile, and it determines this on the basis of the actual state of affairs."[109] We draw premature conclusions from our observation of this state of affairs, and that is how we arrive at mistaken thoughts about God.[110] This "theology"

---

[103] In his biography of Luther, Oberman depicts him as a man "between God and the devil." See Heiko A. Oberman, *Luther, Mensch zwischen Gott und Teufel* (Berlin: Severin und Siedler, 1982). See also the paragraph in Althaus's *Theologie*, 144-150: "Der Mensch zwischen Gott und Satan." It is Calvin's commentary on the Psalms which indicates how this characterization also applies to Calvin as he describes the position between God and the devil as characteristic of the situation for every believer.

[104] Ps. 76:11 (*CO* 31, 709).

[105] Ps. 32:24 (*CO* 31, 313).

[106] Ps. 16:5 (*CO* 31, 154).

[107] "Iam quum eodem telo appetitus fuerit filius Dei, nihilo magis fidelibus, qui eius membra sunt, parcet Satan," Ps. 22:8 (*CO* 31, 225).

[108] Ps. 77:6 (*CO* 31, 713).

[109] Ps. 22:2 (*CO* 31, 220). Cf. Ps. 27:5 (*CO* 31, 274): "...quo docemur non metiri Dei auxilium externa specie, vel externo modo...."

[110] Ps. 44:24 (*CO* 31, 448).

poses a threat to the faithful when they conclude based upon their need that God has forgotten them or that he has even turned against them.

> It is a heavy affliction when someone measures God's favor by earthly well-being because then it is not such a surprise that great confusion arises under these circumstances.[111]

Meanwhile, Calvin notes, the strategy of Satan is to intentionally spread a different theology. The Reformer explains,

> This is the devil's approach: since he is not capable of eradicating in one single step every religious sensibility from our hearts, he tries to dissuade us from our conviction by presenting to us the ideas that we must seek a different God (*alienum Deum*) from the God we have thus far been worshipping, or that we need to be reconciled with him in a different way, or that we need to gain the assurance of his grace in a different way than from the law and the gospel.[112]

Therefore, Calvin's remedy to the devil's tricks is our adherence to God's theology as opposed to the theology of Satan. By "the law and the gospel" Calvin means the conviction of sin and grace evident in his observation that Satan wants to keep people away from God by removing from them the realization of their misery.[113] Without any conviction of sin, one will not seek God. A struggle thus takes place in one's heart, and Satan tries to merely keep the heart occupied with mistaken ideas about God and ourselves.[114] He is out to provide people with a rather different "*cognitio Dei et hominis.*" Calvin suggests that is the devil's handiwork to bring people to fabricate false gods.[115] The heart is a workshop where all sorts of thoughts are continuously framed, and if God does not keep watch over it Satan can easily direct the thoughts to his liking.[116]

According to Calvin, "Satan has countless tricks to plunge us into darkness," and so we consequently have eyes only for the disorder in this

---

[111] Ps. 17:13 (*CO* 31, 166).
[112] Ps. 44:20 (*CO* 31, 445).
[113] "...miseriae nostrae sensum nobis adimat...," Ps. 32:2 (*CO* 31, 318).
[114] "...Satan fallaciis corda nostra occupans...," Ps. 32:2 (*CO* 31, 318).
[115] Ps. 73:25 (*CO* 31, 688).
[116] Ps. 141:3 (*CO* 32, 393).

world, and we no longer recognize that God is providing for this earth.[117] Moreover it is part of his strategy to bring chaos to our thought so that our attention is divided and we can no longer direct ourselves toward God alone.[118] Calvin affirms that chaos and disorder are to be seen as largely the work of Satan. This then poses a clash between "the flesh" and our faith, a struggle that takes place in the heart of the believer. In such situations, he observes, "the knowledge of faith" (*fidei cognitio*) stands in opposition to "the logic of the flesh" (*carnis ratio*) by which the flesh wants to make us believe that God has closed his eyes towards us.[119] In the heart of the believer there are two voices: that of God and that of God's enemy. God's voice may be heard in the promise giving hope, but the other voice points out the circumstances in order to bring one to despair of God.[120] Furthermore, that which the flesh calls absurd, such as trusting in God in situations like this, is the highest wisdom to faith.[121]

Calvin sees clear evidence of this internal conflict in the psalmist's words of Psalm 22: "My God, my God, why have you forsaken me?" It seems to be a contradiction here since the author confesses his unbelief saying that God has forsaken him while first confessing his faith by twice calling God "my God." According to Calvin though this is the daily experience of the believer, and this contradiction is characteristic of the life of faith.[122] In Calvin's thought, this also reflects a *"theologia crucis"* as it is evidenced when he says that "It is indeed quite hard to keep in mind that God is gracious towards us in the moment when he is angry or that he is close in the moment when he is far away."[123] When circumstances are against us, the flesh concludes that God has rejected and abandoned the believer, but faith clings to God's invisible grace. It also reassures one of God's presence since he is near to us even when he seems to be far away.[124]

Faith is always in motion since the tension between hope and fear is ever-present. Believers are always faced with two feelings. On the one hand they

---

[117] Ps. 73: introduction (*CO* 31, 673).

[118] "...conatur Satan hucque et illuc distrahere," Ps. 41:11 (*CO* 31, 423).

[119] Ps. 13:4 (*CO* 31, 133).

[120] Ps. 3:2 (*CO* 31, 53).

[121] "Et certe nihil carni videtur magis absurdum...hanc esse optimam prudentiam," Ps. 14:6 (*CO* 31, 141).

[122] Ps. 22:2 (*CO* 31, 220).

[123] Ps. 69:15 (*CO* 31, 645).

[124] "...ut certi statuamus, etiam quam longissime abesse videtur, eum nobis propinquum es," Ps. 16:8 (*CO* 31, 155).

are torn by feelings of fear and worry, and on the other hand God inspires them with a hidden joy which helps to keep them from being overwhelmed by the other feelings.[125] While it might appear that these are mutually exclusive feelings which cannot be found in a single heart, Calvin declares that "experience teaches that hope can only truly reign where fear also keeps part of the heart occupied."[126] Hope does not function where there is a restful state of mind, but it springs into action when everything comes down upon one.

The temptation to adopt this way of thinking, Calvin says, is perhaps particularly strong when our adversaries employ this theology by implying that God is apparently not taking care of us anymore, having turned from our ally into our foe.[127] Behind these enemies sits Satan. He is the one bringing us to despair in such situations with the suggestion that God is no longer supporting us with his Spirit nor wanting to provide for our salvation.[128] If the faithful would just completely trust in God, Satan would be unable to harm them. Yet the problem is that the many deaths which threaten them bring about doubt, fear and unrest so that for even the most experienced believer nothing is more difficult than to recognize that God remains gracious towards us.[129]

According to Calvin, every believer faces this quandary daily.[130] In this inward struggle one discovers two things: the weakness of one's flesh and the presence of faith. This dichotomy in the experience of faith brings the believer into a peculiar position between God and Satan. The devil will construe adversity as a sign of God's wrath which proves that God has abandoned the believer. Thus Satan attempts to bring the believer to despair that he might expunge faith in God.[131] Calvin writes,

> Quite cunningly he tries to bring us to despair and entices us with the notion that God has taken away the help of his Spirit and that he has stopped providing for our salvation.[132]

---

[125] Ps. 94:18 (*CO* 32, 27).

[126] Ps. 56:4 (*CO* 31, 548).

[127] Ps. 3:2 (*CO* 31, 53).

[128] "Hac vero occasione Satan astute nos ad desperationem sollicitat et impellit...," Ps. 55:5 (*CO* 31, 536).

[129] Ps. 91:5 (*CO* 32, 3).

[130] "Idem quotidie quisque fidelium in se experitur...," Ps. 22:2 (*CO* 31, 220).

[131] Ps. 22:2 (*CO* 31, 220). Cf. Ps. 41:13 (*CO* 31, 424).

[132] Ps. 55:5 (*CO* 31, 536).

On the other side, however, there is God who promises the faithful that he will indeed show his fatherly countenance again. Faith remains standing by seeking in God's promises something to which it may really cling.[133] Satan, of course, also concerns himself with God's promises, but he merely seeks to convince the faithful that they are empty. Behind the enemies who mock believers, saying, "Where is your God now?," Calvin believes the devil is at work. "Satan has no more deadly an arrow with which to wound the heart than his tries to chase our hope away by making God's promises laughable."[134] He endeavors to destroy faith, Calvin details, with the stinging taunt that, given the circumstances, one is calling upon God in vain.[135]

As noted above, Satan advocates a "theology from beneath," attempting to bring us to conclusions about God on the basis of that which befalls us here and now. This is a theology in keeping with our flesh, Calvin writes, since the flesh "assesses God by what it experiences momentarily of his grace."[136] Therefore Calvin highlights the "antithesis" which lies between "the pernicious delusions that Satan whispers to us" on the one hand and the affirmation that God is gracious towards us and that he guards our faith on the other.[137]

When faced with these circumstances, faith knows a different theology, not one which surveys heaven from earth, but one which surveys earth from heaven. Calvin writes in this context about "an evidence of faith to obtain light from heaven when on earth we are surrounded by darkness in order to continue along the way of the hope of salvation."[138] The Reformer is convinced that "when faith directs itself towards heaven, it is easy to rise above despair."[139] Furthermore, Calvin teaches that he who listens to God well is armed against the wiles of Satan.[140] However, he who does not rest in the *doctrina Dei* is an easy prey for Satan.[141] Accordingly, the struggle against Satan clearly has a cognitive dimension in Calvin's thought.

---

[133] Ps. 22:2 (*CO* 31, 220).

[134] Ps. 22:8 (*CO* 31, 225).

[135] Ps. 22:8 (*CO* 31, 225).

[136] Ps. 14:6 (*CO* 31, 141).

[137] Ps. 73:1 (*CO* 31, 674).

[138] Ps. 11:4 (*CO* 31, 123). Another discussion of *fidei probatio* occurs also in Ps. 31:14 (*CO* 31, 308).

[139] Ps. 119:87 (*CO* 32, 252).

[140] "Si enim attenderent ad vocem Dei, probe contra omnes Satanae insidias muniti essent," Ps. 119:3 (*CO* 32, 216).

[141] Ps. 119:11 (*CO* 32, 219).

Yet faith never actually knows rest since it is continually moved to and fro.[142] God's children are also constantly tossed about by the waves of temptation.[143] Whenever they want to patiently trust in God in the midst of a situation where he is training them by means of a cross, Satan comes to entice them towards impatience, hoping that they will thus rise up against God. The highest they can reach is the state of the sea right before a storm. In other words, there are no big waves, but there is already a discernible swell. At that moment, Satan often starts inciting new unrest.[144] Furthermore, he elevates his attacks correspondingly when we raise our efforts to obey God.[145] This is also the reason for not panicking when we feel all sorts of temptations and longings arise in our hearts. Calvin gives quite an elaborate meteorological illustration here. Just as bad weather develops as a result of the sun's heat rising from the earth and colliding with the clouds, a similar phenomenon occurs with believers who direct themselves toward heaven. The clouds of the flesh try to block this and that leads to acute afflictions.[146] Yet Calvin thinks that it is just as well that this happens because if our thoughts were able to direct themselves towards heaven unhindered, many vain thoughts could also arise. According to Calvin, the faithful often stumble when Satan envelops them in such a solid darkness that the word of God means almost nothing to them any more.[147] This explains why Calvin mentions Satan by name in his exposition of Psalm 119 roughly as many times as he does in all the other psalms combined. Satan seeks to prevent us from walking in the way of God's law, and so he will always try to lure us away from it.[148]

For those with whom things are going well, Satan has a different tactic. With them he aims to convert their strength in faith to mere self-confidence, thereby paralyzing their faith.[149] That's how it goes with many, with whom things are going all right in the world, but who forget God's judgments

---

[142] "Scimus non ita compositas esse piorum mentes, quin saepe alternis fluctuationibus iactari contingat," Ps. 62:1 (*CO* 31, 585). Cf. Ps. 62:6 (*CO* 31, 587): "...nunquam ita bene pacatas esse mentes nostras quin sentiant caecos motus."

[143] Ps. 116:7 (*CO* 32, 194).

[144] Ps. 62:6 (*CO* 31, 587).

[145] Ps. 119:173 (*CO* 32, 293).

[146] "...nubes autem oppositae dum liberum cursum impediunt ipso conflictu tonitrua generant. Idem et piis contingit...," Ps. 39:4 (*CO* 31, 398).

[147] Ps. 116:11 (*CO* 32, 197).

[148] Especially in the interpretation of such verses as 3, 5, 9, 29, 60, 61, 69 and 104.

[149] "Haec enim Satanae astutia est, ex virtute fabricare carnis confidentiam quae torporem inducat," Ps. 17:5 (*CO* 31, 161).

because of that. Calvin argues that a spiritual torpor then sweeps over the faithful and turns their prayer cold. Their dependence upon God's favor diminishes, and at the same time their trust in transient well-being increases.[150] Calvin sees this as a process in which Satan slowly pries one loose from God.

In contrast with Luther, it is noteworthy how rarely Calvin relates affliction to the question of whether one is a child of God.[151] This does not mean that the issue is not present, but rather it is present much less since the questions of Calvin and his readers in this matter are differently defined. In Calvin's thought it is not in the first place the struggle with personal sin that brings one to affliction. It is setbacks and difficulties that bring one to the question whether one has indeed received forgiveness from God. Doubt about one's reconciliation with God sets in when the signs of reconciliation (such as deliverance from hardship) are lacking.[152] Satan then tries to bring people to the point where, because of their circumstances, they convince themselves that God is apparently not gracious or that he does not provide for their salvation.[153] Against this notion, Calvin recalls the words of Psalm 32:1, observing that "the Holy Spirit confirms and authenticates the forgiveness of sins with an abundance of words so that, amidst all the events which befall the faithful, they will not be overcome by despair."[154]

Another different in comparison with Luther is that Satan brings sins into plain sight in Luther's thought, but Calvin remarks that Satan makes us blind to our sins. Satan knows how to ensnare people in all kinds of traps so well that, according to the Genevan, there is scarcely anyone with an adequate conviction of sin. Believers as well can be so deceived that they may not regard even gross sin to be so.[155] In this way the devil keeps people from God since those who have no conviction of sin will not fear God's judgment nor seek God's forgiveness.

In conclusion we can observe what Calvin says in his commentary on the fourth psalm. To believe, he explains, means to descend into the arena where

---

[150] "...ne inter laetos successus blanditiis suis nos fascinet Satan," Ps. 30:7 (*CO* 31, 296).

[151] For Luther, see Horst Beintker, *Die Überwindung der Anfechtung bei Luther* (Berlin: Evangelische Verlagsanstalt, 1954).

[152] Ps. 109:26 (*CO* 32, 157).

[153] "Ita subest antithesis inter pravas imaginationes quas suggesserat Satan...," Ps. 73:1 (*CO* 31, 674).

[154] Ps. 32:1 (*CO* 31, 316).

[155] Ps. 19:12 (*CO* 31, 204).

battle must be done with one's enemies. However, believers know that "God is on our side," and this is why our enemies will never win.[156]

8. The Weakness of the Believer

It is not only Satan's work which promotes unrest since he would offer no threat at all if only the faithful offered more resistance and were not so weak. Satan has an important and loyal co-conspirator in our "flesh" (by which Calvin means the New Testament concept of *sarx*). Calvin writes, "When we are well, each of us seems to be an invincible soldier, but as soon as the battle begins in earnest our weakness becomes openly apparent, and that is the moment when Satan seizes the opportunity."[157] Believers are unstable, and they are more susceptible to all kinds of spiritual commotion than is good for them.[158] As they are too sinful and too weak to be resistant against the enticements of Satan, they continually need God's grace and power.[159] Believers are, as Calvin puts it, "inclined towards distrust and unfaithful doubt," and therefore they must always be reminded of God's promises.[160] Their weaknesses prevent them from being able to consistently resist attacks, and so there can be times of backsliding.[161] Moreover, however much they try to suppress their feelings of doubt, believers keep struggling with their weakness,[162] and Satan characteristically strikes at precisely our weakest moments.[163] Various afflictions related to the weakness of our faith often develop when we observe the apparent well-being of those who do not bother themselves with God. At those times, the conviction that someone who has obtained the forgiveness of sin is blessed becomes a hard pill to swallow.[164] The believer who sees how well things are going for those who live without God, "comes under the serious temptations not only to criticize God tacitly that he does not regulate such matters but also to give in to the opportunity to sin since this can apparently go unpunished."[165]

---

[156] Ps. 4:3 (*CO* 31, 59).
[157] Ps. 55:5 (*CO* 31, 536).
[158] Ps. 62:6 (*CO* 31, 587).
[159] Ps. 119:37 (*CO* 32, 230). Cf. Ps. 119:43 (*CO* 32, 233).
[160] Ps. 12:7 (*CO* 31, 129).
[161] Ps. 17:15 (*CO* 31, 168).
[162] Ps. 22:2 (*CO* 31, 221).
[163] Ps. 146:6 (*CO* 32, 423).
[164] Ps. 32:1 (*CO* 31, 316).
[165] Ps. 73:2 (*CO* 31, 675).

To deter this outcome, Calvin presents the reader again with the example of David the psalmist, who "is aware of his own vulnerability and at the same time knows of the numerous wiles which Satan likes to employ."[166] The weakness, Calvin explains, must not utterly discourage a believer. Calvin denounces that which he calls the merciless doctrine of perfection. When we do not manage to serve and praise God as we would want to do, we must not despair because, even though our praise is deficient, that does not mean that it necessarily displeases God. After all, God is not looking for perfection but for sincerity.[167] Yet Calvin does not have a particularly positive view of the believer since, though one may know that he or she has been created to praise God, in practice very little is carried out to this end. When it comes to the praise of God, the faithful are cold and lethargic, and they constantly need to be urged.[168]

9. Means against Affliction

The differences between Luther and Calvin on the nature of affliction are also evident when it comes to the *remedy*. Whereas Luther cautions against facing these things while alone,[169] Calvin specifically advises that solitude be sought. Amongst others, he argues, one's thoughts can become confused and divided, but when alone one can quietly find oneself, abhor one's deeds and find the way back to God. Thus the believer can come to his senses.[170]

Calvin is in *agreement* with Luther however when he notes that calling God "my God" is a weapon against afflictions.[171] When a person has any doubt over the question of whether God is still favorably inclined towards them, Calvin advises that one start with the general covenant promise given to the entire church, and then from there he recommends that one apply it

---

[166] Ps. 39:2 (*CO* 31, 396). According to Barbara Pitkin there is a tension here in the way that Calvin sets up David as an example: "the Christians who are to imitate his faith, though they have by virtue of their historical situation the advantage of a superior and clearer manifestation of God's mercy and favor, appear to be so much more blind," *David's Paradigm*, 861.

[167] "...si modo non simulate enitimur ad praestandum hunc pietatis cultum," Ps. 111:1 (*CO* 32, 167).

[168] "...sed interim iacet inter nos eius gloriam," Ps. 113:1 (*CO* 32, 177).

[169] See, amongst others, *WA* 40 I, 493, 19-21; and *WA* 42, 501, 35-41.

[170] "...reditus ad sanam mentem...," Ps. 4:5 (*CO* 31, 61).

[171] "...quod Iehovam appellat Deum suum, sed hoc velut agere opposito tentationum fluctus repellet," Ps. 7:2 (*CO* 31, 80). For Luther, see Beintker, *Überwindung*, 115-31.

personally.[172] If God is indeed the protector of the church, then he is also the protector of the individual believer. In such situations, therefore, the important thing is "that everyone applies to himself that which God has in general promised to his church."[173]

Afflictions, however, are not assessed by Calvin as purely negative though since he also sees them as a means by which faith is tested and strengthened. He observes that faith often bears fruit when it must battle to remain standing in the midst of dangers.[174] Furthermore, faith is only able to prove itself when the struggle in which we are caught is so intense that "it seems as if hell is opening its doors to swallow us in."[175] For this reason, Calvin considers it a good thing to test one's own faith by first finding oneself and then doing some soul searching without others present. At that time the believer will be forced to face the question as to whether God is still enough for him or whether he is letting himself be strongly influenced by that which the people around him think.[176] Therefore, it is not a question as to whether or not there is still faith, but instead whether faith is still completely aimed towards God. Another invincible weapon against afflictions is the knowledge that God is almighty.[177] God's nature as God is thus a remedy to affliction, and thus Calvin seeks to go back even further than the promise to God himself.

10. Doubt over God's Grace

As it was already observed, the commentary on the Psalms provides proportionately little attention the question of the assurance of salvation. This is not surprising though since Calvin emphasizes the fact that God is gracious according to his very nature. Given the nature of God and the essence of his grace make every form of doubt entirely unnecessary.

Calvin makes this point in the only place where he discusses the question of the assurance of salvation with any detail—his comments concerning Psalm 130:4. Here he remarks about his contemporaries that "there are so few people living with the conviction that the grace they need is also

---

[172] "...a generali promissione incipere...," Ps. 121:4 (*CO* 32, 301).

[173] Ps. 125:1 (*CO* 32, 313).

[174] Ps. 27:3 (*CO* 31, 272-3).

[175] Ps. 46:4 (*CO* 31, 461).

[176] "Nam haec vera demum fidei probatio est, dum se quisque colligens, absque testibus animum suum examinat...," Ps. 91:9 (*CO* 32, 4).

[177] "...sed si probe de eius omnipotentia persuasi essemus, contra omnes tentationum insultis invicta nobis futura esset," Ps. 93:1 (*CO* 32, 16).

available to them."[178] Among those who have no assurance, there are certainly some who simply lie sleeping in their sin without letting grace bother them, but there are also those who are tossed this way and that by various doubts. This latter group of people is aware of their own sin and is remorseful about it, but they lack faith. The cause, as Calvin sees it, is a theology in which God has been divorced from his mercy, as if mercy does not quite belong to God's nature. Furthermore, this is connected with the Roman Catholic doctrine in which the grace of God is mixed up with the worthiness and adequacy of man. For the one who seeks God in terms of this theology, still encounters his own sins in God's grace. Therefore, Calvin suggests, it is little wonder that people under the papacy do not continually call upon God in prayer. Prayer places one before God, confronting him or her quite directly with guilt. When God is considered apart from his mercy, prayer only increases the anguish over sin. Calvin then says that prayer, as the sinner's appearance before God, becomes something like placing wood on the fire. Against this notion, Calvin states that one may trust in God's forgiveness because God is God.[179] God is gracious because he is God, and therefore every prayer starts with forgiveness.

Calvin accuses Rome of needlessly scaring the believers in her fold. Consider his severe charge concerning the absence of assurance:

> Sure, they have long sermons about the fear of God, but, because they keep miserable souls trapped in their doubts, they may be building but without the foundation.[180]

For Calvin, that foundation is the gracious nature of God. To those who would serve him, God never proves to be anything but reconciliatory.[181] The reason for this attitude is God's own honor. God knows that if he were to only make himself known as the wrathful judge "there would remain no piety in the world at all," and "without a trust in the reception of forgiveness there would also be no more worship of God."[182] In the Reformer's mind, it is clear

---

[178] Ps. 130:4 (*CO* 32, 334).

[179] "...certoque persuasus sim te ideo misericordem esse quia Deus es," Ps. 130:4 (*CO* 32, 335).

[180] Ps. 130:4 (*CO* 32, 335).

[181] "...et nunquam in medium prodire quin se placabilem servis suis offerat," Ps. 103:4 (*CO* 32, 335).

[182] Cf. Ps. 103:4 (*CO* 32, 336): "Unde sequitur, Deum nunquam recte coli absque notitia gratiae eius."

what happens when people are only confronted with God's wrath and when the message of God's grace does not precede it:

> They all flee from him and become frightfully scared of his countenance. Inasmuch as they do not exactly turn their backs on him, they vigorously try to hide themselves from him. In short, the realization of God's judgment without the hope of forgiveness creates a fear that will automatically turn into hate.[183]

Calvin so seldom deals with the difficulty of *accepting grace* because this matter, he assumes, belongs to Roman Catholic theology. Moreover, unlike Luther, he hardly knew this sort of affliction personally. Calvin acknowledges that there could be doubt, but at the same time he quite emphatically denounces the idea, calling it "the delusion of Sorbonne,"[184] that the faithful may not be sure whether they will keep the faith throughout their lives. He notes that the scriptures establish our confidence that the grace of God encompasses the rest of one's life,

> ...and we would certainly find ourselves in a miserable condition if we had to again be afraid all of the time that God's grace could all of a sudden not be there for us anymore![185]

Furthermore, it is impossible for a believer to sin such that he changes from being a child of God to being an enemy of God once more. In saying this, Calvin rejects the doctrine of mortal and venial sins and looks to 1 Peter 1:23 and 1 John 3:39 for support. Sometimes, he states, it may appear as if God is rejecting someone, but in hindsight it is evident that God's grace has nonetheless been upon him even if the signs of his grace are temporarily hidden. When David prays, "Do not take your Holy Spirit from me," he does not mean to imply that the Spirit can completely withdraw but rather that a believer might fear this upon the realization that his sins have in essence been an attempt to snuff out God's grace.[186] Calvin is not consistent in his reasoning and usage of the text. He creates the impression that he wants to

---

[183] Ps. 103:4 (*CO* 32, 335). Compare this to Luther's observation that there was a time in his life when he hated God.
[184] "...sorbonium illud commentum...," Ps. 16:8 (*CO* 31, 155).
[185] Ps. 16:8 (*CO* 31, 155).
[186] Ps. 51:12 (*CO* 31, 518).

use this text as the proof for his doctrine. For example, in connection with the twelfth verse of Psalm 51, Calvin observes that the word "create" denotes that the heart of man is utterly corrupt and that one must therefore be completely renewed.[187] The implication of this interpretation would then be that David therefore must be completely renewed after his sin since he would have fallen from the state of grace. Calvin, however, does not want to follow through with this implication, and so he insists that grace cannot be lost. Calvin apparently interprets verse 12 as the words of the unregenerate and verse 13 as the prayer of the regenerate when, in fact, it is all the prayer of the same person!

11. Predestination

Both in his catechism of 1537 and in the last edition of the *Institutes* (1559) Calvin discusses election in connection with the origin of faith and doubt.[188] For this reason predestination is discussed in these places after the treatment of faith (see, for example, the *Institutes*). This also conforms to Calvin's habit of speaking about the faithful as the elect and the outcast as unbelievers in this commentary. Calvin thus arrives at his doctrine of election by way of experience, which is to say *a posteriori*.

God is completely able to fill all the earth with his love, and yet the majority of humanity is imprisoned in a deathly darkness. This reality has no other explanation than the fact that "God does not look upon all people with friendly and fatherly eyes, and he does not open all eyes to the fact that the source of all joy can only be found in him."[189] Furthermore, experience shows that God does not elect everyone to grace.[190] In discussing the sixty-fifth Psalm, Calvin asks what other explanation there could be for the fact that God does not let all alike come to him other than that "his gracious election

---

[187] "Unde sequitur totum cor hominis, ubi in sua natura consideratur, contortum esse et perversum: quia si ulla esset a natura rectitudo vel mundities, non hanc vocaret David spiritus donum, illam vero Dei creationem," Ps. 51:12 (*CO* 31, 518).

[188] For Calvin's teaching on election and a summary of the literature on this aspect to his thought, see Richard A. Muller, *Christ and the Decree: Christology and Predestination in Reformed Theology from Calvin to Perkins* (Durham, NC: Labyrinth Press, 1986); Cf. Faber, *Symphonie*, 199-215.

[189] Ps. 16:11 (*CO* 31, 158).

[190] "...et experientia eorum inscitiam coarguit, qui communem omnibus sine delecti Dei gratiam esse garriunt," Ps. 65:5 (*CO* 31, 605).

distinguishes one from the other."[191] Although the situation of all people is essentially equal, by his election God separates them into two kinds.[192] Elsewhere he explains that God is not the savior "of all indiscriminately but only of his chosen people."[193] Likewise, Christ offers himself to the entire human race as a brother, but he recognizes as brothers only the faithful.[194] The recognition of the latter group, though, is not a restriction of the former offer: "Christ warmly invites all to conversion."[195]

Christ's invitation is not in the foreground when Calvin mentions the book of life. The Reformer writes, "Even before the creation of the world God wrote the names of his children in the book of life, but he considers them to be in the list of his own only when he puts his mark on them when they are born again through the Spirit of adoption."[196] In the Bible this list is called "the book of life," and it is "none other than the eternal decree of God by which he has elected his own unto salvation."[197] When the Bible mentions the writing down of those who are added to God's people, it concerns that which was recorded even before the foundation of the world. God however speaks about this being writing down in time as a form of "*accommodatio*."[198] God adapts his speech to our capacities because otherwise his election would be incomprehensible to us.[199] Similarly, this also applies when David speaks of the names of those who reject Christ as being erased from the book of life.

Between election and the moment of regeneration in the individual person, Calvin identifies the time of calling.[200] The order in this is clear in one passage of Calvin's commentary: "He [God] declares his love towards us in his call after he has chosen us."[201] Calling therefore comes to all of the covenant people, but Calvin writes that it is not effective with all.[202] The

---

[191] Ps. 65:5 (*CO* 31, 605).

[192] Ps. 87:6 (*CO* 31, 804).

[193] Ps. 130:8 (*CO* 32, 338).

[194] Ps. 22:23 (*CO* 31, 232). Note that Calvin is speaking about *fideles*— not *electi*.

[195] Ps. 18:38 (*CO* 31, 188).

[196] Ps. 87:6 (*CO* 31, 804). Calvin's references to "*catalogus*," "*recensere*" and "*nota*" bring to mind a census during which all those who belong to the people are officially registered as such.

[197] Ps. 69:29 (*CO* 31, 650).

[198] "Est quidem improprie loquutio, sed quae ad nostrum modulum non male accommodatur...," Ps. 69:29 (*CO* 31, 650).

[199] "Sed quia incomprehensibilis est aeterna Dei electio, respectu humani sensus scribi dicuntur...," Ps. 69:29 (*CO* 31, 650).

[200] "...ad vocationem pertinet...," Ps. 87:6 (*CO* 31, 804).

[201] Ps. 65:5 (*CO* 31, 606).

[202] "...quia neque omnes efficaciter ad se vocaverat Deus...," Ps. 65:5 (*CO* 31, 606).

explanation for the difference between those who only hear and those whose calling also penetrates the heart is the hidden election of God.[203] Therefore, the distinction in no way lies in some particular quality of man. The basis for this effectual calling does not lie in something outside of God but only and completely in his grace.[204] Election is therefore always followed by outward calling, and consequently none of the elect remain invisible but all that are his will join to the congregation.[205] To the one whom God has chosen to call unto salvation, God will also give the unique gift of getting the right view of him.[206] God's voice resounds over all the earth, but it only penetrates into the heart of those whom he has predestined unto salvation.[207]

Election is necessary because of the situation in which man has found himself since the fall into sin. Unless God first changes their heart of stone into a heart of flesh, it is impossible for anyone to convert himself to God out of free will. Here Calvin follows Augustine, who says that the conversion of a man is a greater work than his creation.[208] To be sure, faith and prayer *are* the means of reconciliation with God, but even the means do not come from man. By faith we accept the promise, and by prayer we call upon God as father, but, Calvin inquires, "Where else do faith and prayer come from if not from the grace which connects God to us who by nature are alienated from him?"[209] In short, we cannot decide to make him our God unless his grace precedes that.[210] Election accentuates the primacy of grace. God's grace precedes everything. Man is not even able to choose in favor of God by himself. Calvin writes, "The principle is to be firmly adhered to that there is for us no communion with him [God] at all unless he comes first with his grace."[211] The cause of the forgiveness of sins is the grace wherewith God wants to freely embrace in his fatherly favor people who have not deserved it.[212] To Calvin this implies the general rule that our access to God remains

---

[203] "Interim ex forte arcanae electionis manat hoc discrimen, ut in paucorum corda verbum penetret, aliorum aures verberet duntaxat," Ps. 81:14 (*CO* 31, 766).

[204] Ps. 105:6 (*CO* 32, 100).

[205] Ps. 65:5 (*CO* 31, 606).

[206] Ps. 19:7 (*CO* 31, 199).

[207] Ps. 40:8 (*CO* 31, 412).

[208] "...imo renovatio haec (ut scite Augustinus docet) ipsa creatione praestantior est," Ps. 81:14 (*CO* 31, 766).

[209] Ps. 65:5 (*CO* 31, 605).

[210] "Neque enim in arbitrio nostro est facere ut sit Deus noster, donec gratis nos praeveniat," Ps. 143:10 (*CO* 32, 405).

[211] Ps. 33:12 (*CO* 31, 330).

[212] Ps. 65:5 (*CO* 31, 605).

blocked for as long as he does not let us taste his goodness, and nobody can even pray well if he has not first experienced God's grace.[213]

The distinction between the elect and the rest of the world goes back to the good pleasure of God.[214] The archetypal expression of this, according to Calvin, is the election of Israel, who was no better than other peoples of the earth.[215] The Israelites were just as much enemies of God as the rest of Adam's descendants.[216] The only advantage that the Jews had over other peoples though was that God had accorded them the particular grace of his election.[217] Seen from the standpoint of God's judgment, the situation of all people in the world is equal. The source of the distinction between Israel and the others is thus purely one of God's grace. God discriminates, yet he does so without making the distinction dependent on anything in the elect themselves.[218] God's election therefore did not rest on the dimension or the quality of Israel. Initially there was only the family of Abraham who himself was infertile.[219] In Calvin's thought one could say that predestination as truly as creation may be characterized as God's work *ex nihilo*.

Election runs its course within the framework of the covenant of grace. David, for example, directs himself to the promise of the covenant and concludes from it that he belongs to God's church. In going by the promise, he incorporates himself, one might say, into God's church.[220] In the framework of the covenant, the question of the individual's responsibility also takes its place. Election plays no dominant role such that it would render every human activity either redundant or impossible. Calvin says that there are people who have fallen from the service of God and thereby made themselves unworthy of receiving God's favor.[221] In his interpretation of Psalm 16:7, Calvin points out that it is only due to the grace of God that one receives faith, thus becoming an heir to life. At the same time, however, he states that God "invites both the outcast and the elect unto himself, but the former rob themselves of this through their ingratitude."[222] Nevertheless

---

[213] Ps. 5:8 (*CO* 31, 69).

[214] Ps. 44:4 (*CO* 31, 439).

[215] Ps. 105:6 (*CO* 32, 100). Cf. Ps. 147:19 (*CO* 32, 432).

[216] Ps. 148:14 (*CO* 32, 436).

[217] Ps. 65:5 (*CO* 31, 605).

[218] "Unde sequitur discrimen in Dei amore esse…," Ps. 105:6 (*CO* 32, 100).

[219] "Unica fuit domus Abrahae, et quidem sterilis…," Ps. 105:12 (*CO* 32, 102).

[220] "…sicuti David in Dei ecclesia se includit," Ps. 22:5 (*CO* 31, 224).

[221] "…qui desciverant a Dei cultu: ideoque paterno Dei favore erant indigni," Ps. 73:1 (*CO* 31, 675).

[222] Ps. 16:7 (*CO* 31, 154).

Calvin does not say that God is a shepherd for the elect alone, but that he only wants to be a shepherd for those who seek shelter in him and want to be led by him.[223]

The most essential motive for Calvin's adherence to the doctrine of predestination though is that only this gives all the praise to God because "it is not permitted to share the praise between us and God."[224] In fact Calvin calls it a "sacrilege" to let salvation depend "even for just a single drop" upon us.[225] Any denunciation of predestination consequently poses a violation of the first commandment as a sin against God's being God. If the actions of men were to precede God's grace, there would not remain election by God.[226] Predestination upholds the link between the honor of God and the salvation of man: Calvin explains, "He wants his grace to radiate in our salvation."[227] We are close to him because his hand has pulled us up from the depths.[228] In this way election is an expression of God's love. Considering it nearly a synonym for the concept of grace, Calvin speaks of God's *love* as the basis for election. There is no other source for God's benevolence than his love, and the reason for his love by no means lies outside of God.[229] In short, God's love is the reason for the distinction he makes among people.[230]

12. The Scope of Election

The purpose of God's election which Calvin states in the Psalms commentary is that God "wants a people on earth who calls upon him and honors him."[231] God wants to be served. This is the purpose of creation, and this is also the purpose of election.[232] Apart from election there would not be anyone who serves God anymore. This also makes election certain because God simply

---

[223] Ps. 23:1 (*CO* 31, 238).

[224] Ps. 60:13 (*CO* 31, 580).

[225] "...quanto minus tolerabile est sacrilegium, in salute promerenda vires liberi arbitrii, spiritus sancti gratiae opponere ac si aequalis esset concursus?" Ps. 60:13 (*CO* 31, 580).

[226] Ps. 65:5 (*CO* 31, 605).

[227] Ps. 109:21 (*CO* 32, 155).

[228] Ps. 65:5 (*CO* 31, 606).

[229] Ps. 105:12 (*CO* 32, 103).

[230] Ps. 148:14 (*CO* 32, 436).

[231] Ps. 105:44 (*CO* 32, 115).

[232] "Et certe hic electionis nostrae finis est, quod Deus populum aliquem vult habere in terra a quo invocetur et colatur," Ps. 105:44 (*CO* 32, 115).

wants there to be a people who serve him. Election is therefore both in our interest and in God's interest because, as Calvin puts it, "he wants to preserve us in order that we may glorify his name."[233] God desires to be a father to his people, and therefore he elects children for himself.[234] A noteworthy implication for Calvin is that God indeed must give people faith since otherwise there would be no use in offering himself to them.[235] We are accepted as God's children because he wants us to honor him for all he gives us. His honor is his only ground for helping us. Therefore there is no other cause for our preservation than the honor of God's name.[236] Advancing this honor should then also become the goal in all of our deeds.[237] For Calvin, the doctrine of election gives new definition to God's purpose in creation. Therefore predestination, in establishing the purpose of creation, does not merely or even primarily pertain to our redemption from the consequences of sin in this life as much as to our service in this life now.

The purpose of making election known, Calvin explains, is to strengthen faith. In the Bible this "immutable decree of God" is revealed in order that faith may be supported amidst all the commotions in the world.[238] Election puts the faithful at rest since God does not choose his people for nothing. The Reformer holds that God chooses out of faithfulness to his covenant in order to maintain his people.[239] Calvin also sees a clear correlation between election and protection since the elect are assured of God's protection.[240] Moreover, when God seems far away the doctrine of election offers comfort since it is fixed and it rests on grace alone. Even one's sins cannot nullify the certainty of election.[241]

Rightly understood, Calvin writes, predestination does not hinder the spread of the gospel: "God descends to us through his word and, by inviting all without exception, disappoints no one. Whoever comes is admitted and will find that he has not been called in vain."[242] Although the calling comes to all, only the elect will come. The outward calling only becomes effectual

---

[233] Ps. 115:1 (*CO* 32, 182).

[234] Ps. 105:1 (*CO* 32, 98).

[235] "Nihil enim prodesset, Deum se nobis liberaliter offerre, nisi fide eum reciperemus...," Ps. 16:7 (*CO* 31, 154).

[236] Ps. 31:3 (*CO* 31, 302).

[237] Ps. 122:4 (*CO* 32, 305).

[238] Ps. 2:4 (*CO* 31, 45).

[239] Ps. 149:2 (*CO* 32, 437).

[240] See, for example, Ps. 44:4 (*CO* 31, 439) and Ps. 46:2 (*CO* 31, 460).

[241] "...sed potius gratuitae Dei electioni innititur...," Ps. 69:15 (*CO* 31, 645).

[242] Ps. 81:14 (*CO* 31, 766).

when God also draws to himself those whom he is calling.[243] Calvin denounces as foolish the notion that God allots his grace to all until they reject it. The faithful indeed dearly want all people to be saved, but they know that there are enemies of Christ so incorrigible that their destruction is assured.[244] Calvin finds the basis of their destruction not in the fact that God has rejected them but in their rejection of Christ.

The big question however remains: "What prevents God from bringing all hearts to obey him?"[245] Calvin does not know the answer, but he urges caution and warns the reader not to trespass into the secret decrees of God. We must be satisfied, he says, with God's will revealed in his word, and if it says there that God wants all people to be saved then we must proceed from that word.[246] This also ought to move the faithful to pray for the salvation of all people. Calvin writes,

> Because it is not ours to distinguish between the elect and the outcast, we must learn to pray for the good of all who make things difficult for us, we must learn to wish that the entire human race will be saved, and we must be concerned for the salvation of every single person.[247]

13. Election and Rejection

Calvin hardly speaks at all about God's active rejection of some. He asserts that "the treasure house of the forgiveness of sins is locked to the outcast."[248] In the commentary on the Psalms only a single passage may be found which speaks of an active rejection by God. In his exposition of Psalm 110:1 Calvin says that the entire human race by nature struggles against Christ, but the Son nevertheless "restrains some and humbles them into voluntary obedience to exalt them afterwards into communion with his glory. Others however he fells such that they remain lying in eternal destruction."[249]

---

[243] "Quanquam non sola vox externa sufficeret, nisi efficaciter ad se traheret quos vocavit," Ps. 81:12 (*CO* 31, 765).

[244] Ps. 79:6 (*CO* 31, 749).

[245] Ps. 81:14 (*CO* 31, 766).

[246] Ps. 81:14 (*CO* 31, 766).

[247] Ps. 109:16 (*CO* 32, 153).

[248] Ps. 145:9 (*CO* 32, 415).

[249] "…alios autem prosternit, ut in ruina perpetuo iaceant," Ps. 110:1 (*CO* 32, 161).

The point of departure is the state of enmity and damnation of all people. Calvin does not speak in this context about an election and rejection occurring prior to the fall into sin. On the contrary, Calvin clearly articulates that God chooses his own "from the lost offspring of Adam."[250] Originally all people were meant to be children of God, but because of sin the father-child relationship disappeared. "Therefore we are all by nature in a state of misery until God by his grace adopts us, and there is no other door to happiness than his election of unworthy people solely upon the basis of his good pleasure."[251] Calvin takes here an infralapsarian stance. In all other cases he speaks about God passing by those who are not saved. The rejected are the unworthy from whom God withholds his grace.[252] When God elects Israel, he passes by all the other peoples.[253]

The combination is thus not election and rejection, but rather election and passing by. The ultimate fate of unbelievers is only mentioned in one place and there only in summary form since Calvin does not say more than that "all unbelievers will completely go under through God's just judgment."[254]

According to Calvin the number of true believers is indeed quite limited. The unfaithful make up the majority, and the number of people who truly serve God is always small.[255] Most people for example *do* pray, but he questions how many do so sincerely. Calvin's terse generalization puts it well: "The fear of God is extremely rare."[256] The number of the elect is therefore not great in light of the whole of humanity. However, he considers it a wonder that people are saved at all from this fallen mass, and equally remarkable that there are so many being born again.[257] The faithful may be recognized by the confession of their faith since, in Calvin's view, faith cannot remain concealed.[258] He points again to the inseparable connection between belief in the heart and confession by the mouth through quoting Jesus' words, "What God has put together let no man tear asunder." It is the Holy Spirit who has established this "holy bond" between the heart and

---

[250] Ps. 105:1 (*CO* 32, 98).

[251] Ps. 33:12 (*CO* 31, 330).

[252] "...si gratiam...ab indignis subducit...," Ps. 21:11 (*CO* 31, 218).

[253] "...Deus reliquis praeteritis adoptare dignatus est," Ps. 147:19 (*CO* 32, 432).

[254] Ps. 145:20 (*CO* 32, 420).

[255] "...impios, quod numero praevalerent: sicuti exiguus semper est piorum numerus qui reverenter Deum colant," Ps. 119:51 (*CO* 32, 236).

[256] Ps. 25:12 (*CO* 31, 257).

[257] Ps. 110:3 (*CO* 32, 163).

[258] "...fidem non posse in cordibus mortuam latere quin emergat," Ps. 116:10 (*CO* 32, 196).

mouth. The external distinction between the faithful and the unfaithful is found in that the faithful seek God's countenance.[259] The actual reason for the distinction however is the *"adoptionis privilegium."*[260] For Calvin there are three groups of people: the faithful (the group he always denotes with "we" and "us"), the hypocrites, and those hardened despisers of the gospel.[261]

Because they can be recognized, there is no doubt about who the outcasts are in contrast to the elect. A distinction between the faithful and unbelievers is evident in their way of life. Calvin, of course, also knows how to describe "the antithesis between the outcast and the faithful" such that the division between the two groups is manifest. In fact, he juxtaposes the two against each other in a comprehensive list. The outcasts reveal themselves by their promiscuity and narcissism. They cover their sins, and they reject every judgment. Even as they lie in their beds they continuously hatch evil plans, and they take pleasure in despising God. The faithful, in contrast, show themselves by their modesty and self-condemnation, they confess their sins, and they place themselves under God's judgment. When alone, they busy themselves with self-examination, and they occupy themselves in the loathing of their sin.[262] The reprobate meanwhile violently oppose the faithful, but Calvin portrays the elect as "the good and the straightforward."[263]

14. Conclusion

Calvin's conception of faith is largely determined by the father-child relationship, resulting in Calvin's definition of faith as knowing, loving and trusting. This relationship, however, is rooted in the reconciliation between God and man since guilt before God is man's essential problem. For Calvin, the assurance of faith and the joy of faith are inseparably connected. Yet a struggle is also experienced in faith because the believer continuously finds himself in the midst of a battle between God and Satan, and the resultant afflictions can only be endured when faith persistently seeks God and his promises.

By his commentary on the Psalms, Calvin also shows that predestination is not a dogma springing from rationalsim, but it is rather an existential

[259] "…hac proprie nota discerni fideles a profanis hominibus…," Ps. 105:4 (*CO* 32, 99).
[260] Ps. 46:2 (*CO* 31, 460).
[261] Ps. 32:2 (*CO* 31, 317).
[262] Ps. 36:4 (*CO* 31, 361).
[263] Ps. 31:20 (*CO* 31, 311).

doctrina. The latter character is guaranteed by election's purpose being adoption into a living relationship with God as one's father. This aspect to Calvin's view of election, of course, seriously challenges many of the prevailing stereotypes about the Reformer regarding this doctrine.[264] Finally, Calvin's exposition of the Psalter shows that predestination is not so much a distinction between merit and grace as one between man and God, human honor and God's honor. Just as creation does, predestination also ascribes all the glory to God and none to us.

---

[264] In *Die Probleme der Theologie Calvins* (Leipzig: Hinrichs, 1922), 81, Bauke points out that "die Lehre doch im Verlauf der Geschichte der Calvinischen Kirche und Theologie infolge des konfessionellen Gegensatzes ein grösseres Gewicht bekommen, als sie im Rahmen der eigentlichen Theologie Calvins hat."

Conclusion

1. The Theology of Calvin

The concentration on the *Institutes* in Calvin studies has indeed produced much valuable material, but at the same time it has not always adequately accounted for the particular character of the *Institutes*. Calvin did not intend the work to be a summary of his theology, but rather he produced it as a theological glossary to accompany his commentaries. Calvin was not a man of just a single book, and therefore the *Institutes* by no means gives a complete representation of his theology.

The study of his commentary on the Psalms proves that there are themes in Calvin's theology which occur in his commentaries though they are not found in the *Institutes*.[1] At the same time, there are also matters which are only briefly noted in the commentaries since Calvin expounds upon them at length in the *Institutes*. This does not mean that in the commentaries we encounter a different Calvin from the writer of the *Institutes*. Instead the difference can be explained by the careful distinction which Calvin himself makes among literary genres. Not only language and style but content as well is impacted by the issue as to whether Calvin is writing a sermon, a commentary or a theological discourse. Furthermore Calvin keeps a target group in mind during his composition of each: is the aim to instruct students of theology or to encourage persecuted fellow-believers? Past research has often largely overlooked this distinction between genres.

For the remainder of this study, we will seek to compare the *Institutes* with the commentary on the Psalms, an obvious consideration seeing as that only two years lie between the appearance of the commentary on the Psalms (1557) and the publication of the last Latin edition of the *Institutes* (1559). Given certain passages which are duplicated nearly verbatim in both works, it is noticeable that Calvin worked on both books simultaneously.

---

[1] See Muller's criticism of the assertion that the commentaries present nothing more than the *Institutes*: Muller, *Unaccommodated*, 106-8.

In light of the distinction in genre and reading audience as well as the correspondence in content, I would like to define the commentary on the Psalms as a pastoral variation of the *Institutes*. In this commentary in particular Calvin applies himself to the main themes of the *Institutes* and gives them form so that they are directly applicable to the practice of living in faith. This would also explain why Calvin sometimes brings issues into consideration during his exposition which neither appear in the text of the Psalm nor seem to directly relate to it, and meanwhile Calvin makes far fewer references to contemporary events and situations than other commentators from the era do.[2] Hence discussions of such things as the Lord's Supper and the Trinity do not occur at all, and the matter of election scarcely occurs.

At the very least this study made clear that many new possibilities for research on Calvin still exist if only the sermons and commentaries of the Reformer would be given more attention by scholars.

In the past scholars sought to identify the *Leitmotif* of Calvin's theology. Both the doctrine of predestination and the glory of God were at various times suggested as his central themes although neither of these possibilities found general acceptance. Indeed the theology of Calvin is such that a leitmotif is very hard to find.

On the basis of his Psalms commentary, though, one might want to consider the "*deitas Dei*" as a possible leitmotif. Calvin continually busies himself with the questions of God's nature and acts, and he even tries to defend God's being God while at the same time responding to the questions and objections which people might voice about the "*deitas Dei*." God is in the center of the issues Calvin and his fellow believers have to deal with. Meanwhile Calvin holds that God must also be in the center of our actions, thoughts and beliefs. In fact, everything revolves around God, and God keeps everything revolving.

The divine nature of God is also the background for the heated debate over the "*extra calvinisticum*," where Calvin endeavors to safeguard God's freedom while maintaining the connection between the deity and true humanity of Christ. This safeguarding of God's freedom is also the reason why he does not want to bind Christ's divinity indissolubly with Christ's humanity, nor with the sacramental bread, nor binding the Spirit to the church service. By this, he aims to guard against the idolatry of trusting in external matters.

---

[2] For example, Melanchton. See Gosselin, *King's Progress*, 91.

In his analysis of the *Institutes* Marijn de Kroon concludes that Calvin's thought is dominated by the honor of God and the salvation of man.[3] Further investigation into the commentary on the Psalms in this study has also confirmed this conclusion, albeit with the qualification that the primary emphasis falls on the honor of God. This raises the question though whether it is correct then to speak of Calvin's theology as being so emphatically Christocentric.[4] After all, in the Psalms commentary it is not Christology but rather the question of God which stands as central. Calvin's theocentrism has been argued already by Bohatec[5] as well as Doumergue.[6] Subsequently, however, when Calvin research was influenced by Karl Barth, Calvin's was presented as a decidedly Christocentric theology. In recent years the study of Calvin's theology has also been affected by a renewed interest in the thought of Schleiermacher, resulting in the allegation that Calvin also took man as his point of departure in approaching the questions of God and faith.[7] Calvin's commentary on the Psalms, though, dispels the myth of a Barthian Calvin just as it also dismisses the notion of a Schleiermacherian Calvin. It is more accurate to say that Calvin's theology is not Christocentric (let alone anthropocentric!), but it is utterly *theocentric*.

2. Calvin and Luther

This investigation into Calvin's Psalms commentary did not set out to prove his similarities with Luther, yet it did establish numerous similarities between the two Reformers which are beyond dispute. In his exposition of the Psalter Calvin mentions Luther by name only one time, mentioning his agreement with the German Reformer's exegesis of a verse under consideration.[8] The

---

[3] Marijn de Kroon, *De eer van God en het heil van de mens: Bijdrage tot het verstaan van de theologie van Johannes Calvijn naar zijn Institutie* (Roermond: J. J. Romen, 1968; Leiden: J. J. Groen en Zoon, 1996).

[4] See Niesel, *Theologie Calvins*, 235: "Jesus Christus beherrscht nicht nur den Inhalt, sondern auch die Form des Calvinischen Denkens."

[5] Bohatec, *Vorsehungslehre*, 344, 348.

[6] E. Doumergue, *Jean Calvin. Les hommes et choses de son temps, tome quatrième. La pensée religieuse de Calvin* (Lausanne: G. Bridel & Co., 1910), 428-30.

[7] Ilka Werner's *Calvin und Schleiermacher im Gespräch mit der Weltweisheit. Das Verhältnis von christlichem Wahrheitsanspruch und allgemeinem Wahrheitsbewußtsein* (Neukirchen-Vluyn: Neukirchener, 1999) serves to illustrate this new approach. Werner is of the opinion that both Calvin and Schleiermacher ask the question: "Wie können wir wieder fromm werden?" See also "Calvin und Schleiermacher gehen von der Gottbezogenheit, nicht von der Gottfremdheit des Menschen aus," 280.

[8] Ps. 132:14 (*CO* 32, 350).

fact that Calvin mentions the man from Wittenberg only once is not odd, though, considering that the names of theologians (with just a single exception) do not occur in this commentary at all. The one occurrence however does at least confirm that Calvin used Luther's writings as a reference in composing his own commentary.

The close connection between a theologian's biography and his exegesis means that in comparing Calvin's and Luther's theology one must take Calvin's historical context into account just as it would be necessary with Luther's exegesis. The growing concern of persecution, for example, brings a dimension to Calvin's interpretation that is not present to the same degree in Luther's while the "existential" dimension of a personal struggle of faith for Luther occurs far less prominently in Calvin's writings. As a result of their differing situations, Luther's exegesis very clearly has a *"pro me"* character while the exegesis of Calvin reflects a theology *"pro nobis."*

In two respects however Calvin clearly shows himself to be a good pupil of Luther.[9] The first and prime commonality is the theocentric character of Calvin's theology. The title of an important book about Luther's theology might as well have been the title of a book about Calvin's thought: *Let God be God!*[10] Just like Luther, Calvin wants to put God at the center and then approach all other *loci* from that starting point. Particularly when the profound questions of election and providence or of evil and free will are under consideration, Calvin shouts out just as Luther does that people must let God be God. In the work of both Reformers, a warning against theological *"superbia"* is issued, urging readers not to transgress the boundaries into that which God has not revealed.

A second point of agreement is found in each thinker's "theology of the cross." Even if Calvin does not speak as extensively about the contrast between *"theologia crucis"* and *"theologia gloriae,"* this does not make the matter any less present. God's way of working is only clearly seen at Golgotha. There God reveals himself as the God who is known in Christ, especially in the suffering and death of Christ. From there Calvin also draws a line towards the suffering of the Christian, who by partaking of Christ shares in the cross of Christ. In and through suffering the Christian comes to know God better, and thus God reveals himself to us in suffering.

---

[9]   "Calvin ist der größte und wohl auch einzige Schüler, den Luther wirklich gehabt hat, d.h., der ihn zutiefst verstanden, und von ihm ausgehend, das Werk der Reformation mit einer eigenen Durchdringung der Botschaft des Evangeliums fortgesetzt und zu einer eigenen kirchlichen Gestalt gebracht hat." Peter Meinhold, "Calvin und Luther," in *Lutherische Monatshefte* 3 (1964): 94.

[10]   Philip S. Watson, *Let God Be God!* (Philadelphia: Muhlenberg Press, 1949).

DISCOUNT drug mart PRESCRIPTIONS

4006 73682000

PHARMACY#: 1   RECEIPT

Rx: 673682

BROWN, DENVIL
309 FURNACE ST
VANCOCIN HCL 250 MG PULVULEVIR
04/11/07 SENIOR

EL/1 Dr. CARSON, DENNIS

500 ABBE ROAD
ELYRIA   OH   44035
440 365' 8319

322 0450
66593-3126-02

PATIENT COUNSELING

	AMOUNT	DISCOUNT	PRICE
	1002.29	100.23	902.06
		0	08/08/1926

FILLED: 04/11/07

902.06

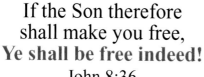

If the Son therefore
shall make you free,
Ye shall be free indeed!
John 8:36

*If the Son therefore
shall make you free,*
**Ye shall be
free indeed!**
John 8:36

***Come hear how
Chaplain
Mike Swiger
was truly set free!***

Sunday
March 25, 2007
9:30 AM

Held at
The Gospel House
14707 Alexander Road
Walton Hill, OH 44146
(440) 439-6555

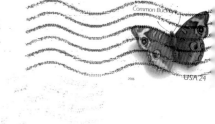

While acknowledging Luther's influence on Calvin and the great similarity between their respective theologies, however, the differences are not to be overlooked. The question, though, is whether one can speak of differences or whether, considering each man's theocentric character and the extent of their similarities, one should rather speak of variations by the Reformers within a same framework.

3. The Spirituality of Calvin

Careful study of Calvin's works yields a great amount of information about him as a person. Contrary to the stoic and lifeless caricatures of the Reformer which are so often assumed, we encounter instead a human being with emotions and afflictions of faith. Calvin does not appear as a cool rationalist, nor a mere architect of a dogmatic system, and certainly not as Geneva's feared tyrant who rules his subjects with an iron fist. Rather, the commentary on the Psalms shows that Calvin was a human being who struggled with himself, being aware of his impatience and irritability and yet seeking the ideal of "*interior tranquillitas.*" He was one who, as a believer, faced the immensely troubling questions of life and yet sought to hold onto something stable in the "*providentia Dei.*" Calvin's commentary on the Psalms is also a record of the struggle that Calvin himself experienced with the "*deitas Dei.*" Where his conception of God is concerned, Calvin straddles the dividing line between the Middle Ages and the new era—just as Luther does. On the one hand he emphasizes the fatherhood of God and the evidence of God's love and mercy, but on the other hand he speaks about the terror of God in his wrath and punishment. This does not suppose a contradiction between love and wrath in God, for Calvin knows how to relate God's righteousness and his mercy with complete harmony. However, this dynamic lies behind utterances in which one is told that one does not have to fear God while other passages seem to assert the very opposite.

The question of whether Calvin was a person plagued by fear cannot be answered by a simple yes or no. That he knew many terrors may be deduced from the text of the commentary, but it is not clear that he was utterly controlled by them.[11] The following passage illustrates the complexity of Calvin's own spirituality as a conjunction of his biography and theology:

---

[11] De Kroon sums up his evaluation of Bouwsma's book on Calvin with the observation that "Fearfulness plays a notable roll in Calvin's thought yet not as dominant a role

When dense vapors occupy the sky it is just as if the clouds are pressing down on us. And not only that, but it is also just as if the majesty of God draws closer to frighten us. Terror grips us, though we were so merry when the sky still looked cheerful. Let us not forget, meanwhile, that the image of a dark cloud is used to describe God's wrath to us. When the sky is clear it seems as if God's countenance cheers us up, but when the sky is ominous it looks as though God is threatening to come down upon us with a furrowed brow, and whether you like it or not you are going to look on despondently and sadly.[12]

From this passage one may infer how Calvin experienced the weather and how rather dramatic changes in the weather challenged both his sense of stability and his faith. At the same time though these words reveal some of the questions in Calvin's conception of God: when God's countenance frightens us, is he then actually like that or is it but his mask?

The commentary on the Psalms also confirms the fact that in Calvin's thought there is no trace of a stoic ideal of life. Calvin assumes a large role for feelings and the emotions in human experience, and this is precisely why the Psalms so powerfully speak to him. In fact, there is no biblical book in greater conflict with stoic ideals than the book of Psalms. Living under God's providence brings rest without taking away all unrest. Thus, while Calvin assumes a role for the emotions, it is a role with clear boundaries. He frequently reiterates a warning against giving free rein to feelings, whether they are positive or negative. The warning arises from his conviction that sin can take possession of one's feelings until one would lose sight of God. In the case of negative feelings this would mean "*desperatio*," and in the case of positive feelings, carelessness.

Although there is no sign of a stoic ideal, there are indeed unmistakable elements of humanistic ideals. Bouwsma's judgment that Calvin's moral values, shaped as they were by humanism, hinder him in his objectivity as an exegete, accordingly deserves closer inspection.[13] However the question should also be asked whether *any* exegete could perform his task so objectively that personal preferences and influences play no role at all.

More than once one observes difficulty in Calvin's exposition as he balances his two interests of putting God at the center while at the same time pastorally addressing the questions of a believer. Calvin is markedly hesitant

---

as Bouwsma would indicate in his chapter on Calvin's fearfulness." See his *Eer van God*, 211.

[12] Ps. 18:14 (*CO* 31, 177).

[13] Bouwsma, *Calvin*, 93

to leave incomprehensible matters alone, and he seems compelled to anticipate and answer his reader's possible question as to *why* something is so. The conviction that God has a purpose in everything and that this purpose can become clear to us brings its own distinctive character to preaching and pastoral care in Calvinism. He who is inclined to speak about God's purposes while not wanting to accuse God of injustice must, in the end, arrive at personal guilt. At the same time, when criticizing Calvin's approach, people have too often failed to see that Calvin's struggle for an explanation is driven by pastoral concern and not by a fondness for speculation.

The commentary on the Psalms however contains several themes which are worthy of comparison with Calvin's other commentaries. Here one thinks of the relationship between penance and forgiveness. Calvin's view of history also deserves closer attention. The unique way in which he sets David, Christ and believers of all times on one line as well as his well-known emphasis on the unity of the Old and the New Testaments both strongly point to an unequivocally static view of history. To what degree is there actually a history for Calvin and what is the benefit of the incarnation when the old and the new covenants differ not in substance but only in "*administratio*"?

4. The Spirituality of Calvinism

There is no doubt that Calvin's theology of the Psalms has left an impact on the spirituality of Calvinism. Yet, how closely has Calvinistic spirituality adhered to that of Calvin himself? This question emerges in even a superficial inspection of the Reformed tradition, where, for example, theatre attendance has often been anathematized despite the Reformer's positive mention of the theater in some contexts of his writings. Has not a kind of misrepresentation taken place? Are Calvin's "*Weltoffenheit*" and his impulses towards scientific understanding not strongly reduced among his theological heirs? Has his own tension between a dynamic view and a static view of God not been replaced for the tensionless acceptance of the latter view? These questions need to be asked, just as they need to be answered with definitive evidence from the Reformer's writings.

Negative life experiences have, as Calvin himself put it, left their stamp on his interpretation of the Psalms. The question which emerges then is whether Reformed spirituality, which is so indebted to the Psalms, has also shared in the same negative streak. Although it is still perhaps premature for us to pose an answer to this question, it is safe to say that the context of Calvin's interpretation has not received sufficient attention. By using Calvin's commentary in modern times, have the Reformer's remarks about his own experiences been under-appreciated as an important part of his exposition? Has Calvin's reading audience even been adequately taken into account thus far, or is his interpretation simply read as if it did not speak to a situation where there is high infant mortality, frequent outbreaks of mortal disease and severe religious persecution?

At the same time, though, Calvin has had an influence on the spirituality of Calvinism directly related to his theology even apart from its context. Here one should think of Calvin's attempt to bring a connection between sin, guilt and punishment. In his defense of God's righteousness and goodness, Calvin characteristically seeks a cause of suffering in man and his sin. My evaluation is that this stems from Calvin's emphasis on the unity of the Old and the New Testament. When this unity is emphasized so strongly, the possibility that *no* distinction will be made between God's actions before and after the coming of Christ is certainly a danger. Therefore, the connection that Calvinism has often made between floods, wars, and epidemics on the one hand and God's punishment on the other, between the sins of the people and perceived judgments of God in human history, certainly relates to the levelling of historical circumstances from that aforementioned unity. Consequently, the Calvinist may hold today that, in response to disobedience and idolatry, God still metes out punishment to the church in the same way that he did with Israel.

On the other hand, certain aspects of Calvin's theology and spirituality have obviously disappeared in Calvinism, or they have at any rate received much less attention than would be expected on the basis of Calvin's work. In his commentary on the Psalms Calvin emphasizes the assurance of faith, he asks for diligence regarding growth in faith and the joy of faith, and he defines belief in terms of love. In the contemporary expression of Calvinism these emphases do not occur unless in certain rare exceptions. This is also somewhat true in the ambivalent character of Calvin's theology. Calvin has a way of speaking solemnly about God only to remark a moment later that he asks himself who God actually might be. Calvin therefore struggles with the question of the nature of God. The questions of "why" from his own life and from the lives of his fellow believers always brings him to the question of "Who is God?" Calvin needs to know that there are certainties about God in order for him to remain standing (to say nothing of his concern for others). Yet these certainties in fact seem to call forth new questions in him. The question of whether Calvinism is a religion with a clear (albeit somewhat static) conception of God also deserves to be investigated more closely. At the very least, it does not seem to match up with Calvin's own conception of God. Calvin speaks of God's fatherly emotions, and at the same time he fears those emotions as possible changes in God.

In summary, his Psalms commentary indicates that Calvin sees no choice but to make do, content to live with the paradoxes between the divine word and our daily reality, between God's *ordo* and this worldwide chaos, between the heavenly rest and our inward unrest, between God's mercy and his wrath, between God's promise of salvation and man's miserable experience, between God's "*praesentia realis*" and God's hiddenness, and between faithful trust in God and the "whys" that scream out to us. Ironically, this struggle seems to bring Calvin closer to Luther than to those later theologians known as "Calvinists." This struggle also brings Calvin much closer to man today.

Bibliography

Primary Sources

Beze, Theodore de. *Correspondence de Theodore de Beze*, 2 vol. Genève: Droz, 1996.

Calvin, John. *Het boek der Psalmen verklaard door Johannes Calvijn, vertaald en uitgegeven onder toozicht van den weleerw. heer J. Boer Knottnerus V. D. M.* 1898; W. A. de Groot-Goudriaan, 1970.

———. *Teksten uit de INSTITUTIE van Calvijn*, trans. Willem van 't Spijker. Delft: Meinema, 1987.

———. *Commentaires sur le livre des Pseaume Ceste traduction est tellement reveuë, & si fidellement conferee sur le Latin, qu'on la peut iuger estre nouvelle.* Genève, 1561.

———. *Institutio christianae religionis.* Genève, 1559.

———. *Le livre des Pseaumes exposé.* Genève, 1558.

———. *Ioannis Calvini Opera, quae supersunt omnia,* ed. Wilhelm Baum, Edward Cunitz and Edward Reuss. Brunsvigae-Berolini: C. A. Schwetschke et filium, 1863-1900.

———. *Auslegung der Heiligen Schrift, in deutscher Übersetzung, Die Psalmen*, 2 vol. Neukirchen: Buchhandlung des Erziehungsvereins, 1930.

———. *Der Psalter auf der Kanzel Calvins,* bisher unbekannte Psalmenpredigten herausgegeben und eingeleitet von Erwin Mülhaupt (Neukirchen-Vluyn: Neukirchener Verlag, 1959).

———. *Psalmpredigten, Passions-, Oster- und Pfingstpredigten*, ed. Erwin Mülhaupt. Supplementa Calviniana, vol. VII. Neukirchen-Vluyn: Neukirchener Verlag, 1981.

———. *Calvins Commentary on Seneca's De Clementia*, ed. and trans. Ford Lewis Battles and André Malan Hugo. Leiden: Brill, 1969.

———. *Commentary on the Book of Psalms,* 5 vol., ed. and trans. James Anderson. Edinburgh, 1845-1849.

———. *A Commentary on the Psalms*, 4 vol., trans. Arthur Golding. London, 1571. Revised and edited by T. H. L. Parker. London: James Clarke, 1965.

Luther, Martin. *D. Martin Luthers Werke. Kritische Gesamtausgabe.* Weimar: H. Böhlau, 1883-1987.

Secondary Sources

Althaus, Paul. *Die Theologie Martin Luthers.* Gütersloh: Gütersloher Verlagshaus, 1980.

Angenendt, Arnold. *Geschichte der Religiosität im Mittelalter.* Darmstadt: Wissenschaftliche Buchgesellschaft, 1997.

Bakker, K. *Opmerkingen over Kalvijn's voorrede bij den commentaar op de psalmen.* Amsterdam, n. d.

Balke, Willem. "Calvijn over de geschapen werkelijkheid in zijn Psalmencommentaar." In *Wegen en gestalten in het gereformeerd protestantisme*, ed. S. van der Linde, 89-103. Amsterdam: Ton Bolland, 1976.

―――. "The Word of God and *Experientia* according to Calvin." In *Calvinus Ecclesiae Doctor*, ed. W. H. Neuser, 19-31. Kampen: Kok, 1978.

Bandt, Helmut. *Luthers Lehre vom verborgenen Gott*. Berlin: Evangelische Verlagsanstalt, 1958.

Battles, Ford Lewis. *Interpreting John Calvin*. Grand Rapids: Baker Books, 1986.

Bauke, Hermann. *Die Probleme der Theologie Calvins*. Leipzig: Hinrichs, 1922.

Beeke, Joel R. *The Quest for Full Assurance: The legacy of Calvin and his successors*. Edinburgh: Banner of Truth, 1999.

Beintker, Horst. *Die Überwindung der Anfechtung bei Luther*. Berlin: Evangelische Verlagsanstalt, 1954.

Bieler, André. *La pensee economique et sociale de Calvin*. Genève: Librairie de l'université, 1961.

Blaser, Emil. "Vom Gesetz in Calvins Predigten über den 119. Psalm." In *Das Wort sie sollen lassen stahn: Festschrift für D. Albert Schadelin*, eds. Hans Dürr, Alfred Fankhauser, and Wilhelm Michaelis, 67-83. Bern: H. Lang, 1950.

Bohatec, Josef. "Calvins Vorsehungslehre." In *Calvinstudien-Festschrift zum 400. Geburtstage Johann Calvins*, ed. Joseph Bohatec, 339-441. Leipzig: R. Haupt 1909.

Bonhoeffer, Dietrich. *Schöpfung und Fall*, ed. M. Rüter and I. Todt. München: Chr. Kaiser, 1955.

Bouwsma, William James. *John Calvin: A Sixteenth Century Portrait*. New York/Oxford: Oxford University Press, 1988.

Büsser, Fritz. *Calvins Urteil über sich selbst*. Zürich: Zwingli Verlag, 1950.

De Greef, Wulfert. *Calvijn en het Oude Testament*. Amsterdam: Ton Bolland, 1984.

―――. *Calvijn over de Bijbel. Enkele brieven, inleidingen en hoofdstukken uit de Institutie*. Houten: Den Hertog, 1998.

De Jong, James A. "'An Anatomy of all Parts of the Soul': Insights into Calvin's Spirituality from his Psalms Commentary." In *Calvinus Professor*, ed. W. H. Neuser, 1-14. Grand Rapids: Eerdmans Publishing Company, 1994.

De Kroon, Marijn. *The Honour of God and Human Salvation: a contribution to an understanding of Calvin's theology according to his Institutes*. Edinburgh: T&T Clark, 2001.

Dellsperger, Rudolf, Rudolf Freudenberger und Wolfgang Weber. *Wolfgang Musculus (1497-1563) und die oberdeutsche Reformation*. Berlin: Akademie Verlag, 1997.

Denzinger, Heinrich Joseph Dominicus. *Enchiridion Symbolorum*. Freiburg: Herder, 1953.

De Rover, Piet Adriaan . *Calvijn, de reus van Noyon*. Den Haag: Voorhoeve, 1962.

Dowey, Edward Atkinson, Jr. *The Knowledge of God in Calvin's Theology*. Grand Rapids: Eerdmans Publishing Company, 1994.

Engammare, Max. "Plaisir des mets, plaisir des mots: Irdische Freude bei Calvin." In *Calvinus Sincerioris Religionis Vindex—Calvin as Protector of the Purer Religion*, ed. Wilhelm H. Neuser and Brian G. Armstrong, 189-208. Sixteenth Century Essays & Studies, vol. XXXVI. Kirksville, MO: Sixteenth Century Journal Publishers, 1997.

Erikson, Erik Homburger. *Young Man Luther: A study in psychoanalysis and history.* New York: Norton, 1958.

Faber, Eva-Maria. *Symphonie von Gott und Mensch: Die responsorische Struktur von Vermittlung in der Theologie Johannes Calvins.* Neukirchen-Vluyn: Neukirchener Verlagshaus, 1999.

Gamble, Rick Craig. "Current Trends in Calvin Research, 1982-1990." In *Calvinus Sacrae Scripturae Professor,* ed. W. H. Neuser, 91-112. Grand Rapids: Eerdmans Publishing Company, 1994.

Ganoczy, Alexandre. *Le jeune Calvin: Genèse et évolution de sa vocation réformatrice.* Wiesbaden: F. Steiner, 1966.

Gerrisch, Brian Albert. "'To the Unknown God": Luther and Calvin on the Hiddenness of God." In *The Old Protestantism and the New: Essays on the Reformation Heritage.* Chicago: University of Chicago Press, 1982.

Gosselin, E. A. *The King's Progress to Jerusalem: Some Interpretations of David during the Reformation Period and their Patristic and Medieval Background.* Malibu: Undena Publications, 1976.

Graafland, Cornelis. *Het Vaste Verbond: Israël en het Oude Testament bij Calvijn en het Gereformeerd Protestantisme.* Amsterdam: Ton Bolland, 1978.

———. "Hat Calvin einen *ordo salutis* gelehrt." In *Calvinus Ecclesiae Genevensis Custos,* ed. Wilhelm H. Neuser, 221-244. Frankfurt am Main: Lang, 1984.

Hamm, Bernd. *Promissio, Pactum, Ordinatio—Freiheit und Selbstbindung Gottes in der scholastischen Gnadenlehre.* Tübingen: J. C. B. Mohr, 1977.

Hesselink, Ira John. *Calvin's Concept of the Law.* Allison Park, PA: Pickwick Publications, 1992.

———. *Calvin's First Catechism, a Commentary.* Louisville, KY: Westminster/John Knox Press, 1997.

Jones, Serene. *Calvin and the Rhetoric of Piety.* Louisville, KY: Westminster/John Knox Press, 1995.

Kohls, Ernst-Wilhelm. *Die Theologie des Erasmus.* Basel: F. Reinhardt, 1966.

Kolfhaus, Wilhelm. *Von christlichen Leben nach Calvin.* Neukirchen: Buchhandlung des Erziehungsvereins, 1949.

Kooiman, Willem Jan. *Luther en de Bijbel.* Baarn, 1977.

Kraus, Hans-Joachim. "Vom Leben und Tod in den Psalmen: Eine Studie zu Calvins Psalmen-Kommentar." In *Biblisch-theologische Aufsätze,* 258-77. Neukirchen: Neukirchener Verlag, 1972.

Ladurie, Emmanuel Le Roy. *Le siècle des Platter (1499-1628).* Paris: Fayard, 1995.

Lienhard, Marc. "Les Épicuriens a Strasbourg entre 1530 et 1550 et le problème de l'épicurisme au XVIe siècle." In *Croyants et sceptiques au XVIe siècle.* Strasbourg: Librairie Istra, 1981.

Lillback, Peter. *The Binding of God: Calvin's role in the Development of Covenant Theology.* Grand Rapids: Baker Books, 2001.

Loewenich, Walter von. *Luther's Theology of the cross,* trans. H. Bouman. Minneapolis: Augsburg, 1976.

Lohse, Bernard. *Luthers Theologie.* Göttingen: Vandenhoeck & Rupecht, 1995.

Lülsdorf, Raimund. *Die Zukunft Jesu Christi: Calvins Eschatologie und ihre katholische Sicht.* Paderborn: Bonifatius, 1996.

Martin-Achard, Robert. "Calvin et les Psaumes." In *Approche des Psaumes*. Paris 1969.

Mays, James Luther. "Calvin as an Exegete of the Psalms." In *Calvin Studies IV: Presented at the Colloquium on Calvin Studies at Davidson College and Davidson College Presbyterian Church, Davidson*, eds. J. H. Leith and W. S. Johnson, 95-104. 1988.

Millet, Olivier. *Calvin et la dynamique de la parole: Étude de rhétorique réformée.* Paris: H. Champion, 1992.

———. "L'humanité de Calvin." In *La Revue réformée* 191 (1996/5): 9-24.

Moehn, Wilhelmus Hendricus Theodorus. *God roept ons tot Zijn dienst: Een homiletisch onderzoek naar de verhouding tussen God en hoorder in Calvijns preken over Handelingen 4:1-6:7.* Kampen: Kok, 1996.

Muller, Richard A. *Christ and the Decree: Christology and Predestination in Reformed Theology from Calvin to Perkins.* Durham, NC: Labyrinth Press, 1986.

———. "The Hermeneutic of Promise and Fulfillment in Calvin's Exegesis of the Old Testament Prophecies of the Kingdom." In *The Bible in the Sixteenth Century*, ed. David C. Steinmetz, 68-82. Durham: Duke University Press, 1990.

———. "Scholasticism in Calvin: A Question of Relation and Disjunction." In *Calvinus Sincerioris Religionis Vindex—Calvin as Protector of the Purer Religion*, ed. Wilhelm H. Neuser and Brian G. Armstrong. Sixteenth Century Essays & Studies, vol. XXXVI. Kirksville, MO: Sixteenth Century Journal Publishers, 1997.

———. *The Unaccommodated Calvin: Studies in the Foundation of a Theological Tradition.* New York: Oxford University Press, 2000.

Naphy, William G. *Calvin and the Consolidation of the Genevan Reformation.* Manchester; NY: Manchester University Press, 1994.

Neuser, Wilhelm. "Theologie des Wortes—Schrift, Verheissung und Evangelium bei Calvin." In *Calvinus Theologus: Die Referate des Europäischen Kongresses für Calvinforschung*, ed. W. H. Neuser, 17-37. Neukirchen-Vluyn: Neukirchener Verlag, 1976.

Nijenhuis, Willem. *Calvinus Oecumenicus: Calvijn en de eenheid der kerk in het licht van zijn briefwisseling.* 's-Gravenhage: M. Nijhoff, 1959.

Oberman, Heiko Augustinus. *Luther, Mensch zwischen Gott und Teufel.* Berlin: Severin und Siedler, 1982.

———. "Die '*Extra*'-Dimension in der Theologie Calvins." In *Die Reformation: Von Wittenberg nach Genf*, 253-82. Göttingen: Vandenhoeck & Ruprecht, 1986.

———. *De erfenis van Calvijn.* Kampen: Kok, 1988.

———. "The Pursuit of Happiness: Calvin between Humanism and Reformation." In *Humanity and Divinity in Renaissance and Reformation: Essays in Honor of Charles Trinkaus*, ed. J. O'Malley *et al.*, 251-83. Leiden: Brill 1993.

———. "'*Subita conversio*': The 'Conversion' of John Calvin." In *Reformiertes Erbe*, vol. 2, eds. Heiko A. Oberman, *et al.*, 279-95. Zürich: Theologischer Verlag, 1993.

———. "'*Initia Calvini*': The Matrix of Calvin's Reformation." In *Calvinus Professor*, ed. W. H. Neuser, 113-54. Grand Rapids: Eerdmans Publishing Company, 1994.

Olson, Jeannine E. *Calvin and Social Welfare: Deacons and the Bourse Francaise.* Selinsgrove, PA: Susquehanna University Press, 1989.

Opitz, Peter. "'*Asperges me Domine hyssopo, et mundabor*': Beobachtungen zu Sadolets und Calvins Exegesen von Psalm 51 als Frage nach dem '*proprium*' reformierter Schriftauslegung." In *Reformiertes Erbe*, vol. 2, eds. Heiko A. Oberman, *et al.*, 297-313. Zürich: Theologischer Verlag, 1993.

———. "Ein Thorapsalm als ABC des christlichen Glaubens: Beobachtungen zu Calvins Predigten über Psalm 119." In *Calvin's Books: Festschrift für Peter de Klerk*, eds. Wilhelm H. Neuser, Herman J. Selderhuis, Willem van 't Spijker. Heerenveen: J. J. Groen, 1997.

Parker, Thomas Henri Louis. *John Calvin: A biography*. Philadelphia: Westminster Press, 1975.

———. *Calvin's Preaching*. Louisville, KY: Westminster/ John Knox Press, 1992.

———. *Calvin's Old Testament Commentaries*. Louisville, KY: Westminster/John Knox Press, 1993.

Payne, John Barton. "Erasmus's Influence on Zwingli and Bullinger." In *Biblical Interpretation in the Era of the Reformation*, ed. Richard A. Muller and John L. Thompson, 61-81. Grand Rapids: Eerdmans, 1996.

Peter, Rudolphe. "Calvin et la traduction des Pseaumes de Louis Budé." In *Revue d'histoire et de philosophic religieuses* 42 (1962): 175-92.

Peter, Rudolphe et Jean-Francois Gilmont. *Bibliotheca Calviniana: Les oeuvres de Jean Calvin publicées au XVIe siècle. Écrits théologiques, littéraires et juridiques*, 2 vols. Genève: Droz, 1991-1994.

Peters, Albrecht. *Kommentar zu Luthers Katechismen, vol. 2: Der Glaube*. Göttingen: Vandenhoeck & Ruprecht, 1991.

Peuckert, Will-Erich. *Die Grosse Wende: Das apokalyptische Saeculum und Luther*. Darmstadt: Wissenschaftliche Buchgesellschaft, 1966.

Pfisterer, Ernst. *Calvins Wirken in Genf*. Neukirchen: Verlag der Buchhandlung des Erziehungsvereins, 1957.

Pitkin, Barbara. "Imitation of David: David as Paradigm for Faith in Calvin's Exegesis of the Psalms." *Sixteenth Century Journal* 24 (1993): 843-63.

Puckett, David Lee. *John Calvin's Exegesis of the Old Testament*. Louisville, KY: Westminster/John Knox Press, 1995.

Richel, Pieter Johannes. *Het kerkbegrip van Calvijn*. Franeker: Wever, 1942.

Russell, S. H. "Calvin and the Messianic Interpretation of the Psalms." *Scottish Journal of Theology* 21 (1968): 37-47.

Scheld, Stefan. *Media Salutis: Zur Heilsvermittlung bei Calvin*. Wiesbaden: Steiner, 1989.

Scholl, Hans. *Der Dienst des Gebetes nach Johannes Calvin*. Zurich: Zwingli Verlag, 1968.

Schreiner, Susan Elizabeth. *The Theater of His Glory: Nature and the Natural Order in the Thought of John Calvin*. Grand Rapids: Baker Books, 1995.

Schützeichel, Heribert. "Ein Grundkurs des Glaubens. Calvins Auslegung des 51. Psalms." *Catholica* 44 (1990).

Seeberg, Reinhold. *Lehrbuch der Dogmengeschichte*, vol. IV.2. Erlangen: A. Deichert, 1920.

Selderhuis, Herman Johan. *David, Calvijn en ik*. Barneveld: De Vuurbaak, 1996.

———. *Calvijn als asielzoeker*. Apeldoornse Studies 35. Apeldoorn: Theologische

Universiteit Apeldoorn, 1997.

Sharples, R. W. *Stoics, Epicureans and Sceptics: An introduction to Hellenistic Philosophy*. London and New York: Routledge, 1996.

Stauffer, Richard. *Dieu, la création et la Providence dans la prédication de Calvin*. Bern and Las Vegas: Peter Lang, 1978.

Van der Haar, Jan. *Het geestelijke leven bij Calvijn*. Utrecht: De Banier, 1959.

Van der Linde, Simon. "Gereformeerde Scholastiek IV, Calvijn." *Theologia Reformata* Jaargang XXIX (1986/3): 244-66.

Van der Vegt, Willem Hendrik. *Verbond en verkiezing bij Calvijn*. N. p.

Van Eck, Johannes. *God, mens en medemens: Humanitas in de theologie van Calvijn*. Franeker: Van Wijnen, 1992.

Van't Spijker, Willem. *Luther en Calvijn: De invloed van Luther op Calvijn blijkens de Institutie*. Apeldoornse Studies 20. Kampen: Kok, 1985.

―――. "'*Extra nos*' en '*In nobis*' bij Calvijn in pneumatologisch licht." *Geest, Woord en Kerk*, eds. C. Augustijn, W. H. Neuser en H. J. Selderhuis, 114-32. Kampen, 1991.

Walchenbach, John Robert. "The influence of David and the Psalms on the life and thought of John Calvin." Th.M. thesis, Pittsburgh Theological Seminary, 1969.

Wendel, Francois. *Sources et évolution de sa pensée religieuse*. Geneva: Labor et Fides Paris, 1975.

Witte, J. L. *Het probleem individu-gemeenschap in Calvijns geloofsnorm*, 2 vols. Franeker: Wever, 1949.

Wolf, Hans Heinrich. *Die Einheit des Bundes: Das Verhaltnis von Altem und Neuem Testament bei Calvin*. Neukirchen: Verlag der Buchhandlung des Erziehungsvereins, 1958.

Wolff, Christian. "Strasbourg, cite du Refuge." In *Strasbourg au coeur religieux du XVIe siècle: Hommage à Lucien Febre*, 321-30. Strasbourg: Librairie Istra, 1977.

Wright, David Frederick. "Calvin's Accommodating God." In *Calvinus Sincerioris Religionis Vindex—Calvin as Protector of the Purer Religion*, ed. Wilhelm H. Neuser and Brian G. Armstrong, 3-19. Sixteenth Century Essays & Studies, vol. XXXVI. Kirksville, MO: Sixteenth Century Journal Publishers, 1997.

Index